Ben Sira's View of Women

Program in Judaic Studies
Brown University
BROWN JUDAIC STUDIES

Edited by

Jacob Neusner
Wendell S. Dietrich, Ernest S. Frerichs,
Alan Zuckerman

Number 38

BEN SIRA'S VIEW OF WOMEN: A LITERARY ANALYSIS

by Warren C. Trenchard

BEN SIRA'S VIEW OF WOMEN: A LITERARY ANALYSIS

by
Warren C. Trenchard

Scholars Press
Chico, California

Ben Sira's View of Women:
A Literary Analysis

by
Warren C. Trenchard

Library of Congress Cataloging in Publication Data
Trenchard, Warren C.
Ben Sira's view of women.

(Brown Judaic studies ; no. 38)
Bibliography: p.
1. Women—Biblical teaching. 2. Bible. O.T. Apocrypha. Ecclesiasticus—Criticism, interpretation, etc. I. Title. II. Series.
BS1199.W7T73 1982 229'.4083054 82-16755
ISBN 0-89130-593-9

Printed in the United States of America

To Marilyn,

whom Ben Sira should have known.

Warren C. Trenchard, born in St. Johns, Newfoundland, Canada, holds the B.A., M.A., and B.D. from Andrews University, and a Ph.D. from the University of Chicago. He is presently Chairman of the Humanities Division at Canadian Union College in College Heights, Alberta, Canada.

TABLE OF CONTENTS

PREFACE ix

INTRODUCTION 1

Chapter

I. WOMAN AS GOOD WIFE 9

Introduction 9
26:1-4, 13-18 9
36:21-26 19
7:19 26
7:26a 27
9:1 29
25:1 31
25:8a 33
28:15 35
40:19, 23 37
Conclusion 38

II. WOMAN AS MOTHER AND WIDOW 39

Introduction 39
3:1-16 40
7:27-28 47
23:14 48
41:17a 49
15:2a 50
Miscellaneous Mother-Related Expressions 51
4:10 52
35(32):14-15 54
Conclusion 55

III. WOMAN AS BAD WIFE 57

Introduction 57
26:5-9; 25:13-26 57
9:2 87
33:19ab (30:28ab) 88
47:19 89
7:26b 91

37:11a 92
42:6 93
Conclusion 94

IV. WOMAN AS ADULTERESS AND PROSTITUTE 95

Introduction 95
23:22-26 95
9:8-9 108
26:9 115
9:3-4, 6-7 118
19:2-3 122
42:8ab 124
41:20b, 21c, 22a, 22b 125
Conclusion 127

V. WOMAN AS DAUGHTER 129

Introduction 129
7:24-25 129
22:3-5 134
26:10-12 140
42:9-14 146
9:5 162
Conclusion 163

CONCLUSION 167

Appendix
1. NUMERICAL SAYINGS 175

2. THE TEXT OF SIR 40:18-20 179

NOTES 183

BIBLIOGRAPHY 315

INDEX OF SUBJECTS 333

INDEX OF SIRACH PASSAGES 337

PREFACE

My interest in the view of women reflected in Hellenistic Jewish literature began while I was enrolled in a graduate course at The University of Chicago. I became especially fascinated with the wisdom materials from that period and with Ben Sira in particular, since his declarations on women were both the most numerous and the most controversial of the Hellenistic Jewish wisdom tradition. After I discovered that no thorough study had been made of this material in Sirach, I decided to engage in just such a project as a doctoral dissertation for the Dapartment of New Testament and Early Christian Literature. This book is a slightly revised version of that endeavor.

I am particularly grateful to Dean Jonathan Z. Smith, who served as my principal advisor. His penetrating critiques and creative suggestions were invaluable in the development of this study. My thanks also extend to Professors Robert M. Grant and Nancy P. Helmbold for their encouragement and helpful advice.

In addition to the Regenstein Library at The University of Chicago, which purchased and secured many materials for my use, I wish to gratefully acknowledge my access to library collections at Andrews University, Ballarmine School of Theology, Bethany Theological Seminary, The Chicago Theological Seminary, Lutheran School of Theology at Chicago, McCormick Theological Seminary, Notre Dame University, Saint Mary of the Lake Seminary, and Union Theological Seminary in New York.

Several persons at Canadian Union College deserve special credit for their assistance in the preparation of this book:

Mrs. Gale Milovanov for her careful typing, Mrs. Bonnie Johnson for her helpful proof-reading, and Professor Paul Lee for his word processing equipment.

My deepest appreciation go to my wife and three sons, who have all too often been without a husband and father because of this research. Without their understanding and support this study would never have materialized.

INTRODUCTION

The book of Sirach contains discussions of a wide variety of topics that arise from everyday life in Palestine in the second century B.C. These include descriptions of and counsel concerning various classes of people, such as physicians, scribes, friends, counselors, enemies, craftsmen, rich, poor, wisemen, and fools.[1] However, one of the most prominent features of Sirach is the rather large amount of space that it devotes to the discussion of women. Of the 1390 verses in Sirach, 105, or about 7 percent, deal with women. While some of the units concerning women are isolated distichs, about two-thirds of the material is found in sections of five verses or longer. One such section contains thirty-two verses.

In view of its quantitative significance, it is indeed curious that to date no one has produced a comprehensive treatment of this material about women in Sirach. The commentaries[2] on the book are understandably inadequate. In the course of their treatment of the whole work, they provide important textual, linguistic, and exegetical data on the texts that relate to women. However, they do not consider the problem of women in Sirach in any thoroughgoing, systematic way. The only studies specifically devoted to the topic of women in Sirach are two very short articles in Expository Times. One[3] is from just before the turn of the century and the other[4] almost eighty years later. The brevity and general nature of these articles disqualify them as serious attempts to understand the issue. The same can be said of the Festschrift article by

Kenneth E. Bailey,[5] which compares Ben Sira's view of women to that of the NT.[6]

Despite the paucity of specific studies on the issue of women in Sirach, scholars have offered various opinions on the nature of Ben Sira's view. These opinions tend to fall into two groups. Some have expressed the notion that Ben Sira is personally negative toward women.[7] Others have interpreted his remarks about women as balanced[8] or merely a reflection of his sources and contemporary conditions.[9] Yet, none of these scholars has seriously attempted to support these claims. Their opinions on Ben Sira's view of women take on more the character of a priori remarks than genuinely informed statements.

The purpose of this study is at once general and specific. In a general sense it is designed to fill the gap of scholarship on the issue of women in Sirach. Thus, I will systematically analyze all the material concerning women in the book, providing detailed exegesis in each case. More specifically, I will endeavor to resolve the question of the nature of Ben Sira's view of women. This will involve an examination of the evidence to determine whether or not Ben Sira was personally negative toward women.[10]

In the early stages of my investigation of the issue I did not know the direction that my resolution of the problem of Ben Sira's view of women would take. However, after a preliminary examination of the initial data that I had gathered, I was able to detect a developing tendency in the evidence. It was then that I formulated the following working hypothesis for this study: Ben Sira is personally negative toward women. Thus, in addition to reviewing and analyzing all his remarks about women, I will seek to test the reasonablity of this hypothesis in view of the evidence of the text.

As I prepare to analyze certain portions of Sirach, it will be helpful to briefly review several matters of introduction. Unlike most Jewish treatises from this period, the book contains the identification of its author. According to 50:27 his name was Joshua the son of Eleazar the son of Sira.[11] Since the last of these three designations in Heb is ben-sîrā', in Jewish circles and beyond it has become customary to refer to the author as Ben Sira. I will follow this practice in the present study and use the name Ben Sira in reference to the author of the book. When I refer to the book itself or cite material from it, I will use the title Sirach.[12] The author was apparently the master of a school,[13] which was probably in Jerusalem.[14]

Scholars are generally agreed on placing the date of composition around 180 B.C.[15] This is determined largely by the statement of his grandson in the Prologue to the Gr translation that he went to Egypt in the year 132 B.C. and translated his grandfather's work sometime thereafter.[16] The other main factor in dating the composition is its reflection of a generally tranquil urban society. This would require a date prior to the outbreak of the Maccabean Revolt in 168 B.C.; in fact, probably before 171 B.C., when Antiochus Epiphanes appointed Menelaus as high priest.

The book of Sirach is easily classified in general terms as an example of wisdom literature. In this respect it most nearly resembles the OT book Proverbs. Scott[17] notes that wisdom was a phenomenon common to all the ancient Near Eastern societies as "the fine fruit of a tradition originally rooted in the mores of family and tribe and local community." It includes simple domestic sayings and grandiose proclamations of kings, traditional folk maxims and literary masterpieces.[18]

In recent years some scholars[19] have come to view Sirach more specifically as a textbook for young men studying in Ben Sira's school. It is seen not so much as a book of elementary instruction but as a work to support progressive learning.[20]

Perhaps the most important development in Sirach research that related to the purpose of this study has been the recognition that the book is a composite corpus consisting of compiled traditional materials woven into the text at numerous points and Ben Sira's own compositions. This was early recognized by Box-Oesterley,[21] who saw Ben Sira using OT words and ideas as springboards for his own views. More recently, scholars have 4 expanded this to include Gr sources as well.[22] However, in most cases what appears to be traditional material in Sirach cannot now be identified with extant literature.[23] Such material may often be recognized in the text by its formal discontinuity with surrounding material. This includes cases where poetically designed distichs (traditional) are followed by one or more loosely formed distichs which elaborate on or qualify the theme of the first distich (compositional). Traditional material may also be detected through a repetition of various formal elements in a series of distichs. Forms like Zahlensprüche[24] are generally regarded as traditional.

Ben Sira has left clues concerning his compositional technique. In 33:16-18 (30:25-27)[25] he describes himself as "one who gleans after the grape-gatherers" and who fills his wine press "for all who seek instruction."[26] In 39:1 he notes that the student of the law "will seek out the wisdom of all the ancients." In 18:29 he suggests that those who study sayings become capable of producing proverbs themselves. Thus, both by his testimony and by the evidence left in the text itself we are safe to consider the book a composite of traditional materials and his own composed materials.[27]

Ben Sira originally wrote in Heb, and his grandson produced a translation in Gr. However, apart from certain rabbinic citations,[28] the Heb text was lost until near the end of the nineteenth century, when about two-thirds of it was discovered among the Cairo Geniza materials.[29] Another MS from the Geniza was published in 1931.[30] But the most dramatic and significant discovery came in 1964, when a Sirach scroll containing portions of 39:27-44:17 was found during the excavation of Masada.[31] This MS has been dated in the first half of the first century B.C.[32] The Geniza MSS by comparison are medieval. Several fragments of Sirach have also been discovered among the Dead Sea scrolls.[33]

The grandson's Gr translation apparently lies behind the LXX text of Sirach,[34] which became the standard text of the book during the centuries when the Heb was lost. It continues to serve this function for those sections where the Heb is still not extant. The Gr has survived in two major recensions. The shorter text, which is generally held to be the original Gr version, is usually designated GrI. The longer text, with its scattered additional distichs and sections and which is dated to about 70-60 B.C., is designated GrII.[35] Most of the text has also been preserved in the Syr Peshitta,[36] which was probably translated from the Heb, but often influenced by the Gr. Another important witness to the text is the Old La,[37] which was translated from the Gr and which exhibits a text much like GrII. The text also survives in Cop, Arm, and Eth.

My final note of introduction to Sirach concerns the organization of the book. In a recent study Roth[38] has argued for a progressive development of Sirach. He sees 1:1-23:27 and 51:1-30 as Ben Sira's original book. To this Ben Sira added three successive sections: 24:1-32:13; 32:14-38:23; 38:24-50:29. It is beyond the scope of this study to address the issue of Ben Sira's progressively developing his book. However, the organization which Roth identifies seems sound.

Before proceeding to the text itself, let me offer a few remarks concerning the methods I have employed in this study. The first has to do with the plan of approach to the material needing to be analyzed. I have chosen to assemble all of Ben Sira's material related to woman into the five categories of good wife, mother (and widow), bad wife, adulteress (and prostitute), and daughter. These five categories will in turn constitute the five chapters of the study. In a loose sense they are arranged to progress from the most positive to the most negative. I will analyze each text within a given category and ascertain its contribution toward the verification of my working hypothesis. These individual findings will be summarized in a conclusion to each chapter. The conclusion at the end of the whole study will review these data for all the categories from the perspective of the various types of evidence observed.

The first step in any responsible exegesis of a text is the determination of the actual reading of the text. This work, of course, may be left to text critics and editors of published texts, with the exegete merely accepting their decisions. However, there is still need for the exegete to periodically make textual decisions. This is especially true when the number of witnesses is small and when important MSS have been recovered since the publication of standard critical texts. Both these conditions exist with regard to the text of Sirach. Thus, I will prepare a critical translation for each unit of the Sirach text which I will discuss. By this, I mean a translation of the text based on what I perceive to represent most accurately the original text. I will provide extensive notation to the translations with readings from the three principal textual sources, Heb, Gr, and Syr, as well as occasional references to the La, and discussions of the various potential readings.

This study will be limited to a literary analysis of Sirach in an effort not only to catalog Ben Sira's remarks on women but especially to determine the nature of his view on women. Thus, my methods of approach to the study will be related to the literature. Beyond this literary limitation I have not chosen to conduct a study based on any particular analytical technique, such as form criticism. Instead, I have decided to permit the phenomena of each text to dictate the methods necessary for the proper interpretation of that text.

Foremost among the approaches that I will use is tradition-composition analysis. I indicated above that Sirach is a composite work, containing both traditional materials and those composed by Ben Sira himself. I am especially indebted to the work of Werner Fuss, noted above, for the classification of these materials, though I have not always followed his conclusions. I will show that the way Ben Sira arranges, edits, deletes, and expands traditional materials in his discussions of women provides important evidence concerning his view of women.

Ben Sira was influenced by both biblical and extrabiblical sources. Principal among these was the OT, especially its widsom literature like Proverbs. Most of his vocabulary and many of his phrases and figures are drawn from the OT. For this reason it will be necessary for me to periodically employ comparative analysis in relating Ben Sira to his biblical idea source. I will compare and contrast his topic choices, tone, application of figures, and assertions concerning women to those of the OT. The value of these observations lies not so much in their establishment of the veracity of my working hypothesis but in their potential for confirmation.

Much of the task of unlocking the meaning of the texts that I will consider involves standard exegetical practices. These include contextual analysis, grammatical and linguistic analysis, historical analysis, form analysis, and, in its literary sense, structural analysis.[39]

Through the application of these various techniques I will explore Ben Sira's numerous and variegated remarks concerning women and will present them in a systematic and organized fashion. Furthermore, I will demonstrate that Ben Sira wrote about women as he did, because he was motivated by a personal, negative bias against them.

CHAPTER I

WOMAN AS GOOD WIFE

Introduction

The first category we shall consider in analyzing Ben Sira's view of women is the good wife. His material on the good wife is of two types. First, we shall treat two major texts that represent extended discussions of the good wife and that reflect Ben Sira's conscious and considered opinions on the topic. Secondly, we shall note and discuss several miscellaneous references to the good wife which are scattered throughout Ben Sira's writings on various matters. Together these will provide a picture of Ben Sira's view of women through his assessment of the good wife both in his deliberate discussion of the topic and in his more random allusions.

26:1-4, 13-18

1 A good wife--blessed is her husband,[1]
And the number of his days[2] is doubled.
2 An excellent wife[3] gladdens her husband,[4]
And he will complete his years in peace.[5]
3 A good wife--a good portion;[6]
And she will be allotted[7] to him who fears the Lord.[8]
4 Whether rich or poor, his heart is glad;
At all times his face is cheerful.
13 A wife's charm[9] pleases her husband;[10]
Her prudence[11] will fatten his bones.[12]
14 A silent wife[13] is a gift from the Lord,[14]
And priceless is a restrained voice.[15]
15 A modest wife--charm upon charm;[16]
And there is no price worthy[17] of a self-controlled soul.[18]
16 As the sun rising in the heights of the Lord,[19]
So is a beautiful woman[20] in the arrangement of her home.[21]

17 As the lamp burning on the holy lampstand,[22]
So is the beauty of a face[23] on a stately figure.[24]
18 As golden pillars on a silver base,[25]
So are beautiful legs[26] on firm heels.[27]

Before undertaking an analysis of this section, let us consider the place that it holds in the whole discussion of women in 25:13-26:18. I shall also justify the collocation of vv. 1-4 and 13-18.

The most thoroughgoing analysis of the structure of this passage was done by Josef Haspecker,[28] who treats these verses as part of a larger piece, 25:1-26:27.[29] For Haspecker the controlling and determinative concept in Sirach is Gottesfurcht--the fear of the Lord. He sees this concept as primary in the interpretation and structuring of 25:1-26:27.[30]

According to Haspecker the overall theme is stated in 25:1d, which he considers to be the conclusion[31] of a Zahlenspruch--numerical proverb: "A wife and husband who share each other's company." He organizes the structure as follows: 25:1-11 (fifteen distichs consisting of three Zahlensprüche and a section on old age); 25:13-26 (fifteen distichs forming a negative contrast concerning the evil wife); 26:1-27 (thirty distichs of material concerning the good wife, the evil wife, and daughters). As it presently stands, the last section consists of four distichs (good wife), ten distichs (evil wife and daughter), six distichs (good wife), and ten distichs (evil and good wives). Haspecker takes 26:1-18 to be a redaction of the original order, which he reconstructs as: 26:5-12 (ten distichs on the evil wife) and 26:13-18, 1-4 (ten distichs on the good wife).

I consider Haspecker's case for the inclusion of 25:1-11 in this section to be very weak. Only one of the two opening Zahlensprüche contains a reference to a woman.[32] In the third Zahlenspruch only one of the ten elements concerns a woman.[33] Vv. 3-6 deal with the experience of the aged, suggested by 25:2d. There is thus very little in 25:1-11 that can be reasonably connected with 25:13-26:18 in the sense of determining structure. At best, the section contains two unrelated references to women, which may have suggested the inclusion of a more extensive treatment of the topic.

Haspecker's contention that 26:1-18 was originally ordered differently from its present form is well taken. However, the reconstruction must extend to the whole section, 25:13-26:18.[34] Its present structure alternates uneven blocks of material about evil wives, good wives, and daughters.[35] By placing 26:1-4 after vv. 13-18 Haspecker at least consolidates all the good wife material. However, it seems more reasonable to place 26:1-4 before vv. 13-18.[36] Haspecker's arrangement is motivated by a desire to bring the section to a conclusion on the theme of Gottesfurcht. But, even if this were significant, which itself is unconvincing, the Gottesfurcht reference is in v. 3, not in v. 4. Thus, it would not conclude the passage in any case.

A further realignment is necessary, since the whole section, 26:1-4, 13-18, appears to be out of place. It would seem to fit best after 25:11.[37] In 25:7-11 a positive Zahlenspruch describes what makes a man happy. The section on the good wife, 26:1-4, 13-18, is a natural expansion of 25:8a and would follow the Zahlenspruch. After this section would come the material concerning the evil wife, which begins with 26:5-9. Thus, both the good wife and evil wife sections open with a Zahlenspruch. Next would come 25:13-26, followed by the material on the daughter in 26:10-12. The former ends with two imperative distichs and the latter begins with two imperative distichs, which is a natural transition. In this arrangement[38] both the good wife and evil wife (and daughter) sections end with figurative descriptions.[39]

There remains the question of the genuineness of 26:19-27. Haspecker[40] sees no reason to consider these verses secondary.[41] He holds that they render a Heb Vorlage and exhibit a conscious structure.[42] For Haspecker vv. 19-21 "fittingly follow the statement of a woman's excellence in 13-18, and are absolutely indispensable according to the structure of the entire piece from 25:13."[43] Finally, he cannot imagine Ben

Sira concluding his discussion of a suitable wife "with a description of her pretty legs (26:18)."[44]

The section, 26:19-27, is not extant in Heb, La, or GrI (SAB). It appears only in some witnesses to GrII (the Lucianic recension, 743[45]) and in Syr. Arm has v. 27ab. Clement of Alexandria quotes v. 22.[46] Haspecker, who seems motivated by his concern to preserve two Gottesfurcht statements (vv. 23b, 25b), completely ignores the external evidence against the genuineness of these verses. I would not dispute the contention that this incompletely attested GrII piece renders a Heb Vorlage. GrII is generally conceded to have stemmed largely from a first century B.C. Heb expansion of Sirach.[47] However, its Hebraic quality need not suggest an origin with Ben Sira.

The structure of the passage does not exhibit the precision that Haspecker suggests. Its arrangement of positive and negative assessments of women is quite out of character with Ben Sira's large blocks on the good wife and evil wife in 25:13-26:18. Here these are sprinkled freely and randomly throughout, with several distichs in antithetical form.[48] Furthermore, the section does not divide neatly into two groups of five distichs each. There is, for instance, a clear break after v. 21. Box-Oesterley[49] give a more realistic division of the distichs: 3 + 4 + 1 + 1 + 1. While Ben Sira employs antithetical parallels, he does so sparingly.[50] But of the ten or eleven[51] distichs in 26:19-27, five are antitheses, far more than one would expect from Ben Sira. This section gives the impression of being an awkward addition, which makes use of material and ideas like Ben Sira's but not in his type of arrangement. Because of such reasons I cannot accept the genuineness of these verses. Accordingly, I shall not treat the statements in this section in the analysis of Ben Sira's view of women.

Sir 26:1-4, 13-18 is Ben Sira's longest statement on the good wife. Vv. 1-4 introduce the subject with the general declaration that a good wife is good for her husband.

Ben Sira begins by stating in v. 1 that the husband of a good wife (<u>'šh ṭwbh</u>) is blessed. This construction, as reflected in the translation, is an example of what Tadeusz Penar calls <u>casus pendens</u>.[52] In line <u>b</u> the blessing is explained in terms of the husband's life being doubled. This is a description of his quality of life with a good wife in comparison to life with an evil wife,[53] which he will consider later. In vv. 13-15 Ben Sira is more specific concerning the benefits of a good wife to her husband that could make his life more pleasant and his days seem longer. Here he is content merely to make a general statement. We may note that, while the wife is good, the husband is the one blessed, and it is his days that are doubled.

The assertion in v. 2 is essentially a restatement of v. 1. Here the wife is called "excellent" (<u>ḥyl</u>[54]). But as in v. 1, her quality is stated in relationship to her husband--she makes him glad (<u>euphrainei</u>[55]). V. 2b reinforces the positive state of the husband's quality of life introduced in v. 1--"He will complete his years in peace." This, of course, implies that his wife will not cause him trouble so as to disturb his tranquil existence. Thus, the wife's excellence is established and measured in terms of her benefit to her husband or, at least, her lack of trouble for him.

The next two distichs, vv. 3-4, must be considered together, since the second is clearly dependent on the first. The form of v. 3a parallels that of v. 1a.[56] In fact, both begin with the same independent phrase, "a good wife." As in vv. 1-2, the wife here is merely labeled "good" without qualification. This is another general declaration. But unlike vv. 1-2, the husband is not explicitly mentioned, though he is clearly implied. The wife in question is "a good portion" (<u>mnh ṭwbh</u>) who "will be allotted (<u>wbḥlq . . . tntn</u>) to him who fears the Lord."[57] Thus, a good wife is the lot of the God-fearing man. So, again Ben Sira mentions a good wife in the context of her husband, here a good husband. In effect, he receives her as a piece of desired property. V. 4 notes the effect this has on him--no matter what his economic condition, he is content and ever cheerful.[58]

For Haspecker, who interprets 25:13-26:27 against the background of Gottesfurcht, v. 3 is a major text.[59] As we have seen, he would end the discussion of the "good wife" with this theme.[60] One cannot deny the prominence of the Gottesfurcht concept for Ben Sira. However, it cannot be used subjectively for textual reconstruction and the evaluation of divergent readings. Nor can it be employed in a reductionistic manner, as though it were the controlling hermeneutic for the book. The term is sufficiently widespread[61] in Heb thought to render this unlikely.[62]

For those scholars who have tried to preserve Ben Sira's positive assessment of women even in the face of such texts as 42:14, these verses, 26:1-4, provide welcome relief. For example, Gaspar calls this section a "note of high appreciation."[63] Eberharter sees these verses as reason to declare: "Jesus Sirach was no fundamental hater of women."[64] Likewise, Spicq on the basis of this passage concludes: "Ben Sira is not an obstinate misogynist."[65]

However, as we have seen, vv. 1-4 contain nothing more than a general statement on the "good wife." Furthermore, Ben Sira does not mention the good wife here outside the context of her husband. He is blessed and has his days doubled (v. 1). He is gladdened and lives in peace (v. 2). He receives her as an allotment from the Lord, making him content (vv. 3-4). While I would not argue that Ben Sira has no place in his thinking for a good wife, I would conclude that even his consideration of the good wife in this section is tainted by the fact that he does not evaluate her in her own right. His view of woman's status is such that she can be adjudged positive only in the context of her benefit to a man--in this case, her husband.

In vv. 13-15 Ben Sira becomes more specific on the traits that characterize the good wife. The first item that he mentions is her hn "charm" (v. 13). This represents those qualities that make her desirable.[66] But as in the foregoing general statements, Ben Sira here considers this trait of the good wife only in relationship to her husband. Her charm pleases (mṭyb[67]) him. In v. 13b the author extends this idea to a more specific function: "Her prudence will fatten his bones." Here the parallel to ḥn is śkl. The verb form means "to have insight, act with insight." Hence, as a noun it denotes "insight, prudence." The term is used in a wide variety of settings, with meanings ranging from "good sense" in general to particular skill in doing certain things.[68] Ben Sira uses śkl here to describe a good wife's trait. This characteristic is displayed as she fattens his bones.[69] The metaphor suggests more than her providing her husband with good food. It extends to the whole idea of healthful well being.[70] A good wife will preserve her husband's health. In this setting śkl no doubt refers to the wife's sensitivity to her husband's health needs and her ability to provide for them. Again the object and context of the positive assessment of the wife is her husband.

From what a good wife does (v. 13), Ben Sira moves to what she does not do (vv. 14-15). These two verses contain material about a wife's silence and modesty. However, these elements are mixed in the witnesses to the text as follows:

	Heb C	Gr	Syr
14	(not extant)	silent wife restrained soul	good wife restrained throat
15	modest wife sealed mouth	modest wife self-controlled soul	modest wife restrained mouth

It appears likely that all these witnesses reflect various stages of corruption of the text at this point. Ben Sira's stylistic tendency in this context[71] would suggest that the material on the silent wife should be grouped together and that the material on the modest wife should be grouped together. Smend[72] recognizes this and suggests that the Gr psychēs "soul" in v. 14b came into the text from v. 15b. He postulates that behind both pepaideumenēs (v. 14b) and egkratous (v. 15b) lay the same Heb word, mysrt "disciplined."

By comparing the witnesses to vv. 14-15, one notices that (1) there are two concepts considered, silence and modesty, (2) all the witnesses are agreed on the placement of "a modest wife --charm upon charm," and (3) the extant witnesses to v. 14 contain some reflection of "silence" in that verse. These observations suggest the following reconstruction:[73]

14 A silent wife is a gift from the Lord,
And priceless is a restrained voice.[74]
15 A modest wife--charm upon charm;
And there is no price worthy of a self-controlled soul.

The first thing that the good wife does not do, is talk (v. 14). Her characteristic of silence is declared to be a gift from the Lord.[75] In fact, such a trait in a wife is priceless. This, of course, makes sense only in the context of the husband. He is the one who is either advantaged by having a silent wife or disadvantaged by having a talkative one. The gift that is mentioned is given to him. The value placed on her is value to him. Therefore, a silent wife is good because her sience is a benefit to her husband.

Ben Sira next considers a wife good who is modest (v. 15). But this also represents something she does not do--she does not behave indecently. The Heb word here was probably bwyšt[76] "shamefaced, modest." This implies more than shy, retiring behavior. Rather, she does not conduct herself in a manner that would attract the sexual interests of other men. Such a trait of active reserve is for Ben Sira the highest kind of charm.[77]

V. 15b echoes the thought of v. 14b with only a change in the object of worth. It also follows naturally after the superlative idea in v. 15a. Here the priceless trait is "a self-controlled soul." As Ben Sira constructed this,[78] the "self-controlled soul" clearly refers to the wife who in v. 15a is termed "modest." This confirms the contention that the subject of v. 15 is that of a woman's conscious effort to avoid acting indecently, so as to invite sexual advances. However, as in v. 14b, the value of this trait is priceless to the woman's husband, not to herself. She is his property, and the more faithful[79] she is to him, the greater is her value to him.[80]

We have seen that the section consisting of vv. 13-15 continues to view the good wife solely in reference to her husband. In both what she does (v. 13) and what she does not do (vv. 14-15), she is positively regarded because of her benefit to her husband.

In the final section of this text, vv. 16-18, Ben Sira moves from the good wife's conduct to her beauty. However, he does not consider it directly. Instead, he expounds a woman's beauty through a series of comparisons.[81] The first distich is general, followed by two distichs that consider particular parts of a woman's body.[82]

The general simile, v. 16, compares a beautiful woman to the sun. In her[83] home she is like "the sun rising[84] in the heights of the Lord." Edersheim expresses the comparison thus: "What the sun is in the house above, woman is in that upon earth."[85] But this does not refer to any woman. She is specifically termed a beautiful woman. The emphasis in vv. 16-18 is on a woman's eye appeal and not on her moral appeal. The context in which she is lauded is that of her home or, as the text puts it, "in the arrangement of her home."[86] This does not suggest that she is beautiful because she has efficiently or aesthetically arranged her home.[87] Rather, this is merely the setting in which she is being viewed. As a woman, she may be beautiful, but she is worthy of praise for such beauty only as she appears in the domestic environment of her home.

Ben Sira becomes more specific about a woman's beauty in vv. 17-18, where he compares her body parts to appropriate parts of the temple.[88] The mention of the sun in v. 16 gave rise to the extension of the light motif to the lampstand in the temple (v. 17).[89] This first temple comparison suggests that the radiance of the burning lamp on the lampstand in the Holy Place[90] is analogous to the radiance of a face on a stately figure.[91] Of course, in this context the face is that of a beautiful woman. Her beautiful face adorns her statuesque body.[92] Ben Sira's concern is for her appearance or sex appeal.

The second temple comparison and the last consideration of the good wife in this section concerns the pillars and a woman's legs (v. 18). The "golden pillars on a silver base" probably refer to miscellaneous gold-covered columns in the Zerubbabel temple complex.[93] The simile concerns pillars/columns and bases, to which are compared legs and heels/feet.[94] As in v. 17, so also here, the context suggests that these body parts belong to a woman. Ben Sira thus completes this aesthetic assessment of the good wife by extolling her shapely legs and attractive feet.[95]

In vv. 16-18 Ben Sira makes glowing and complimentary statements about a wife's beauty. However, he is not so much concerned about her as a woman, as he is about her appearance to others, particularly to her husband. The more beautiful she is, the more sexually appealing she will be to him. Again the husband is the focus of this discussion about a good wife.

We have seen that our text, 26:1-4, 13-18, considers the good wife from the point of view of her husband and in relationship to him. This is true whether the material is general (vv. 1-4) or specific (vv. 13-18). A wife is considered good if she meets her husband's needs, makes him happy, pleases him sexually, remains silent, and looks beautiful. She is not assessed in her own right. Thus, Ben Sira here views even the good wife negatively, since she is made secondary to her husband. Even Gaspar, who is more laudatory of Ben Sira's view of the good wife, admits that she is seen only in the context of her home.

> The author extols her beauty, not for its own sake, but because it is a worthy concomitant of a wife graced with such <u>home-making</u> qualities. Her sphere of activity, her social milieu, is the home, in which--as the sun in the heavens--she is chief ornament and light.[96]

Gaspar further notes that the only "career woman in the Wisdom literature is . . . a good wife and mother."[97]

<u>36:21-26</u>

21 Any man[98] will a woman accept,[99]
Yet one woman[100] is more pleasant[101] than another.[102]
22 The beauty of a woman[103] brightens[104] the countenance[105]
And excels every desire of the eye.[106]
23 And if she possesses[107] a soothing tongue[108]
Her husband[109] is not like other men.[110]
24 He who acquires[111] a wife gets[112] his best possession,[113]
A helper suiting him[114] and a pillar of support.[115]
25 Without a fence the vineyard is destroyed,[116]
And without a wife a man is a wanderer and a fugitive.[117]
26 Who will trust a troop of soldiers[118]
That springs from city to city?[119]
So is the man who has no nest[120]
Who settles[121] where evening finds him.[122]

The section of text that concerns us here is part of a two level structure. From 36:18-39:11 Ben Sira considers various members of society and advises his students on how to relate to each. He discusses wives (36:21-26), friends (37:1-6), counselors (37:7-15), teachers (37:16-26), physicians (38:1-15), the dead (38:16-23), craftsmen (38:24-34), and scribes (39:1-11). At the head of this section stands a three distich introduction concerning the principle of discernment among people.

However, 36:21-26 forms a unit within a secondary context. This section, 36:18-37:15, is characterized by a consistent pattern used to introduce each of the four subsections. Each distich, which opens these subsections, contains <u>kl</u> at the beginning of line <u>a</u> and <u>ʼk yš</u> at the beginning of line <u>b</u>.[123] The general idea conveyed by this pattern is that, while there are many kinds of food, wives, friends, and counselors, not all are equally desirable. As Smend[124] notes, this necessitates the making of wise choices.

The passage, 36:18-20, which opens this entire section is unique in its treatment of a thing, i.e., food, in contrast to the variety of people considered in what follows. This fact, together with its position at the head of the section, suggests that the idea of food is here to be taken as metaphorical and introductory. Thus, the statement--the stomach receives all food alike, but the mouth distinguishes between tastes[125]--and its accompanying discussion in 36:18-20, sets the tone for what follows.[126] It is a symbolic introduction to the necessity of careful decisions in human relations.

After this introduction, the first specific human relation which Ben Sira considers is one's dealing with his wife. That he treats the wife first is significant. For Ben Sira the most important distinguishing choice one must make in society is his selection of a wife. This is evident because of the negative experiences that can result from a poor choice.[127]

This treatment of the wife has the following internal structure: the theme statement (one distich--v. 21); a good wife's characteristics (two distichs--vv. 22-23); a good wife's contributions (four distichs--vv. 24-26). Let us consider each part in turn.

The theme statement of v. 21 is no doubt a traditional piece, as Fuss suggests.[128] But it is one that Ben Sira has altered to fit his particular view. This is clear from a comparison of this distich to the other three that together form the four traditional statements around which 36:18-37:15 is built. Note the formal construction of these distichs:[129]

36:18	Any food . . . /	Yet there is a food . . . .
36:21	Any man . . . /	Yet there is a woman . . . .
37:1	Any friend . . . /	Yet there is a friend . . . .
37:7	Any counselor . . . /	Yet there is a counselor . . . .

The first line of each distich makes a statement about every member of a particular class. The second line declares that some members of that class are more desirable than others. However, this pattern breaks down in v. 21.[130] Its formal relationship to the other distichs would suggest that we should expect:

Any man will a woman accept,
Yet one <u>man</u> is more pleasant than another.

Instead, Ben Sira has substituted in line <u>b</u> the word "woman" (<u>'šh</u>) for "man" (<u>zkr</u>). Thus, he took a statement about the levels of desirability of men as husbands and altered it to consider women as wives in this sense. While this section as a whole treats woman as good wife and has a positive surface, the theme statement itself is negative. Its negativeness results from Ben Sira's deliberate alteration of a traditional statement that, at worst, conveyed a neutral view of women.

As it now stands, v. 21 reflects the prevailing oriental custom, where at marriageable age the woman accepted the husband given her by her father.[131] The man (or his family) chose his wife, not the reverse. But not all candidates were equal. Some were more beautiful and congenial than others, as vv. 22-23 suggest. This required the future husband to choose with discrimination and wisdom.[132]

The first of two characteristics of the good wife that Ben Sira considers in this section is beauty (tw'r). This is the only instance where he uses tw'r[133] in a positive sense when related to women. In 9:8 and 42:12 the term is used to denote a negative characteristic.[134] In fact, Ben Sira seems to suggest that beauty in a woman is more of a problem than a blessing, because of its seductive potential. This is clear from 9:8 and 25:21, where in the latter he uses another word for beauty, ypy.[135] He does, however, convey a positive impression by using the adjective yph[136] "beautiful" in 26:16 and by the two verses that follow. Thus, Ben Sira is, at best, ambivalent regarding beautiful women. In a wife beauty is positive, but in other women it is negative.

A wife's beauty brings joy to her husband[137] or, as the text reads, "brightens the countenance."[138] Her looks surpass the eyes' greatest desire. Here, as in 26:13-18, the focus is on a beautiful wife, but only in terms of the pleasure she brings to her husband. He is the one who is benefitted by her pleasing characteristics. Thus, even Ben Sira's positive statement about a wife is found in the context of her subordinate role and sexual potential.

Fuss[139] considers this distich to be traditional and hence material taken over by Ben Sira. If this is the case, then its original reference was to a beautiful woman in general and not specifically to a wife. In such a setting it would retain the notion of woman as a sex object, though not necessarily viewed in a subordinate marital role.[140] But in its new context, linked to v. 23, which according to Fuss[141] is Ben Sira's composition, the traditional statement is made to reflect a beautiful wife, who is desired by her husband. Ben Sira has given the traditional material a negative coloring, despite its originally neutral impression and its present location in what is superficially a positive look at the good wife.

In v. 23 Ben Sira notes the second characteristic of a good wife. She should possess a soothing tongue. While he would prefer a wife to be silent (26:14), he will at least settle for one who speaks gently. He will not permit a wife to speak boldly (25:25). Thus, a wife's quality of speech is more significant than the quality of her looks.[142]

This characteristic of a good wife is also viewed in the context of its value to her husband. As a wife's silence is a gift to her husband from God (26:14), so her soothing speech gives him an advantage over most men. Her speech qualities are lauded not in terms of her own self-worth but in terms of their value to her husband. Furthermore, the statement implies that if a good wife possessed a soothing tongue, it would indeed be an unusual phenomenon, since it would set her husband apart from most men.[143]

Ben Sira moves from the wife's characteristics to discuss her contributions to the home. V. 24 opens with the declaration: "He who acquires a wife gets his best possession." The verb qnh, employed here in participle form, means "to acquire, buy." Usually the meaning assumes an actual business transaction, where valuables are exchanged.[144] While this is not the usual word for the establishing of a marriage,[145] it is confirmed in this sense by Ruth 4:10: "Also Ruth the Moabitess, the widow of Mahlom, I have bought (qnyty) to be my wife."

The word qnyn "possession, property" also deserves attention. In the OT it is used to denote items of personal property and is frequently found in combination with cattle and beasts.[146] However, while a wife is listed along with items of a man's personal property,[147] she is never specifically termed a qnyn. Thus, Ben Sira's use of the word in this connection represents a view of the wife's status which is lower than that portrayed in the OT.

The terms qnh and qnyn in this line suggest that, at least in Ben Sira's mind, the basis of Heb marriage was the purchase of the wife by the husband or his parents. The custom involved a transaction between the two sets of parents, whereby the husband[148] or his parents[149] sealed an agreement for him to marry another man's daughter by paying him the agreed upon price (mhr).[150] At that moment she became the husband's betrothed, an intermediate state toward marriage but closer to marriage than present day engagement.[151] After the marriage ceremony she passed fully under the control of her husband and into his household.[152]

Most students of Heb marriage hold that, though the transaction involved the presentation of something valuable to the father of the bride, the bride was not actually "sold" to her husband.[153] Rather, the mhr was a compensation[154] paid to the bride's family for their loss of a daughter. Outwardly, this resembled purchase, and thus the language of buying and selling[155] continued to be employed for the marriage transaction.[156] But in reality the wife was not sold into marriage.[157]

Ben Sira, however, goes beyond the appearance of purchase, which is reflected in the OT, and, by employing the terms qnh and qnyn,[158] suggests that marriage--and he has in mind a good marriage--is a matter of buying property. The fact that he calls the wife the best[159] property does not soften this assertion. He has taken OT and contemporary transactional language, which was used to some extent in a figurative way for marriage, and applied it with literal meaning through language that heightens that meaning.[160]

V. 24b notes two additional benefits of acquiring a wife. First, she is described as a "a helper suiting him."[161] This term was also used for the relationship of Eve to Adam (Gen 2:18, 20). It is a role the wife plays in relationship to her husband. He is the center of the expression. She is described in terms of him. Next, Ben Sira calls her "a pillar of support." This may recall the temple pillars,[162] for which the term _mwd_ was regularly used. In general the object of this support is the home. But the context would suggest that her husband is the specific object. He is the building which she supports. She does this by upholding his directives and not countering his wishes.

We see that the good wife in v. 24 is considered among her husband's possessions. He has purchased her along with other items. Her value is in her help and support[163] to him and not in any independent quality. She is evaluated solely in terms of her relationship to him.

Vv. 25-26 contain three distichs that treat the plight of a man who has no wife/home. Conversely, a wife is assumed to be a stablizing influence on a man. In v. 25a we have what seems to be a traditional proverb, which has no connection with a wife in the home. This is a piece of rural wisdom based on the same social condition that gave rise to the legislation in Exod 22:5.[164] Ben Sira uses this proverb to introduce the statement about a man without a wife in line _b_. But the comparison is forced and awkward. The fence in the original setting surely had no reference to a wife. But Ben Sira implies this, though he does not specifically make the comparison.[165] Instead, he suggests that the unmarried man "is a wanderer and a fugitive."[166] This hendiadys term is taken from the picture of Cain (Gen 4:12, 14). The wandering, unmarried man does not destroy the home, as line _a_ would suggest if this parallel were a closer one. Rather, line _b_ should be taken in its own right without regard to line _a_. The meaning is simply that an unmarried man is prone to behave like Cain, wandering from place to place with no roots.

In fact, this is the theme that Ben Sira pursues in the two distichs of v. 26. The first distich states the condition to which he attaches the comparison[167] of the wandering bachelor in the second distich. Just as no one will trust a roving band of Greek mercenary soldiers[168] looting from city to city, so no one will trust[169] a homeless man. Such a man is described as one "who has no nest."[170] Ben Sira already had before him in Prov 27:8 the figure of a nest in reference to a home.[171] A homeless man will wander from place to place (v. 25) and will spend the night wherever he happens to be. Such a person does not inspire confidence.[172]

In v. 26cd there is no mention of a wife nor the man's lack of one. But since v. 26 is an expansion of the theme of v. 25b, the homeless man of v. 26cd is understood to be wifeless as well. Furthermore, the implication of v. 26d is not only that such a man is wifeless but also that he cohabits[173] with whatever woman he happens to be with when evening falls.

The underlying suggestion of vv. 25-26 is that a wife will prevent a man from leading a roving, rootless existence. Such a condition would be socially unacceptable. Thus, a wife is necessary for a man to reach a respectable level in society.[174] This is her contribution. But it is a contribution that centers on the husband. Without her, he is distrusted as unstable and is socially incomplete.

Schilling[175] considers this entire section to be evidence of Ben Sira's positive stand on women. He points particularly to the contention that where there is no woman in the house there is no home. However, as we have seen, this is not the case. The fact that Ben Sira discusses a good wife in terms of positive phenomena such as beauty, good speech, helpfulness, support, and social acceptability is noteworthy. But these constitute a veneer beneath which we have seen his controlling, negative assessment of women. He has altered traditional proverbial material to suit his opinions. Furthermore, he describes the good wife only in relationship to her husband.[176] She satisfies him by her looks and words and becomes his best piece of property. Without a wife he would be socially deficient and suspect. Everything centers on the husband, with the wife leading a dependent existence solely for his good.

In addition to the two major texts discussed above, Sirach contains several miscellaneous reflections of the good wife. All are short statements in contexts that usually do not concern the question of women. I shall discuss each one briefly. The first group contains prohibitives.

7:19

Do not reject[177] a wise wife;[178]
And a charming wife[179] is above pearls.[180]

The context of this statement is first a formally[181] related set of twenty-two distichs (7:1-21), which constitutes a series of negative counsels on general social and religious themes. However, the statement is thematically related to vv. 23 (or possibly 22)-28,[182] which consider domestic matters. We may further note that both the initial twenty-two formally related distichs and vv. 22-28 are part of a larger section, 7:1-9:16. This section is characterized more by content--counsels on social relations--than by form.[183]

Gaspar[184] takes this statement to be a reference to divorce. Accordingly, Ben Sira counsels that husbands should not divorce wise wives. However, this does not appear to be the case. The imperative here is tm's "reject, despise," which is translated by the LXX with astochei "depart from, deviate from." The OT uses this with reference to a woman in Isa 54:6; Jer 4:30 but not with the notion of divorce.[185] The usual OT words for divorce are grš (verb) and krytwt (noun). These are rendered respectively by the LXX with ekballō and to biblion tou apostasiou. Thus, neither the Heb nor the LXX reading in this statement clearly suggests the idea of divorce. Instead, what is intended here is counsel to a husband not to despise or reject a wise wife.[186]

While our text is an isolated and undeveloped reference to women in the larger context of social relations, it does fit Ben Sira's patterned view of the good wife. He views her in the context of her husband and in terms of her usefulness to him. This does not mean that she is prized for her wise advise. In fact, her "wisdom" no doubt lies in her silence and docility. Elsewhere, Ben Sira considers a silent wife to be a gift from the Lord, while a babbling or outspoken wife is deplored.[187] If a wife is charming in addition to her "wise" restraint, she serves to meet her husband's desires.[188] He will value her "above pearls." Again the focus of this material concerning the good wife is really the husband. She is presented in terms of her relationship and value to her husband.

7:26a

Do you have a wife?[189] Do not abhor her.[190]

This text has several things in common with 7:19, which we discussed above. It shares the same extended context,[191] involves a similar prohibitive, and has also been taken as a reference to divorce. The immediate context of this statement is a series of counsels on domestic relationships.[192] But Ben Sira has probably fashioned this on a core of formally related, traditional[193] distichs, of which 7:26 is one. The others are vv. 22, 23, 24,[194] which deal with cattle, sons, and daughters respectively.

The first line of each of these four distichs begins by mentioning the category under consideration followed by lk. This forms a question ("Do you have . . . ?"). The line continues with a brief exhortation, followed by a complementary statement in the second stich. We may further note that vv. 22a, 23a, and 24a have the following pattern: category + lk + verb + object or prepositional phrase. In each case the exhortation which follows the question is positive. However, while v. 26a parallels the first lines of the other three traditional distichs in the question (category + lk), it departs from them in the pattern of the rest of the line. Its pattern is: category + lk + negative + verb (with pronominal suffix). Here the exhortation which follows the question is negative.

These traditional distichs contain second stichs which complement the positive exhortation of the first. But here also v. 26 departs from this pattern. Line b reads:

But do not trust in a wife whom you hate.

This line is antithetical and does not fit the analogy of the other distichs.

These incongruities of v. 26 to the other three traditional distichs suggest that Ben Sira has edited the original distich concerning women. We cannot reconstruct the original from what now exists. However, it is likely that the second half of line a was a positive exhortation to preserve the marriage, with line b complementing this suggestion and retaining the positive stance.

In considering the implications of this apparent redaction, I will deal here only with v. 26a.[195] One may argue that the exhortation which now stands in line a is positive, since it is something of a double negative ("do not abhor"). However, at best the present statement is neutral. It represents a distinct toning down of what we would expect, based on the pattern of the other traditional distichs. It is not a positive exhortation.

As mentioned above, this text has been understood to be a statement on divorce.[196] In fact, this is apparently the way the grandson understood it. Not only did he use the usual LXX verb for divorce (ekballō), but he also added the qualifying phrase kata psychēn to "wife." This allowed for divorce under certain circumstances.[197] However, the Heb verb is tʿb "abhor." It is never used for divorce, nor does the LXX, with this exception, render it with ekballō. As pointed out in our discussion of 7:19,[198] the Heb verb for divorce is grš which is always translated ekballō[199] by the LXX. Furthermore, line b, which is Ben Sira's antithetical redaction, does not suggest divorce for the hateful wife as we would expect if line a cautioned against divorce. Line a, then, does not refer to divorce but exhorts the married man not to abhor his wife.

Ben Sira appears to have softened the expected positive exhortation in the traditional distich represented by v. 26 to what is now a neutral statement.[200]

9:1

Do not be jealous[201] of the wife of your bosom,[202]
Lest[203] she learn[204] evil against you.[205]

Unlike the other miscellaneous texts considered here, this one occurs in a context that concerns women. This distich opens an eleven distich set of warnings about women (vv. 1-9). We may organize them either according to content or form, since the two do not completely coincide. Vv. 1-2 deal with one's own wife; vv. 3-4 concern loose women; v. 5 is about a virgin; vv. 6-7 warn against harlots; v. 8 considers beautiful women; v. 9 treats married women. The distich pattern, however, is: 2 (vv. 1-2) + 2 (vv. 3-4) + 2 (vv. 5-6) + 3 (vv. 7-8) + 2 (v. 9).

This section is related to 8:1-19 both in terms of the general tone of caution in social contacts and in the form of composition.[206] However, it is also part of the larger context of 7:1-9:16, with its counsels on social relations.[207]

Fuss[208] considers vv. 1, 3-6 to be traditional distichs incorporated by Ben Sira into the section, 9:1-9. These share a distinct form[209] in contrast to vv. 2, 7-9. The former have the pattern: ʼl / pn ("do not" / "lest"). V. 2,[210] however, has the form: ʼl / l- ("do not" / "to").

Do not give yourself to a wife
To cause her to tread upon your heights.

This is the only departure from the former pattern in the first six distichs. It is no doubt the result of Ben Sira's redactional addition.[211] I will consider the implications of this addition after a discussion of the meaning of v. 1.

The center of this statement is a prohibition against jealousy towards one's wife. This calls to mind the one biblical example of trial by ordeal (Num 5:11-31).[212] A husband who suspected his wife of conjugal infidelity could take her to the priest to determine her guilt or innocence. She was given a potion to drink and subjected to curses. If innocent, she would not be affected by the potion, but if guilty, she would suffer infertility and disgrace.[213] In our text the injunction is not against valid suspicion of infidelity but is a caution against groundless jealousy.

The wife is characterized here by the expression "the wife of your bosom" (<u>'št</u> <u>ḥyqk</u>).[214] It is not used in any paticularly endearing sense. Rather, like its OT uses, it merely constitutes a poetic reference to one's wife. Furthermore, it may be used here to fill out the meter of the line.[215]

Most commentators interpret line <u>b</u> assuming the LXX reading, i.e., that groundless jealousy "may promote the realization of the thing feared."[216] However, the Heb, which is to be preferred,[217] gives quite a different impression. The husband tempted to be groundlessly jealous of his wife is warned that she may, in fact, discover some marital infidelity on his part. Should this happen and should she expose him, he would suffer public embarrassment and disgrace. He could be held liable for violating another man's wife. The whole affair could result in both economic and political loss to him.

This traditional proverb adopted by Ben Sira is itself not very complimentary to women. At best it is a neutral assessment. The husband is counselled to avoid groundless jealousy against his wife but only for selfish reasons--she may be aroused to discover an impropriety on his part. But Ben Sira is even uncomfortable with this statement. Thus, he annotates it with the added distich (v. 2), which now stands as a corrective to the sweeping prohibition of v. 1. He can then say that, while groundless jealousy of one's wife is inadvisable, he should never submit to her attempts to dominate and deceive him.

The second group of miscellaneous references to the good wife contains positive statements in contrast to the foregoing prohibitives.

25:1

Three things my soul desired,
And they are beautiful in the sight of the Lord and of men:[218]
Harmony among brothers, and friendship among neighbors,
And a wife and husband[219] who share each other's company.[220]

This two distich piece is associated with v. 2, another two distich stanza, in both content and form. Both concern social elements that either please (v. 1) or displease (v. 2) their author(s). Together they stand at the head of a section, 25:1-11, that introduces a lengthy discussion of social responsibilities (25:13-32:13), the first major topic of which is devoted to women (25:13-26:18). They are preceded by the hymn to wisdom in chapter 24.[221]

Vv. 1-2 are also related formally. Both are Zahlensprüche of the single number variety (X).[222] They are built around the number three and are parallel in structure, though antithetical in content. Both stand out sufficiently from Ben Sira's usual aphorism style to warrant the conclusion that they are traditional. This is further suggested by their relationship to the material that follows.[223]

Some[224] interpret this proverb from the premise that Zahlensprüche reach a climax with the final item mentioned in the list that follows the introductory formula. This leads to an understanding of the proverb which approximates Gaspar's[225] paraphrase: "More lovely than harmony among brothers and friendship among neighbors are husband and wife suited to each other." However, as we shall see later in our fuller consideration of Zahlensprüche, the above mentioned premise is unwarranted.[226] Zahlensprüche are not predetermined to be either progressive or climactic. In fact, 25:1 is an example of a Zahlenspruch which is clearly not progressive towards a climax. The three elements, brothers, neighbors, spouses, do not represent a progressive order. Thus, the mention of wife and husband is of no more significance to the author[227] of the proverb than the other elements. These are merely three social phenomena that are characteristic of congeniality.

The mention of wife and husband in that order according to Gr is doubtlessly correct. The scribal tendency would be to give the more socially acceptable order, which is reflected in the other versions.[228] This order, however, is of little significance for our purposes, since the Zahlenspruch as a whole is probably traditional and does not reflect Ben Sira's preferences. It is surprising though that he did not alter the order to reflect his usual bias, since he has edited traditional material elsewhere.[229]

The relationships that are commended in 25:1 are not particularly noteworthy. However, they were not always present in society, and this gave rise to the sage's words. The description of the ideal wife and husband must not be understood in isolation, but as part of a threefold picture of desirable social relationships. The three entities are natural social units, and only as these units maintain internal compatibility can the social order survive. Thus, we find here a general reference to marital harmony,[230] which is one of several necessary ingredients to social stability.

This reference to the good wife is quite neutral, since it assumes that the normal and expected, though not always realized, role of a woman in marriage is one of compatibility and cooperation. It is likely a traditional proverb that Ben Sira has incorporated into his composition. However, in this case we see no evidence that he altered it. It thus reflects his viewpoint only insofar as he has inserted the piece. Nevertheless, the generality and basic neutrality of the implication is such that would not be out of harmony with his usually negative bias. He may have even read the statement with the view that the wife's submissive subordination is the element necessary for marital harmony, though, of course, the text itself does not suggest this.

25:8a

Blessed[231] is he who possesses[232] a wise wife.[233]

This beatitude is one of two (see also v. 9a) that comprise a ten element Zahlenspruch, which, along with the two previously noted Zahlensprüche, stands at the head of a long consideration of social relationships (25:1-32:13).[234] This particular Zahlenspruch contains a list of items that please the author, including domestic, social, intellectual, and religious phenomena. Like the other Zahlensprüche in this setting, this one appears to be traditional. This is suggested not only by its distinctive form but particularly by Ben Sira's editorial comments in v. 11 on the final element (v. 10b).

The form of this Zahlenspruch differs from that of those in vv. 1-2. While the latter are single number Zahlensprüche (X), this one is a double number type (X/X+1). The introductory formula (v. 7ab) reads:

With nine thoughts I have gladdened my heart,
And a tenth I shall tell with my tongue.

Though it cannot be predetermined for all Zahlensprüche[235] of either the double or single number varieties, this one does appear to reach a climax with the final element that mentions the one who fears the Lord (v. 10b).

The most immediate problem with this Zahlenspruch is the fact that the Gr has preserved only nine of the ten elements which are called for in the introductory formula.[236] Spicq[237] suggests that the author considers the ninth element, the fear of the Lord, to be supreme and a résumé of all the other elements. Hence, it is also termed the tenth. We must reject this solution, since there is no such analogy among Zahlensprüche. The mutilated text of HebC and the Syr would appear to solve the problem. Each of these contains an additional stich after v. 8a:

And he who does not plough[238] with ox and ass.[239]

Thus, HebC and Syr contain ten elements, and so the problem is solved for most scholars.[240]

Those who read the text in this way generally interpret v. 8b as an enlargement of the idea of v. 8a or as a related idea suggested by v. 8a. Both views assume that the reference is metaphorical for sexual intercourse and/or marriage.[241] The enlargement idea is supported by the Syr, "and who does not plough . . . ."[242] However, this understanding is unlikely, since none of the other elements of this Zahlenspruch completes the idea of the one before it.

The Heb is more consistent with the pattern of the construction and supports the view that line b represents a separately commended man, with the subject matter suggested by line a. The interpretations of the metaphor include marriages that involve: adultery or a heathen wife;[243] a poor husband and a rich wife or quarrelsome wives;[244] a sensible husband and a stupid wife.[245] No matter which view of the relationship between lines a and b one holds, the fact remains that line b stands in awkward contrast to the remaining elements of the Zahlenspruch. Not only is it the only metaphorical expression among direct statements, but its cryptic nature makes it unique and totally unexpected in this context. Thus, it would appear that line b was part of neither the traditional Zahlenspruch nor Ben Sira's composition, since the Gr does not know it.

However, since the Gr does know an introductory formula that calls for ten elements, we cannot simply say that the original Zahlenspruch had but nine elements. To account for these phenomena I offer the following hypothesis. The traditional Zahlenspruch incorporated here by Ben Sira contained ten elements. However, the particular text that served as the archetype for the grandson had one element, namely 25:8b,[246] missing.[247] The Gr reflected its archetype faithfully at this point even to the inconsistency between the introductory formula and the number of elements. The Syr represents an attempt to overcome this inconsistency by inserting an element after the third to complete the number. But the Syr did not insert a new idea. Rather, it enlarged on the idea already expressed in v. 8a. HebC followed Syr but conformed the inserted element to the others by making it a category related to, but separate from, line a.[248]

Whether or not this hypothesis is sound, the point seems certain that 25:8b is secondary to both the original Zahlenspruch and to Ben Sira. Thus, we need not concern ourselves further with its meaning, since it does not reflect Ben Sira's view.

V. 25:8a does stand in the text and does reflect Ben Sira's view. The participle[249] is a form of the verb b`l, whose predominant meaning in the MT is "take possession of a wife."[250] Ben Sira is comfortable with the view that a wife is a possession[251] and feels no impulse to alter the text of this traditional statement.[252] In our discussion of 7:19 we dealt with the implication of passive restraint suggested by Ben Sira's own use of the expression 'šh mśklt "a wise wife."

28:15

The third tongue[253] has cast out[254] courageous women[255]
And deprived[256] them of their labors.[257]

This distich is part of a section, 28:13-26, which deals with the dangers of the tongue. Along with vv. 14, 16 it specifically considers slander, "the talk of a third party" (NEB). Among the effects of slander Ben Sira notes the following: many are shaken and scattered internationally; cities and prominent families are overturned; those who listen to it find no rest.

In the middle of this discussion v. 15 declares that slander has caused courageous women to be cast out. As we noted in our consideration of 7:26a, the word ekballō employed here is the regular LXX verb for divorce.[258] The expected Heb term would be grš. Unlike 7:19 and 7:26a[259] the reference in 28:15 is to divorce. This is suggested not only by the use of ekballō but also by the implication of v. 15b and the analogy of v. 14.

The particular women/wives mentioned are termed andreias. This word, which basically means "pertaining to a man" or "manly," was sometimes used with reference to women in the sense of "courageous."[260] Though it may have a negative connotation ("stubborn"[261]), it would seem to be positive in this context. The implication is that innocent wives have been slandered before their husbands by rival wives or other third persons. The injured wives endure such slander but are nevertheless expelled from their households. The effect of these divorces is that such women are cut off from their labors or, more likely, the fruit of their toil.[262] The latter no doubt refers to both the children they have produced and the wealth they have accumulated during their marriages.[263]

Since this section, vv. 13-26, is not extant in Heb, we should be cautious in considering the question of source based on the constructions in Gr. Yet, we notice certain characteristics that would suggest that this piece, or at least parts of it, appears to be traditional. Note the clear contrast between cursing (v. 13 and the negative implications in vv. 14-18) and blessing (v. 19 and the positive implications in vv. 20-22) and also the identically beginning stichs of v. 17.[264] Whether or not these indicate a traditional origin is secondary to our interest here. What is noteworthy is the fact that vv. 14-16 constitute a rather tight subsection of vv. 13-26, consisting of two strophes of two distichs each. Both strophes begin with the phrase glōssa tritē, followed by the direct object and the verb. The first strophe is tighter than the second, but each seems poetically conceived. It would appear reasonable to cautiously conclude that at least vv. 14-16 are traditional to Ben Sira.

If this conclusion holds, then the view expressed is not directly Ben Sira's. However, he has included it here, and we have no evidence that he altered it. While he has no hesitation suggesting divorce for a rebellious wife,[265] he readily sees the value of an obedient and desirable wife, as we have seen in this chapter. Thus, for unfair slander to break up a good marriage would be as distasteful to Ben Sira as to the author of these apparently traditional words.

40:19, 23

19 A child and a city establish a name,[266]
But better than both is he who finds wisdom.
Young cattle and planting cause food to flourish,
But better than both is a devoted wife.[267]
23 A friend and a companion[268] will lead at the right time,[269]
But better than both is a wise wife.[270]

These three distichs are among ten[271] formally related distichs that constitute vv. 18-26b. In each distich line a notes two desirable and related items, while line b declares that a third item, usually unrelated to the first two, is better than both.[272] Because the items in line b of each distich are rather unrelated to those in the corresponding line a, one may be tempted to conclude that the former are Ben Sira's set of priorities appended to a traditional list of desirable items. But the entire piece is rather tightly constructed, suggesting that it was a conscious creation as a unit. Furthermore, the listing of items in the initial distich lines is sensible only in the context of the statements of superiority in the second distich lines. It is more reasonable to take the whole construction as traditional,[273] with Ben Sira's characteristic expansion of the Gottesfurcht idea[274] in vv. 26c-27.

I have included v. 19ab only because in Gr vv. 19a and 19d form a distich with 19bc missing.[275] However, since lines ab do not fall within our area of concern I shall not discuss them further.

In v. 19cd the comparison is between two food sources, cattle and crops, and a devoted[276] wife, with the latter declared to be superior. Though it is likely traditional, this reference to a devoted wife is not antithetical to Ben Sira's understanding of a wife's expected stance toward her husband.[277] Her role is husband oriented.

The comparison in v. 23 is between the counsel offered by a friend and a companion and the superior quality of a wise wife. We have already discussed Ben Sira's own use of this phrase in 7:19[278] and found it to essentially reflect the notion of passive restraint. Thus, this traditional use of the phrase fits well with Ben Sira's view.

The impact of these miscellaneous references to the good wife on our working hypothesis is minimal, since most of the statements appear to be traditional.[279] Ben Sira is usually comfortable with their rather neutral[280] or slightly negative[281] posture toward women. However, in two cases he has apparently altered the traditional statements[282] or appended his own material[283] to negatively color the originals. These serve to underline Ben Sira's negative bias.

Conclusion

In the two major texts that we have considered in this chapter, Ben Sira discusses the virtues of the good wife. However, he treats her only in relationship to her husband. The husband obtains and maintains her as valuable property. Her physical appearance and sexual attractiveness stimulate him. But she will be prized most if she remains silent. Without her in the home he would suffer social stigma. In short, she has no existence independent of her husband.

Furthermore, we have noted Ben Sira's redaction of pieces of traditional material, which he incorporated into his composition. At times, he altered positive or neutral statements on women to make them negative in their new setting. He does use unedited traditional material concerning women but mostly in contexts where the mention of women is incidental to the larger themes. Such references are neutral to slightly negative and are not antithetical to Ben Sira's negative bias.

In a setting where we might expect Ben Sira to be positive, we have in fact found him to be negative. While the good wife has virtues, the fact that she is a woman is for him a negative status. He measures her goodness only in terms of the tangible benefits she represents to man.

CHAPTER II

WOMAN AS MOTHER AND WIDOW

Introduction

Ben Sira's material concerning women includes reflections of the categories of mother and widow. In this chapter I shall construct a profile of his view of women in relationship to these related categories. First, I shall examine his remarks concerning mothers. This will include both his major, extended statements and his incidental references. I shall also note and discuss a group of miscellaneous expressions that relate to mother. Finally, I shall treat his two remarks concerning widows. This will provide a basis for summarizing Ben Sira's view of woman as mother and widow.

Before we consider the first section of Sirach which contains references to mother, we must note an important phenomenon. Ben Sira never discusses mother as an independent category.[1] He refers to literal mothers[2] in only two ways.[3] The most frequent form involves distich parallelism, in which reference to father in the first stich is accompanied by reference to mother in the second. We also find Ben Sira using the expression "father and mother." Thus, he mentions mother only in relationship to father. This suggests that Ben Sira is not concerned with a woman's particular role as mother. Instead, he introduces her as part of a parallel construction or compound expression that represents a literary convention which means parents.[4] We may also observe that in these constructions mother is subordinate to father, since she always appears second in the parallel or the expression.

3:1-16

1 Listen to me your father, O children;[5]
And act accordingly, that you may be kept in safety.
2 For the Lord honored[6] the father above his children,
And made firm[7] the authority[8] of the mother over her sons.[9]
3 He who honors[10] his father atones for sins,[11]
4 And he who glorifies[12] his mother is like one who stores up treasure.[13]
5 Whoever honors his father will be gladdened by his own children.
And when he prays he will be heard.
6 He who glorifies[14] his father will prolong his life,[15]
And he who gives his mother rest[16] renders good to God.[17]
8 Honor your father by word and deed,
That a blessing from him may come upon you.
9 A father's blessing establishes a root,[18]
But a mother's curse[19] uproots the plant.
10 Do not glorify yourself by dishonoring your father,
For your father's dishonor is no glory to you.
11 A man's glory is the glory[20] of his father,
But he who dishonors[21] his mother multiplies shame.[22]
12 O son, help your father in his old age,
And do not grieve him as long as he lives.
13 Even if he is lacking in understanding, show forbearance;
In all your strength do not despise him.
14 For kindness to a father will not be forgotten,
And against your sins it will be credited to you,
15 In the day of your affliction it will be remembered in your favor;
As frost in fair weather, your sins will melt away.
16 He who forsakes[23] his father is like a blasphemer,[24]
And he who provokes[25] his mother is cursed[26] by God.[27]

This section, which contains fourteen distichs,[28] is an expansion of Exod 20:12. As a whole, the section treats one's responsibilities to his parents.[29] Haspecker[30] considers it one of Ben Sira's most careful and perhaps independent compositions, reflecting an individualization of the traditional promise of blessing and a thoroughgoing transposition into personal religion. In each distich there is a direct or indirect reference to father.[31] But in six distichs (vv. 2-4,

6, 9, 11, 16) the mention of father in line a is paralleled by the mention of mother in line b.[32] We will be concerned here with only these six distichs.

However, before we discuss these distichs, it is necessary to consider the genuineness of v. 7:

He who fears the Lord will honor his father,
And will serve his parents as masters.

The textual evidence is as follows: the entire distich is missing in Heb and Syr; line b is included in GrI (with the exception of 421, 755) and in La; line a is found only in GrII (Origenistic recension, Lucianic recension, 694, 743, 768) and La.

As Haspecker[33] aptly notes, the question of genuineness must relate to the whole distich, since a tristich (6ab + 7b) is unimaginable in this section. Most scholars[34]--some hesitantly--accept the entire distich as genuine. Haspecker,[35] however, argues for it most extensively. He asserts that v. 7b requires v. 7a, and that both are required on grounds of the structure of the entire section. For him v. 7 has the central transitional role of linking the general statements before it to the more direct parenesis after it. But his main and thinly veiled reason for including the distich is its reference to Gottesfurcht,[36] which for him is the hermeneutical key to Sirach.

However, we must consider the formidable evidence against the genuineness of v. 7. Haspecker himself admits that this distich disturbs the connection of v. 8 to vv. 3-6, with v. 7 introducing a new element, obedience, as opposed to the general call for respect and care. He also notes a formal objection. The rest of the section alternates between distichs about father and those which include a parallel involving father and mother. V. 7 breaks this pattern. But apart from the considerable textual problem, which Haspecker completely ignores, the most potent objection to this distich lies in the use of the term tois gennēsasin auton "to those who begat him" (RSV "his parents") in v. 7b. Not only does this break the above mentioned pattern, but it also represents a term which is totally uncharacteristic of the LXX rendition of the Heb OT. The latter has no word for "parents" and reflects the idea through the phrase "father and mother."[37] This expression is translated literally by the LXX. The aorist active participle of gennaō is never used alone for "parents."[38] It is unlikely that we should expect a Heb Vorlage of "father and mother" behind the Gr "those who begat" mentioned in the same stich. Furthermore, if v. 7a from GrII were admitted, the first stich would contain a reference to "father." The complement in line b should be "mother," if the analogy of vv. 2-4, 6, 9, 11, 16 were followed. Otherwise, we might expect the continuation of the father idea, as in vv. 1, 5, 8, 10, 12-15.

For these reasons I take the entire distich identified as v. 7 to be secondary to Ben Sira. It was no doubt added to the text in stages. That v. 7 is early is evident from its inclusion in GrI. It was probably an expansion of the notion of obedience in v. 6b (Gr). This left the text with an uncharacteristic tristich, a situation which gave rise to the GrII addition of v. 7a to restore the distich pattern.

The first distich in 3:1-16 to mention mother as a parallel to father is v. 2. It functions as the motivation for complying with the imperative of v. 1.[39] Why should one honor his parents? One should do so because the Lord himself honored the father and the mother. This is probably a reference to the decalogue item[40] that the writer of the Epistle to the Ephesians termed "the first commandment with a promise."[41] The distich is a tight parallel with "the Lord" serving as the subject of both stichs. Consequently, there is nothing particularly significant about what is assigned to father as opposed to mother. The predicates "honored . . . above . . . children" and "made firm the authority . . . over . . . sons" mean virtually the same thing. Furthermore, as we have seen, the reference to father and mother is simply the Heb way of saying parents[42]—a way convenient to poetic parallelism.[43]

The term krisis in v. 2b stands in the LXX most frequently for mšpṭ. This Heb word for judgment may also mean "right, claim, due," especially the right of the oppressed.[44] Ben Sira uses the word (and Gr follows with krisis) in 38:16, where he encourages the living to bury a dead person with the "honor due" him. Thus, the expression "made firm the authority" conveys the notion of divinely established parental right or honor over their children.[45] The fact that it is said of the mother is not significant, as we noted above.

Vv. 3-4 constitute the second distich of the strophe, vv. 2-4. Like v. 2, each stich of this distich contains three units that are parallel to each other: "he who honors" / "he who glorifies"; "his father" / "his mother"; "atones for sins" / "is like one who stores up treasure."[46] The storing up of treasure is clearly to be understood metaphorically as the accumulation of meritorious credit worthy of divine favor in the day of judgment.[47] This expression is a parallel equivalent to the atoning for sin in v. 3.

Box-Oesterley[48] see here an early stage in the development of the Jewish doctrine of atonement. To honor one's parents is to fulfill an injunction of the decalogue, producing a meritorious act toward atonement. This idea is repeated and enlarged in vv. 14-15, where the act is "kindness to a father."[49] Thus, the motivation for favorable treatment of parents is the prospect of advantage that one will have in the judgment. It does not arise from any larger ethical concern but from self-interest.[50]

This distich, like the previous one, continues the father and mother parallel to mean parents. The statement about the mother, therefore, has no independent value, except that a mother is accorded an important place of honor along with a father. However, she is not treated separately and is characteristically listed second.

Following v. 5, which treats only the father, the two distich strophe continues in v. 6 with another father and mother parallel. However, this parallel is not as tight as those we have already observed.[51] Apart from "father" / "mother," the other phrases represent complementary, but looser, parallels. To "he who glorifies his father" line b parallels "he who gives his mother rest," and to "will prolong his life"[52] line b gives "renders good to God."

The expression "to give rest" is based on Smend's emended reading mnyḥ.[53] In Hif`il I the predominant idea behind the verb is the giving of rest as freedom from distress in its various forms. Most frequently the distress is war[54] or enemies[55] but may also be misfortune,[56] pain, turmoil, or hard service.[57] Thus, unlike the active glorifying of the father in v. 6a, the giving of rest to the mother is more passive--keeping her from distress and things negative. This is hardly an expression of piety that is "more tender and more delicate toward the mother,"[58] compared to the glorifying of the father.

The result of this rest-giving is that one "renders good to God." If this reconstruction of the Heb based on the Syr[59] is sound, then the term used here was gml "render (good, evil) to." While the positive use of this word with reference to God is without parallel in the OT, the rendering of evil to God is expressed in Deut 32:6 and Joel 3:4 (4:4 Heb). The context[60] of the former in particular suggests a state of rebellion, abandonment, and disobedience of Israel toward Yahweh. Thus, in our text the opposite, rendering good, would suggest faithfulness and obedience to God, as the free translation of the Gr correctly divined.[61] Such an idea would be related to the miṣwāh orientation of the whole distich, which is especially evident in a line a.

The parallel use of father and mother again reflects the Heb idiom for parents. Nothing here stated about the mother is noteworthy apart from her role as parent along with the father.

The next mention of mother is in v. 9,[62] the second half of a two distich strophe. This distich is the first antithetical parallel that we encounter in the section. We will meet another in v. 11. The antitheses are related and tight:

"father's blessings" / "mother's curse"; "establishes a root" / "uproots the plant." The first pair continues the practice of paralleling father and mother to equal parents. We may, therefore, understand this general idea for both stichs.

The parents are here portrayed as regents who transmit divine blessings and curses.[63] That Ben Sira sees God as the real source of parental authority is evident in vv. 2 and 16. But blessings and curses presuppose positive and negative behavior on the part of children toward their parents,[64] especially their relationship to the suggestions Ben Sira offers in this section. He may be thinking particularly of one's duties to aged parents,[65] since it is in old age that parents usually bless their children.[66]

The figures of planting and uprooting are here employed as general metaphors of prosperity and adversity,[67] arising from parental blessings and curses. Children can expect to prosper under parental blessing but to fail under parental curse.

As noted above, v. 11 is the second of two antithetical parallels in this section. Together with v. 10 it forms a two distich strophe, which is built on the contrast between honor and dishonor to parents.[68] The first distich is directed to the reader (or listener) and is probably from Ben Sira. V. 11, however, is a related epigram addressed to no one in particular and is probably traditional. The first distich is negative, dealing with dishonor to one's father, while the second is mixed, considering honor to one's father and dishonor to one's mother.

The elements of antithesis in v. 11 are: "a man's glory" / "he multiplies shame" and "the glory of his father" / "who dishonors his mother." While these are not tight, formal parallels, like some that we have seen in this section, they represent, nevertheless, genuine idea parallels expressed antithetically. Line b expresses the negative side of line a and, therefore, offers no special insight. The parallel mention of father and mother, as before, merely equals parents.

The strophe as a unit conveys the idea that honor to one's parents is honor to oneself.[69] Conversely, dishonor to one's parents brings no honor to a person and leaves him in shame and disgrace.

The concluding distich in the section, v. 16, is another synonymous parallel. However, unlike the other such parallels that we have treated, this one deals exclusively with negative material.[70] The paralleled expressions are: "he who forsakes his father" / "he who provokes his mother" and "is like a blasphemer" / "is cursed by God." The former is tight and continues the characteristic father and mother parallel, which together means parents. The latter, however, is less tight, with line _a_ assuming God to be the object and line _b_ identifying God as the source of the action. More significant is the fact that a God-oriented idea is found in both stichs.

In effect, the entire section is inclosed by two God-related distichs. In v. 2 the Lord is said to have honored and authorized parents. The present distich concludes the discussion by having God curse the one who provokes his mother.[71] The motivational function of the latter for the enactment of the advice in the preceding verses is obvious. The threat of divine curse is an even stronger motive than the prospect of parental blessing.[72]

As we noted above, the parallel of father and mother means simply parents, which implies that there is no independent meaning to the mother statement in v. 16b. Instead, the motivational function of the distich is that to forsake or provoke one's parents is to blaspheme God[73] and be cursed by him.

In summarizing our findings for this section, we note that the focus centers on one's responsibilities to his parents. Characteristically, the notion of parents is expressed by the parallel involving father and mother. Mother is not here mentioned apart from father. Reference to her is merely a convention that equals the second half of a parallel, which together means parents. However, since he is always mentioned first in this parallel, father is predominant and more characteristic of parenthood for Ben Sira.[74]

We have also seen that where the father and mother parallel is employed the statements concerning mother exhibit no independent value. Rather, they usually echo closely the material related to father in the first stich of the parallel. This is not to deny that the juxtaposition of mother to father in this section represents an important and honored role ascribed to women who attain the status of motherhood. Such exaltation is universal, ancient and modern. Yet, this is because of the mother's obvious role in the preservation of the name and the family lineage.

This section is dependent on Exod 20:12. We may note, however, that in the distich which most nearly reflects the decalogue commandment, v. 8, Ben Sira does not refer to mother. His advice is simply, "Honor your father."

One should not conclude that Ben Sira is negative on motherhood in this section. Nevertheless, despite the elevated position of a woman who is a mother--meaning particularly the mother of a son--he does not treat her independently of her husband or of her partnership in parenthood. Even in the latter she is always number two.

<u>7:27-28</u>

27 With your whole heart honor your father,[75]
And do not forget your mother who bore you.[76]
28 Remember, that if they did not exist, you would not exist;[77]
And what shall you return to them that compares to what they have given you?[78]

This counsel concerning parents is part of a section that considers domestic matters (vv. 22-28).[79] These include statements about animals, sons, daughters, wives, and parents. The first distich, v. 27, would appear to be a traditional exhortation, modeled to some extent on Exod 20:12. If this is valid, then Ben Sira has incorporated a proverb that reflects the typical Heb father and mother parallel, that expresses the equivalent of parents.[80] That this is the intention of the parallel is confirmed by the double use of the word "them" in v. 28.

The second distich is no doubt Ben Sira's elaboration of the general theme introduced in v. 27. He insists on gratitude and respect toward one's parents by pointing to their priority in time, their role in bearing their offspring, and their incomparable gifts of life and development to their children.

This section offers no new insights into Ben Sira's view of mother. He mentions her only in relationship to her husband, who is a father. The traditional material that he appears to incorporate is a discussion of parents expressed as father in parallel with mother. Ben Sira's own extended discussion does not even repeat the terms father and mother but refers to parents together simply as "them." As in 3:1-16, mother is here mentioned second to father and is not given any independent consideration.[81]

23:14

Remember your father and mother[82]
When[83] you sit in council[84] among great men;[85]
Lest you stumble[86] in their presence
And be regarded a fool[87] because of your manner;[88]
And you will wish you had never been born,[89]
And you will curse the day of your birth.

Before treating this verse in particular, we must consider its setting. The text is part of an instructional section, which consists of 23:7-15. This is preceded in 22:27-23:6 by a prayer, which calls for control of one's mouth (words), mind (ideas), and eyes (desires--lust and gluttony).[90] The prayer clearly serves to introduce the instructional material that follows.[91]

The section on language contains two subsections. Vv. 7-11 provide counsel on oath-taking. This is followed in vv. 12-15 by instruction on avoiding insolent speech.[92] While these subsections are not equal in length,[93] they are arranged according to an identical pattern. Each contains in order an introduction, a negative imperative, an illustration, and a motivation statement.[94] What concerns us here is v. 14, the illustration material in the second subsection.

In v. 14a Ben Sira makes reference to parents with the characteristic expression "father and mother."[95] He suggests that one should not disgrace his parents by negative behavior in public, especially by his manner of speaking. The setting that he describes is no doubt the council of the elders,[96] in which the reader is likely to participate. To use insolent speech in such a context would dishonor one's parents. Thus, for Ben Sira the remembrance of one's parents should serve as a deterrent to using such language in public. If one should "stumble" in this way, he would regret it to the point that life itself would seem meaningless.[97] Such despair does not result from the act itself, which may have only temporary consequences, but comes from the disgrace brought upon the family.

This text sheds little light on Ben Sira's view of mother. As in the texts that we have discussed above, mother is mentioned here only as the second element in the literary convention "father and mother" (or in some places father in parallel with mother) which stands for parents. Therefore, 23:14 says nothing about mother, apart from the fact that she is a parent. Along with father, she may act as a deterrent to a person's negative behavior in public.

<u>41:17a</u>

Be ashamed[98] of[99] insolence[100] to[101] father and mother.

This stich is part of a section on shame (41:14-42:8) and a subsection on things concerning which one should show shame (41:17-23 <u>RSV</u>).[102] It contains the verbal imperative that is understood for the entire subsection, with each succeeding stich merely adding the object of the shame. The stich is also a part of a smaller unit, vv. 17-19a, which is characterized by its formal construction. Each stich in this unit contains an indication of the context in which or the object to whom a particular negative, shameful act is performed.[103] This is followed by the designation of the act itself.[104] Using this pattern, the unit describes insolence to father and mother (v. 17a), lying to a prince and a ruler (v. 17b), conspiracy toward a master and a mistress (v. 18a), transgression in an assembly and a people (v. 18b), unfaithfulness to a partner and a friend (v. 18c), and theft in the place where one lives (v. 19a).

We may further observe that in all but the last of these six stichs the context or object is expressed by two parallel terms. In each case these terms are so closely related that we may safely conclude that they are hendiadys expressions, referring, in fact, to a single reality. Thus, the expression "father and mother" equals parents. We have seen this to be the typical Heb (and Ben Sira's) way of designating parents. But here we have the added confirmation of such a meaning based on the analogy of similar hendiadys expressions in the immediate context.

The behavior that is condemned in our text is different from the insolent speech in 23:12-15. Both refer to insolence and to parents, but the contexts are different. In the latter the insolent speech is displayed in the public assembly, against which display the thought of one's parents serves as deterrent. Here, however, the insolent behavior is directed toward one's parents themselves, as the parallel items in the context show. What is described here is more like the situation reflected in 3:11b[105] where dishonor of a parent brings shame.

Our text has nothing distinctive to say about mother. As in the previous discussions, we find here that mother is mentioned along with father only as a literary convention that means parents. As a parent she is to be honored, and to be insolent toward her is to bring shame upon oneself.

15:2a

And she will meet him like a mother.

We have already treated the setting of this text and found the simile to represent personified Wisdom,[106] who comes to a person like his mother.[107] This is the only mention of mother in Sirach, apart from birth-related expressions, that is not juxtaposed to father. Here mother is paralleled to wife (v.

2b). Both serve merely to describe personified Wisdom. Ben Sira has nothing to say here about the role or status of woman as mother, apart from the allusion to her tender regard for her children implied in the simile.

Miscellaneous Mother-Related Expressions

Besides the direct references to mother in the texts that we have discussed, Ben Sira also employs several expressions that relate to mother. Chief among these is the term womb. Every reference is to origin or birth. In 1:14 Wisdom is said to have been created with the faithful "in the womb."[108] God has allotted man much labor "from the day of his coming forth from his mother's womb" until his death[109] (40:1). In praising famous men, Ben Sira notes that Jeremiah was "a prophet preserved from the womb" (49:7).[110] And at the end of this section he places a benediction (50:22-24), which contains the notion that the God of all "exalts man from the womb" (v. 22).

Two additional birth ideas are found in Ben Sira's use of the words ḥyl "to suffer the pain of childbirth" (cf. Gr ōdinō) and yld "to bring forth a child" (cf. Gr tiktō). Each is used in a purely figurative way. In a description of various elements of the weather in 43:17 Ben Sira declares, "The voice of his thunder makes his earth have birth pains (yḥyl)."[111] We also find a simile using the Gr equivalent (Heb is not extant) in 34(31):5, where the emptiness of divinations, omens, and dreams are compared to the imaginings of "a woman with birth pains (ōdinousēs)."[112] The second word is reflected metaphorically in 8:18. Here Ben Sira cautions against trusting a secret to a stranger, "for you do not know what he will bring forth (yld) in the end."[113] In 10:18 reference to "man" in line a is paralleled in line b by the periphrastic expression "one born of woman" (ylwd ʾšh). In two cases Ben Sira employs both terms in close context. The description of the people of Jerusalem under the threat of Sennacherib[114] includes the statement in 48:19 that their pride was shaken "and they writhed (wyḥylw) like a woman with birth pains (kywldh)." While Heb is not extant in 19:11, Gr reflects the same dual figure:

A fool will have birth pains (ōdinēsei) because of a word,
Like a woman in labor (hē tikousa) because of a child.[115]

In both these examples the texts use the metaphor of birth pain, followed by the simile of a woman bringing forth a child.

These miscellaneous references to mother add nothing to our understanding of Ben Sira's assessment of woman as mother. They are merely conventional literary figures used to convey ideas of origin and birth, as well as the notions of discomfort and pain.

We turn now to the category of widow, which is a minor one in Sirach. Because the two categories are inherently related, I have chosen to treat Ben Sira's two isolated references to widows at the end of this chapter on his view of mother.

4:10

Be like a father to orphans,[116]
And instead of a husband[117] to widows;[118]
And God will call you a son[119]
And will be gracious to you[120] and will deliver you from the pit.[121]

These two distichs complete a section, 4:1-10, which contains general counsel on one's duty toward the poor and oppressed. This group is identified in many ways,[122] with the distichs often noting two categories in parallel.[123] The orphan/widow distich (v. 10ab) is the last in the section which identifies particular classes of the oppressed. It is more specific than the other distichs. This leaves v. 10cd as the conclusion to the entire section. It is a motivation clause to encourage the behavior suggested. I have included it here solely because Gr reads "mother" in line d.[124]

Both the identification of widows as a class and the consciousness that the group needed special social protection have been evident in legal and wisdom literature since early times.[125] Such is also the case in the OT, where we may add the testimony of the prophets as well.[126] All agree that a widow was a formerly married woman whose husband had died, and who had not remarried. While some[127] limit the definition to this, others[128] add that only those women who, having met the above characteristics, also were found to be without financial support and legal protection were classified _ʼlmnwt_ "widows." It is not my purpose here to enter this debate on definition, apart from observing that the OT use of _ʼlmnh_ appears to be sufficiently general so as to sometimes describe simply a woman bereaved of her husband without further qualification.[129] That she was often the victim of social and legal exigency is evident from the widespread counsel for her support. Otwell may only slightly exaggerate when he calls her condition "the gravest extremity in which the Israelite woman might find herself."[130]

For Ben Sira the one who would be a son of God or of Wisdom[131] must, among other things, support and protect orphans as though he were their father and widows as though he were their husband. This counsel is not to be understood as a call for the adoption of orphans and the marriage of widows. Nor is it a command to fulfill the levirate responsibility. By supporting and protecting all the oppressed, and in particular the orphans and widows, one will be called God's son. This is appropriate, since the ultimate protector of these classes is God himself. Such a theme is prominent in the OT[132] and is also reflected in Ben Sira.[133]

Otwell argues that, since they are regularly grouped not only with orphans but with resident aliens, widows have a status equal to at least certain males. He observes that "a male sojourner had no advantage over the Israelite without family."[134] All three groups lacked participation in an Israelite family[135] and its accompanying economic and legal security. Such reasoning with regard to the status of women in the OT is shaky at best.[136] But for Ben Sira it would be quite unfounded, since here widows are directly related only to orphans,[137] who as children were always classed with women as the weaker, minor members of a household.

Ben Sira is not concerned here with the status of women as widows. He merely recognizes the existence of such a class of women and, in harmony with the standard legal and wisdom traditions, calls for their support. To uphold and protect them is part of the universal social conscience of the ancient Near East.

35(32):14-15

14 He will not ignore the groaning[138] of the orphan,[139]
Nor the widow[140] when she pours out[141] her chatter.[142]
15 Do not the tears[143] flow down on the cheek[144]
And sigh[145] against the one who causes them to fall?[146]

After discussing acceptable (34[31]:18-26) and unacceptable (35[32]:1-11) sacrifices and associated circumstances, Ben Sira extends the latter into a contemplation of God who is the judge of social injustice. This section, 35(32):12-20, opens with a two distich introduction of God as impartial judge (v. 12).[147] The next two distich strophe (vv. 13-14) particularizes the introductory assertion by relating God's impartial judgment to specific oppressed groups in society. The groups[148] mentioned here also occur in the more extensive listing found in 4:1-10.[149] The rest of the section includes the cry of the oppressed (vv. 15-16), the prayer of the weak (v. 17), God's vengeance on social evil (vv. 18-19), and the welcomeness of God's mercy (v. 20).

We have noted the relationship between this section and 4:1-10. As in the earlier pericope, the mention of orphan and widow here is the most specific for the groups discussed. Here also orphan and widow are introduced in parallel stichs and in the same order as in 4:10. It is, therefore, not necessary for us to review the juxtaposition of orphan and widow or the definition, status, and Near Eastern consciousness of the latter. These we have done when considering 4:10.[150]

One difference between 35(32):14 and 4:10 is that in 35(32):14 God is seen as the protector of the orphan and the widow, while in 4:10 the sage calls for God's sons to fulfill this role. As we have seen,[151] both ideas are evident in Heb thought, though the latter is more prominent.

A more significant difference between 35(32):14 and 4:10 lies in the tone of the reference to the widow. The mention of widow in 4:10 is neutral. However, 35(32):14 refers to the "widow when she pours out her chatter." While śyḥ, which I have translated "chatter," may have a positive or neutral meaning ("complaint" or "story"), it is used here with Ben Sira's typical pejorative sense, "empty talk."[152] It means more than that the widow was wordy.[153] Ben Sira sees her as verbally overbearing with her constant stream ("pours out"[154]) of empty words. But God listens anyway.

I have included v. 15 here because in Gr the reference to widow extends into it.[155] However, as we have seen, v. 14, with its mention of oppressed classes and God's care for them, is best linked with the parallel v. 13. Each class is merely noted in a single stich as in 4:1-10. An extension of the discussion of widow into v. 15 would be uncharacteristic. Instead, v. 15 should be read with Heb and be connected to v. 16, as a two distich reference to the cry of the oppressed in general.[156]

As in 4:10, Ben Sira is here concerned with the existence of certain oppressed social classes and the need for their protection and support. He is not expounding on the status of women who happen to be widows. However, in 35(32):14 he may be seen to have revealed, even if ever so slightly, his negative bias against women by characterizing the widow as one who "pours out her chatter."

Conclusion

With one exception, Ben Sira always treats mother as part of the twofold expression "father and mother" or the parallel involving father and mother. In either case the effect is equivalent to the term parents. This is the regular Heb idiom meaning parents and is so employed in the OT. The fact that father always precedes mother is also reminiscent of the OT. The father is more characteristic of the concept of parents, since he is often mentioned alone when parents in general are intended. A mother has the honor of being a partner in parenthood. However, unlike the OT,[157] Ben Sira never treats her independently from her husband, the father. While he does not overtly show negative regard for woman as mother--not even a misogynist is a mother-hater--he avoids reflecting on mother as an independent, positive role for a woman. His negative bias against women is evident, though only faintly, in his silence.

The one exception to Ben Sira's consistent treatment of mother together with father is his comparison of Wisdom coming to a person like his mother. But this is merely a figure paralleled to another concerning a young wife, neither of which contributes to Ben Sira's view.

The miscellaneous mother-related expressions dealing with the womb and other birth language are equally uninstructive for our purposes. They are but conventional literary images of origin, birth, and pain.

Finally, in his references to the widow Ben Sira reflects a common Near Eastern and OT identification of the widow as one of the oppressed social classes, which need protection and support. Only his slight annoyance with her empty wordiness could be construed as evidence of his negative bias against women.

On the whole, in mentioning mother and widow Ben Sira conforms to well established Heb patterns. Except for the few hints that I have noted, the evidence is rather neutral with regard to our working hypothesis of Ben Sira's personal, negative bias against women.

CHAPTER III

WOMAN AS BAD WIFE

Introduction

Ben Sira devotes his most extensive discussion of women to the topic of the bad wife. In this major unit of his work he considers a wide variety of negative domestic scenarios ranging from drunken wives to wives who are overly talkative, from wives hard to control to those who support their husbands financially, from suppression to divorce. The major portion of this chapter will be an investigation of this important section of Sirach. I will also consider several minor statements scattered throughout Ben Sira's work which also fall into this category.

26:5-9; 25:13-26

5 With three things my heart[1] is concerned,
And with a fourth[2] I am afraid:[3]
An evil report in the city, and the assembly of the people,[4]
And a false accusation[5]--all are worse[6] than death.[7]
6 There is grief of heart[8] and sadness[9] when one wife is the rival of another,[10]
And a tongue-lashing[11] shares it with everyone.[12]
7 An evil wife[13] is like[14] the bars of a yoke;[15]
He who takes hold of her[16] is like one who grasps a scorpion.[17]
8 A drunken wife[18] causes great wrath,[19]
And she does not conceal[20] her nakedness.[21]
9 A wife's fornication shows in the excitement of her eyes,
And by her eyelids she will be known.[22]
13 Any wound,[23] but not a wound of the heart.[24]
Any wickedness,[25] but not the wickedness of a wife.[26]

14 Any attack,[27] but not an attack from those who hate.[28]
Any vengeance,[29] but not the vengeance of enemies.[30]
15 There is no head[31] worse than the head of a snake,[32]
And there is no wrath[33] worse than the wrath of a wife.[34]
16 It is better to dwell[35] with a lion and a dragon[36]
Than to dwell[37] with an evil[38] wife.[39]
17 The wickedness of a wife[40] blackens[41] her appearance[42]
And darkens[43] her face[44] like a bear.[45]
18 Her husband[46] sits[47] among the neighbors[48]
And involuntarily[49] sighs[50] bitterly.[51]
19 Little wickedness[52] is like the wickedness of a wife.[53]
May a sinner's lot fall upon her.[54]
20 Like[55] a sandy[56] ascent[57] to the feet[58] of the aged,[59]
So is[60] a babbling wife[61] to a humble man.[62]
21 Do not fall[63] because of[64] the beauty of a woman,[65]
And do not be caught[66] because of her possessions.[67]
22 For it is hard[68] slavery[69] and a disgrace[70]
When a wife supports[71] her husband.[72]
23c[73] Drooping hands[74] and tottering knees[75]--
d A wife who[76] does not make her husband[77] happy.[78]
24 From a woman[79] was the beginning of sin,[80]
And because of her we all die.[81]
25 Do not allow an outlet to water[82]
Nor outspokenness[83] in an evil wife.[84]
26 Unless she goes[85] as you direct,[86]
Cut her off from your flesh.[87]

The section that we are about to consider is the only major unit in Sirach devoted to the treatment of the bad wife. However, this piece is of such length and variety, both in form and content, though it has been edited and rearranged, that it can be said to genuinely represent Ben Sira's considered thought on the matter. Thus, this section must be given priority when one seeks to determine Ben Sira's view of woman as bad wife.

I have already argued the case for the rearrangement of 25:7-26:18.[88] This rearrangement involves the grouping of materials on the good wife (26:1-4, 13-18) and those on the bad wife (26:5-9; 25:13-26). Furthermore, I have treated the issue of the genuineness of 26:19-27,[89] which includes several stichs devoted to the bad wife.[90] My conclusion on genuineness was negative. Therefore, I will not discuss this material here.

The structure of this section falls into two distinct patterns, with that of 26:5-9 differing rather widely from 25:13-26. Such a difference may have afforded a ready point of division when the section was split and its parts set in their present place within 25:7-26:18. What is now 26:5-9 contains six distichs, with the structure 3 + 3.[91] I have already discussed the distich pattern of 25:13-26.[92] It is characterized by a series of subsections involving 2 + 1 + 1.[93]

The first strophe of the subsection, 26:5-9, is a three distich Zahlenspruch[94] comprising vv. 5-6. In its present form the Zahlenspruch represents the double number variety (X/X+1), involving the expression, "With three things. . . and with a fourth." The introductory formula indicates that this is a negative construction, since the sage declares with reference to the appended list that his "heart is concerned" and he is "afraid." This Zahlenspruch, like the others in Sirach, represents traditional material that Ben Sira has molded into his discussion.[95]

As the text now stands, three elements of the Zahlenspruch are clear--"an evil report in the city, and the assembly of the people, and a false accusation." These are items that reflect general social concerns.[96] The fourth element is not so evident. In fact, it appears that the original fourth element is now missing from the present text. This is clear from the fact that following the three elements already noted, the Zahlenspruch contains what is obviously a concluding formula--"all are worse than death." But Ben Sira does not intend for the Zahlenspruch to end with this formula. Instead, he includes a fourth element in v. 6 by introducing a wife who is envious of her rival.

That Ben Sira's fourth element on the envious wife was not originally part of the traditional Zahlenspruch is established from three observations. As we have already noted, the Zahlenspruch in its present state contains a terminal formula after the third element, rendering the fourth element a highly doubtful member of the original piece. Furthermore, the form of the fourth element is quite different from that of the others. Each of the first three elements is a compact phrase, containing in the original language only one or two words, as one might expect in this literary form. In contrast, the fourth element comprises an entire distich, which is quite out of character with the model. Finally, the content of the fourth element speaks against its original inclusion in this Zahlenspruch. The first three elements represent situations in the community where one's name may be sullied by negative assessments of his character or behavior. However, the fourth element treats the domestic problem of an envious rival wife. Furthermore, the terminal formula for the first three elements suggests that they are considered "worse than death," while the present fourth element merely leads to "grief of heart and sadness." We must recognize that Ben Sira does his best to integrate this into the whole by including in v. 6b the notion that such a wife expounds the issue to the community. Nevertheless, the transparency of his manipulation remains.

It is apparent that Ben Sira has chosen to introduce his treatment of the bad wife with a traditional Zahlenspruch (v. 5), to which he has added a distich concerning an envious wife (v. 6). The original Zahlenspruch may have contained only three elements,[97] in which case Ben Sira may have added the term "fourth" in v. 5a. It is also possible that the original read "with two things. . . and with a third," followed by the three elements and the terminal formula in v. 5cd.[98] I consider it more likely, however, that Ben Sira altered the original Zahlenspruch in a minimal way by merely deleting one of the four original elements and by adding his own element after the terminal formula. But for my purposes it is unimportant which of these scenarios is valid. What seems certain and significant is that Ben Sira has altered the traditional Zahlenspruch to fit it into this section on the bad wife.

The original Zahlenspruch is an expression of fear so intense that the sage considers the negative circumstances indicated to be worse than death. Thus, when Ben Sira chose a

Zahlenspruch to head this section, as he had done for the previous section,[99] he found one which was extremely negative. By adding his own material on the rival wife to the traditional form, he sought to bring the former under the negative aura of the latter. Furthermore, this dark picture is made to set the tone for the entire lengthy consideration of the bad wife.

It is also evident that in this Zahlenspruch, as reconstructed by Ben Sira, the fourth element on the rival wife is featured and made to serve as the climax of the piece. The reason for this is not because Zahlensprüche, especially the double number type (X/X+1), predictably climax in the last element.[100] Rather, the fourth element climax[101] is here justified by the fact that Ben Sira has deliberately added it to the original Zahlenspruch, and by the fact that he placed the whole construction at the head of a major discussion of a topic that in general arises out of that element. For him, though not for the author of the original, the problems caused by the rival wife situation are even worse than the three conditions already described as being "worse than death."

The woman featured in v. 6 is termed in Gr an antizēlos, which means "a rival wife."[102] The picture is that of a husband with two or more wives, a situation that inevitably produces jealousy and conflict. That it was of particular concern to Ben Sira is evident from the fact that he refers to such rival wife problems at least two and probably three times.[103] This frequency is remarkable in contrast to the paucity of direct references to rival wives in the OT.[104]

While polygamy generally causes hostility and grief for the rival wives themselves, this is not Ben Sira's concern. The "grief of heart"[105] and "sadness" to which he refers belong to the husband. He has to live in the negative environment of jealousy and strife, and the result for him is emotional distress. Ben Sira may tolerate a good marriage, but polygamy is too much marriage and intolerable.

Conversely, if the distress belongs to the husband, the "tongue-lashing" is the activity of one or more of his wives with him as the object. The wife is hardly pictured here in a passive role, cringing under her husband's rule. Apparently, she freely criticizes him for showing favoritism to her rival. But the most damaging aspect of such behavior is the time and place of her performance. She puts on her act in public or at least outside the family confines, resulting in the broadcast of the domestic problems to everyone. This, of course, adds embarrassment and humiliation to the husband's emotional distress.

Vv. 7-9 constitute a three distich subsection. The first distich (v. 7) treats "an evil wife," the second (v. 8) considers "a drunken wife," and the third (v. 9) discusses a wife who plays the harlot. Fuss[106] understands these verses to be traditional, with v. 7 coming from the same source as the animal comparisons in 25:13-16. But 25:13, 15, 16 have the animal comparisons in the first line of each distich, with the mention of the wife in the second line. The order is reversed in 26:7. It does not appear that they come from the same source. In fact, I will argue below that 25:15, 16 are not traditional at all. The question of the source for the variegated material[107] of 26:7-9 is more complicated. I will consider this for each verse individually.

We may note that Ben Sira has arranged this material in such a way as to form a negatively progressive look at the bad wife. His order of treatment is: a bad wife in general (v. 7), a drunken wife (v. 8), and an adulterous wife (v. 9).

As we have noted, Ben Sira follows the Zahlenspruch with the subject of "an evil wife" in v. 7. The expression "evil wife" is used by Ben Sira to refer to a wife seen to have negative characteristics in general without specific identification. We find the term used in various contexts. In 25:16 (gynaikos ponēras) the emphasis is on incompatibility. In 25:25 (gynaiki ponēra) the wife's outspokenness is featured. In 42:6a ('šh r`h[108]--the only use with extant Heb) the focus is on untrustworthiness.[109] Ben Sira also uses the related expression "the wickedness of a wife"[110] with the same general meaning.

It is significant that the term ʾšh rʿh is almost nonexistent in the OT. The only exception is the construct form in Prov 6:24 ʾšt rʿ. However, this reading is not totally certain. The LXX reads gynaikos hypandrou "married woman," which, as in 6:29, would represent ʾšt rēʿa instead of ʾšt rāʿ. However, the presence of nkryh "foreign woman" in v. 24b would seem to require something like ʾšh zrh "strange woman" in line a, as the editors of BHS have proposed. Such a parallel with this order is common in Proverbs.[111] But for our purposes it matters little whether we read with MT, the LXX, or the BHS conjecture, though the latter is probably preferable. The context of 6:24 involves a discussion of adultery and not a general reference to a bad wife, as in Ben Sira's work.

Thus, Ben Sira goes beyond the OT in general and Proverbs in particular when he employs the term ʾšh rʿh as a broad description of a bad wife. This is not to say that the term originated with him. But it is sufficiently used by him in contrast to the OT that we can safely claim it to be characteristic of his writing. Therefore, I understand v. 7 to represent Ben Sira's composition.

The evil wife is compared to "the bars of a yoke." The yoke is a frequent OT metaphor of oppression and restriction. This particular expression is found in Lev 26:13 and Ezek 34:27, where Yahweh either reviews or promises the breaking of the bars of Israel's yoke of slavery. The emphasis of the simile in our text, however, does not seem to be the oppression of a man by his evil wife.

It may be that the present comparison is no longer clear, as Schilling observes.[112] Nevertheless, this has not prevented scholars from offering their suggestions on its meaning. The views include: an unsteady yoke caused by animals pulling in different directions;[113] an ox and an ass plowing together as in 25:8b (Heb and Syr);[114] an ill-suited yoke of oxen;[115] a badly fitting yoke that hinders work;[116] a yoke that rubs and irritates the animals.[117] The meaning of the symbol does not seem to lie in the defectiveness of the yoke or its placement. Nor does it suggest anything about the nature or cooperation of the animals so yoked. While the OT meaning of oppression is too strong here, it nevertheless offers the suggestion that the yoke image used in 26:7 is to be understood in a general negative sense.

One particular OT use of the yoke symbol, however, may be instructive. In 1 Kgs 12:11, 14 (= 2 Chr 10:11, 14) we find Rehoboam under the advice of his companions declaring, "My father made your yoke heavy, but I will add to your yoke; my father chastised you with whips, but I will chastise you with scorpions." It is immediately evident that this text shares the elements of "yoke" and "scorpion" with our text and treats them in the same order. Here "yoke" may mean oppression in a general sense, but in a more particular sense it means burden.[118] The young king planned to increase the burden of the people through greater tax levies, etc. This is the meaning of the "hard service," against which the people complained (v. 4). For our text, then, the evil wife may be understood as a restricting burden to her husband.[119] This is further explained in the following line.

In line b Ben Sira continues his discussion of the evil wife by means of another comparison. He states that one "who takes hold of her" compares to a person holding a scorpion. The reference to taking hold of her (ho kratōn autēs) does not mean marriage here,[120] though the expression itself has that potential. Both the Gr and the apparent Heb Vorlage[121] express a more general meaning. In the context the emphasis seems to be on the issue of control. Ben Sira observes that attempts to control an evil wife bring negative results.[122]

These negative results are symbolized by the mention of a scorpion. Some[123] hold that Ben Sira is referring to the evil wife's biting speech, as though this distich continued the topic of v. 6. In the OT scorpions represented deadly danger.[124]

But in 1 Kgs 12:11, 14, while the yoke symbolizes a heavy burden, the scorpion is used in a setting of punishment--punishment more severe and deadly than the whip. This idea is echoed by Ben Sira in 39:30. Among the things created for vengeance and judgment on the wicked are "the teeth of wild beasts, and scorpions and vipers."[125] The scorpion is a symbol of a severe wound.[126] To grasp a scorpion is to be stung. The comparison that results is: to control an evil wife is as impossible as controlling a scorpion in your hand.

In v. 7 Ben Sira seems to have been influenced by the juxtaposition of yoke and scorpion in 1 Kgs 12:11, 14, although the former figure reflects the form of expression in Lev 26:13 (a reference to slavery in Egypt) and Ezek 34:27 (a statement of restoration from Babylonian captivity). V. 7 asserts that control of an evil wife is an impossibility, which results in a heavy burden to her husband.

The focus of v. 8 shifts from the evil wife in general to a more specific phenomenon, the drunken wife. Like the former, this expression[127] appears to be characteristic of Ben Sira. The only OT reference remotely comparable to our text is 1 Sam 1:13. There the priest Eli mistook Hannah's silent praying for an indication that she was intoxicated. However, she was not drunk as suspected. Thus, this account does not serve as a genuine analogy to Ben Sira's expression. Elsewhere, women and drinking are related in various contexts. In Judg 13:14 the expectant mother of Samson is forbidden to drink wine or strong drink. In Job 1:13, 18 Job's daughters are described as drinking wine, though no mention is made of drunkenness. The same may be said for the wives and concubines of Belshazzar in Dan 5:2-4, 23. However, none of these texts describes these women or wives as "drunken."[128] It seems reasonable, therefore, to cautiously consider Sir 26:8 to be the product of Ben Sira himself. Accordingly, we see him pointing to a negative aspect of female behavior that had not been developed by the biblical writers before him.[129]

As we noted above, vv. 7-9 contain a view of the bad wife that progresses negatively. V. 8 represents the midpoint of this development. For Ben Sira the drunken wife is worse than the general picture of the evil wife in v. 7[130] and is the natural transition to the adulterous wife of v. 9.[131]

Both the appearance and the behavior of a drunken wife "causes great wrath." This doubtlessly refers to the anger and disgust of those who observe her. However, as the context of this material would suggest, the wrath is especially that of her husband. He is both saddened by her conduct and embarrassed among his colleagues.[132] In view of the progressive nature of vv. 7-9 and the concern of v. 7 with a husband's attempts to control an evil wife, v. 8 presents a picture of an extended loss of control.

The reason for the husband's wrath is not only the generally negative conduct of his intoxicated wife but also, as line _b_ indicates, her disgraceful display of nakedness.[133] In her drunkenness Ben Sira pictures her losing control of herself to the point of shedding her clothes, either by accident or design. This, of course, may serve to prepare the ground for the adultery discussed in v. 9. At least this is how Ben Sira appears to have envisioned the situation.

Since I will treat v. 9 in chapter IV, which deals with adultery and prostitution, I will not consider it here beyond the general references already made regarding its relationship to the other verses in the strophe (vv. 7-9).

To summarize our findings in vv. 7-8, we have noted Ben Sira's employing the expressions "evil wife" and "drunken wife," which are not used in the OT. By doing so he has gone beyond the OT in his characterizations of the bad wife. This is not so much because women were less well behaved in his day but presumably because of his antifeminine bias. He also refers to the control of the evil wife by using the particularly harsh figure of the scorpion. He does not appear to be especially concerned with bad wives themselves but with the damage they do to their husbands.

Before proceeding with an analysis of the rest of the section, 25:13-26, let us make some preliminary observations concerning the source and content of vv. 13-14. In a textual note to v. 13 we have already seen that b. Šabb. 11a contains material that follows the same pattern that we find in vv. 13-14: any "A," but not the "A" of "B." Furthermore, the Tal. text also presents some subject matter which is similar to the Sirach text.[134] Scholars[135] have almost universally credited the Tal. with a loose quotation of Sirach at this point. Such a conclusion is supported by the rather widespread reflection of Ben Sira in rabbinic literature.[136]

The form and content similarities are impressive, but they do not demand the conclusion that the rabbis are quoting from Sirach. It is, in fact, more likely that both Ben Sira and the rabbis are quoting from a third body of material. Vv. 13-14 represent a form that is structurally distinct from adjacent material--a characteristic typical of the traditional material that Ben Sira weaves into his presentations. These verses also exhibit the usual traditional verbal compactness and patterned composition. Fuss[137] considers v. 13 to be traditional but strangely takes v. 14 to be an out of place composition of Ben Sira. In my judgment this latter conclusion is untenable. In fact, the dissimilarity of v. 14 to Ben Sira's general theme at this point speaks eloquently in favor of its traditional nature and not of its composition by Ben Sira. Thus, I consider vv. 13-14 to be traditional material used by Ben Sira.

We may also observe that Sir 25:13-14 and b. Šabb. 11a contain both similar and dissimilar material. Each has four examples of the form. Two of these are common to both, while the other two are unique to each. Let us compare them:

b. Sabb. 11a	Sir 25:13-14
sickness of bowels	
pain of heart	wound of heart
ache of head	
wickedness of wife[138]	wickedness of wife
	attack of haters
	vengeance of enemies

The most reasonable explanation of these similarities in form, content, and order, as well as the differences in the topics treated is that both Ben Sira and the rabbis have independently and differently drawn from a common source.[139]

With this in mind, we must consider Smend's important textual emendation in v. 14.[140] The point at issue centers on the Gr genitives misountōn "those who hate" (line a) and echthrōn "enemies" (line b) and the expected Heb Vorlage. It is Smend's contention that Gr mistakenly read śn'(ym) "hater(s)" instead of śn'h (śenu'ah) "a woman who hates" and ṣr(ym) "enemy(ies)" instead of ṣrh (ṣarah) "rival wife." His analogies are 7:26b (śenu'ah) for the former and 37:11 (ṣrh) for the latter. Let us discuss these suggestions separately.

Initially, we observe that both in the LXX generally and in Sirach in particular the usual Heb word behind miseō is śn'. We may reasonably expect a form of śn' in v. 14a. However, I reject Smend's suggestion that the form of śn' must be the precise expression śenu'ah. There is always a problem in restoring nonextant Heb. But the difficulties are compounded and the certainties eroded when one tries to establish that the Gr misread the nonextant Heb. While we may grant that a form of śn' stood in v. 14a, this does not eliminate other possibilities. The Gr miseō translates other Heb words in Sirach, e.g., 'wṣ "to urge"[141] (7:15) and g`l "to abhor" (31[34]:16). This is true even when Ben Sira is discussing women. In 42:9b, while Smend[142] restores HebB to read [tśn'], Yadin[143] restores HebM to read ṫ[nš]ḣ "be forgotten" (cf. HebBmg) or ṫ[sk]ḣ "be forgotten." Smend appears motivated to reconstruct the Heb as he does in order to bring this distich into conformity with the context that deals with the bad wife. But as we have seen, vv. 13-14 are doubtlessly traditional, coming from a source that contained a series of miscellaneous identifications of particularly undesirable phenomena. Only one of these references clearly deals with women.[144] Thus, we need not force the topics treated in v. 14 into any particular subject mold, including that of the bad wife.

This nullification of the motivation to conform v. 14 to Ben Sira's overall topic for the section undercuts Smend's postulation of the Heb reading ṣrh in line b. But there is further evidence against such a reading. From a frequency perspective we might expect a form of śn' behind echthros, as is the case seven times in Sirach.[145] But this is untenable, since śn' was no doubt in line a. The next most frequent Vorlage is 'yb "enemy."[146] Smend's suggestion ṣr lies behind echthros only twice.[147] Where ṣrh does occur (37:11), Gr translates with the technical term antizēlos.[148] Thus, if ṣrh had been used in 25:14b there would be no reason for the translators to misunderstand it. The most likely Heb word behind echthrōn is 'ybym.

In further support of the readings involving forms of śn' and 'yb in v. 14 I offer the fact of the frequent OT representation of parallels involving these terms. The parallel 'yb / śn' with corresponding LXX echthros / miseō is found about fourteen times.[149] The reverse order, as in our text, is also found, but less often.[150] In contrast, the parallel ṣr / śn' with LXX echthros / miseō occurs only in Deut 32:41cd and Ps 44:10.[151] The reverse order that Smend would require is never used.

Let us now look at v. 13. This distich contains two of the four traditional stichs that Ben Sira incorporated into his treatment on the bad wife in this strophe. As we have seen, these four lines represent only a portion of the original piece. The first stich declares "a wound of the heart" to be the worst of wounds. This phenomenon is generally interpreted in the light of line b as emotional stress caused by a bad wife.[152] In fact, Smend[153] specifies that an evil wife herself is a heart wound.

However, we have seen that the original source from which Ben Sira drew this material contained a series of miscellaneous topics. Some may be loosely related, e.g., sickness of the bowels, pain of the heart, and aching of the head (all from the rabbinic citation) and attack from haters, vengeance of enemies (from Sirach). The nature of such a form and the variety of the topics treated would speak against the legitimacy of interpreting one line of the original in terms of another. Furthermore, the rabbinic quote would suggest that the line which refers to the heart wound was originally associated with and ordered within the group of topics noted above: bowels, heart, and head. Thus, it was probably not in the same distich with the topic of a wife's wickedness.

This is not to say that Ben Sira himself did not wish to convey a relationship between these lines and between this distich and the next. In fact, we note that he has apparently relocated the stich involving the heart wound so as to bring it into the same distich as the wife's wickedness. Thus, what originally had nothing to do with women is now made to appear complementary to the topic at hand, the bad wife. Whereas in the original a wound of the heart represented emotional distress, for Ben Sira it came to refer to the particular distress caused by a bad wife.

Line b, of course, contains the topic that motivated Ben Sira's use of this traditional material. It declares that no wickedness is as bad as a wife's wickedness. The phrase "wickedness of a wife" (r`t 'šh) occurs several times in this section (vv. 17 [r` 'šh], 19) and, along with the related expression "evil wife" (the Heb would be 'šh r`h as in 42:6a) found in 26:7; 25:16, 25, would seem to characterize the section. We have seen that the latter expression is particularly associated with Ben Sira. It may be that he developed the more all-inclusive "evil wife" from the more restricted traditional phrase "wickedness of a wife" found here in his source.

I have argued that v. 14 represents two stichs of traditional material that originally had nothing to do with women. I have also rejected Smend's efforts to reconstruct the missing Heb so as to relate the distich to the bad wife theme. Thus, the original traditional focus of these lines centered on the seriousness of attacks from adversaries. But, as we saw in v. 13, Ben Sira has so arranged this material in this particular context to leave the impression that all these topics are dependent on and enlargements of the theme of the wife's wickedness in v. 13b. Thus, for him the haters and enemies of v. 14 stand for bad wives.[154]

In v. 15 we find the ingredients of a structure like that of vv. 13-14. Each stich of v. 15 mentions a particular class of negative item followed by a specifically qualified mention of that class which is considered particularly undesirable. The symbolic representation would be: there is no "A" worse than the "A" of "B." We may assume that either these three distichs were originally part of the same source or that Ben Sira has loosely modelled v. 15 after vv. 13-14, which he found in his source. In either case v. 15 would reflect the work of Ben Sira, whether through redactional alteration or compositional modelling.

Because neither of the stichs of v. 15 is echoed in the Tal. material, which I have argued is source material common to both Ben Sira and the Tal. and not a quote from Ben Sira, I consider this verse to be Ben Sira's composition.[155] This distich makes the "A" of "B" element in each stich the worse possible form of the "A" element. Such an assertion is considerably stronger than the more oblique model found in the four stichs of vv. 13-14: any "A," but not the "A" of "B."

Thus, it would appear that Ben Sira has headed this portion of his discussion on the bad wife with a two distich excerpt (vv. 13-14) from a traditional piece on various kinds of negative conditions. He used it because one of its stichs is devoted to the subject of a wife's wickedness. To this he added his own distich in v. 15, loosely modelled after the traditional material. In this way he heightened the negative assessment of women.

We have already noted the similarity between our text and Gen 3, with the shared elements of snake, including snake's head, and woman.[156] This, along with the obvious reference of Sir 25:24 to the Gen 3 story, would suggest that Ben Sira was not only influenced here by the Genesis material but has consciously reflected its elements in his composition. It may be tempting to treat each stich of v. 15 separately, since they may appear to be distinct ideas. However, we should probably consider the two stichs to be merely a parallel reflection of the Genesis story of the fall, with its principal negative protagonists, the snake and the woman. Ben Sira's focus, of course, is on the woman. The snake's head with its poisonous biting potential[157] is noted. But for Ben Sira the real center of the fall story is the woman with whom sin began (cf. v. 24).

While Ben Sira appears to have drawn his material for v. 15 from Gen 3, he is not expounding here on the role of woman in the fall. Rather, he is merely employing these elements to reflect on a wife's anger.[158] For him this is the most negative kind of anger. He does not elaborate on this, except possibly in vv. 17-19. But even there he does not indicate what has made her angry or how her anger is displayed. Presumably, the object of her wrath is her husband, as in 26:6.

V. 16 contains another animal comparison. In this case Ben Sira declares that to dwell with a lion and a dragon is better than to dwell with an evil wife. We have already discussed the significance of the expression "evil wife" and have seen it to be characteristic of Ben Sira.[159] Therefore, it is reasonable to take this distich to be his composition.[160]

We noted that this text is at least partially dependent on Prov 21:9, 19; 25:24.[161] This is particularly true of the opening formula: "It is better to dwell" (<u>twb</u> <u>lšbt</u>). Also both the Proverbs texts and our text express the preference for dwelling in some undesirable situation over dwelling with a negative wife. It is evident that Ben Sira was influenced by the Proverbs material.

However, Ben Sira has gone beyond Proverbs. Not only has he employed his characteristic term "evil wife" in contrast to the less pejorative "contentious wife,"[162] but he has also sharpened the harshness of the comparison. The Proverbs texts speak of dwelling in "the corner of the housetop"[163] and in "a desert land."[164] Ben Sira speaks of dwelling "with a lion and a dragon." What for Proverbs is an inconvenience, for Ben Sira is a disaster. To live with a lion and a dragon would be not to live at all. Yet, Ben Sira says that this would be better than living with an evil wife.[165]

It is tempting to give full weight to the Gr synoikēsai in the sense of "to be married to." The term reflects that meaning in 25:8; 42:9, 10. It is clearly the implication of the Gr in our text as well. However, as we have seen, this composition of Ben Sira's reflects similar Proverbs distichs, all of which begin with the general expression twb lšbt "better to dwell." The LXX translates these quite literally with kreisson / kreitton oikein. As we argued above,[166] the expression twb lšbt no doubt stood in our text. If this is the case, then the Gr has translated the Heb by resorting to the more specific expression involving synoikeō. Therefore, although this distich assumes a marriage situation, it would not be warranted to force the text to say that Ben Sira would rather be married to a lion and a dragon than to an evil wife.

The next portion of the material involves the unit consisting of vv. 17-18. Fuss[167] considers v. 17 to be traditional, with v. 18 an expansion by Ben Sira. I find no reason to dispute this assessment. We have already seen that the expression "wickedness of a wife" is found in the traditional material in v. 13b. Furthermore, the idea of darkening something and the use of a bear[168] in comparison are not found elsewhere in Sirach. Even though v. 18 is clearly an extension of and dependent on v. 17, it is not a continuation of the same literary fabric. V. 17 involves a loose chiastic structure, that includes a rather obscure comparison. In contrast, v. 18 is a straightforward description, that is more prosaic than poetic. Thus, I concur with Fuss' judgment on the origin of these verses.

The feature of v. 17 is the expression "wickedness of a wife." As we have seen, this phrase is also found in v. 13b.[169] In considering its use there, we noted that this phrase (r` 'šh[170]), which appears to be traditional, is more restricted than the broader "evil wife" (*'šh r'h*), which is characteristic of Ben Sira. There is no way of determining the exact referent of this phrase. Thus, we must be content to understand the expression in the general sense of negative behavior on the part of a wife.

The text states that this wickedness blackens the wife's appearance (line *a*) and "darkens her face" (line *b*). In some sense this makes her look like a bear. Both the meaning of the description and the nature of the comparison are rather obscure. The only OT use of the verb *šḥr* I, employed in line *a*, is found in Job 30:30. There Job declares that his skin "turns black" and falls off, suggesting decay. The *Hif'il* of the verb *qdr* in line *b* is found in Ezek 32:7, 8, with reference to Yahweh making the stars and heavenly luminaries dark.[171] The comparison involving a bear is even more problematic. Which is featured, the bear's color, its disposition, or its face? One could probably make a case for any of these. On the basis of the double reference within the distich, face appears most likely. But this does not really elucidate the comparison. The problem remains as to how a woman's darkened face resembles a bear's face. About all that can be said for this distich is that the wife's negative behavior is said to show in her grim, cold look, which resembles the look of a bear.[172]

We have observed that Ben Sira appears to have extended the traditional material of v. 17 by appending his own distich (v. 18). In this addition the expression "her husband," of course, refers to the husband of the woman described in v. 17. He is said to involuntarily and bitterly sigh while in the presence of his neighbors.[173] The traditional statement (v. 17) refers to a wife's negative behavior and its effects on her appearance. It mentions nothing about who observes her or what effect she has had on others. Nor does it indicate that this is the object of discussion within or without the home. But where the traditional distich is silent, Ben Sira speaks openly. In his material (v. 18) the wife's negative behavior becomes the object of her husband's complaint and sorrow, which he expresses in the neighborhood. Thus, what was traditionally described without a specific setting now takes on the air of a community context, with all its accompanying judgments.

Let us turn to the meaning of the husband's sighing or groaning. The term used here is the Hitpa`el of 'nḥ. This form of 'nḥ, which is not found in the OT, is not uncommon in Sirach. In 12:12 it refers to one's sighing after not heeding the sage's plea. Its use in 30:20[174] refers to the groaning of a eunuch when he is unable to copulate with a maiden. These uses in Sirach reflect the two predominant ideas of sorrow and frustration that accompany the OT use of 'nḥ, which is consistently in the Nif`al.[175] In the present context I prefer to see the idea of sorrow in our text as the best meaning. Accordingly, Ben Sira describes the husband as so distraught by his wife's negative behavior that he spontaneously groans with sorrow and pours out his complaint among his neighbors.[176]

V. 19 stands in isolation as a single distich. Fuss[177] is somewhat ambivalent on its derivation. On the one hand, he observes that this verse stands close to the theme of vv. 13, 15, 16, all of which he considers traditional.[178] On the other hand, he holds that the severity of the language and the religious curse suggests Ben Sira as the author.

In my judgment it is possible to be more decisive on the matter of origin. But to do so we must consider each stich separately. Line a has a form that parallels that of vv. 13-14, which I take to be traditional. It also includes the expression "wickedness of a wife" (r`t 'šh), which appears to be from Ben Sira's source(s).[179] Thus, we may reasonably conclude that line a is traditional. However, line b does not continue the crisp construction and distinctive form of line a, as in the case of vv. 13-14 and even, for that matter, v. 15. Nor does it follow the kind of parallelism offered in the traditional v. 17. Thus, on formal grounds I take line b of our text to be the work of Ben Sira. Its harsh language does not prove it to be Ben Sira's composition, as Fuss suggested. But once its compositional status has been determined on the basis of its form, line b can be seen to be typical of Ben Sira's view of women. Thus, he appears to have placed in the text a traditional stich (line a), to which he added his own anathema (line b).

The meaning of the traditional line a is quite general. In our discussion of vv. 13b, 17 we noted that the expression "wickedness of a wife" was less restricted than Ben Sira's phrase "evil wife" and points in general to a wife's negative behavior. Here also the sage echoes a sentiment very much like v. 13b. In fact, the implication of v. 19a is even less pejorative than v. 13b. Here the text allows for the possibility of other forms of wickedness worse than a wife's wickedness.

In contrast, Ben Sira pronounces on such a wife a rather severe religious curse (line b). He calls for her to receive a sinner's lot (gwrl ḥwṭ'). The term gwrl often refers to a stone used in the casting of lots to secure a decision as well as to the decision itself. But it is also used for an inheritance[180] received by such lot casting and hence for the idea of destiny.[181] The particular expression "sinner's lot" is not found in the OT. However, we may gain a general idea of what Ben Sira means with this expression by noting some elements of the sinner's fate or destiny that are reflected in the OT. Sinners will be destroyed.[182] This is particularly true of their fate in the judgment.[183] Ps 104:35 is especially interesting for our purposes since, like our stich, it is cast in the form of a curse:

> Let sinners be consumed from the earth,
> and let the wicked be no more!

We cannot, of course, unlock exactly what Ben Sira had in mind by assigning a sinner's lot to the woman in our text. But as our look at the OT description of the fate of sinners has shown, such a wish can only be viewed negatively.[184] In doing this he went beyond the OT, which never assigns such a fate to a woman in particular.[185]

V. 20, like v. 19, is an independent distich without strophic relationship to what goes before or after. Fuss[186] considers it to be traditional. The independence of the distich as well as its proverbial character would tend to support this contention.

Line a of the distich contains a simile, which in line b is applied to a "babbling wife" in relationship to a "humble man," presumably her husband. That relationship is said to be like "a sandy ascent to the feet of the aged."[187] The focus here is on the difficulty of walking up a sandy slope, especially when the person involved is old. Such a situation is wearisome[188] and requires patience.[189]

The figure of the climb of sand by old feet refers to a particularly negative relationship between a wife and her husband. That relationship is clearly caused by the wife's undesirable characteristics or behavior. She is described as a "babbling wife" (ʼšt lšwn[190] literally "a woman/wife of tongue"). We find the related expression ʼyš lšwn referring to a man or a person generally in 8:3 and 9:18 as well as in Ps 140:11. The phrase appears to imply different things in all these places[191] and would seem, therefore, to be somewhat plastic, with its precise meaning dependent on its context. In our text the expression ʼšt lswn stands in contrast to ʼyš ʽny "a humble man." I understand the latter phrase to mean a quiet, nonassertive man, who in this setting is a husband. Thus, ʼšt lšwn is pictured as the talkative, domineering counterpart. Although Ben Sira has inserted this apparently traditional distich into his work, I can hardly think that he is comfortable with the scenario of this retiring husband. We will see, in fact, that he continues the idea of a husband's subordination in the next strophe. However, he does so by concluding the material with his own negative assessment of the situation.

It is not warranted to consider ʼšt lšwn as a reference to the wife's abusive speech.[192] The problem implied is merely that of an endlessly talking wife. This is clear from the comparison. It is as difficult and wearisome for a quiet man to live with a talkative wife, as it is for an old man to climb a sandy slope.

The next strophe involves the two distichs of vv. 21-22. I follow Fuss'[193] contention that v. 21 is traditional and v. 22 is Ben Sira's composition. The former is a tight, formal parallel in prohibition form with slightly differing topics. In contrast, the latter is a more prosaic comment on the topic introduced in v. 21b. The strophe is thus devoted to the idea of a husband who is financially supported by his wife. Ben Sira introduces the discussion with a traditional distich, one stich of which contains the topic he wishes to pursue.

The traditional material, v. 21, treats two topics: falling because of a woman's beauty and being caught because of her possessions. The reader is admonished to avoid both. The verbs <u>npl</u> and <u>lkd</u> suggest the idea of falling into a trap and being caught thereby. Ben Sira sounds a similar warning, using these same verbs with regard to a strange woman and a woman musician in 9:3, 4.[194]

The idea of beauty is common in Sirach. Some of the references[195] deal with beauty in general, while others relate specifically to a woman's beauty. The latter are divided equally between positive and negative statements made about good wives[196] and bad wives/women[197] respectively. Our text falls into the negative category. The beauty of a woman is pictured as a trap into which the unsuspecting man may fall and thus suffer the consequences of sin. The behavior of the woman involved is not specified as in 26:10-12. It is unclear whether she is active or passive.

In its traditional setting line <u>a</u> refers to a woman, married or unmarried, whose beauty is the potential cause of downfall for a man who is not her husband. However, both the topic of this entire section as well as the implication of Ben Sira's expansion in v. 22 suggest that he desired to convey the impression that the women of v. 21 were bad wives. He clearly keyed on v. 21b in this regard and added his own comment on it accordingly (v. 22). But this left v. 21a, with its clear reference to woman and not wife, out of harmony with the section.

As we have seen, Ben Sira included this traditional material because of line b. Just as the beauty of a woman may cause a man to fall, so also the attraction of her possessions may entrap him. As far as it goes, this statement is rather general and originally referred to a woman and not necessarily to a wife. But in the light of v. 22, which Ben Sira added, it is made to imply a wife supporting her husband. Thus, he has taken material which originally had nothing to do with the bad wife and inserted it somewhat awkwardly[198] into this discussion on the bad wife.

We have noted that Ben Sira extended the notion of a man's being caught by a woman's possessions by adding what appears to be his own composition in v. 22. In this way he refined the general condition of v. 21b by applying the idea to a husband's being supported by his wife. He characterizes this situation as "hard slavery" and "a disgrace." Ben Sira was certainly aware of the use of the former phrase in the OT. The expression "hard slavery" (ʿbdh qšh) is used with regard to three negative periods in Israel's history: slavery in Egypt;[199] oppression in the time of Solomon;[200] and captivity in Babylon.[201] Thus, Ben Sira employs a phrase which the OT uses with reference to periods of severe national oppression to describe the effect of a wife's economically supporting her husband.[202] The implied comparison is unreasonably severe.

Ben Sira also suggests that "disgrace" or shame results from a husband's being supported by his wife. The idea of shame (bwšt, as here, and the verb bwš) is very common in Sirach. However, its implication here is probably best illuminated by the scenario in 13:4-7. There Ben Sira pictures a wily rich man, who exploits those who think they are being supported by him. According to Gr,[203] the rich man shames the dependent with his foods, while he drains him repeatedly and finally derides and forsakes him. Likewise, in our text the wife uses her support as a means of emasculating her husband, leaving him inept[204] and powerless.[205] This is one of the worst possible conditions for Ben Sira, who considers it paramount for a husband to be in control.[206]

V. 23cd[207] is structured very much like v. 22. Each distich contains a double characterization in line a. In line b each distich begins with a reference to a wife, continues by identifying a certain negative condition, and ends with the mention of a husband. Both distichs contain phrases that are common in the OT. In Heb and Syr the sentence structures are cryptic.[208] Both distichs probably represent compositions by Ben Sira.[209] Despite these similarities, however, the two distichs do not fall in the same strophic subsection. V. 22 is clearly an extension of v. 21 and must be grouped with it. This leaves v. 23cd along with v. 24 as independent distichs in the distich pattern.[210]

The situation described in this verse is one in which a wife does not make her husband happy or, in an equally plausible translation, does not call her husband blessed. The phrase refers to the showing of proper respect and the extolling of appropriate praise. We may note that this common OT idea expressed in the word 'šr is never used of a wife with regard to her husband. This is not to deny that the reality existed but merely to observe that it is not so stated. In Prov 3:18 the one who possesses the personified Wisdom is called blessed, though not necessarily by her.[211] Sometimes women are called blessed/happy, as in the cases of Leah[212] and the young lover of Canticles.[213] But the most startling contrast to Ben Sira's composition lies in Prov 31:28, where the industrious wife is called blessed not only by her children but also by her husband.

Line a characterizes this situation by means of the double metaphor "drooping hands and tottering knees." The figure of "drooping hands" is frequently employed in the OT as a symbol of discouragement and despair.[214] It is so used by Ben Sira in 2:12, where the related expression is "timid hearts." Sometimes the phrase is associated with the idea of weak knees as in our text.[215] It is understandable, therefore, that some translations[216] attempt to overcome the cryptic structure of this verse by inserting something into line b or by rearranging the material to give the impression that the wife in question causes her husband to despair and be discouraged.

We must note, however, that the word which I have translated "tottering" (kšlwn) is not elsewhere associated with knees.[217] Its only OT use is in Prov 16:18, where it means "fall" or "stumbling." The word is figurative for a calamity or disaster.[218] It may be reasonable, therefore, to consider the entire double metaphor as a reference to disaster. Ben Sira seems to have drawn this compound idea from Isa 35:3. But he verbalized it more like the "hands" expression in Jer 47:3. His particular formulation dealing with knees is unique. All this would suggest that we are not bound by the OT implications of these metaphors when seeking their meaning as employed in our text.

Ben Sira does not seem to be conveying the notion that a husband who is not made happy by his wife falls into discouragement and despair. That picture of a husband would be foreign to him. Instead, he appears to imply that when a wife does not make her husband happy or call him blessed she has created a calamity, a situation of disaster.[219] For Ben Sira marriage demands that the wife show her husband proper respect and extol him with appropriate praise.

V. 24, like the previous distich, is independent in the distich pattern. It treats a topic that is unrelated to what precedes or follows it, except in the general theme of the section. Fuss[220] is undoubtedly correct in assigning its composition to Ben Sira. We have already seen the influence of the Gen 3 material on him in v. 15.

This is the earliest extant piece of Jewish writing that ascribes the beginning of sin and the resultant death particularly to Eve.[221] Malina[222] demonstrates that the majority view contemporary with Ben Sira was that sin derived from the fall of evil angels and their cohabitation with women, according to the interpretation of Gen 6:1-4.[223] Rabbinic theology usually regarded Adam as responsible for sin and death.[224] But for Ben Sira, in the words of Spicq,[225] "the mother of life is the cause of the death of her children."

Von Rad[226] may be justified in denying that this verse is a definitive pronouncement by Ben Sira on the issues of sin and morality, but he is not correct in characterizing it as a passing statement. The author has deliberately traced the evil of women and their evil influence to a woman's role in the origin of all evil.[227] In fact, he has placed this assertion here as a kind of climax to this entire section on the bad wife, with what follows functioning as a denouement.

Hughes[228] observes that while the Gr <u>archē</u> in our text may be either temporal or causal, the Heb <u>tḥlh</u> is only temporal, meaning "beginning." From this Hughes argues that Ben Sira does not picture a woman as the cause of sin, but merely its historical starting point. But, as Tennant[229] notes, whatever the meaning of line <u>a</u>, line <u>b</u> is definitely causal. Ben Sira does not seem to be making any fine distinctions here between beginning and cause. We should read the distich as a unit, which attributes to a woman the origin of sin and death, both of which have accrued to succeeding generations. The emphasis is on the role of the woman in this negative event and not on the technicalities of the event itself.

We need not be concerned with what Ben Sira here means by sin.[230] The concept is extensively reflected in his book as the anthithesis to wisdom[231] and <u>Gottesfurcht</u>. He does not have any esoteric intent in our text, where, as we have observed, the focus is on the negative role of a woman. Likewise, the relationship between sin and death should not be seen as central to our text or even a problem to be solved.[232] Ben Sira is content to reflect the sin and death[233] elements of the Genesis story as the negative results of a woman's act. He is the first to have made this emphasis.

The final strophe of this section is the two distich unit consisting of vv. 25-26. According to Fuss,[234] v. 25 is traditional, followed by Ben Sira's compositional expansion in v. 26. However, I have argued that the expression "evil wife" is characteristic of Ben Sira,[235] and thus I prefer to assign the entire two distich strophe to his compositional activity. Fuss no doubt concludes that v. 25 is traditional based on its figurative language and tight parallelism. This cannot be ignored. It may be that Ben Sira found some of the material, such as line a, in his source and then reworked it, either by composing line b or by modifying it with an expression especially his own. In any case, I take v. 25 in its present form to be Ben Sira's composition.

The focus of v. 25 is on an evil wife's outspokenness. This is not the endlessly talking wife described in v. 20. Nor does it refer to public criticism from a rival wife as in 26:6. Here the use of the word parrēsia would suggest a wife who speaks to her husband with an arrogant boldness. She speaks in a way that challenges his authority.

Ben Sira advises a husband not to tolerate such behavior. He introduces the counsel with a cryptic metaphor about not allowing water, presumably a lake or pond,[236] to have an outlet. For Peters[237] the meaning of this parallel is that as only a dam holds the water in place, so only the constraint of a husband's rule holds the wife in the right path.

In v. 26 Ben Sira continues the discussion initiated in the previous distich by further defining the problem and offering his advice on its resolution. He opens with a statement of condition: "Unless she goes as you direct (literally according to your hands)." This reinforces and particularizes the wife's arrogance suggested in v. 25. Her outspokenness runs counter to his control. Thus, vv. 25-26 involve a discussion of the husband's authority in the home in general and over his wife in particular.

Ben Sira's apodosis in v. 26b is particularly abrupt when he calls for his readers who may be in such a situation to divorce their wives.[238] He expresses this through a rather unique metaphor: "cut her off from your flesh." The use of apotemnō for divorce is unconventional, having no parallel in the LXX[239] or classical literature.[240] However, the regular Heb term for divorce, krytwt, comes from the root krt, the verb form of which means "to cut." Since this verb is not unknown to Ben Sira,[241] we may reasonably postulate that it stood in our text. In fact, I would further suggest that Ben Sira himself has coined the use of the verb in relationship to divorce.[242]

While most scholars[243] see this verse as a reference to divorce, they are not agreed on the meaning of "cut her off from your flesh." Ryssel is content to see in the idea a presupposition of the "one flesh" concept of marriage stated in Gen 2:24. Box-Oesterley consider the statement as the equivalent to a bill of divorcement. However, Smend understands the metaphor as relating to the dowry or the wealth of the rich wife of vv. 21-22, which is lost because of divorce. Thus, the divorce settlement is like cutting off a piece of one's body. Peters rejects this notion and counters that the figure refers to the loss of the wife herself, who has become part of the husband's flesh.

The expression "from your flesh" is a translation of the Gr apo tōn sarkōn sou. The plural of sarx denotes flesh in the mass in distinction from the singular, which implies the substance itself.[244] In the LXX the plural is frequently employed where the underlying Heb is singular. The Heb in our text was undoubtedly a form of either bśr, which usually lies behind sarx in the LXX, or š'r. Both terms are well represented in Sirach,[245] although bśr is more frequently translated by sarx.[246] It is not particularly critical to chose between bśr and š'r for our text, since they may be used as synonyms. Both can mean "flesh," "body," and "relative."[247] However, we may express a slight preference for š'r for the following reason. Of the four instances where the LXX translates š'r with sarx, in three cases it uses a plural form of sarx.[248] This is also true of the one instance where Gr translates š'r with sarx in Sirach.[249] When sarx translates bśr in Sirach it is always singular. If š'r stood in our text, it no doubt conveyed the idea of one's body or oneself. The latter is reflected in Prov 11:17. This suggests that Ben Sira employed the metaphor "cut her off from your flesh" to mean simply "cut her off from yourself." In other words, "divorce her."[250]

We may also note two contrasting assessments of Ben Sira's attitude toward women as reflected in this distich. Gaspar[251] claims that the divorce discussion alludes "to the intimacy and strength of the bond that is being broken." Conversely, Snaith[252] sees Ben Sira anticipating those rabbis who later argued for a rather free application of divorce. For him "Ben Sira seems remarkably liberal--perhaps because of his prejudice!"

We have already seen that Ben Sira has probably initiated the use of the verb krt in reference to divorce. This would indicate more than a passing interest in the subject. But before we can make a precise judgment on this attitude here, it is necessary to look further at the use of krytwt in the OT. Of its four uses[253] only two (Deut 24:1, 3) are concerned with literal divorce. The Deuteronomy material is legal case language that assumes a divorce, in fact two divorces,[254] as the case condition.[255] It is concerned with the prohibition of a twice-divorced woman being remarried to her first husband. Furthermore, in 24:1 the condition assumes that the woman was divorced because her husband "found some indecency in her." The Heb term is ʿrwt dbr and is found elsewhere only in Deut 23:14 (15 Heb) with reference to excrement. However, the word ʿrwt has the well attested meaning "nakedness" or "genitals."[256] Note also the related words ʿrh "to lay bare," ʿrwm "naked," and ʿryh "nakedness." Thus, the divorce situation in Deut 24:1[257] results from behavior on the part of the wife that is considered sexually lewd and suggestive and, therefore, unacceptable.[258]

Ben Sira's call for divorce in the face of a wife's arrogant disdain for her husband's authority stands in stark contrast to the material in Deuteronomy.[259] He counsels the dissolution of the marriage union on grounds far less serious than those he found in his national tradition. Snaith has said it well.

In these forty lines of text devoted to the bad wife, Ben Sira has introduced his characteristic phrase "evil wife." This non-OT expression appears in the first distich after the introductory Zahlenspruch (26:7) and is the point of reference in the last two distich strophe of the section (25:25-26). We also find it in the middle of the material (25:16). We could justifiably entitle this section "Reflections on an Evil Wife."

Ben Sira's negative bias against women may be detected in his use of the expression "evil wife." But his bias is even more evident in other areas. He goes beyond the OT when he employes the harsh OT images of yoke (= slavery) and scorpion (= deadly danger) to the problem of controlling an evil wife (26:7). His consideration of the topic of the drunken wife (26:8) is without parallel in the OT. When he describes dwelling with an evil wife (25:16), he outstrips his literary models from Proverbs by changing the figure from those of inconvenience to one of disaster. His severe religious curse on a wife because of her wickedness (25:19) has no counterpart in the OT. He characterizes a wife financially supporting her husband (25:22) by using a metaphor which the OT applies to major periods of national oppression. Whereas Ben Sira is critical of a wife who does not call her husband blessed (25:23), the OT never pictures a wife in this role, though the reverse is true. He also exceeds the OT when he calls for the divorce of a wife who does not live within the bounds of her husband's control (25:25-26). But Ben Sira's most notable extension of the OT lies in his original assignment of the responsibility for the introduction of sin and death to a woman (25:24).

In addition to these conceptual phenomena, we may review certain formal factors that illustrate Ben Sira's negative bias against women. He has altered the traditional Zahlenspruch, which he placed at the head of the section, by the addition of an element describing a negative situation involving rival wives (26:5-6). This he followed with a three distich progression that moves from a bad wife in general to a drunken wife to one who is promiscuous (26:7-9). Next he rearranged the stichs of some general traditional material so as to imply that all the stichs referred to the bad wife mentioned in one of them (25:13-14). He included traditional material on the negative behavior of women in general and applied it to wives in particular (25:17-18, 21-22).

Thus, both in his unique conceptual creations and adaptations as well as in his formal adjustments and structuring Ben Sira has resoundingly revealed a negative bias against women in 26:5-9; 25:13-26.[260]

In addition to the main section of Sirach that deals with the bad wife, which we have just considered, we find several miscellaneous passages where the topic appears. I will discuss each of these isolated references under two categories: (1) women who rule men, and (2) bad wives variously described. Each group contains three texts.

9:2

Do not give[261] yourself[262] to a wife[263]
To cause her to tread[264] upon your heights.[265]

I have already discussed the context and form of this distich when treating 9:1 in chapter I.[266] We may note here, however, that vv. 1-2 form a strophe of two distichs, which are devoted to the topic of relating to one's own wife. In the earlier discussion we also concluded that v. 1 is traditional and that v. 2 is Ben Sira's composition.[267] We saw that the latter functions as a corrective to the apparent broad call for trust of one's wife in the former.

It is not possible to understand the meaning of "give yourself to a wife" apart from line b. But before I discuss line b I wish to make a brief observation about the verb ntn "to give." This verb is sometimes used in the OT in a technical construction ntn . . . l'šh with the meaning "to give (a person to someone) as a wife."[268] Even though he does not employ this technical expression or its masculine counterpart in our text, Ben Sira appears to have the idea of marriage in mind.

However, he advises against a man's giving himself to a woman. This is language that is rather foreign to the OT. Of course, as we shall see, he is offering negative counsel against a particular kind of marriage relationship.

The figurative language of line _b_ explains the specific situation that calls for the advice in line _a_. Gr and Syr progressively unlock the Heb metaphor "tread upon your heights" to convey the idea of "usurp your power."[269] This is not just any marriage. It is a marriage in which the husband has surrendered his authority and rule to his wife.[270] In terms of line _a_, such a husband would be given in marriage to his wife, rather than the reverse.

We see then that Ben Sira has appended to a traditional distich that advises against jealousy of one's wife a distich of his own that qualifies the traditional material. One should trust his wife, but he should not permit her to overtake his authority and rule.[271] Otherwise, the husband becomes the passive figure who is given in marriage, rather than the one who actively receives the wife.

33:19ab (30:28ab)

A son or a wife,[272] a brother[273] or a friend,[274]
Do not let rule[275] over your life.[276]

This distich is part of the section, 33:19-23,[277] which offers advice against a person's surrendering his authority and independence to others while he is still alive. Ben Sira identifies the potential power usurpers as a son, a wife, a brother, a friend, and any creature.[278] Presumably, these are people over whom the advisee has some control. This is certainly true of the son and wife. Thus, to allow any of them to gain power over oneself would involve the untenable situation in which the subordinate gains control of the superior.[279]

The implications of this section and of this distich in particular are similar to 9:2. While there the advice was couched in metaphorical language--don't allow her to tread upon your heights--here the counsel is direct. However, 9:2 is a limited and specific reference to a wife, whereas 33:19ab

(30:28ab) includes the wife as one of a group to whom control over oneself should not be given. Our text, then, does not single out the wife. It is something of a summary statement on an issue which he treats elsewhere in terms of some of its component parts. He discusses the wife and control in 9:2[280] and the son and control in 30:1-13.[281]

Although Ben Sira is not specificaly discussing wives in our text, he does include a wife among those subordinates to whom one should not surrender control. The verb which he uses here is m̲š̲l̲ II + b̲- "to rule over." In Gen 3:16 the first woman is told that her husband shall rule over her. Thus, as far as the wife in our text is concerned, for her to rule over her husband would reverse the divinely determined domestic order. Isaiah pictures the lamentable and vulnerable posture of Judah by declaring that it is oppressed by children and ruled over by women (Isa 3:12).

This distich contributes little to our understanding of Ben Sira's view of the bad wife. It is a general statement of advice against surrendering one's authority and control to others, including a wife. This mention of wife echoes 9:2 and anticipates 47:19, 20.

<u>47:19</u>

But you gave[282] your loins[283] to women[284]
And let them rule[285] over your body.[286]

The setting for this distich is Ben Sira's eulogy of Solomon in 47:12-22, which is a unit in his extended celebration of biblical notables in chapters 44-49. In this section he notes Solomon's building the temple (v. 13), his well-known wisdom (vv. 14-17), his wealth (v. 18), his life of folly (vv. 19-20), the resultant national division (v. 21), and the continuity of the Davidic lineage (v. 22). The strophe of three distichs that constitutes vv. 19-20 deals with Solomon's negative life style in general and his amorous adventures in particular. In v. 19 Ben Sira laments a specific Solomonic behavioral trait, and in v. 20 describes the results.

The particular problem that Ben Sira has in mind is Solomon's surrender of control over himself to women. In line _a_ he is certainly thinking of the biblical descriptions of Solomon in 1 Kgs 11:1-3. But Ben Sira departs from the biblical material in two ways. First, he exceeds the simple statements of his source that "Solomon loved many foreign women" and "clung to these in love," having "seven hundred wives, princesses, and three hundred concubines." In contrast, Ben Sira erotically charges, "you gave your loins to women."[287] Secondly, as 1 Kgs 11:1-3 confirms, the real problem with Solomon's behavior was the idolatry which resulted from his contact with foreign women. But Ben Sira avoids discussion of idolatry when he deals with Solomon and women. In fact, he does not mention idolatry at all in the section devoted to Solomon.[288] One may be tempted to dismiss this lacuna as characteristic of Ben Sira's relative silence on the question of idolatry. But it is strange that he praises only those judges "whose hearts did not fall into idolatry (46:11)."[289] For Solomon, he uses no such criterion. Instead, despite Solomon's well documented idolatry,[290] Ben Sira sings his praises, except for criticism of his surrender of control to women.[291]

The meaning of v. 19a is clarified by line _b_. To give one's loins to women means to give them control over oneself. The verb _ntn_ "to give" in line _a_ echoes 9:2, while the construction _mšl_ II _b_- "to rule over" is reminiscent of 33:19ab.[292] Thus, this distich with its historical example forms a kind of summary of Ben Sira's advice to men on not surrendering their control to their wives or to any women, for that matter.

Ben Sira extends this condemnation by noting in v. 20 the results of Solomon's behavior. These include: staining his honor, defiling his bed,[293] bringing wrath on his offspring, and causing sighing on his couch.[294]

We have seen in this distich that Ben Sira uses the occasion of condemning Solomon's negative behavior to summarize his advice on a wife's controlling her husband. But in doing so he handles his biblical source in a way that puts women into a more negative light than did his source. He also chooses to deal only with Solomon's "women" problems and not with Solomon's problems of idolatry, which clearly are the major concerns of the biblical source. This treatment reveals Ben Sira's negative bias against women.[295]

7:26b

But do not trust[296] in a wife whom you hate.[297]

This is the first of three miscellaneous texts that treat bad wives in various settings. It is the second line of a distich whose context I have already discussed when considering 7:19 in chapter I. I also dealt in the same chapter with the first line of this distich, which advises a man not to abhor his wife.

The key term in this line is śnw'h, which means "a hated wife." This technical expression is not uncommon in the OT.[298] Sometimes it is used in a context that implies bigamy.[299] But it is also found in a more general sense where dislike and disdain of one's wife is the focus.[300] It is in this latter sense that Ben Sira employs the term here, since there is no contextual evidence to indicate that he is contemplating a situation of polygamy. We should avoid the temptation to become highly specific concerning the type of woman he is describing here. Is she a wife who has been released[301] or a woman loved illegitimately?[302] Such characterizations arise from either a misunderstanding of or an ignoring of the context. This line is merely a corrective, added to line a to dampen the effect of what could be taken as an unconditional injunction against abhoring one's wife. Ben Sira is saying that such an injunction does not apply if one has a wife whom he disdains. He gives no hint as to the cause for such disdain. If she is disliked for whatever reason, she should not be trusted.[303]

We have noted that v. 26b stands as a corrective to the more universal line a. In chapter I[304] I showed that vv. 22-24, 26 share a common structure, but that v. 26 deviates in several ways from the pattern of what appears to have been traditional material. The deviation that concerns us here is the relationship of v. 26b to v. 26a. Vv. 22-24 are formulated as complementary parallels. V. 26, however, is antithetical. When discussing v. 26a, I argued that this distich has been edited by Ben Sira. It appears that his source contained a complementary positive statement in line b, reinforcing the counsel of line a. But he has apparently replaced that line with his own composition which acts to qualify and soften the impact of the broad statement of v. 26a. He is content to pass on advice concerning not abhoring a wife only after he has qualified it by excluding wives who are disliked.

37:11a

(10a Do not consult[305] . . .)
11a With a wife[306] concerning her rival.[307]

This injunction is part of a section (vv. 7-15) which deals with good and bad counselors. The arrangement of the distichs is as follows: four distichs present the opening formula (v. 7)[308] and general advice on distinguishing among counselors (vv. 8-9); six distichs (vv. 10-11) contain a series of individuals who cannot give unbiased or informed counsel on particular matters; two distichs (v. 12) describe a godly law keeper as a trusted counselor; two distichs (vv. 13-14) suggest that one's heart is his own best counselor; one distich (v. 15) adds that a person should consult God. Our line refers to a person who is an unproductive counselor, due to her prejudiced position. As Kearns[309] puts it, "Interested parties make poor counsellors."

The wife is disqualified if called upon to give advice concerning her ṣrh. As I have already demonstrated,[310] ṣrh is a technical term referring to a rival wife.[311] It is unclear whether our text understands this particular ṣrh as a potential rival wife--one whom a man may be planning to take[312]--or an actual rival wife.[313] In either case a wife would hardly provide objective counsel concerning the woman in question.

In this subsection Ben Sira includes the example of a wife as a kind of counselor to be avoided in a paticular situation. This is the only explicit example that he offers from within the close family circle. In fact, she stands at the head of the list that follows the introductory distich (v. 10). But we must avoid making too much of these rather minor details. It is enough to observe that in this material concerning unproductive counselors Ben Sira includes a wife as an advisor concerning her rival.

42:6

Upon a wife[314] who plays the fool,[315] a seal;[316]
And where there are[317] many[318] hands,[319] a key.[320]

This distich is in the middle of a section (42:1-8[321]) which contains a series of things concerning which one need not be ashamed. The section opens with an introductory distich and closes with a distich of conclusion. The remaining eight distichs include five (vv. 2, 3, 4a, 5a, 4bc, 8ab) which have <u>ʿl</u> at the beginning of each line,[322] introducing the various items of which one should not be ashamed. However, this pattern is broken for vv. 5bc-7, where <u>ʿl</u> at the beginning of line <u>a</u> of each distich means "upon." Strugnell[323] identifies the two patterns as: (1) "(Do not be ashamed) concerning (<u>ʿl</u>) X and Y;" and (2) "Upon (<u>ʿl</u>) an X (put--<u>vel</u>. <u>sim</u>.) a Y." Our text, of course, falls into the second category.

I am concerned here with the meaning of only line <u>a</u> in this apparently traditional distich.[324] The expression "a wife who plays the fool" (<u>ʾšh</u> <u>mṭpšt</u>), which is not found in the OT, no doubt should be taken in the general sense of an irrational or irresponsible wife.[325] The sage suggests that it is no shame to put a seal on such a wife. By seal (<u>ḥwtm</u>) he does not mean a signet ring or a cylinder seal[326] but a device that prevents entry into or escape from something.[327] In this case the term is used metaphorically to convey the notion of control and limitation. Thus, if a man has an irresponsible wife, he is well advised to place upon her whatever restrictions that are necessary to control her activities.[328]

The sentiments of this traditional stich contribute little to our mosaic of Ben Sira's view of the bad wife. He is comfortable with its implications, since he himself expresses similar concerns for the dominance of a husband's control over his wife and not the reverse.[329]

Conclusion

In this chapter we have observed many instances where Ben Sira has revealed his negative bias against women when discussing the bad wife. Most of the evidence for such a bias arises from the way he negatively exceeds the general or specific implications of his sources whether biblical or extra-biblical.

In considering the bad wife Ben Sira employs terms[330] and discusses issues[331] that are not found in the OT material on the subject. Furthermore, he applies to bad wives several metaphors which the OT uses in particularly pejorative or harsh settings, but never for women. He also criticizes Solomon for his amorous affairs, without mention of the idolatry which they caused. This is in contrast to the OT account, which centers its attack on the latter.

Ben Sira's handling of extrabiblical sources is even more revealing. We found that he reconstructed a Zahlenspruch to include negative material on women. He rearranged traditional material and applied general statements to specific situations in an effort to darken his picture of the bad wife. We also noted that he qualified traditional statements on the good wife, by both replacing a positive parallel stich with a negative corrective and adding his own negative distich to soften the impact of a preceding positive distich.

All that Ben Sira says about the bad wife is, of course, negative. In this sense he is certainly not unique. What we have seen, however, is that he has a unique, personal, negative bias against women which is evident in the data that we have reviewed.

CHAPTER IV

WOMAN AS ADULTERESS AND PROSTITUTE

Introduction

In this chapter I will discuss Ben Sira's reflections on women in two negative categories that relate to illicit sexual activity. The first group of texts contains references to adulteresses, actual or potential. The second group involves assertions or counsels regarding prostitutes. At the end I will consider a text that may be seen as a type of summary regarding both these categories, as well as a statement about a maidservant.

23:22-26

22 So it is also with a woman[1] who leaves her husband[2]
And produces[3] an heir[4] by a stranger.[5]
23 For first, she disobeyed[6] the law of the Most High;[7]
Second, she committed an offense[8] against her husband;[9]
And third, she committed adultery through fornication[10]
And produced[11] children[12] by a strange man.[13]
24 She will be led away[14] unto the assembly,[15]
And punishment will fall[16] on her children.[17]
25 Her children[18] will not spread out[19] roots,[20]
And her branches[21] will not bear fruit.[22]
26 She will leave[23] her memory for a curse,[24]
And her disgrace[25] will not be blotted out.[26]

This section constitutes Ben Sira's major discussion of the adulteress. The material is part of a larger unit that begins in v. 16. There we find a Zahlenspruch[27] (vv. 16-17) that serves to introduce a two part discussion of sexual immorality. The first part deals with an adulterer (vv. 18-21), while the second part involves our text. At the end stands a statement (v. 27) which concludes not only the adultery material but also the portion of the text that begins in v. 7.[28] Let us examine this context more closely.

Haspecker[29] has creatively analyzed the extended section, 23:7-27, with which we are concerned here. He demonstrates that this material is a tight knit composition, whose formal characteristics are consciously determined. The distichs are arranged in two symmetrical groups around the Zahlenspruch of vv. 16-17. The pattern of distichs is as follows, with 4 representing the Zahlenspruch: 2 + 6 + 7 + 4 + 7 + 6 + 2. On one side of the Zahlenspruch stands material that deals with verbal sins, while on the other side we find a consideration of sexual evils. The section opens with a two distich heading (vv. 7-8) and closes with a two distich practical application (v. 27). Working inwards we find two six distich segments. One is on swearing (vv. 9-10), the other is our text concerning the adulteress (vv. 22-26). On each side of the Zahlenspruch are two seven distich units. One deals with lewd talk (vv. 12-15), the other describes the adulterer (vv. 18-21). Haspecker notes that both six distich groups contain a similar casuistry, while both seven distich units appeal to authority figures as deterrents to negative bahavior.

We are especially concerned here with the the second half of this long section. As we have noted, this opens with a Zahlenspruch, which I take to be traditional.[30] As it now stands, this Zahlenspruch reads as follows:

16 Two sorts of men multiply sins,
And a third will bring on wrath.
A heated person like a burning fire
Will not be quenched until he is consumed.
A man who commits fornication with his near of kin
Will never cease until the fire burns out.
17 To a fornicator all bread is sweet,
He will never rest until he dies.

The three elements of this double number (X/X+1) Zahlenspruch are: (1) a heated person, (2) one who commits incest,[31] and (3) a fornicator.[32] Ben Sira uses this traditional piece as an introduction to his two prong discussion of adultery--the adulterer (vv. 18-21) and the adulteress (vv. 22-26). Before we consider our text, which is the second of these, it will be necessary to look at material on the adulterer in considerable detail. This will allow us to compare Ben Sira's handling of these related topics.

The first segment of this discussion concerning the adulterer contains three parts. In the first part (vv. 18-19a), which consists of three distichs, Ben Sira describes a man who commits adultery and justifies the act by claiming that no one sees him. The exact nature of this man's act and the identity of his partner are veiled in cryptic language. Ben Sira merely says that he "turns aside from his bed" (v. 18a).[33] There is no mention of the man violating a particular moral or civil law. Nor is he said to commit an offense against his wife. That Ben Sira intends his readers to understand that this man was engaged in adultery seems certain from the parallel nature of this material in relationship to the discussion of the adulteress that follows. After the section opens in v. 22 with the expression houtōs kai "so also," the woman is said to have "committed adultery" (v. 23c). The effect of this is to suggest that the man described in vv. 18-21 was also engaged in adultery. But since we are not told whom the man offended by his behavior, we are left to conclude that Ben Sira sees his offense being against the institution of marriage itself, of which the man is the head and personification. It is therefore against himself.

The second part of the section on the adulterer (vv. 19b-20), also including three distichs, contains Ben Sira's treatise on the all-seeing divine eye. The adulterer may think that his actions are concealed by the walls of his own house (v. 18cd). But the sage declares that God sees all things everywhere, even in the hidden places (v. 19e). In fact, God is said to see things twice. First, he observes events in their primeval, predetermined state (v. 20a), and second, he sees them in their historical occurrence (v. 20b).[34] Ben Sira avoids calling the man's action a sin against God, even though the man himself recognizes that he is sinning (v. 19a). Rather, he is content to merely describe in general terms how God will see him. He seems to suggest that the prospect of God's passive observation will be a deterrent to such behavior.

The third part of this section, expressed in a single distich (v. 21), alludes to the adulterer's punishment. The offender will be unexpectedly seized and will be punished in the streets. As in the other parts of this section, Ben Sira is again vague when he mentions the man's punishment. The text contains no reference to execution or any specific kind of penalty.[35] Instead, it seems to imply public seizure or detection. That is to say, the offender who took care for his secrecy will be publicly exposed, accompanied by the disgrace that will follow.

Having described the setting in which our text is found, let us now turn to a few final remarks before we examine the text itself. Fuss[36] considers this material to be largely the result of Ben Sira's own composition. However, he holds that vv. 22 and 24 may have formed a traditional casuistic unit which Ben Sira inserted in a separated form into his material. He offers a similar assessment of vv. 18ab and 21 in the section on the adulterer. It seems clear that some form of the Zahlenspruch which stands in vv. 16-17 is traditional. However, I am not convinced that Fuss' suggestions concerning vv. 18ab, 21, 22, 24 are valid. They do not appear to be traditional in their present form. This is certainly the case for v. 18ab, where line b easily flows into the following lines. Furthermore, vv. 22 and 24 do not stand out in the section either formally or conceptually but occupy natural places in the logically developed material. Therefore, I take this section to represent Ben Sira's work.

We have noted that Haspecker places our section into one strophe of six distichs. This needs a little refinement, however. Actually, the material lies in two subsections, each involving three distichs. The first unit (vv. 22-23) describes the offense of the adulteress, while the second (vv. 24-26) concerns her fate.

In the first strophe Ben Sira pictures the offense of the adulteress in terms of three elements. First, she left her husband (v. 22a). Second, she committed adultery through fornication (v. 23c). Third, she provided an heir by a stranger (v. 22b).

This is not the usual triangle that we might expect. The case is quite different from that of the adulterer described above.[37] He violated his marriage by secretly committing adultery in his own house. His motivation appears to be gratification of sexual desire. Our text mentions nothing of this sort with regard to the woman in this section. There is no triangle. Instead, there is a quadrangle. The added element is an heir. As Buchler points out, "The sin of the adulteress was in this instance not prompted by lust, but by her desire to have a child."[38] This, of course, presupposes that the couple had no children of their own. Such a presupposition is not disputed by the text.[39]

W. Frankenberg[40] sees v. 22 reflecting a common practice where a childless wife sought to produce an heir for the household. He looks on Ben Sira's pains to show such behavior to be offensive and punishable as evidence that ordinary people would not hold this act to be particularly sinful. An heir was held in such high regard and possessed such legal prerogatives that a childless wife was often disfavored by her husband.[41]

Further evidence that the desire for motherhood was the probable motivation for this woman's offense is seen in the repeated references to children throughout the section. I have already discussed the mention of an heir in v. 22b, where the offense is described. The third judicial conviction in v. 23cd refers to her bringing forth children (<u>tekna</u>[42]). These children share in their mother's punishment and fate in vv. 24b, 25a.

The use of the plural <u>tekna</u> in v. 23d raises the question of whether this woman mothered more than one illegitimate child in her quest for an heir, or whether the text beginning in v. 23 becomes a discussion of general principle rather than a specific incident. It is not possible to answer this question with certainty. We may more safely conclude that the woman's primary motivation for her act or acts was the desire to have children of her own. The prospect of an heir was probably her rationalization, since an heir would be an asset to her husband. The references to tekna would reflect her true motivation. It is unimportant whether or not the plural is to be taken literally, i.e., whether or not she "left her husband" on more than one occasion. What is significant is her quest for motherhood.

Wis 3-4 contains material that elucidates this woman's offense. In 3:13 the sage declares:

> For blessed is the barren woman who is undefiled,
> who has not entered into a sinful union;
> she will have fruit when God examines souls.

This woman is said to be barren. But in reality it is probably her husband who is sterile. She does not try to conceive children by another man. Her "fruit," the reversal of her childlessness, will come in the judgment. In 4:1 he comforts such a woman:

> Better than this [a grievous end] is childlessness with virtue,
> for in the memory of virtue is immortality,
> because it is known both by God and by men.

These texts contain a reference to childlessness and a warning for women not to enter extramarital relationships to conceive children. In 3:16-19; 4:3-6 we learn that children conceived in this way will have both social and eschatological troubles. The adulteress in our text should be seen in the same domestic setting as these women in Wisdom.

Gaspar[43] considers the woman in this section to be the same as the "strange woman"[44] of Proverbs. He gives a long description of Gustav Boström's[45] theory that this is an expression referring to a cult prostitute. In his challenge to this view Gaspar asserts that the "strange woman" is an Israelite adulteress, who is further described not only in Sir

23:22-26 but also in 26:19-24.[46] Upon inspection, however, I cannot support such a correlation.

The first and obvious fact is that our text does not contain the term "strange woman."[47] But it is more significant to note how the women in question differ. In Proverbs the "strange woman" is married[48] but acts like a prostitute.[49] However, she is especially singled out for her seductive behavior, particularly the seductive words by which she allures young men to her bed.[50] Her motivation is purely the desire for sexual gratification and/or gain. As we have seen, this is not the case regarding the woman in our text. While she is married and her activity is described by Ben Sira in v. 23c as committing adultery en porneia "through fornication (or harlotry)," she is not accused of seductiveness. No one is warned against her enticements. Rather, she is condemned for illegitimate child-bearing. Her motivation was a desire for motherhood, not sexual activity as an end in itself. She is not an example of the "strange woman" of Proverbs.

The use of the term klēronomos in v. 22b raises the question as to whether or not the offspring of an adulterous union involving a married woman would be an heir to that woman and her own husband. Chaim Tschernowitz in his study of inheritance of Jewish illegitimate children asserts that Israel, like most other nations of antiquity, made "no great distinction . . . between blood relationship (cognation) and artificial kinship (agnation)" such as adoption.[51] Whomever the father accepted as a son, legitimate or illegitimate, was a full son and an heir.[52] Polygamy provided children from several wives and concubines, but all were heirs.[53] Tschernowitz sees the Tal. as confirming this situation of liberal interpretation of inheritance laws. He notes that when R. Akiba pronounced any child from a forbidden union to be a bastard (mmzr),[54] he was opposed by majority rabbinic opinion. The latter limited this category to offspring from incest.[55]

The implications of v. 22 are that the woman can provide an heir by another man, and that the child can indeed be an heir either solely or along with sons born legitimately.[56] Ben Sira does not nullify the woman's efforts by declaring that such offspring are not in fact heirs. He does not indicate that she cannot legally accomplish her wish. The sage simply declares her act to be an offense against God, her husband, and her illegitimate offspring (v. 23). The description of her children's fruitlessness and share in her punishment (vv. 24-25) does not nullify their being potential heirs. The former is figurative, as we shall see, and not legal. These children can be more accurately described as potential heirs, since, as Tschernowitz[57] points out, only those children which the husband so identified were considered heirs.

That the woman is able to provide an heir through an illicit union with another man does not mean that she shares equal legal status with her husband in this regard. On the contrary, it shows that she is subordinate to him. He owns her. Therefore, he also owns anything that she produces. Furthermore, he has the right to claim or reject as his own her offspring from whatever source.

After describing her offense in v. 22, Ben Sira enumerates in v. 23 those whom the woman has offended. These two distichs are in the form of a judicial distinction in which the injured parties are listed individually.[58] The list proceeds from the greatest to the least of those injured. First, she is condemned for disobeying "the law of the Most High" (v. 23a). The law in question is probably the seventh prohibition of the Decalogue.[59] Nothing is mentioned about an attempt to conceal her act from God, as in the case of the adulterer.

The adulteress is next said to have "committed an offense[60] against her husband" (v. 23b). She has mistreated her "owner" by offering herself to another man (v. 22). The verb is used in much the same way in 26:11,[61] where the potential offender is a daughter who is likely to commit an offense against her father--her "owner." Again we may note the contrast between Ben Sira's description of the adulterer and that of the adulteress. In the former there is no mention of the offended spouse. In the latter, apart from God himself, the spouse is the chief victim.[62]

The third article of indictment is not as clearly stated as the first two. It contains two elements. There is reference to her act of "adultery through fornication" (v. 23c) and to the fact that she "produced children by a strange man" (v. 23d). As in v. 22, I prefer to take the second half of the distich as a statement of the purpose of the first. Thus, the purpose of her adultery was to produce children. But this does not solve the problem of the identity of this third offended party. Some possibilities include: the community in general, the woman herself,[63] her husband's family,[64] her illegitimate children.[65] The last possibility seems most likely, since the bearing of children is central to v. 23cd and to the entire discussion of her offense. Furthermore, they are said to share her fate (vv. 24-25) and are, therefore, tangibly offended.

The second strophe in this section involves the three distichs of vv. 24-26, which deal with the woman's fate. In v. 24a Ben Sira declares that the adulteress "will be led away (exachthēsetai) unto the assembly (ekklēsian). Unfortunately, he does not elaborate on why she is brought before the assembly or on the nature of the sentence. Scholars have taken various positions concerning what this line means. Büchler[66] contends that she receives the death sentence, with the assembly acting as God's agent. Weber[67] sees her receiving a sentence of divorce, expulsion from her home, loss of her property, and public scourging. According to Spicq,[68] the assembly merely examines her and establishes the illegitimacy of her children, in order to remove them from her husband's family and from the religious community. Box-Oesterley[69] simply have her brought to the assembly "for punishment."

The critical questions in interpreting this line are: did Palestinian Jews have the authority to use capital punishment in this period, and, more importantly, if they did have the authority, was such punishment used in cases of adultery? The answer to the first question is inconclusive. The sources for the

Ptolemaic and early Seleucid administration of Palestine are meager. Sirach itself is one of the few witnesses to the period. Middendorp[70] finds in Sirach, among refrences to several classes of government officials, mention of a magistrate (šlṭwn ʿyr),[71] who has the power to kill.[72] He sees this Stadthaupt as a kind of police chief or security officer. It is not clear whether this official was native or Greek. It does not seem likely, however, that his death power was a judicial function. He appears to have an executive or military authority that includes execution. But his responsibility is probably only to the Greek overlords, with no regard to internal questions of native law.

While the answer to the second question is also rather uncertain, there is at least more data. Let us consider the broader problem of adultery and punishment in the OT. The numerous references may be divided into groups based on whether adultery is literal or figuative, and whether punishment is literal, figurative, or eschatological. The first group, literal adultery/no punishment mentioned, includes the prohibitions of the Decalogue[73] as well as that of Lev 18:20 in the expanded discussion of forbidden sexual relations. Since they do not refer to punishment, these texts cannot help us here.

Group two, literal adultery/literal punishment,[74] is the most important for our problem. In Lev 20:10 and Deut 22:22 the law calls for the execution of both parties involved in adultery. Deut 22:23-27 suggests that the mode was probably to be stoning.[75] There are also several references to adultery or possible adultery that include a death warning. Abimelech was told in a dream that he was "a dead man" because he mistakenly took Abraham's wife.[76] In similar circumstances he later took Isaac's wife. When he discovered that Rebekah was married, he ordered that if anyone touched either Isaac or Rebekah he "shall be put to death."[77]

In the discussion of the "loose woman" in Proverbs there are several references to death. Her house is called "the way to Sheol" in 7:27.[78] This, however, is the antithesis to the "path of life," which she does not know,[79] and which her partner will not regain.[80] By itself it can hardly refer to execution. In 5:23 we find that one who consorts with such a woman "dies for lack of discipline." The parallel in line b reads: "and because of his great folly he is lost." This appears to be the general result of all unwise behavior.[81] The mention in 6:32 of an adulterer destroying himself is in a context that includes "wound," "dishonor," "disgrace," and jealous revenge.[82] The declaration, "it will cost him his life" in 7:23, is probably related to the figurative description in v. 26:

> For many a victim has she laid low;
> yea, all her slain are a mighty host.

None of these references can be taken as evidence that their author had judicial execution in mind as the penalty for adultery. This seems clear not only from what we have already seen but also from the important fact that in no instance is the "loose woman" herself given such a penalty. Instead, she lays low "many a victim."[83]

Literal adulterers/adulteresses receive a variety of literal punishments or consequences. These include: sterility,[84] imprisonment,[85] wounds,[86] dishonor,[87] miscarriage,[88] divorce,[89] rejection of offerings,[90] revenge,[91] and punishment in general.[92]

The other categories, literal adultery/eschatological punishment,[93] figurative adultery/literal punishment,[94] and figurative adultery/figurative punishment,[95] are of little value for the present discussion. However, let us make a few observations concerning some texts that fall into the last group. Jer 3:8 mentions "a decree of divorce" and may reflect the literal background for its figurative use here. It is further possible that adulteresses had their genitals publicly exposed. Such a punishment may have been the basis for the prediction in Jer 13:26, where Judah is told:

> I myself will lift up your skirts over your face,
> and your shame[96] will be seen.

Likewise, Hos 2:3 refers to the figurative stripping of clothes from unfaithful Israel.[97]

From this look at the biblical relationship of adultery to punishment, it is evident that, while the law demands death, the cases observed and the various discussions of the subject do not support a practice of execution. Rather, such cases and discussions allude to various penalties and consequences. The OT records no example of an adulterer or an adulteress being executed.

The account of Susanna in the Apocrypha deserves our mention. This second century B.C. legend[98] contains the story of a Jewish wife who was falsely accused of adultery. She was convicted by the congregation[99] and sentenced to death. But on the way to execution she was saved by a lad named Daniel, who demanded her retrial. He showed that the witnesses had perjured themselves, and Susanna was vindicated, while her accusers were themselves executed. The references to death as a penalty are in vv. 22, 28, 41, 43, 45. If this piece of fiction was created by Pharisees attacking the lax judicial procedure of the Sadducees, as some[100] have suggested, then it is understandable that the account conforms to the law, without regard to its contemporary application. The author(s) could hardly create a legal case without including the legal penalty which is set down in the Torah. Besides, it makes a much better drama this way. If, however, the account was based on a simple non-Jewish folk tale with the Jewish details added, as Pfeiffer[101] suggests, then we are free to dismiss the story as having any reflection of contemporary Jewish custom. In any event, Susanna is not useful for either an understanding of adultery and its penalty or an insight into the role of the assembly in cases of adultery.

If Ben Sira were aware of the contemporary practice of execution in adultery cases, he would certainly have mentioned it in connection with his discussion of adultery. This would be particularly so with regard to the adulteress, since he treats her offense in greater detail than that of the adulterer.

Whatever penalty Ben Sira has in mind, it does not appear to be execution.[102]

The assembly (ekklēsia) in v. 24 is probably the qhl, or popular assembly, in contrast to the `dh, or congregation. Our text suggests that it had jurisdiction in matters pertaining to the Mosaic law. In 42:11 a father is counseled to strictly watch his daughter, lest she cause him to be publicly ridiculed and disgraced. In conjunction with this, Ben Sira quotes a line from a traditional Zahlenspruch which reads: "An evil report in the city, and an assembly of the people (wqhlt `m)."[103] Middendorp[104] holds that this refers to the possibility of the daughter's having to appear before the assembly on the charge of adultery. However, it probably means no more than general public disgrace like the kind experienced by the adulterer in Prov 5:14.[105] About all that we can say for certain is that the woman in v. 24 is taken to the assembly for some kind of examination to determine the details of her offense.

The only mention of punishment is with regard to her children (v. 24b). But again this is quite general. The term used is episkopē "visitation," rather than ekdikēsis, which is the usual translation of nqm in Sirach.[106] Smend[107] suggests that the children's punishment is the assembly's decision that they are illegitimate. If this is the case, then the assembly hearing may have been for the purpose of the husband's publicly rejecting them as his own. We have already seen that he apparently had the right to identify children not actually his own to be his heirs. While we cannot prove that this was the reason for the appearance before the assembly, it is at least plausible.[108]

V. 25 figuratively develops this punishment by declaring that these children will "not spread out roots" and "will not bear fruit."[109] These predictions simply represent pious, wishful thinking and should not be interpreted in any legal or biological way. Thus, Spicq's[110] assertion that this verse refers to the penalties of premature death and sterile unions is untenable.

The final element in the fate of the adulteress is the disgrace that will accompany her name even after her death (v. 26). For her mistakes she will live in dishonor during her life. And when her life ends, she will still be remembered with contempt, and her memory will still be cursed.

Her fate is complicated. She is examined by the assembly. After being found guilty of adultery, she may be divorced or beaten. She is certainly publicly disgraced. Her children from the illicit union are found to be illegitimate. For this she will always be cursed, even in death. Such is the sorry end of her quest for motherhood.

In this discussion we have seen that Ben Sira treats the adulteress with more severity than the adulterer. His offense is vaguely against his own bed, which in general is against the marriage that he personifies. She has specifically left her husband, committed adultery, and mothered children by a stranger. In so doing, she broke God's law, offended her husband, and imperiled her illicit children. On the other hand, he is loosely condemned for not recognizing that God sees his secret behavior. But God does not punish him. Rather, he is merely detected and exposed in the community. In her case she is specifically summoned to the assembly, where she is examined and disgraced. Her children are declared illegitimate and share her dishonor. Even in death her memory will be cursed. This contrast appears all the more striking when we remember that her motivation for adultery appears to have been her desire for motherhood. He merely wanted sexual gratification. Ben Sira has left his mark of negative bias against women on this material.

<u>9:8-9</u>

8 Hide[111] your eye[112] from a charming woman,[113]
And do not look on[114] beauty that is not yours.[115]
By the beauty of a woman[116] many have been ruined,[117]
And thus love[118] is kindled[119] like a fire.[120]

9 Do not stretch out the elbow[121] with a married woman,[122]
And do not mix[123] wine with her,[124]
Lest your heart[125] turn aside to her,[126]
And in blood[127] you go down[128] to the Pit.[129]

These four distichs occur at the end of the eleven distichs of miscellaneous counsels concerning women in 9:1-9. I have already discussed the context, both immediate and extended, as well as the structure of this section.[130] Because he judges it to be disproportionately verbose, Fuss[131] considers these verses to represent Ben Sira's composition. This conclusion seems reasonable.

We must note at the outset that this material is not actually a discussion of an adulteress. Like all of 9:1-9, it is set in the form of advice to a man, probably a young man, concerning his dealings with women of various sorts and roles. These verses treat his relationship to married women, i.e., the wives of other men.[132] The sage counsels the reader to avoid conduct around such women that would intensify the chance of his engaging in illicit sexual activity with them. If this should happen, the offense would be adultery, since they are married. The married women discussed here are potential adultresses. Thus, it seems reasonable to consider this material within this particular category.

This unit consists of two subsections. Two distichs (v. 8) constitute advice not to look at a beautiful, married woman. This is followed by two distichs (v. 9) which counsel the reader not to eat or drink with a married woman. In each case failure to heed the advice may lead to uncontrollable sexual desire, which, in turn, will result in negative consequences. The second subsection reflects a more intense situation than the first, both in terms of the danger of adultery and in terms of the description of the results.

The focus of the two distichs of v. 8 is the seductive characteristic of a woman's beauty. Ben Sira displays a considerable interest in the beauty of women. His discussions employ three principal terms, each used in both positive and negative settings. It is significant that lines a-c of our text contain each of these terms. This makes v. 8 a rather comprehensive statement of Ben Sira's view of a woman's beauty, at least in negative settings such as this one.

The first "beauty" word is ḥn (v. 8a). Its essential meaning is "charm, elegance." Ben Sira uses it for a good wife in 7:19 and probably in 26:13.[133] It is a quality that relates to her sexual attractiveness to her husband. In our text the word is used in the expression ʾšt ḥn literally "a woman of charm." It is to be understood negatively, since the reader is advised to hide his eye from her. In the OT we find ḥn used for women both positively[134] and negatively,[135] but we find no counsel against looking at a woman who has this characteristic.

The second word for beauty is ypy (v. 8b). While it is extant only in the Heb of Sirach here, it probably also occurred in 25:21; 26:17.[136] The first text, found in the discussion of a bad wife, is negative. The second is a description of a good wife's attractiveness to her husband. This word is a standard Heb term for a woman's beauty. The OT employs it in both positive[137] and negative[138] settings. However, it contains no advice concerning not looking at a woman with ypy. In our text Ben Sira tells the reader not to look on ypy that does not belong to him, i.e., the beautiful wife of another man.

The third word for beauty which Ben Sira uses is tʾr (v. 8c). This term refers particularly to "form," but it is used several times by Ben Sira in the sense of the form or beauty of a woman. In 36:22 (24 Heb, 27 Gr) he describes a good wife whose tʾr brightens her husband's countenance. However, in 42:12 he advises a father not to allow his daughter's tʾr to be exposed to any man. The OT uses this word in relationship to women only positively.[139] In our text, on the other hand, Ben Sira suggests that through a woman's tʾr "many have been ruined."

This reference to many being ruined (hšḥtw rbym) is not a reflection of capital punishment. We will discuss this below in relationship to v. 9d. In fact, the expression probably does not imply any kind of punishment as such. Instead, it is best understood in the light of the following line, which conveys the likely consequence of looking at beautiful, married women. The verb, which is a Hof'al from the root šḥt, means "to be spoiled, ruined."[140] Thus, the line suggests that the beauty of a woman has been the means for many men to be corrupted, i.e., to become involved in illicit sexual activity. This is confirmed by line d.

In v. 8d Ben Sira declares that the result of gazing at a beautiful woman is bound to be the arousal of sexual desire.[141] Such passion, according to the sage, flames up like a fire. Several scholars[142] have noted the play on words in these lines, involving the terms ʾšh "woman" and ʾš "fire." What Ben Sira seems to be implying here is that if one continues to watch a certain physically attractive, married woman, he will come to desire her sexually and will no doubt fulfill his desire. This, of course, would corrupt him morally and socially, as well as put him in jeopardy with her husband.

In v. 9 Ben Sira moves from counsel that relates to watching a beautiful, married woman (v. 8) to the consideration of an advanced level of involvement with a married woman. His advice concerns a person's behavior in relationship to eating and drinking with such a woman. This certainly does not reflect a situation where a man would be dining alone with another man's wife.[143] Such a secret restaurant scene would be grossly anachronistic! Instead, this no doubt involves a general banquet setting--a scenario common to Ben Sira.[144]

The counsel part of this two distich subsection is contained in the first distich, lines ab. While these lines together constitute a hendiadys reflection of dining at a banquet, each line has its own particular notion. In line a Ben Sira suggests that a man should "not stretch out the elbow with a married woman." In this setting it appears that the cryptic expression refers to not eating with a married woman, the corollary of not mixing or drinking wine with her (line b).

However, the same construction occurs in 41:19c. There, in a section dealing with things of which one should be ashamed,[145] we find this exhortation: "(Be ashamed) of stretching out the elbow at bread."[146] From this it is clear that the expression "to stretch out the elbow" cannot mean "to eat" or even "to recline at table." A person would not need to be ashamed of either. But from both 9:9a and 41:19c it is evident that the expression refers to some kind of behavior or activity that is considered improper in the context of a meal, probably a banquet. Since the elbow would be used in propping oneself up while reclining on a dining couch, the expression probably refers to some type of indecent reclining or behavior while in this position.[147] A more precise explanation is not possible.[148] This much is clear: Ben Sira advises his reader not to behave around a married woman at a banquet in such a manner as to induce sexual arousal.

In line b the meaning is more evident. Ben Sira advises a person not to "mix wine" with a married woman. It seems reasonable to assume that the setting is still the banquet pictured in line a. But Ben Sira is not particularly concerned about the mixing or drinking of wine as such. With that he is quite comfortable.[149] What troubles him here is the juxtaposition of wine and women, particularly married women. Elsewhere, he recognizes that the overindulgence of wine is conducive to sexual irresponsibility and promiscuity.[150]

The distich of counsel (v. 9ab) is followed by a distich dealing with consequences (lines cd). The result of excessive familiarity with a married woman at a banquet is described in two ways. One concerns the man with the woman; the other concerns the man himself. In line c Ben Sira indicates that the person who disregards the advice in lines ab is likely to "turn aside to her." We might have expected him to use the verb śṯh "to turn aside" in this situation. This is the verb used in Prov 7:25, which along with vv. 26-27 has undoubtedly influenced Ben Sira in lines cd. Except for Prov 4:15, śṯh is used only in reference to illicit sexual intercourse.[151] However, in our text Ben Sira uses a similar sounding synonym nṭh. The reason for this may lie in the fact that nṭh can mean either "to stretch out" or "to turn aside." He has used the verb with the former meaning in line a (to stretch out the elbow) and in line c with the latter meaning. But the meaning in line c is equivalent to śṭh in Prov 7:25. The verb nṭh itself is not normally used with sexual connotations. However, it occurs in Gen 38:16 in such a context. There Judah turns aside to negotiate a sexual encounter with his daughter-in-law, Tamar, whom he thought to be a prostitute. It would appear that Ben Sira selected the verb nṭh in our text in order to play on its two meanings. The effect of this is to imply that the nṭh of the elbow with a married woman (line a) produces the nṭh of the heart to her (line c). In other words, if one behaves indecently with a married woman at a banquet, he will surely find himself joining her in sexual activity.[152]

Ben Sira indicates the second consequence in line d when he states that the man who does not heed his advice will go down in blood to the Pit. This reference to the Pit (šḥt) is clearly related to the idea of death, as its use elsewhere with Sheol (š'wl) confirms.[153] Furthermore, the mention of blood would suggest violent death.[154] In view of this, many scholars[155] have taken line d as an indication of the penalty of execution that awaits an adulterer. They see at work here the application of the legal code reflected in Lev 20:10 and Deut 22:22, which calls for such execution. Others[156] prefer to see here the retaliation of the offended husband, who slays the offender. In either case, this is taken to be a reflection of Prov 7:23-27.

There are several problems with these interpretations, which see line d as specifically referring to literal death, particularly death due to capital punishment. This line is part of a set of miscellaneous prohibitions regarding women (9:1-9). Thus, it is not the place where we would expect an account of adultery as explicit as the one found in 23:16-27, which is Ben Sira's most complete treatment of the topic. It would be unusual, therefore, to find reflected here a specific reference to a death penalty, when such is not the case in 23:16-27, as we have seen.[157] We have noted the relationship of our text to material in Prov 7. But, as we have previously observed,[158] Prov 7:23-27 cannot be taken to reflect a death penalty for adultery, since the woman involved accumulates "many a victim" and is obviously not executed. If she is not executed, then her lovers are certainly not the victims of capital punishment.

We have already explored the matter of Jews and capital punishment in this period and the relationship of this to adultery, with the conclusion that Ben Sira is not aware of a contemporary practice of execution for adulterers or adulteresses. In our text he draws on the material in Prov 6 and 7 that describes the consequences to come to the man who engages in adultery or consorts with prostitutes. But the Proverbs material is uneven. Sometimes death is implied.[159] At other times the offender is the victim of revenge or tries to offer compensation.[160] Nevertheless, Ben Sira employs these reflections in hyperbolic manner for the purpose of motivation. Thus, the allusion to violent death should be seen as a metaphor which represents the various destructive consequences that inevitably accompany adultery. These may include public exposure and disgrace,[161] legal or retaliatory action on the part of the offended husband,[162] and, of course, divine disapproval and judgment.[163]

In this section Ben Sira views woman as a sex object. Although she is not pictured here actually committing adultery, she is nevertheless presented in the light of that potential. In fact, Ben Sira implies that illicit sexual activity is the probable result of a man's gazing at a beautiful, married woman or reveling with her at a banquet. Neither of these situations is featured in the OT. By contrast, this makes Ben Sira more negative toward women. However, we should assess this material with restraint, since by itself it reflects very little of Ben Sira's view of women. The most that we can say is that it fits well with the Tendenz that we have observed in Ben Sira, not only to relegate women to second level status, but to do so under the particular motivation of a personal, negative bias.

<u>26:9</u>

A wife's fornication[164] occurs[165] by the lifting up of her eyes,[166]
And by her eyelids[167] she will be known.[168]

This verse is not an isolated distich relating to women, as its appearance here would seem to indicate. It is found in the midst of Ben Sira's most extensive discussion of women, located in chapters 25 and 26. I have already dealt with the matter of rearrangement of this material.[169] According to my proposed scheme, this text is part of the section devoted to the bad wife, which is now found in 26:5-9; 25:13-26.

This distich is also part of a subsection, 26:7-9, which makes three assertions about a bad wife. As we noted in discussing vv. 7-8, Fuss[170] considers the three distichs of this subsection to be traditional. However, after examining vv. 7 and 8 individually, I have concluded that they are more likely the product of Ben Sira himself.[171] Furthermore, I would extend this assessment to v. 9 as well. This situation would be expected in the company of Ben Sira's own material in vv. 7-8.[172] Furthermore, the verse contains expressions that are not uncommon to Ben Sira's style. These include <u>porneia</u>,[173] and <u>meteōrismos ophthalmōn</u>.[174] Thus, the whole subsection, vv. 7-9, appears to be Ben Sira's composition.

We also noted in our discussion of vv. 7-8 that the subsection, vv. 7-9, seems to reflect a progressively negative look at the bad wife. This starts in v. 7 with a description of a bad wife in general. V. 8 is more specific with its view of the drunken wife. The progression culminates in our text by referring to "a wife's fornication."

The expression <u>porneia gynaikos</u> clearly refers to the adulterous activity of a wife. Chapters 25 and 26 are dealing with good and bad wives in particular and not with good and bad women in general.[175] Thus, the <u>gynē</u> in our text is a married woman. The term <u>porneia</u> can refer to prostitution, as it does in 42:8. A prostitute may be a married woman, or a married woman may, for one reason or another, play the role of a prostitute. This is reflected in Prov 7. However, our text does not seem to have this meaning in mind. In 23:23 Ben Sira describes a married woman who "committed adultery"[176] en porneia. In that context, as we have seen,[177] porneia does not mean "prostitution." The wife is seeking to mother a child, even if through a man other than her husband. Her act is called adultery. Thus, en porneia must mean "by means of fornication." This general use of porneia seems more reasonable in our text than the specific meaning prostitution.

If this understanding of porneia is granted, then the distich may be seen to reflect a chiastic structure. Accordingly, line a begins by mentioning sexual activity, followed by a remark about the woman's eyes. Line b starts with a reference to her eyes and ends with a circumlocution for sexual activity. This last item is the expression gnōsthēsetai "she will be known." The verb "to know" is a common OT euphemism for sexual intercourse.[178] It is possible, of course, that Ben Sira is thinking of this expression in a double sense--both literally and figuratively. But in this context, at least, the latter seems secure.

The recognition of this distich as a chiasm is helpful in the interpretation of the references to the woman's eyes. The "eye" expression in line a has proved the most enigmatic to scholars. Smend[179] suggests that en meteōrismois ophthalmōn means "by the impact of her eyes." Hamp[180] takes the expression to mean "by her uncontrolled glances." For Middendorp[181] the meaning here, as in 27:22, deals with the dangerous winking of the eye. Robert Renehan[182] notes the similarity of this expression to rhipsophthalmos "casting the eyes about (at the object of one's desire)" and especially to hypsēlophthalmos "raising the eyes (to better see the object of his desire)."

It is clear from the context that the term meteōrismos is being used in our text more like its application in classical Gr than in the rest of the LXX. In the latter, the word is used to translate the Heb mšbr "breakers, waves."[183] The only exception to this is its use in the late 2 Mac 5:21 with the meaning "arrogance." The classical meaning is "a lifting up, swelling."[184] None of these appear to relate the term to eyes. However, Ben Sira has just such a combination in 23:4b. The RSV translates the expression meteōrismon ophthalmōn as "haughty eyes." Smend[185] is no doubt right in rejecting this as the meaning of the phrase in our text.

We should, however, consider the possibility that "haughty eyes" is not the best rendering of meteōrismon ophthalmōn in 23:4b. We may note that the line of which this phrase is a part combines with the following line (v. 5) to form a parallel. The petitions in these lines constitute a section of a prayer found in 22:27-23:6. In v. 4b the petitioner asks that meteōrismon ophthalmōn not be given to him. He follows this in v. 5 by urging that God take away epithymian from him. These simply represent two ways of praying that he be kept from some negative characteristic(s). It seems reasonable to assume that both these expressions are referring to the same basic reality. The word epithymia means "desire" and is clearly to be understood here in the negative sense. It follows that meteōrismon ophthalmōn must have a similar meaning. When viewed from this perspective, the expression metaphorically conveys the notion of lusting for something, i.e., the lifting of the eyes to observe the object of one's desire.[186]

This understanding of meteōrismon ophthalmōn in 23:4b may be helpful in the interpretation of the similar phrase in our text. If we insert this meaning into 26:9a, we have a line which conveys the notion that a wife's fornication occurs, in part, through her lustful, seductive eyes. This sense is both consistent with the context and in line with the expression in 23:4b. The same meaning is reflected by the expression en tois blepharas autēs "by her eyelids" in line b of our text. In this distich the woman's eyes are taken to be her chief seductive weapons.[187] This may include both the way she uses her eyes and the manner in which she decorates them.[188]

We have seen that this distich is the final element in a three distich subsection that describes the bad wife from a progressively negative prospective. Ben Sira refers to a bad wife in general (v. 7), pictures a drunken wife (v. 8), and culminates with a statement about an adulterous wife (v. 9). The relationship between the latter two is quite tight, since the drunken wife is said to "not conceal her nakedness."[189] Ben Sira seems to imply that the next level of negative activity is adultery.

By itself this distich does not reveal a particularly negative bias against women on Ben Sira's part. As we have seen, the OT reflects the same relationship between a woman's eyes and her sexual desire. However, when this text is viewed within the negative progession of vv. 7-9, we detect Ben Sira's apparent implication that a bad wife will eventually disgrace herself through drunkenness and will finally descend to the depths of adultery. If this is his what he is consciously or unconsciously reflecting, then it does betray his negative bias.

The second group of texts that we will consider in this chapter contains references to woman as prostitute. These include texts that mention the strange woman, a female musician, and the prostitute herself. The distinction of some of these from the adulteress is not always easy to maintain. Therefore, the placement of some texts in this part of our discussion is somewhat arbitrary.

<u>9:3-4, 6-7</u>

3 Do not meet[190] a strange woman,[191]
Lest you fall[192] into her nets.[193]
4 Do not consort[194] with a female musician,[195]
Lest you be caught[196] by her flatteries.[197]
6 Do not give yourself[198] to a prostitute,[199]
Lest you lose[200] your inheritance.[201]
7 Do not look around[202] in the alleys[203] of a city,[204]
And do not wander about[205] in its deserted places.[206]

These verses are found in the midst of a group of distichs that offer various counsels concerning women. I have already discussed the context and some of the formal characteristics of

9:1-9.[207] It seems appropriate at this point to gather the material from this section which appears to reflect counsel concerning prostitutes and to consider the distichs together.

Fuss[208] identifies three of these distichs, vv. 3-4, 6, as traditional. Along with vv. 1, 5, they exhibit a consistent form. Each distich is a self-contained unit of thought, dealing with a unique topic. This is in contrast to v. 7 which departs from the form and is dependent on v. 6 for meaning in this setting dealing with women. Fuss considers it to be Ben Sira's composition, along with vv. 2, 8-9.[209] These judgments seem reasonable.

In the first traditional distich, v. 3, the counsel centers on the _ʾšh zrh_ "strange woman." We have already discussed the strange woman, featured several times in Proverbs.[210] There she appears as a married woman who acts like a prostitute. Through seductive behavior and speech she allures young men to her bed for sexual gratification. It seems likely that the reference to the strange woman in our text reflects the same picture as that of Proverbs. If this is true, one could make a case for discussing 9:3 under the category of the adulteress, since the woman involved is probably married. However, because she behaves like a prostitute it is equally justifiable to consider our text here.[211] This is what I have chosen to do.

In the words of this traditional distich Ben Sira advises his readers not to meet a strange woman. The idea of meeting, from the verb _qrh_,[212] is not itself a reference to sexual intercourse, since the strange woman's catching her victim is the consequence expressed in line _b_.[213] Instead, line _a_ conveys the notion of a person's rendezvousing with the woman in question for the purpose of sexual activity. The meeting is clearly not by accident, but by design and arrangement. Otherwise the counsel would be senseless.

The sage suggests that if a person disregards his advice he will fall into the woman's nets. We have already noted the seductive techniques that such women employ. The person who arranges to meet her will surely be caught. Line _b_ refers primarily to the man's becoming involved in sexual activity with the strange woman. However, it may also convey the notion of his being entrapped by her in a long term relationship.

The second traditional distich, v. 4, advises the reader not to consort with a female musician. It is possible that this reference to a female musician is intended to picture a female singer or instrumentalist[214] whose morals are low[215] and who may seduce the unsuspecting. However, this text immediately follows a distich that deals with a strange woman and comes two distichs before one concerning a prostitute. Thus, it is more likely that the female musician in v. 4 represents a prostitute also. Here she is seen in one of her seductive roles, employing one of her alluring techniques. The prostitute who uses both instrumental and vocal music to attract her customers is reflected in Isa 23:15, 16.[216]

The sage urges that his readers not consort with a female musician, since she may capture them by her flatteries. If a form of ḥlqh "flattery" stood in line b, as I have read the text,[217] then we have an additional confirmation that the female musician here is describing a prostitute. Several times in Proverbs, ḥlqh or a related term is used in connection with prostitutes.[218] To be caught in this way is to fall victim to her seductiveness, much like the reflection of the previous distich.

In v. 6 we have the third distich in this section that relates to prostitutes. In this traditional material the sage advises his reader not to give himself to a prostitute (zwnh). The expression "do not give yourself" ʼl ttn . . . npšk is also found in 9:2, which we have taken to be Ben Sira's composition.[219] In that setting it means not to permit a wife to usurp one's authority. Here it conveys the picture of a person submitting to the seductiveness of a prostitute by engaging in sexual intercourse with her.

The consequence of failure to follow this advice is expressed in line b. We have seen that the negative consequences in vv. 3 and 4 suggest the idea of sexual involvement with the women in question. Here, however, such involvement is reflected in line a. The negative consequence in this distich describes the results that will follow a sexual encounter with a prostitute. The offender will lose his inheritance. This does not mean that he will fail to receive his inheritance due to some dishonor or disgrace. Rather, it suggests that he will waste that which he has inherited and lose it through the practice of purchasing sexual favors.[220]

With an apparent desire to reinforce these traditional counsels on not becoming involved with prostitutes, Ben Sira adds his own advice in v. 7. This distich does not specifically refer to a prostitute or, for that matter, to a woman at all. However, in this section of miscellaneous material on women in general and in a setting which follows a distich that deals with a prostitute in particular, the meaning is clear: Don't walk around town looking for a prostitute.[221] Historically, the street has been the prostitute's domain.[222] Often she is described plying her trade in the open, as in the case of Tamar.[223] But here Ben Sira pictures a person wandering into alleys and deserted places to find a prostitute. He does not indicate the negative consequences of failing to follow his advice as do the traditional distichs. Instead, he merely intensifies the notion by constructing line b in synonymous parallelism with line a.

Like most of the material in this section, these distichs concerning prostitutes contribute very little to our understanding of Ben Sira's view of women. The counsels crisply echo the more extensive discussions found in Prov 5-7. Three of the four distichs are traditional and seem to have been incorporated by Ben Sira without being altered. In view of his own particularly negative bias against women, he is comfortable with the generally negative tone of the material.

19:2-3

2 Wine and women[224] make the heart lustful,[225]
And he who clings[226] to prostitutes[227] perishes.[228]
3 Decay[229] and worms[230] will inherit him,[231]
And an insolent soul[232] will destroy its owner.[233]

These verses are part of a three distich unit (19:1-3) which deals with wine and women. V. 1 concerns drinking; v. 2 mentions both wine and women; v. 3 is limited to the consequences of consorting with a prostitute. The previous unit (18:30-33) is somewhat related in its exhortation to self-control.

The compositional status of our text is mixed. Fuss[234] maintains that v. 2 is traditional and v. 3 is Ben Sira's composition. I find it easy to concur with this assessment as far as v. 2 is concerned. It is a self-contained unit that can easily stand alone. In contrast to this, v. 3 requires v. 2 in order to be sensible. Thus, it displays the characterisitcs of a composition by Ben Sira, designed to elaborate one of the notions in v. 2. We could leave the discussion of tradition and composition at this, were it not for the fact that in Heb v. 3b is virtually identical to 6:4a.[235] This suggests that, while Ben Sira may well have added v. 3 to the traditional v. 2, he apparently did so by including a line (line b) from another traditional source, different from v. 2.[236] Thus, I consider v. 2 to be traditional from one source, v. 3a to be Ben Sira's composition, and v. 3b to be traditional from another source, but edited into the present unit by Ben Sira.

The traditional v. 2 appears to treat two topics. In line a it mentions wine and women, and in line b it makes a note about a prostitute. We have already discussed the relationship between wine and women earlier in this chapter.[237] In 9:9 the woman with whom one was not to drink wine was married. Here we have a general statement that wine and women produce a lustful heart. The women here are not specifically defined. It is likely, however, that the sage equates "women" in line a with prostitutes in line b. The resultant relationship of prostitutes to wine would be in line with a well established OT theme.[238]

There are two implications reflected in the observations of v. 2. Line a implies that the effect of a person's becoming simultaneously involved with wine and women is the intensification of his sexual desire. In 9:9 a similar situation involving a married woman is said to result in one's heart turning aside to her. The second implication is the notion in line b that the person who "clings" to prostitutes will perish. The same idea is reflected in v. 3.[239]

The ideas of perishing, decay[240] and worms,[241] and destruction are clear references to death. Are such statements to be taken literally or metaphorically? Weber[242] suggests that these refer to the premature death which comes upon the offender as a punishment. But this seems unlikely. The person mentioned in v. 26 is said to be involved with prostitutes (plural). He is also described as one "who clings" (ho kollōmenos) to prostitutes. These two facts suggest that the sage is describing a kind of persistent behavior and not a single act.[243] If punishment were intended by these "death" references, we would expect a setting dealing with individual acts, not with persistent behavior. It is more likely that the author of v. 2b, as well as Ben Sira who follows him in v. 3, is using the "death" references metaphorically to convey the notion of the whole complex of destructive consequences that accompany such behavior.[244] Ben Sira's contribution is one of intensifying and reinforcing this figuratively expressed result. This hyperbole has the effect of heightening the motivation for the reader to avoid the behavior described.

This material on prostitutes reflects little of Ben Sira's particular attitude toward women. The ideas are largely determined by the traditional distich which he uses here. He has merely intensified the motivational "death" element. Taken as a whole, the lines convey a summary of the consequences of the similarly conceived behavior reflected in Prov 5-7.

42:8ab

(. . . do not be ashamed)[245]
Of admonishing[246] the simple[247] and foolish,[248]
A tottering old man[249] occupied[250] with prostitutes.[251]

This verse is part of a group of distichs that describe things concerning which one need not be ashamed. I have already dealt with the matters of context and form for this material (42:1-8).[252] Some of these distichs are traditional.[253] However, our text appears to be a composition by Ben Sira. This is suggested by its somewhat unusual structure. Each line of the other seven specific distichs that relate to the introductory exhortation, "do not be ashamed," is complete in itself. This is not true of v. 8ab. Line b is an extension of line a and requires it in order to be sensible within this setting. The expression mwsr governs both lines a and b.[254] Thus, the meaning of line b is: "(do not be ashamed of admonishing) a tottering old man occupied with prostitutes."

When the distich is understood in this way, the link between lines a and b lies only in the sharing of the expression mwsr. The objects of the admonition are not related. The simple and foolish of line a have nothing to do with the tottering old man in line b.

The focus of line b is the old man. Ben Sira is not so much concerned here with a person's relating to prostitutes as he is with the fact that the person in question is a tottering old man. It is not entirely clear how Ben Sira perceives this man's relationship to prostitutes. Two things tend to minimize the likelihood of sexual activity. In 41:2c Ben Sira refers to a tottering man[255] stumbling over everything. This is within a section that discusses death (41:1-4). Presumably this man is near death. If this is true of the old man in our text, he is not a likely customer of prostitutes. Furthermore, the verb ʿnh II, which means "to be occupied, busied with," is not used elsewhere in a sex-related sense.[256] However, this man cannot be near death, since he is maintaining some kind of contact, real or imagined, with prostitutes. Ben Sira is aware of old men who are not only sexually active but illicitly so.[257] Whether this is true of the old man in our text we cannot determine. It is clear that he is prostitute-oriented, either in thought or in action, either in mere association or in sexual encounter.

Whatever his problem may be, Ben Sira declares that one should not be ashamed of admonishing such an old man. Even respect for age must give way to the condemnation of his behavior.[258] He is a disgrace to both family and community.

Since this line centers on the old man and not on the prostitute, it does not contribute much to our understanding of Ben Sira's view of women. The text implies the familiar condemnation of women who practice prostitution. But, as we have seen earlier in this chapter, such an attitude is certainly not unique to Ben Sira.

<u>41:20b, 21c, 22a, 22b</u>

(Be ashamed . . .)[259]
20b Of looking at[260] a strange woman,[261]
21c And of gazing intently at[262] a married woman,[263]
22a Of meddling with[264] your maidservant,[265]
22b And of violating[266] her bed.[267]

These two distichs occur in the section on things concerning which one should be ashamed (41:17-23[268]). I have already discussed the setting of this material.[269] Fuss[270] is no doubt justified in describing these lines as products of Ben Sira's composition.

In some respects, this two distich unit resembles 9:1-9. Not only do both deal with negative exhortations concerning women, but both also refer to several kinds of women. The earlier section mentions wives (good and bad), prostitutes (including a strange woman and a female musician), a virgin, and other men's wives. Our text reflects several of these types also. Both of these sections represent miscellaneous counsel concerning various kinds of women. In a sense, they are summary statements. It is for this reason that I have chosen to deal with our text at this particular point in the analysis.[271] In this chapter we have looked at Ben Sira's references to the strange woman as a prostitute[272] and to the married woman as a potential adulteress, upon whom one should not gaze.[273] His admonition here concerning these classes of women adds nothing more to the pictures that he has already painted. He merely gathers his advice into a single distich.

The unique materal in this section is found in the second distich (v. 22ab). This is Ben Sira's only mention of a maidservant (špḥh). In line a he counsels against "meddling" with her. The verb ʿśq in postbiblical Heb (ʿsq) has the meaning "to busy oneself." Here it is probably not meant to imply sexual activity. This is also true of the "looking" and "gazing" in the previous distich. However, it clearly reflects preoccupation or familiarity, which may result in sexual intercourse.

This result is reflected in line b. The circumlocation of violating a person's bed is a common figure referring to illicit sex.[274] Ben Sira uses a similar expression in 23:18a. There an adulterer is described as "a man who turns aside from his bed."[275] The bed which in this case is violated is his own. Smend[276] suggests that even in antiquity a person was not permitted to be sexually intimate with his maidservant. But the references he gives are to the violation of virgins.[277] These virgins would be the daughters of other men. To violate a virgin would negatively affect the property of another man. However, a maidservant in one's own house would be his own property. Why would Ben Sira consider sex with one's maidservant to be a shameful thing?

Of the two major Heb words for maidservant (ʾmh and špḥh) the term špḥh reflects the more servile role.[278] Often the špḥh was a household slave.[279] She may be described as belonging to a mistress[280] or to the male head of a family.[281] Laban gave two of his maidservants to his daughters at the time of their marriage to Jacob.[282] Later these maidservants became Jacob's concubines and bore him children.[283] A woman may become betrothed while still a špḥh in expectation of being redeemed. Sexual relations with such a woman were forbidden.[284] This is presumably true even if the betrothed woman was one's own <u>špḥh</u>. These observations suggest that a man may engage in sexual intercourse with his <u>špḥh</u> only if she becomes his concubine. Otherwise, he is forbidden to encounter her sexually. The reason for this probably lies in the fact that even as a <u>špḥh</u>, she is eligible for marriage either within or outside the household. To violate her sexually would be an offense against her future potential husband.[285]

In this two distich unit Ben Sira has assembled several items related to women among his counsels concerning shame. The first distich repeats in summary what he has dealt with elsewhere on the subjects of the strange woman (prostitute) and a married woman (a potential adulteress). In the second distich he discusses one's relationship to his maidservant. This is a category that he does not consider elsewhere. If our understanding of why Ben Sira counsels the reader to avoid sexual contact with his maidservant is valid, then his motive is not as morally honorable as might first appear. The maidservant may in fact be the property of a man, but she is also the potential property of another man, who may take her as his wife, either in freedom or within the environment of slavery.[286] However, even with this reading of v. 22ab, we cannot attribute to Ben Sira a uniquely negative view of women as displayed in this material.

Conclusion

In this chapter we have explored two categories of women discussed by Ben Sira, adulteress and prostitute. We have also noted a single reference to a maidservant, found in miscellaneous counsels that include the two main roles. The evidence from this material relative to Ben Sira's personal attitude toward women is uneven. His discussions of the adulteress reflect his negative bias more than his treatment of the prostitute. We found that he treats the adulteress with greater severity than the adulterer (23:16-26), by describing both her offense and her penalty more specifically than his, even though her motivation seems superior to his. Ben Sira's negative bias is also reflected in his placement of a distich on the adulterous wife (26:9) at the end of what appears to be a progressively negative look at the bad wife. In these three distichs (26:7-9) he moves from a bad wife in general to a drunken wife to an adulterous wife. By implication Ben Sira seems to suggest that this is the predictable route for a bad wife. Even though some of his concerns go beyond the OT, his discussion of married women as potential adulteresses (9:8-9) does not reflect any particularly negative bias.

Almost without exception, the material on prostitutes that we have considered echoes the traditional antipathy to prostitution contained in the wisdom literature, particularly in Proverbs. This is true both where Ben Sira incorporates traditional distichs into his text and where he composes the material himself. He is clearly negative toward prostitutes but not in a way that sets him apart from his environment or his sources.

CHAPTER V

WOMAN AS DAUGHTER

Introduction

The final category under which I will discuss Ben Sira's view of women is that of daughter. His discussion of daughters is found in four multi-distich sections scattered throughout the book. In this chapter I will examine each of these sections and will briefly discuss one minor text concerning virgins.

7:24-25

24 Do you have daughters?[1] Protect[2] their body,[3]
But do not let your face shine[4] upon them.[5]
25 Give a daughter in marriage[6] and trouble[7] will depart,[8]
But bestow her[9] to a man of understanding.[10]

The context of these distichs may be described in several ways. In the extended sense they are part of the long section, 7:1-9:16, which concerns various kinds of social relations. More narrowly, the lines share the theme of domestic matters with 7:22-28 but exhibit a formal relationship to vv. 22-26.[11]

In our discussions of 7:26a and 7:26b we explored the formal relationship among the distichs in vv. 22-26. We noted that vv. 22a, 23a, 24a[12] represent the pattern: category + lk + verb + object/prepositional phrase. The categories include cattle, sons, and daughters. We may further observe that vv. 22b, 23b form positive complementary parallels to their distich counterparts. Such is not the case with v. 24b, which stands in contrast to line a. The positive injunction to protect daughters' bodies is followed by the negative corrective to withhold joy towards them. The discussion continues in v. 25, which departs significantly from the formal pattern of the preceding three distichs. Line _a_ does not introduce a new category but merely extends the consideration of v. 24 by offering an imperative, followed by its consequence. However, v. 25 with its positive imperative is more comparable to vv. 22b, 23b.

Fuss[13] considers vv. 22-24, 26 to be traditional. He also takes v. 25 to be traditional but, because of its formal uniqueness, considers it to come from a different source. However, the matter is not so simple. The formally related material is actually vv. 22ab, 23ab, 24a, 25b. The linking of v. 24a and v. 25b is strengthened by the fact that both v. 23b and v. 25b constitute imperatives that call for certain marriage arrangements for sons and daughters respectively. The formally unique material is found in v. 24b and v. 25a. This suggests that here Ben Sira has incorporated traditional material which originally consisted in three distichs, vv. [22], [23], [24a, 25b], dealing with cattle, sons, and daughters respectively.[14] However, he appears to have split the distich that concerns daughters and inserted his own material, which now stands as v. 24b and v. 25a. We will consider the implications of this redaction below.

Before leaving the matter of tradition and composition with respect to vv. 22-26, we must make a few additional observations. While v. 25b follows the pattern of vv. 22b, 23b generally in form and more specifically in content (at least as far as v. 23b is concerned), it does differ in two respects. Both lines of the distichs in vv. 22-23 reflect plural forms of the categories involved. This is also true of v. 24a with its reference to "daughters." However, v. 25b refers to bestowing "her" to a wise man. This singular would, of course, not fit with the plural of v. 24a to form an intelligent distich. We may also note that, according to my translation, v. 25b, unlike vv. 22b, 23b, stands in a mild adversative relationship to the preceding line in the distich, as the conjunction "but" indicates.

These problems, however, are not as significant as one might first imagine. The latter is the easiest to resolve. The Heb begins with the conjunction w-, as in vv. 22b, 23b,[15] where it is translated "and." The translation must be determined by the content of the line and its relationship to the accompanying line. If v. 25b were attached to v 24a, the content of the second line would easily allow the opening w- to be translated "and."

The problem of the singular of v. 25b in contrast to the plural of v. 24a is more difficult. It is clear that some portions of vv. 24-25 are traditional and some are either composed by Ben Sira or derive from a second source. I have argued that the most defensible assessment finds vv. 24a, 25b to be traditional, originally forming a single distich, with vv. 24b, 25a being material contributed by Ben Sira himself. I reached these conclusions on the basis of both form and content. Therefore, I take these observations for granted when attempting to solve the plural/singular problem of the apparently original distich, vv. 24a, 25b. I would propose that v. 25b in its traditional form originally read gbrym zbdn "(to) men . . . bestow them," as the analogy of v. 23b would suggest. After Ben Sira split the original distich that concerned daughters, he formed a new distich with v. 24a by composing a corrective statement in v. 24b which retained the plural of line a. However, for some reason, he chose to employ the singular "daughter" in his composition of v. 25a. It seems reasonable to conclude that he altered the reading gbrym zbdn in the traditional v. 25b to gbr zbdh, the reading now found in the MSS, in order to conform to his singular in line a.[16]

As we have seen, v. 24 appears to be composed of line a from a traditional distich and line b from Ben Sira's hand. The traditional line a opens with a question that introduces the category under discussion--daughters. It continues by offering the injunction: "Protect their body" (nṣwr š'rm). This advice is extended not so much as a deterrent to loose female morals[17] or as a reminder to fathers that they are responsible for their daughters' virginity and honor.[18] In this context, which centers on marriage,[19] it seems that the imperative reflects the ancient reality that a daughter's marketability as a wife and her virginity were unquestionably related. If a father did not guard his daughter's body, he could hardly expect to marry her to a wise man.[20]

In line b Ben Sira offers a corrective to the positive advice of the traditional line a. The expression "let your face shine" (t'yr . . . pnym) reflects a metaphor that is commonly employed in the OT for God in relationship to people or things.[21] Many of these uses include the parallel ideas of graciousness, blessing, salvation, restoration, and teaching. If our text uses the phrase in this way, the meaning of line b would be: "Do not bless them." The only other OT use of 'wr and pn in combination is Eccl 8:1cd. There God's face is not involved. Instead, a man's wisdom causes his face to shine. We find similar uses in Sir 13:26; 35(32):9.[22] In these texts the idea is one of cheerfulness and joy. Read in this way, our text would express the imperative, "Do not radiate joy toward them." Given both the context of our section and the analogy of Ben Sira's other uses, this understanding of the metaphor seems more likely than the "blessing" motif.

As we have noted, the effect of line b is to qualify the advice given in line a. Ben Sira is content to pass on the material in the traditional line a only if accompanied by his own corrective statement. He agrees that a father must guard the integrity of his daughter. However, he should not go to the extent of cheerfulness toward or rejoicing with her.[23]

We have already observed that v. 25a is the second of two lines that Ben Sira has inserted into the split traditional distich, now represented by vv. 24a, 25b. The content for this line, which deals with giving a daughter in marriage,[24] was no doubt suggested by the theme of v. 25b. The line involves a play on the word yṣ'.[25] To illustrate this, we may translate it thus: "Give away (hwṣ') a daughter, and you will give away (wyṣʼ) trouble."[26] In such a construction a daughter is virtually equated with trouble.

The word "trouble"[27] (ʻsq) has been variously interpreted. Gaspar[28] understands the expression, or more specifically the Gr rendition ergon mega "a great work," in terms of the arranged marriage. Smend[29] suggests that the trouble is that which is reflected in 42:9-11.[30] For Peters[31] the trouble is rearing and supervising a daughter. Both this context and the impact of 22:3-5[32] and 42:9-11 favor the interpretation of "trouble" as more related to the daughter herself than to the task of arranging her marriage. As we have seen, the play on words in the line reinforces the identification of daughter and trouble.

In v. 25b Ben Sira returns to what appears to be the second line of the traditional distich (vv. 24a, 25b). As it now stands, this line represents a positive corrective to line a. But as we saw above, it was originally a complementary imperative attached to v. 24a, forming a distich analogous to v. 23. In that setting the line echoed the advice in v. 23b to give wives to one's sons in their youth.

The traditional distichs devoted to sons and daughters followed an identical pattern. Line a in each distich was composed of two elements, the introduction of the category (sons and daughters) by means of a question and the advice to control them. In both distichs line b offered counsel on arranging their marriages. There is nothing in the original distich dealing with daughters which is not comparable to the distich dealing with sons, and vice versa. Each distich was positive in the advice offered. However, while Ben Sira left the distich dealing with sons intact, he significaltly altered the material dealing with daughters. He split the distich and inserted two lines of his own composition between the traditional stichs. This formed two distichs, each with one traditional stich and one stich from Ben Sira. Ben Sira's material not only distinguishes itself by form, as we have noted, but also by tone. Both v. 24b and v. 25a are clearly negative. In the former he advises fathers not to be cheerful toward their daughters, while in the latter he confesses that to give away a daughter in marriage is to give away trouble. Ben Sira has altered this traditional material only at those points[33] that deal with women, and his alterations have been negative. This is further evidence of his negative bias against women.

<u>22:3-5</u>

3 A father is disgraced[34] by producing[35] an ignorant son,[36]
But a daughter[37] is born[38] to his loss.[39]
4 A sensible daughter[40] will receive her husband,[41]
But she who disgraces[42] is a grief[43] to him who begat her.[44]
5 An insolent daughter[45] disgraces[46] father[47] and husband,[48]
And she will be despised by both.[49]

This text appears in the midst of a rambling discussion of the wise in contrast to the foolish (20:1-22:18). However, our text is part of a parenthesis within the larger section.[50] The full unit consists of vv. 3-6, in which vv. 3-5 constitute a three distich subunit devoted to daughters and v. 6 represents a single distich, loosely related to vv. 3-5 because of its theme of discipline.[51]

The distichs of our text do not share a common form, at least as reflected by Gr. We find here a mixture of contrasts and complements, together with what seems to be an incomplete line in v. 5b. Because of their heterogeneous nature[52] and loose structure, they appear to represent Ben Sira's composition. The two ideas that he consistently explores in the three distichs are daughters and disgrace.[53] These may be seen as the unifying elements in the strophe and the apparent intention of the composition.

It is insufficient, however, to simply say that these verses represent Ben Sira's composition. Many scholars[54] have noted the similarity of our text to Prov 17:21. Indeed, Ben Sira appears to have been influenced by the general content and several specific elements of the Proverbs text, which, according to the rather literal rendering of <u>NASV</u>, reads:

He who begets (yld) a fool (ksyl) does so to his sorrow (ltwgh),
And the father (ʼby) of a fool (nbl) has no joy (yśmḥ).

We may note that, like Prov 17:21, our text begins with the notion of a father and a negative son. That Prov 17:21 was understood to refer to a son in Ben Sira's time is clear from the LXX translation[55] of this verse.[56] In addition to the introductory "son" reference, we may observe the parallel use of ʼb "father" and yld "he who begat" in the Heb that clearly stood behind our text in v. 3a and v. 4b[57] respectively in relationship to a similar, though reversed, occurence in Prov 17:21. Another point of contact between these materials may be a common use of the idea of grief. The Gr for v. 4b relates lypē "grief" to gennēsas "he who begat," much in the same way that Prov 17:21a relates twgh "grief" to yld. However, while the use of yld behind gennēsantos in v. 4b is likely in the Heb original, the presence of twgh is less likely. Ben Sira never uses this rare OT word[58] in the sections that are extant in Heb. Instead, he may have employed here his more characteristic term dwn.[59]

The implications of these points of contact between our text and Prov 17:21 suggest that Ben Sira was loosely dependent on the Proverbs material. The influence, however, while still detectable in the specific items which we have reviewed, was largely that of a general idea source. He used the son idea to introduce our text but then immediately abandoned it to explore the daughter motif in the following five stichs.

Ben Sira opens his discussion of daughters in this section with a reference to sons in v. 3a, which, as we have seen, was probably suggested by Prov 17:21. In the Gr of both texts the son in question is characterized by the adjective apaideutos. The term basically means "uninstructed, uneducated."[60] It may also convey the notion "undisciplined, reckless."[61] For our purposes, it does not matter which of these ideas is reflected in our text, though the former is more likely. What is important is the recognition that not every son falls under this indictment. The son who causes his father to be disgraced is termed apaideutos. A son with this negative characteristic is the focus of the line.

The striking feature of v. 3b is the nature of the reference to a daughter. Not only has Ben Sira switched from the son orientation of what appears to be his idea source (Prov 17:21), but, as our text now reads, he refers to a daughter in universal terms, in contrast to the specifically limited reference to a son in line a. He seems to be saying that, while an ignorant son causes his father to be disgraced, the birth of any daughter is a loss.

This unqualified mention of daughter has produced a number of textual and exegetical innovations, both ancient and modern, to overcome what is perceived to be an untenable social posture. We have already noted some of the textual variations that have developed in Gr, La, Cos, and Eth to qualify the term "daughter" by the addition of various limiting adjectives.[62] Many scholars continue exegetically what the scribes started textually--taking the term "daughter" to actually mean "a bad daughter." Edersheim[63] refers to her as an undisciplined daughter. Spicq[64] calls her a badly raised daughter. Weber[65] characterizes her as unruly. However, Peters[66] has most vigorously argued for this kind of interpretation. While he does not contest the textual reading of line b, with daughter standing unqualified, he does argue that the reference to lack of discipline in line a serves to qualify both son and daughter. For the marriage of such a daughter, Peters claims, a father would have to provide an especially large dowry.

Despite these attempts to justify Ben Sira, it seems to me that we are still left with the fact that he makes a general, unqualified reference to daughter in line b. Smend[67] recognizes this when he notes that what is offensive in line b is a mere daughter. This means that for Ben Sira a negative son is a disgrace, but any daughter is a loss.

The meaning of the term elattōsis "loss" has also generated considerable discussion. We have noted Peters' contention that it refers to the large dowry required to find her a husband. Weber[68] adds that if no one marries her, she will remain the financial responsibility of her father. Eberharter[69] reasons that the loss may be the parents' feeling of sorrow at losing her in marriage and of anxiety that once married she may be untrue.

The Heb term behind ellatōsis, which in the LXX outside Sirach occurs only in Tob 4:13, was probably a form of hsr "to decrease, lack," as in Sir 31(34):4; 40:26. The phrase ep elattōsei should be understood with epi functioning in the sense of result. This gives the meaning: (a daughter's birth) results in a loss. What Ben Sira means by loss is best determined by observing what he says elsewhere about daughters. Most of the problems center on her marriage--trying to keep her as marriageable as possible while she is single[70] and endeavoring to keep her husband happy with her once she is married.[71] She is considered to be trouble[72] and through insolence and negative conduct may cause the family, particularly her father, public disgrace.[73] In summary, she is more likely to disgrace than a son.[74] The idea of loss, then, is not to be understood in the narrow sense of financial loss but in the broader, more metaphorical sense of all the negative situations associated with having a daughter. This makes the whole line general and universal. An ignorant son brings disgrace, but any daughter results in various kinds of pejorative and undesirable circumstances.

Before I consider vv. 4-5, let me make a final observation concerning v. 3. This distich serves an introductory function within the strophe that is devoted to daughters. But since line a concerns a son, under influence from Ben Sira's idea source, the real introduction of the daughter topic occurs in line b. Thus, we may take the declaration that the birth of a daughter represents a loss as a type of heading for the strophe. This means that what follows in vv. 4-5 is an explication of this heading, providing reflections on the meaning of "loss."[75]

The unqualified reference to daughter in this introductory statement is understandable.

The first of the specific references to daughter is found in v. 4a, where Ben Sira notes that a sensible daughter will receive her husband. The expression "sensible daughter" (thygatēr phronimē) may be understood by looking both backward and forward within the strophe. The first point of reference is the word apaideutos in v. 3a. The adjective phronimē is used here as the opposite of apaideutos, as suggested by its use elsewhere in Sirach.[76] Viewed in this way, the term means "wise, sensible." However, to determine the sense in which this particular daughter is considered wise, we must look forward to the rest of the line.

The line continues by declaring that the daughter in question "will receive (klēronomēsei) her husband." This should not be understood to mean that it is the daughter who secures her husband in the marriage. Such an idea would be totally out of character with Ben Sira's concept of marriage.[77] It seems more likely that what Ben Sira means here may be illuminated by reference to 23:22-26 and 42:10b. In the former, a woman is described leaving her husband to engage in an adulterous affair with another man. The latter reflects a father's worry that his married daughter may prove unfaithful to her husband. Given Ben Sira's consciousness of wives repudiating their husbands, it seems reasonable to me that in our text he conveys the notion that a sensible daughter will accept her husband and remain faithful to him.

The expression thygatēr phronimē may thus be understood to mean a daughter who is sensible. But she is described as sensible only in so far as she accepts the husband provided for her and remains faithful to him.

This interpretation of line a is further confirmed by line b, which begins with the expression "she who disgraces" (hē kataischynousa). One is justified in asking, Who is the object of the daughter's shameful behavior? In the light of v. 5 it is clear that both her father and her husband are the recipients.

This would suggest that her disgracing activities reflected in v. 4b relate not only to her father, who is referred to in the line,[78] but also to her husband, who is mentioned in the previous line. To disgrace her husband is the opposite of receiving him. We have seen that Ben Sira elsewhere points to a wife's sexual unfaithfulness to her husband as a particular area of disgrace. As both Box-Oesterley[79] and Weber[80] recognize, any shame brought upon her husband reflects upon her father as well.

If his daughter should behave in this way, a father would experience grief (lypē). In 42:9-10 Ben Sira pictures a father as unable to sleep, in part because of anxiety over whether or not his married daughter will remain faithful to her husband. Here he implies that, if she is indeed unfaithful, the father will have sorrow and grief.

V. 5 is virtually a restatement of the sentiments of v. 4, viewed from a completely negative perspective.[81] Here we enounter a badly behaving daughter who disgraces her father and her husband, as in v. 4, and who is consequently despised by both of them.

In this setting the daughter is termed hē thraseia. The adjective, here used substantively, conveys the notion of one who displays insolent or arrogant behavior.[82] Since she is obviously married, this behavior is directed toward her husband. And since her behavior reflects negatively upon her father and leads both her husband and her father to despise her, the conduct in question must be the type that is feared in 42:10b. There her father worries that she may prove unfaithful to her husband. Thus, we have in v. 5 a reenactment of the situation of v. 4.

This distich, however, makes an additional assertion. Both father and husband despise a woman who behaves in this way. Statements about a husband despising his wife for one reason or another are not uncommon in Sirach.[83] However, this is the only place where a father is said to share such an attitude.

In this three distich strophe we have observed that Ben Sira appears to have used a Proverbs text, which deals with a foolish son, as his idea source. However, after opening the discussion with a reference to such a son, he moves immediately to the consideration of daughters, at times using phrases from the "son" source. But while he finds an ignorant son disgraceful, he terms a daughter--any daughter--a loss. This universal assessment of daughters, in fact, stands out as the conceptual heading of the strophe. He reflects on a sensible daughter as one who accepts and remains faithful to the husband provided for her. However, he devotes most of this treatment to those daughters whose marital unfaithfulness brings grief to their fathers, effects shame upon both their fathers and their husbands, and provokes the negative response of both.

We may summarize all this with the juxtaposition of the words "daughter" and "disgrace," which, as we have seen, are reflected in each of the distichs of this strophe. For Ben Sira to think of a daughter is virtually to think of the potential for disgrace.

<u>26:10-12</u>

10 Keep a strict watch over a daughter,[84]
Lest[85] she find freedom[86] and make use of it.[87]
11 Be on guard[88] against her shameless eye,[89]
And do not be surprised[90] if she commits an offense
against you.[91]
12 As a thirsty traveler[92] opens[93] his mouth[94]
And drinks[95] from any nearby water,[96]
She sits[97] in front of every peg[98]
And opens[99] her quiver[100] to the arrow.[101]

These verses lie embedded within the extensive discussion of women found in chapters 25 and 26. Since the present arrangement with its alternations between material on the good wife and material on the bad wife (and daughter) is unusual, I have argued earlier[102] for the following rearrangement: 25:7-11; 26:1-4; 26:13-18; 26:5-9; 25:13-26; 26:10-12. According to this order, all the material on the good wife precedes the material on the bad wife. The latter logically extends into the section on daughters, with which the entire discussion of women closes. Just as Ben Sira makes his strongest negative statement about women in a section that deals with daughters,[103] so also here he probably concluded this lengthy discussion of women with some thinly veiled figurative language about daughters that constitutes his most obscene remarks.

Fuss[104] considers v. 10 to be traditional material, inserted by Ben Sira at the head of his own composition in vv. 11-12. This judgment is partly valid. The status of v. 10 depends on the recognition that line _a_ is virtually identical to 42:11a. Both are followed by a line which expresses a negative consequence of not strictly watching a daughter. Ben Sira has either repeated his own material, some of it exactly, or he has twice drawn on traditional material. The latter seems more likely. However, he completed the second line of this distich differently on each occasion. In both cases these second lines seem to be Ben Sira's own compositions, possibly following some now lost idea of consequence in the original. His composition in 26:10b is constructed somewhat awkwardly and does not flow smoothly from line _a_, at least in Gr. Ben Sira seems to have composed 42:11b as a transition statement leading into the following distich.[105] This would suggest that he has used a traditional line to serve as a heading for this section, much as he did in 42:11a.[106] The rest of the material in vv. 10b-12 is his own.

We must consider one more preliminary issue before discussing the individual verses of this section. Smend[107] is representative of a group of scholars who understand the term _thygatēr_ in the thematic v. 10 to be used in the sense of "wife," rather than with its normal meaning "daughter." His reason for this conclusion stems from the fact that in the present arrangement of chapters 25 and 26 this section is surrounded by "wife" material.

When we note that this section appears at the end of material which deals with the bad wife[108] and before material which considers the good wife,[109] Smend's interpretation is less likely. It would not be unusual for Ben Sira to digress slightly into a discussion of daughters at this point. However, if we permit the rearrangement of all this material on women according to the scheme which I have summarized above, then the section in question originally came at the very end of the entire discussion.[110] This, of course, would not only further weaken Smend's suggestion; it would virtually nullify it.

In addition to these reflections on the placement of our section, we should observe the way the term thygatēr is used in Sirach. In 7:24-25; 22:3-5; 42:9-14 the word thygatēr with the underlying bt, where the Heb is extant, is found in contexts where father is either mentioned or implied.[111] This limits the term to its natural meaning "daughters" in such places. There is no reason to question this meaning for the term in our setting, even though father is not mentioned. Father may be easily assumed by the nature of the imperative idea of v. 10a. That our section is dealing with daughters in the literal sense of the word is further certified by the fact that v. 10a is identical to 42:11a, which, as we have seen, is in the middle of a section clearly devoted to the topic of daughters.[112]

I will begin my treatment of v. 10 by summarizing some of the observations I have already made. This distich appears to be composed of traditional material in line a and Ben Sira's composition in line b. The former, like its identical use in 42:11a, forms a type of heading. Furthermore, the term thygatēr is to be understood in its natural, literal sense with the meaning "daughter."

To head this section Ben Sira has chosen a traditional line which calls for the careful monitoring of a daughter, presumably by her father. This is a universal statement applying without qualification to any daughter. We probably do not have access to the accompanying line of this traditional piece, assuming that it was originally part of a distich. I have argued above that neither 26:10b nor 42:11b appears to be traditional. If this is the case, then it is not possible to determine the positive or negative nature of the original exhortation. By itself, the line may be understood either positively or negatively. However, Ben Sira has clearly used it to head a section which views a daughter negatively, even obscenely.

Such an understanding begins to develop in line b. Here the father is counselled to strictly watch a daughter, lest she take advantage of any freedom she finds. The word, which I have translated "freedom," is anesis. This rare LXX term is found in Sirach elsewhere only in 15:20: anesin oudeni hamartanein "license for anyone to sin." In our text it seems to be used more with the meaning of relaxation of restraint. The implication is that a daughter is looking for any such indulgence she can find. Ben Sira indicates that, if she finds this kind of liberty, she will "make use of it." The Gr term for this last assertion is a form of chraomai. Ryssel's[113] contention that the expression heautē chrēsētai should be translated "(lest) she abuse herself" and should be taken to imply masturbation is unfounded. Smend is on firmer ground when he declares that the verb means "to cherish sexual intercourse."[114] However, while chraomai can mean "to engage in sexual intercourse," this Sirach hapaxlegomenon is employed in our text with the more general meaning "to make use of something." We should not be influenced by the direction taken in the rest of the material, especially v. 12, to the point where we read too much specificity into this general, introductory distich. Ben Sira suggests that a daughter will grab any liberty she finds.

The generality of v. 10 gives way to Ben Sira's specific reflections in v. 11. But the two distichs are closed related. The second explains the first. V. 11a interprets and concretizes v. 10a, and v. 11b fills out the meaning of v. 10b. We will look at each line separately.

Line a is linked to v. 10a through the verb phylaxai. Note the use of the noun phylakēn in v. 10a.[115] Ben Sira clearly intended to explain the meaning of the "strict watch" of v. 10a through the exhortation of v. 11a. This "watch" is to involve guarding against her "shameless eye." Apart from our text, the adjective anaidēs in the latter expression is found in the LXX modifying ophthalmos "eye" only in 1 Sam 2:29. However, it is often found with prosōpon "face."[116] One of these uses, Prov 7:13, is interesting for our purposes. Chapter 7 describes a married prostitute's solicitation, and this text refers to her "impudent face." In that context the expression anaidei . . . prosōpō clearly refers to her seductive look.[117] Though the word "eye" is used in our text, the meaning is the same. The counsel to the father, therefore, is for him to prevent his daughter from behaving seductively. This is the particularization of the advice to keep a strict watch over her (v. 10a).

In line b Ben Sira specifies the meaning of how a daughter will make use of any freedom she finds (v. 10b). She is likely to commit an offense against her father. The verb plēmmeleō used here is relatively common in the Gr of Sirach.[118] In every instance it is employed in its usual metaphorical sense "to offend, err."[119] However, its use in 23:23 is particularly relevant. There an adulterous woman is described, who, in cohabiting with a man other than her husband and being impregnated by him, is said to have "committed an offense against her husband."[120] It is reasonable to assume that, since illicit sexual conduct on the part of a wife is described in terms of the verb plēmmeleō, the use of the same verb in the context of father and daughter would also imply similar behavior. In 42:10ac such conduct is specifically identified as both premarital loss of virginity and conception. These things would amount to a significant offense against her father. Not only would he be publically disgraced, but she would render herself considerably less marketable in marriage. This would be an economic offense against her father.

Ben Sira does not present this situation merely as an isolated potential. According to him it is likely to happen. He warns the father not to be surprised if his daughter behaves in this way.

If the reader has not yet divined what Ben Sira has in mind in this discussion, he need only continue into v. 12. Here Ben Sira symbolically fills out the scene that he has been developing. The result is the most obscene material of his entire work.

Formally, v. 12 involves a two distich simile. The first distich constitutes the vehicle of the simile, which describes a thirsty traveler. The second contains the tenor or subject of the simile, which refers to the behavior of a daughter.[121] Two assertions are made in each distich. The thirsty traveler (1) opens his mouth and (2) drinks any nearby water. The daughter (1) sits in front of every peg and (2) opens her quiver to the arrow. These assertions may be seen to form a type of chiasm: opening mouth, any water, any peg, opening quiver. However, such a structure is loose at best. The same may be said for the effectiveness of the simile as a whole. The comparison is not particularly tight or well done. We cannot successfully compare the details of the vehicle to those of the tenor. Instead, we are left with a general comparison between a thirsty traveler's indiscriminate drinking of water and a daughter's insatiable lust for sex.

Another thing that makes this simile unusual is the fact that the tenor element is itself metaphorical. The conduct of the daughter is described by reference to her sitting in front of every peg and opening her quiver to the arrow. This, of course, is not to be taken literally. Both the peg (passalos) and the arrow (belos) are metaphors for the penis, while the quiver (pharetra) clearly implies the vagina.[122] Each line of the distich represents a circumlocution for sexual intercourse, or more specifically for the daughter's anxious desire for sex.

In this ribald simile Ben Sira is not describing a daughter who has been previously identified as negative in distinction from good daughters, though this is obviously the case. The way he has composed the section, however, implies that any daughter is likely to behave in this way. He cautions a father not to be surprised at such conduct (v. 11b). I would not suggest that this indictment was valid for all daughters in Ben Sira's day. Nevertheless, Ben Sira discusses the issue as though it were.

Let us review our findings for this section. According to the rearrangement of the material in chapters 25 and 26 which I have proposed, this negative section on daughters comes at the end of the entire discussion of women found in these chapters. It is significant not only that it ends with daughters, but also that the material on daughters is especially negative and untastefully obscene. Ben Sira has apparently chosen to head the section with a universal, traditional statement about guarding a daughter. To this he adds his own explication of why she should be guarded. She will make use of any freedom she finds. She possesses a seductive appearance. She commits an offense against her father by her illicit sexual activity. She insatiably lusts for sexual intercourse. Ben Sira portrays this as a daughter's expected behavior. Finally, we may note that the remarkably explicit metaphors, arrow and quiver (v. 12d), which refer to the sex organs and their use, may represent Ben Sira's obscene adaptation of these terms as they were innocently used in Ps 127:3-5. Ben Sira's negative bias against women reaches its apex when he discusses daughters.

<u>42:9-14</u>

9 A daughter[123] is a treasure of sleeplessness[124] to a father,[125]
And anxiety over her[126] chases away[127] slumber[128]:
In her youth[129] lest she be rejected,[130]
And when she is married[131] lest she be forgotten,[132]
10a In her virginity[133] lest she be defiled,[134]
c And when she is married[135] lest she be unfaithful,[136]
b In the house of her father[137] lest she conceive,[138]
d And of her husband[139] lest she be barren.[140]
11 My son,[141] keep a strict watch[142] over a daughter,[143]
Lest she make fun of you to your enemies[144]--
An evil report in the city,[145] and an assembly of the people[146]--
And shame you[147] in the congregation of the gate.[148]
In the spot where she lodges[149] let there be no window[150]
Or place overlooking[151] the entrance round about.[152]
12 Let her not expose her beauty[153] to any male,[154]
And let her not take counsel[155] among[156] women.[157]
13 For from the garment[158] comes the moth,[159]
And from a woman[160] comes a woman's wickedness.[161]

14 Better[162] is the wickedness of a man[163] than the goodness of a woman,[164]
And a daughter[165] causes fear[166] regarding disgrace more than a son.[167]

This ten distich text constitutes Ben Sira's most extensive statement about daughters. The section is an isolated unit, having little connection to what precedes or follows. Before it stands a lengthy section on shame (41:14-42:8).[168] It is followed by a long statement of praise of God's works in nature, beginning in 42:15. The only possible link of our text with its surroundings would be to the preceding material on shame, but this is very general and loose at best.[169]

Some scholars[170] have suggested that this section is actually a composite of both material on daughters and material dealing with women in general, with the latter beginning in v. 11. When viewed in this way, the term "daughter" is taken in the sense of woman. The section may represent a composite of material drawn from various sources mixed with Ben Sira's own work.[171] We may also detect a variety of subtopics within the section. However, there would seem to be no convincing reason why the term <u>bt</u>, which clearly means "daughter" in v. 9a, should not have the same meaning in vv. 11a and 14b.[172] Thus, I take the entire section to be an essay on daughters.

Before considering each part of our text, let me make a final preliminary comment on the distich pattern. Several things are obvious. Vv. 9cd-10, representing three distichs, are situational extensions of the opening, thematic distich, v. 9ab. V. 11abcd must be taken together. The two distichs of vv. 12-13 are also related, in that v. 13 is a proverbial motivation statement for the advice given in v. 12b. This leaves v. 11ef and v. 14 to stand as independent distichs. When we consolidate these observations, we obtain a distich pattern as follows: 4 + 2 + 1 + 2 + 1.[173] I will discuss the section according to this pattern.

The initial four distich unit opens with the declaration that a daughter causes her father to lie awake worrying (v.

9ab). This distich is followed by three distichs (vv. 9cd-10) which review the various situations envisioned by the sleepless father. Fuss[174] considers the opening distich to be traditional, with Ben Sira appending his own set of various circumstances in the next three distichs. I find no particular reason to dispute this judgment.[175]

The thematic distich, v. 9ab, contains a synonymous parallel about sleeplessness. In line *a* a daughter is said to be "a treasure of sleeplessness" (*mṭmwn šqd*) for her father, while in line *b* his anxiety over her is seen to be the cause of chasing away his slumber (*tnyd nwmh*). The picture is one of a father lying awake at night worrying because of his daughter. When viewed in isolation from the three dictichs added to it by Ben Sira, this distich is rather general. The center of concern would seem to be the daughter herself. If it were standing alone, it could be understood as a reference to an endearing relationship between a father and his daughter. It is this general statement that Ben Sira has selected to stand at the head of his discussion of daughters.

To this traditional introduction Ben Sira adds three distichs which explain why he thinks a daughter's father lies awake worrying about her. Each stich contains its own particular insight. However, the impact of this material is most potent when the three distichs are viewed together before looking at the individual parts.

Ben Sira presents two circumstantial settings in which daughters may be found. They may be unmarried or married.[176] He also offers three perspectives from which daughters may be viewed in each setting. These are marriage, purity, and fecundity. Each of the three distichs is devoted to one of these perspectives, with the first line relating to the unmarried setting and the second to the married setting. This may be easier to visualize diagramatically.

	unmarried	married
marriage:	9c she may be rejected	9d she may be forgotten
purity:	10a she may be defiled	10c she may be unfaithful
fecundity:	10b she may conceive	10d she may be barren

It is evident that these three distichs represent a carefully constructed, tight form.

The first distich, v. 9cd, views the daughter from the perspective of marriage. It is no accident that this is the first perspective considered. The importance of this marriage point of view lies in the fact that the following two perspectives are meaningful only when seen in terms of marriage. The father is really concerned that he be able to give his unmarried daughter in marriage and that she stay married, once she is knotted in wedlock.

The idea of v. 9c is that the father worries that his unmarried daughter may be unable to attract a husband. It is not so much that she may be overlooked, but that she may be considered and rejected (tm′s). The verb m′s I may be used for a wife′s being rejected.[177] However, in Jer 4:30 it is employed in a metaphorical description of a woman who, despite dazzling beautification, is unable to attract and hold her lovers. Like the daughter in our text, she is rejected.[178]

In the second stich, line d, Ben Sira suggests that if the daughter is married, her father will worry that she may be forgotten (tnšh). The textual problem here is difficult, if not impossible, to solve.[179] However, whether one reads tnšh with HebBmg[1] or tśn′ "(lest) she be hated,"[180] as reflected in Gr and Syr, the effect is the same. The scene is that of a wife who has lost favor with her husband. The marriage is in jeopardy.

The next level of perspective involves sexual purity (v. 10ac). If his daughter is unmarried (v. 10a), the father worries that she may be defiled (tḥl). The fact that her status is described by the expression bbtwlyh "in her virginity" confirms that her defilement refers to illicit sexual activity. This use of ḥll I is not uncommon in the OT.[181] If an unmarried daughter lost her virginity, she would greatly reduce her chances of marriage. Her value and marketability would suffer. Her father would sustain social disgrace and economic loss. The latter would be reflected in both his increased difficulity in offering her in marriage and in the continued financial burden of his support of her at home.

The second line of this distich, v. 10c,[182] considers the threat of a daughter's sexual impurity after she is married. Her father worries that she will prove unfaithful to her husband (_tśṭh_ literally "turn aside"). Of the six times that this verb is used in the OT, five reflect illicit sexual activity.[183] One of these[184] advises the reader not to let his heart turn aside to the ways of a harlot. But the most relevant uses of _śṭh_ are its four appearances in the section dealing with the law concerning jealousy, Num 5:11-31.[185] There the wife suspected of adultery is said to have gone astray or turned aside. It is clear that this is also the implication in our text.[186] Her father fears such a situation because it would likely mean divorce, which would deposit her back into his household. Again this would mean disgrace and added financial burden.

The final perspective from which Ben Sira views a father worrying over his daughter is that of fecundity (v. 10bd). In the first line of the distich, v. 10b, the father fears that his unmarried daughter will become pregnant (_tzry`_). The verb _zr`_ literally means "to sow." Here, however, we find it used figuratively, as is sometimes the case in the OT,[187] with the meaning "to conceive." In this setting the daughter has no trouble bearing children. The problem is that she does so outside of marriage, while still living in the father's home. Again this would mean disgrace and further cost to her father. It would also mean that she would be even less marriageable and that the father's financial burden may be endless.

Ben Sira completes this dismal picture in v. 10d by ironically painting the father of a married daughter worrying that she may be sterile (_t`ṣr_). This meaning for the verb _`ṣr_ (literally "to retain, restrain") is represented on occasion in the OT.[188] The daughter who should become pregnant and bear children cannot do so because she is sterile. This father thinks of everything. No wonder he cannot sleep. His worry is not so much for her, however, as for himself. A sterile wife[189] may be released by her husband and sent back to her father's home. Once more he would experience disgrace and have to support her.

We have now seen how three intricately constructed distichs that specify the reasons for his concern have been added by Ben Sira to a rather general traditional statement of a father's sleepless worry over his daughter. A daughter will cause him worry whether she is unmarried or married. His central problem is to get her married and keep her married. Her sexual purity and fidelity, along with her child-bearing in the proper setting, are necessary for the marital state which he wants her to have. But as Davidson[190] has noted, the father is really concerned that as long as a daughter remains unmarried she is a financial burden to him. Furthermore, he would fall beneath this burden again if, for whatever reason, his married daughter was divorced by her husband and sent back to his home.

The second strophe in this section involves two distichs, v. 11a-d. Its distinction from the preceding material is emphasized by the presence in v. 11a of the vocative formula "my son" (bny). However, as we have seen,[191] this does not mean that the topic is no longer daughters. Rather, the emphasis now shifts from the discussion of the worry daughters cause their fathers (vv. 9-10) to the consideration of guarding daughters against negative behavior.[192]

Fuss[193] holds that this unit contains traditional material in v. 11ab, to which Ben Sira added his own composition in v. 11cd. This suggestion is certainly correct as far as v. 11a is concerned. But the matter is more complicated than the simple assignment of the first distich to tradition and the second to Ben Sira. I have concluded earlier that v. 11a is identical to 26:10a and represents a traditional line.[194] Furthermore, I have argued that in both places where he has used this traditional line, Ben Sira has formed a distich by adding his own second line. Elsewhere, we also observed that v. 11c is identical to 26:5c, which is part of a Zahlenspruch.[195]

Ironically, Fuss concluded that this Zahlenspruch is traditional, a judgment in which I have concurred.[196] To be consistent, of course, we must consider v. 11c to be traditional and not compositional, as Fuss has done.

Let us summarize the redactional status of this unit. Ben Sira opened the strophe with a traditional line on watching over daughters. To this line, which he had used elsewhere, he added a complex statement of negative consequence consisting of three lines. The first and third of these added lines (vv. 11b and 11d) directly express the consequence and represent his own composition. The first of these, of course, forms a distich with the opening line. However, his second added line (v. 11c) is also traditional, though from a different source than line a.[197] This inserted line forms a parenthesis between the two lines that state the consequence.

I have already discussed the content of v. 11a, when I considered 26:10a earlier in this chapter.[198] Let me merely review the significant remarks. We saw that this traditional line counsels a father to carefully monitor the activities of his daughter. The statement is universal and applies to any daughter.[199] In its original setting the line may have been intended to be taken positively or negatively. But in Ben Sira's application it is unequivocably negative since the material that it introduces is clearly negative.

The first element of the two part negative statement of consequence that Ben Sira appends to the traditional line is v. 11b. One is to watch his daughter so that she does not make fun of him to his enemies. As it stands, the text implies either that the daughter may directly scorn her father among his enemies or that his enemies may ridicule him because of his daughter's behavior.

To help in solving this problem I would point to Ben Sira's other uses of this idea in 6:4b and 18:31b. We will need to make the comparisons in Gr since the Heb is somewhat corrupt[200] for the first text and is not extant for the second. All three texts contain the same essential words[201] and express the notion "to make fun of someone to his enemies." In both 6:4b and 18:31b the subject of the idea is one's own soul. In the former the soul is termed "an evil soul" (psychē ponēra), which, if one submits to its counsel (6:2), will destroy him (6:4a). The latter is particularly significant. There the sage declares that if one permits his soul to take pleasure in base desire (epithymias), it will make fun of him to his enemies. When we read our text in the light of these other examples of the expression in Sirach, it is clear that just as one's own behavior[202] may cause him to be scorned among his enemies so also the behavior of his daughter may produce the same result.

We may also note that the kind of behavior expressed in 18:31 (taking pleasure in base desire) is probably what Ben Sira had in mind with regard to the daughter in our text. He did not need to specify this since he had already provided concrete examples in the preceding verses.[203] He would surely be scorned by his enemies if his daughter surrendered her virginity or became pregnant while unmarried or was unfaithful while married.

For some reason, at this point Ben Sira inserted a line from a traditional Zahlenspruch before he completed his statement of negative consequence. This line contains two double-word expressions that are rather cryptic. They are clearly intended to reflect something about the negative assessment that the father of an ill-behaving daughter will sustain among his enemies (line b) and in the congregation of the gate (line d).

The first of these expressions, "an evil report in the city" (dbt `yr), is the easiest to relate to our present context. In the OT the term dbh expresses the idea of a negative report,[204] often undeserved.[205] Ben Sira reflects both these nuances.[206] The specific phrase dbt `yr is clearly negative, as its likely inclusion in a negative Zahlenspruch (26:5-6) would suggest.[207] Thus, the expression parallels the ideas of ridicule and disgrace found in Ben Sira's negative statements of circumstance.

The second phrase "an assembly of the people" (qhlt `m), is not so negative in its own right as the first. Its appearance in the above mentioned negative Zahlenspruch, however, would suggest that it too should be understood negatively. The word qhl "assembly," which is a synonym of qhlh,[208] is found at least six times in Sirach, all translated with ekklēsia. One would expect that in each of the thirteen occurences of ekklēsia the underlying Heb was qhl. For our purposes here, one group of these uses is significant. In four places the assembly expresses an opinion. In three of these cases the opinion is positive[209] and in one case the opinion is negative.[210] With this in mind we may suggest that the expression qhlt `m refers, like the other material in this context, to a general erosion of the father's public prestige. If he does not watch his daughter, she may cause him to be publicly disgraced by her behavior.

This interpretation seems preferable to those offered by Spicq[211] and Middendorp.[212] The former suggests that the assembly may meet to condemn and punish the father. But the context speaks of ridicule, an evil report, and shame, not punishment. The latter holds that a daughter can bring a bad reputation upon her father, if she is brought before the assembly for adultery. But the focus of the assembly, as Ben Sira here employs it, is the father, not the daughter. While the negative behavior of the daughter may involve illicit sexual activity, the positing of the specific act of adultery and of an accompanying trial before the assembly is reading too much into this text.

We now turn to the completion of Ben Sira's negative statement of consequence in v. 11d. He advises a father to watch his daughter, "lest she . . . shame you (hwbyštk) in the congregation of the gate" (b`dt š`r). The gate in an ancient city was the civic center--the place of commerce,[213] social intercourse,[214] legal transactions,[215] and judicial decisions.[216] The `dh, which is here related to the gate,[217] may be either the randomly gathering population of the community or the constituted body of elders. Ben Sira uses the term `dh for both.[218] If he is echoing the idea of line b, then the general populace would be preferred. If he is being influenced by the reference to qhlh in the traditional line c, then he may be thinking of a constituted body in our text. But for our purposes, it does not matter which of these alternatives he had in mind. When he refers to shame in relation to the `dt š`r, he is not reflecting a negative judicial decision, nor the father's shame when speaking before the `dh.[219] Instead, he is implying that the father may be disgraced and dishonored in his community because of his daughter's negative behavior.[220]

In this unit Ben Sira has appended to a traditional parenetic statement about a father watching his daughter, three lines that suggest negative consequences that are likely to occur if he should fail to heed the advice. Ben Sira composed two of these lines and inserted between them another traditional line that echoed his own material. The intention of these statements of consequence was to show that a father may be the victim of public ridicule and disgrace because of his daughter's negative behavior. The opening traditional parenesis may be viewed as neutral, even positive. However, in the company of Ben Sira's statements of consequence it is made to reflect negatively upon the daughter.

Whereas the two distich unit, v. 11a-d, advises a father to strictly watch his daughter and provides the negative consequences if he does not, the single distich, v. 11ef, is the first of three specific suggestions of how such a watch should be implemented. With Fuss,[221] I consider this to be part of Ben Sira's own detailed composition, extending from the traditional line (v. 11a) with which he began this part of the text. The distich is not particularly esoteric or complicated. Ben Sira is simply saying that one way of keeping a strict watch over a daughter is to give her a room without windows. This is not to prevent her from looking out but to prevent others from looking in. That this is the intention of line e is clear from line f. There Ben Sira also urges that she be housed where others cannot get a view of the door to her room. This is obviously to prevent her exposure to men by accident or design on the part of either the daughter or her observers--an exposure that could lead to sexual activity.

The second and third of Ben Sira's specific suggestions for strictly watching a daughter, along with a motivation statement, are found in the two distichs represented by vv. 12-13. As part of his extended development of the traditional v. 11a, these distichs reflect his own composition.[222] In v. 12a he advises the father not to permit his daughter to "expose[223] her beauty (t'r) to any male." Ben Sira views a woman's beauty[224] in two different ways. In one's own good wife it is a quality to be desired.[225] But in other women it is to be suspected and feared.[226] Our text, of course, falls into the latter category. This line is a conceptual extension of v. 12. The reason for not allowing windows in a daughter's room is to conceal her beauty from men. In our text beauty may imply the beauty of her naked body. One is reminded of the famous scene in which David was overcome by the beauty of bathing Bathsheba.[227] For a daughter to expose her beauty deliberately would amount to seduction. If she did so accidently, it could lead to rape. Therefore, a father must try to prevent her exposure.

In v. 12b Ben Sira offers his third and final specific suggestion concerning watching a daughter. One should not permit his daughter to socialize and converse with women. It seems likely that by his reference to women he means married women in particular.[228] Since this is a pejorative statement, we must assume that for Ben Sira such women would be a negative influence on young girls. Before we can speculate further on the nature of this influence, we must look at the second distich in the strophe.

Ben Sira continues the notion expressed in v. 12b by providing a motivation statement in v. 13 which explains the reason why a daughter should not be permitted to associate with married women. The first line of this distich, which is really a truncated simile, expresses the vehicle of the comparison:

"From the garment comes the moth." The moth is a frequent OT symbol of destructiveness.[229] It retains this negative connotation in our text as well. However, here the emphasis is not on the damage done by the moth to the cloth but on its emergence from the cloth. This statement may reflect the ancient idea of spontaneous generation. On the other hand, it is more likely to have resulted from astute observation. Clothing moths such as the common Tineola bisselliella and Tinea pellionella lay their eggs in woolen cloth and fur. The larvae feed on this material and pupate on the cloth. Their metamorphosis is complete when they emerge from the case-like pupae as adult moths.[230] Thus, one can say with considerable accuracy that moths come from cloth. But whatever Ben Sira's level of entomological sophistication may have been, his point is clear. Moths emerge from garments.

Ben Sira wishes to suggest that, as moths come from garments, so also wickedness comes from women. He refers to this evil as r'ʿt ʾšh "woman's wickedness." The relationship between women and wickedness or evil is common for Ben Sira.[231] We have seen elsewhere that one of his characteristic expressions is the phrase "evil wife."[232] But in addition to such general references, he has discussed women's negative qualities in considerable detail. This is especially true in his major statement on the bad wife, 26:5-9; 25:13-26. There, he highlights her jealousy (v. 6),[233] uncontrollability (v. 7), drunkenness (v. 8), harlotry (v. 9), anger (v. 15), talkativeness (v. 20), and arrogance (vv. 25-26). Elsewhere, he speaks of her dominance,[234] foolishness,[235] and adultery.[236] In our text he may be thinking of woman's wickedness in general, or he may have in mind a composite of things such as those I have just listed.

One should probably be content with this general interpretation of the line, were it not found in this particular setting. Ben Sira calls for fathers to strictly watch their daughters. He then indicates some specific areas for paternal concern. Fathers should house their daughters in rooms that have no windows and should see that their bodies are not exposed. These counsels are clearly designed to preserve daughters from illicit sexual activity. It seems reasonable that the third specific suggestion, which discourages daughters from associating with married women, has this same goal. Thus, the meaning of v. 13b, which expands the injunction of v. 12b, no doubt centers on woman's wickedness in the realm of sexual activity.[237] Ben Sira implies that an unmarried girl will become increasingly aware of her sexuality through her contacts with married women.

We may note that Ben Sira has made this claim concerning woman's wickedness in the form of a universal statement. This is strong language, but it echoes the same sentiments that he expresses in v. 14a. The universality of the invective may have led the Syr to render this line freely.[238] The same motivation undoubtedly influenced at least one Gr MS[239] to insert the qualifying poněras, which makes the source of woman's wickedness an "evil woman."

Our section closes with an incredible statement which relates a woman's goodness (twb ʾšh) to a man's wickedness (rʿ ʾyš) and compares a daughter's potential for disgrace to that of a son. Some scholars[240] have suggested that this distich concludes the discussion began in v. 12, and that the man and woman are those mentioned in that verse. But this is true only in a loose sense. The link with the preceding material is merely the verbal connection of wickedness and women. From woman's wickedness in v. 13b Ben Sira proceeds in v. 14a to man's wickedness in comparison with woman's goodness. This is certainly a clear transition. But the key to the function of this distich lies with line b. There a daughter is declared to be more worrisome regarding disgrace than a son. This has no direct relationship to vv. 12-13. Instead, it forms a conclusion to the entire section on daughters. As such, it echoes the concerns expressed in the distich which opens the section. There, the father of a daughter experiences sleeplessness and anxiety; here, he fears disgrace.

Fuss[241] considers this distich to be traditional, with line _b_ representing Ben Sira's reworking. However, there are several problems with this assessment. The distich does not present us with a striking or unusual form in this context. Furthermore, it flows easily from the preceding material and understandably concludes the entire treatise on daughters. There is no real discontinuity in either form or content. Finally, line _a_ is such an incomparably negative statement on women that it is easier to attribute its origin to Ben Sira, whom we have repeatedly seen to display an antifemale bias, than to some unknown source. The statement exceeds anything that precedes it in the ancient literature of which I am aware. Thus, I understand v. 14 to be Ben Sira's own work, which he designed to conclude this section on daughters.

Most scholars do not try to interpret line _a_ on its own terms. Instead, they read the line in the light of vv. 12-13. Ryssel[242] sees a man's unkindness and rudeness causing less damage to a daughter than a woman's charming and insinuating ways. Peters,[243] followed by Gaspar,[244] holds that a daughter will be less tainted by bad men than by bad women. Schilling[245] suggests that a man may be repulsive, but he is not as dangerous to a weak spirit as is a woman's surface affection. Hamp[246] considers a rude, unfriendly man less harmful to an unstable maiden than a woman with her enticing talk and dirty mind. Kearns[247] offers the view that a daughter may be shielded against a man's wickedness but is susceptible to a woman's insidious friendship. Spicq[248] thinks that the line is a hyperbole, expressing the notion that a man's frank wickedness is less dangerous than a woman's deceitful kindness.

The main problem with these interpretations is that they start from the premise that Ben Sira's statement must mean something less than what it says. He certainly could not mean what the line actually conveys. Gaspar becomes so concerned to vindicate Ben Sira before the bar of social ethics that he offers the following incredible suggestion: The expression "wickedness of a man" refers to the daughter's father. This he terms an ingenious contrast, wherein the father's "wickedness" is his active attempt to protect his daughter from her unwholesome, "good" friends. He sees this kind of "wickedness" as better than that kind of "goodness."[249] Such an interpretation is without foundation in the context of this negative discussion, as well as in the light of Ben Sira's use of the terms r` and r`h.[250]

This extremely negative statement needs to be understood for what it is, a climactic explosion by one who harbored strong feelings against women. Both Edersheim[251] and Snaith[252] interpret the line in this way. We need not waste our energies trying to salvage Ben Sira's social morality. He has amply displayed his negative bias against women, as we have seen. There is no reason why his blast here should be muted. We should not attempt to unlock his logic, in order to demonstrate just what he may have meant by a man's wickedness and a woman's goodness. He may not have been able to clarify the issue himself. Instead, we should be content to let him say it as he has. The mention of a woman's wickedness in v. 13b has triggered his response that a man's wickedness is better than a woman's goodness. In this way he seems to have merely desired to show the level of wickedness that women represented to him. We must allow him to say it, even though it is utterly indefensible.

After the magnitude of v. 14a, line b seems like a denouement by comparison. But this is Ben Sira's real conclusion to the section. The line does have a point of contact with line a. This lies particularly in the parallel contrasts between males and females. In the way that I have read this line, the resultant structure is chiastic: man / woman : daughter / son.[253]

In three of his four discussions of daughters Ben Sira has directly or indirectly compared them negatively to sons.[254] Besides our text, one of these sections (22:3-5) also features the idea of disgrace. There a daughter's birth is considered worse than the disgrace of producing an ignorant son (v. 3). Furthermore, Ben Sira proceeds to describe the daughter in terms of disgrace (vv. 4-5). Our text reflects a similar notion. By concluding this section with an echo of v. 9ab, Ben Sira suggests that a father has more cause to worry about being disgraced by a daughter than by a son. In the intervening verses he has made a concerted effort to demonstrate why he considers this to be the case. Again, for Ben Sira to think of a daughter is virtually to think of the potential for disgrace. This is his last word on daughters.

In this section we have seen that a father experiences sleeplessness and anxiety over a daughter no matter what her status. If she is unmarried, she may be passed over by prospective husbands for a variety of reasons including, above all, her loss of virginity or an illegitimate pregnancy. If she is married, she may be rejected by her husband for any cause, but especially for adultery or sterility. In either situation the father would have to provide financial and other support for his daughter. This, along with the accompanying social stigma, would represent a significant burden to the father. From this discussion of a father's worry, Ben Sira moves to counsel a father on strictly watching his daughter. He describes several negative circumstances that may develop if she is not guarded. These may be summarized as public ridicule and disgrace. To these he adds three specific pieces of advice for implementing the vigil. She should be housed in a room without windows. She should be kept from exposing herself to men. She should be prevented from associating with married women. The latter are a source of particular wickedness. Finally, he concludes the section with the harshest statememt against women that we have from his pen, along with a final negative comparison between daughters and sons.

This section leaves two major impressions about daughters. First, daughters represent an economic burden to their fathers. This is factually true when they are unmarried. It is potentially true when they are married, because they may be divorced and be returned to their father's support. Second, daughters are sexually irresponsible. Because of this, they are prone to bring public ridicule and disgrace on their fathers. Therefore, they must be guarded.

Before we conclude this chapter, we must include a few remarks on a text which offers counsel concerning behavior toward virgins.

9:5

Do not gaze intently at[255] a virgin,[256]
Lest you be ensnared[257] in fines because of her.[258]

This distich is part of the eleven distichs of miscellaneous counsels concerning women found in 9:1-9. I have already discussed the immediate and extended contexts, as well as the structure of the section.[259] Fuss[260] considers the verse to be part of a homogeneous group of distichs of traditional material utilized by Ben Sira. We will proceed with this assumption.

Out text consists of two parts. Line a offers counsel regarding a virgin and line b provides a statement of negative consequence. The counsel itself bears some resemblance to Job 31:1, as several scholars have noted.[261] However, only the general idea of gazing at a virgin is common to these texts. In Job the speaker resolves not to look upon a virgin in order to show that he not only avoids sin but shuns temptation as well. In our text we have direct advice not to gaze at a virgin. It is not so much the look that is problematic, but the desire which the look produces. This may eventually lead to illicit sexual activity, as line b suggests. In a different form Ben Sira offers the same advice concerning gazing (also from byn) at another man's wife.[262]

The consequence of failure to heed this counsel may lead to the legal penalties associated with sexually violating a virgin. We may presume that the fines in question are those mentioned in deuteronomic law (Deut 22:28-29). There the one who violates a virgin must pay her father fifty shekels, marry her, and be ineligible from ever divorcing her. The law in Exod 22:16-17, upon which the above was no doubt based, merely mentions paying the bride price and marrying the girl, if her father concurs. If not, he is to pay the price anyway.

With Schilling[263] and Hamp[264] we may note that our text emphasizes the financial and social penalties associated wih violating a virgin as a motivation for proper conduct toward her, rather than the morality of chastity. But this can also be said for the biblical legal material that appears to lie behind it. In any case, Ben Sira is certainly not uncomfortable repeating this injunction along with the consequences.[265]

Conclusion

In reviewing our findings let us first look at Ben Sira's redactional activities in the texts that we have considered. His most notable manipulation of traditional material occurred in 7:24-25. There we found that, in contrast to his leaving the distich concerning the son (v. 23) unaltered, he split the traditional, positive, distich concerning the daughter and inserted his own negative material. This gave the resultant two distich unit a distinctly negative tone. We also noted that he applied to daughters in 22:3-5 certain negative material on the son from Proverbs and twice used a general, traditional counsel about guarding daughters to head specific discussions of daughters' disgracingly amorous activities (26:10a; 42:11a).

The general conceptual implications that Ben Sira leaves fall into several areas. Daughters are less significant and more troublesome to a father than sons.[266] Daughters, unmarried or married, represent a real or potential economic burden to their fathers.[267] Daughters are often the source of anxiety and shame to their fathers.[268] Daughters require special monitoring by their fathers.[269] Daughters are to be kept as marriageable as possible or to be kept from divorce.[270] Daughters are sexually irresponsible.[271]

We may also recall that in the context of his discussion of daughters, Ben Sira makes two of his most incredibly negative statements about women. In 26:12 he describes a daughter's insatiable lust for sexual intercourse in terms that are both remarkably explicit and unabashedly obscene. Then in 42:14a he makes the astounding declaration that a man's wickedness is better than a woman's goodness. Thinking about daughters seems to bring out the worst in Ben Sira.

To put these reflections into perspective, it may be useful to make two brief comparisons. First, let us look at the way Ben Sira discusses sons. Of his numerous references to sons, only several seem relevant here. We have already seen that in 7:23 he let stand unaltered a positive, traditional distich about correcting sons and providing them with wives. In 16:1-5 he speaks negatively of unprofitable youth, corrupt children, and presumptuous posterity. In the context these appear to be sons. However, he condemns them for having no fear of the Lord, not for merely being sons. His longest section on training sons is 30:1-13. A father should give great care to his son's development through rigorous discipline and instruction. A son so trained will represent his father after his death, even to his enemies.[272] If a father fails to train his son, he will produce a stubborn, headstrong, mischievous, rebellious, and foolish son who will terrify, grieve, and vex his father. There is no mention of economic burden, disgrace, or sexual irresponsibility.

In these texts Ben Sira speaks of training sons to successfully reach their potential and to positively represent their family. Daughters are guarded so that they may be marketable in marriage and not disgrace the family. Sons have a tendency to be rebellious. Daughters have a tendency to be sexually irresponsible. Sons may bring joy and fulfillment. Daughters bring trouble and anxiety.

Finally, let us note the position of the OT on daughters. The things that we have observed in Ben Sira's discussion of daughters stand in contrast to the material of the OT in several important ways. The most obvious difference lies in the fact that the OT never discusses daughters as an isolated topic, as does Ben Sira. This is even true of the wisdom literature.[273] The OT reflects social differences between sons and daughters, as it does for men and women in general.[274] However, sometimes both are treated equally.[275] On occasion daughters are singled out for particular consideration.[276] Often the term daughter is employed metaphorically as an endearing reference to the covenant people.[277] Ben Sira reflects no such positive attitudes.

Our author seems to reach the climax of his negative bias against women when he discusses daughters. He has virtually nothing good to say about them. What he does say reflects frustration, bitterness, and contempt. He views a daughter as a burden to be unloaded. Thus, 7:25a seems to say it all for him: "Give a daughter in marriage and trouble will depart."

CONCLUSION

The issue that I have addressed in this study concerns the nature of Ben Sira's view of women. The various opinions concerning this matter fall into two general categories. Some claim that Ben Sira was a misogynist. Others hold that he was not a misogynist but merely reflected the low view of women that characterized his age. The first group emphasizes Ben Sira's negative statements about women. The second group feels that his positive statements counterbalance his negative remarks.

Ben Sira's material on women has received only passing treatment in the commentaries and brief considerations in certain monographs on women and social issues in the OT or Judaism. However, the only direct studies of the issue are two short articles, separated by more than seventy-five years. One additional Festschrift article briefly addresses the issue in the midst of a longer consideration of women in the NT. None of these studies has been sufficiently comprehensive or consciously designed to settle the issue of Ben Sira's view of women.

The present study was conducted to meet this need. I have assembled all Ben Sira's material concerning women into categories representing women's various roles. My preliminary reading of the data led me to formulate the following working hypothesis: Ben Sira is personally negative towards women. I have sought to test this hypothesis by carefully analyzing each of Ben Sira's statements about women in its context, through its language and structure, from the perspective of his editorial and compositional activities, and by comparison with his principal wisdom model, the OT.

The conclusion to this study has been developing throughout. At the end of each section of text discussed I have indicated the contribution of that text to an understanding of Ben Sira's view of women and toward the validation of the working hypothesis. I have summarized these findings at the end of each chapter. These chapter conclusions provide statements on his view of women, reflected in his discussions of the various categories of women. It remains now for me to briefly review these discoveries. I will do so from two perspectives.

First, let us look at the categories of women that we have studied in Sirach. Clearly the most problematic category is the good wife. To the casual reader this material appears to be positive regarding women. As we have seen, it is sometimes taken to be so positive that some scholars find it baffling that Ben Sira can at other times be so negative. Scholars have often pointed to this material as evidence that Ben Sira is not personally negative towards women. But as we read Ben Sira's remarks about the good wife more carefully, we found that he does not discuss her as an independent entity. Instead, he sees her only in relationship to her husband. She is his property, as are his children, and is valued to the extent that she serves his needs and meets his desires. Her beauty is lauded as a stimulus to his sexual urges. Her goodness is measured by the degree of her passivity. Her wisdom is the eloquence of her silence.

Some of Ben Sira's remarks about the good wife are actually traditional lines that he has incorporated into his text, with little or no editing. These generally range from neutral to slightly negative towards women. But we have also seen Ben Sira's personal imprint not only in the material that he has composed but especially in the traditional material that he has altered. We have seen in the latter that at times he has reconstructed the positive or neutral material on the good wife from his sources in such a way as to render it negative in its new setting. Thus, Ben Sira's discussions of the good wife which at first appear to be positive are, in fact, negative and reveal him to be personally negative towards women.

Sirach contains several references to woman as mother and two concerning her role as widow. We have seen that Ben Sira mentions mothers in a literal sense only in conjunction with fathers. The expression "father and mother" as well as the appearance of fathers and mothers in parallel stichs is the Heb equivalent of parents. This is the only way in which Ben Sira refers to mothers in a literal sense. Such references are not negative in themselves. After all, a mother is recognized as a parent. But for Ben Sira mother is implicitly a second class parent. She is little more than part of a literary convention. In contrast, fathers are often the subject of his reflection without the mention of mothers. At best, Ben Sira is neutral toward woman as mother. However, his personal, negative bias against woman is dimly revealed in his silence on mothers as a separate topic. His remarks about widows merely reflect the conventional ancient interest in oppressed social groups and offer us little or no insight into his view of women.

The bad wife is Ben Sira's most developed category. He devotes his largest single discussion of women to this topic. In this collection of traditional, edited, and composed material, he ranges widely over the evils of the bad wife. He pictures her as publicly disgracing, uncontrollable, drunken, adulterous, angry, impossible to live with, worthy of a curse, babbling, seductive, emasculating, unpleasing, sin-originating, outspoken and worthy of divorce. Elsewhere, he speaks of the bad wife as domineering and untrustworthy.

Within all of this completely negative material we have seen several things that betray Ben Sira's personal, negative bias against women. He has often altered, rearranged, and supplemented traditional material to reflect negatively on women beyond the implications of his sources. He has at times employed in relationship to women negative metaphors that are found in the OT, but never in contexts which are related to women. We have seen that he appears to have coined certain pejorative expressions relating to the bad wife. He seems to have been the first to lay the blame for sin and death at the feet of a woman. Many others before him and in his day were negative towards bad wives. However, Ben Sira was more than a reflector of this heritage and environment. His writings on the bad wife reveal his own bias against women.

The categories of adulteress and prostitute are related in that both types of women engage in illicit sexual activity. As might be expected, Ben Sira is thoroughly negative towards such women. But in this he is certainly not unique. He echoes the prohibitions and counsels of both the legal and wisdom traditions. This is especially true of his material on prostitutes, most of which is drawn from traditional sources. His major discussion of the adulteress follows a similar treatment of the adulterer and thus conveniently provides for a contextually related comparison. We have seen that in this section Ben Sira describes both the offense and penalty of the adulteress in greater detail than those of the adulterer, even though her motivation may have been superior to his. Ben Sira also implies that adultery is the likely end to the chain of progressively negative behavior on the part of an evil wife. By themselves these reflections would not be enough to establish that he was motivated to write as he does from a personal bias against women. However, once the pattern is certified on other grounds, these materials become more comprehensible and offer added support to our working hypothesis.

If the bad wife is Ben Sira's most extensive category, the daughter is his most negative. Unlike the OT, he devotes several discussions to woman as daughter. These are all negative. He considers daughters to be a great burden, financially and otherwise. They cause more trouble and worry than sons, bringing their fathers anxiety and shame. Since they are sexually irresponsible and seductive, they must be constantly guarded. A father's goal is to give them in marriage and to keep them married. If he is successful in this, he will be relieved of a great trouble. Thus, the object of a father's care of his daughter is to keep her as marriageable as possible. The thought of daughters seemed to bring out the worst side of Ben Sira's negative view of women. In one of his discussions of daughters he painted an incredibly obscene picture of their insatiable sexual desires. Furthermore, at the end of a section on daughters he formulated his most indefensibly negative remark about women. Ben Sira unabashedly disliked daughters. In his discussions concerning daughters he reveals his personal bias against women more clearly than anywhere else. His views are consistent, occurring in various sections of his work. The negative picture seems to be intensified in his final remarks. If we had nothing else about women from his pen but this material on daughters, we could justifiably conclude that Ben Sira exhibits a personal bias against women.

The second perspective from which we will review our discoveries involves the type of evidence considered. We have already anticipated some of this above. Let us look initially at Ben Sira's handling of traditional materials. We have found that in several important instances he altered the intent of the sources from which he quoted statements about women. This resulted either in his making negative what in the sources had been positive or neutral or in his intensifying an already negative remark. When his quotations of traditional pieces included both women and nonwomen material, only the sections concerning women were altered. Ben Sira's redactions of his sources in these settings involve several phenomena such as: rearranging of word or line order; splitting positive distichs and inserting negative material; deleting positive lines and replacing them with negative ones; adding balancing, weakening, or opposing material; reconstructing Zahlensprüche by including a negative unit on women as the climax. We have seen this kind of evidence particularly in Ben Sira's treatment of good and bad wives, as well as daughters. This seems to be the most persuasive data in support of our working hypothesis.

Another type of evidence involves Ben Sira's relationship to his main idea source, the OT. He may be said to parallel the

OT, especially the wisdom literature, in many of his remarks about women. However, his material on women often stands in stark contrast to the OT. We have seen that he mentions negative situations regarding women, such as the drunken wife, and discusses categories of women, such as daughter, where the OT is silent. On the other hand, the OT considers mother as a separate entity, where he is silent. Sometimes in his discussions of women he uses strong, negative OT figures that are not related to women. We have also noted an example of his criticizing Solomon for his sins that relate to women but ignoring his idolatry, while the OT focuses on the latter. This evidence itself may not establish the validity of our working hypothesis, but it clearly supports it.

From the remaining miscellaneous kinds of evidence let me mention just one. Ben Sira was capable of issuing remarks concerning women that stand out as classic pieces of misogynist rhetoric. We alluded to two examples already. But these are so remarkable that they bear repeating here. One case involves Ben Sira's explicitly obscene description of a daughter's insatiable desire for sexual intercourse. The other by itself is sufficient to prove our case: "Better is the wickedness of a man than the goodness of a woman."

Let us summarize what we have seen in this study. Ben Sira is more than passively interested in women. It is a topic that reflects his personal feelings, not merely an environmental phenomenon. Ben Sira is often not content to let traditional material about women, whether positive or negative, stand unaltered in his text. When he edits such material, he does so in a negative direction. He deals with negative topics about women that are not contained in the biblical wisdom or other literature. He makes remarks about women that are among the most obscene and negative in ancient literature. He shows himself to be negative towards women, no matter what type of woman he discusses. This is particularly true of his treatment of the bad wife and climaxes in his consideration of the daughter. We may justifiably conclude, therefore, that Ben Sira exhibits a personal, negative bias against women.

By way of epilogue let me offer a few final remarks. I have deliberately limited the scope of this study to an analysis of Sirach in relation to the issue of Ben Sira's view of women. This has resulted in a description of his view that arises from the evidence of the text. However, there are other issues related to this topic that I have chosen not to address. This decision does not reflect their lack of importance, but my desire to focus the present study. Some of these concerns may be stated as questions. Why did Ben Sira possess this personal, negative bias against women? What kinds of personal experiences did he have with various types of women? What part did this personal, negative bias against women play in his academic instruction? What influence have his views had on later thinkers and writers, particularly Jewish and Christian? How do Ben Sira's attitudes toward women compare to those of his contempories and to the actual status of women in his community? What implications do these findings have for the common notion that wisdom literature reflects social ideals which transcended contemporary social situations? These and related questions may serve to stimulate further investigation into the issues raised by this study.

APPENDIX 1

NUMERICAL SAYINGS

The book of Sirach contains several examples of a common wisdom device, which in German is called a Zahlenspruch, i.e., a numerical saying. The compactness of the German term commends itself, and I have chosen to use it throughout this study. Zahlensprüche occur in various forms. Some are simple epigrams, which include a single number (X)[1] or two numbers, the second greater than the first by one (X/X+1).[2] Others contain two elements. The first part is the introduction or title line, which states the subject of the Zahlenspruch and the number of items to be mentioned. The numerical reference may be to a single number (X) or to a double number (X/X+1). In this type the introduction is followed by a second element, which is a list of words, phrases, and rarely clauses. We will be concerned here only with the Zahlensprüche which contain both numbers and lists.

We may illustrate the X type of Zahlenspruch with the following example from Sir 37:17-18:

> As principles for the guidance of the mind
> Four criteria appear.
> Good and evil, life and death.
> Then it is the tongue that makes known the choice.[3]

Sirach also contains X type Zahlensprüche in 25:1 and 25:2. In the OT this type is found in Job 13:20-21; Ps 27:4; Prov 20:10; 20:12; 22:2; 29:13; 30:7-8; 30:24-28; Isa 47:9; 51:19-20; Jer 2:13; 14:30.[4]

The X/X+1 type of Zahlenspruch is found more frequently in Sirach than the X type. The following example from Sir 50:25-26 is representative of the X/X+1 type:

With two nations my soul is vexed
And the third is no nation:
Those who live on Mount Seir, and the Philistines,
And the foolish people that dwell in Shechem.[5]

We also find this type in Sir 23:16-17; 25:7-11; 26:5; 26:28. For this type in the OT, see Job 5:19-22; 33:14-15a; Ps 62:11-12a; Prov 6:16-19; 30:15b-16; 18-19; 21-23; 29-31.[6]

The antiquity of the X/X+1 Zahlenspruch which contains a list has been traced to Ras Shamra,[7] as this text shows:

For two [kinds of] banquets Baal hates,
Three the Rider of the Clouds:
A banquet of shamefulness,
A banquet of baseness,
And a banquet of handmaid's lewdness.[8]

Other Zahlensprüche without lists representing the X/X+1 type are found in Ugaritic literature, as well as in Sumerian and Akkadian materials.[9]

William Barron Stevenson[10] considers Zahlensprüche to be mnemonic devices employed in the educational context that lies behind wisdom literature. The numbers themselves do not mean simply "a few" or "several," as in the case of two small numbers linked by "or." Rather, they helped students to recall a particular list of items by indicating the number of items in the list.

Stevenson argues that the probable origin of the double number type of Zahlenspruch was the peculiar mannerism of "an influential teacher," who regularly added to the preface number of his list as he thought of an additional element.[11] He accounts for the survival of the form on grounds of its easy accommodation to Heb poetic parallelism. It would be irrational, according to Stevenson, for this form to have developed as a deliberate parallelism, with one number being erroneous.[12] This argument is weak, since, whether rational or irrational, the form is parallel and can be justified as a developing idea, where the second line completes the numerical designation of the first.

It seems more reasonable to conclude that the double number Zahlenspruch owes its existence to the single number form. That the latter was a mnemonic device in education is likely. But when the device moved from oral to written form, the second half of the parallel distich preface began to often include a number, one greater than the number in the first half. This of course required the first number to be adjusted so that the second would reflect the actual number of items in the list.

Roth considers another side of the question of origin regarding Zahlensprüche. He suggests that Stevenson touches the issue only from the point of view of teaching technique. He holds that the sayings in Prov 30:15-31, for example, are "formulations of early Hebrew nature wisdom of encyclopaedic character."[13] As a whole, the pattern is described as a frame pattern, "a pattern which frames several items into a coordinated whole."[14] It occurs wherever reflection on human affairs leads to grouping and classification and is both philosophic and didactic.[15]

Since several of the Zahlensprüche in Sirach contain material about women, it is necessary for us to consider a few issues with regard to their composition and interpretation. The first issue regards parallelism. Most Zahlensprüche contain simple lists of words or phrases. A few include lists in which each item is expressed in a parallel distich.[16] However, such a construction seems out of place in an otherwise compact, didactic form. It is likely that the authors who incorporated these traditional pieces into their texts have expanded the simple lists through parallelism to fit their scheme of composition.[17]

Sometimes the items in the list of a Zahlenspruch are not clear, and scholars have included among the items all or parts of extended discussions that are juxtaposed to it. This is especially true of Sir 23:16-17[18] and 26:5.[19] But both these Zahlensprüche may be understood without reference to the extended discussions. Originally, each contained a simple list of items.[20] If this is recognized, then Sirach provides no analogy to a <u>Zahlenspruch</u> in which one item in the list is an extended discussion. This is also true of the <u>Zahlensprüche</u> of the OT.[21] We can conclude that <u>Zahlensprüche</u> do not contain extended discussions. After all, this would defeat their mnemonic function.

The final issue that concerns us here involves the interpretation of <u>Zahlensprüche</u>. Some scholars[22] have tried to determine the identity of the items in a <u>Zahlenspruch</u> list or to grade their positive or negative impact by assuming or arguing that the items in the list progress toward a climax in the last item. This is considered especially true of the X/X+1 type.

Let us look at the <u>Zahlensprüche</u> themselves to see if they support progression and climax. Not surprisingly, the X type clearly contain no progression or climax.[23] It is not generally claimed that this type is anything more than a simple list.[24] On the other hand, the X/X+1 type invite the view that the second and larger number represents the climax of the list. The evidence from the examples is not as conclusive as for the first type. However, it is sufficient to nullify any thoroughgoing view that all X/X+1 <u>Zahlensprüche</u> progress toward climax. Of the examples in Sirach, three[25] are nonprogressive lists and two[26] may be progressive. The OT examples are also divided. Five[27] are nonprogressive, while two[28] may be progressive. The X/X+1 <u>Zahlensprüche</u> may or may not contain lists that progress toward a climax. Most do not. Therefore, the argument of progression and climax, whether stated or implied, cannot be used either to establish which items comprise a <u>Zahlenspruch</u> list or to advance a particular interpretation of one of these items.

APPENDIX 2

THE TEXT OF SIR 40:18-20

The problem of the differences among the Heb, Gr, and Syr readings of 40:18-20 has moved closer to resolution with the additional witness of the recently discovered MS of Sirach from Masada, HebM. The various readings for these verses according to the witnesses are as follows:

18a	HebB	A life of wine and strong drink is sweet,
	HebBmg	A life of abundance (and) intelligence is sweet,
	HebM	A life of abundance (and) reward is sweet,
	Gr	The life of a self-sufficient (one) and hard-working (one) will be sweet,
	Syr	(missing)
18b	HebB	But better than both is he who finds a treasure.
	HebBmg	But better than both is he who finds a treasure (lit. what has been laid aside).
	HebM	But better than both is he who finds [a treasure] (lit. what has been laid aside).
	Gr	But better than both is he who finds a treasure.
	Syr	(missing)
19a	HebB	Child and city establish a name,
	HebBmg	(none)
	HebM	Child and [city estab]lish a name,
	Gr	Children and the building of a city establish a name,
	Syr	Honor and respect establish a name,
19b	HebB	But better than both is he who finds wisdom.
	HebBmg	(none)
	HebM	But better than both is he who find[s wisdom].
	Gr	(missing)
	Syr	But better than both is he who finds wisdom.

19c	HebB	Young cattle and planting cause a name to flourish,
	HebBmg	(none)
	HebM	[Young cattle and planting cause] food [to flouri]sh,
	Gr	(missing)
	Syr	A building and a plantation restore a name,
19d	HebB	But better than both is a devoted wife.
	HebBmg	(none)
	HebM	(not extant)
	Gr	But better than both is a wife accounted blameless.
	Syr	But better than both is a wise wife.
20a	HebB	Wine and strong drink rejoice the heart,
	HebBmg	(none)
	HebM	(not extant)
	Gr	Wine and music gladden the heart,
	Syr	Old wine rejoices the heart,
20b	HebB	But better than both is the love of friends.
	HebBmg	(none)
	HebM	(not extant)
	Gr	But better than both is the love of wisdom.
	Syr	But better than that is the love of a friend.

V. 18a: I prefer to read with HebM, where w- "and" is understood[1] between ytr "abundance" and śkr "reward." This is reflected in both HebBmg and Gr. The latter is a similar paraphrase with autarkous ergatou "self-sufficient one (and) hard-worker" for ytr śkr. HebBmg reads the same as HebM, except that it substitutes śkl "intelligence" for śkr. HebB reads škr (šēkar) "strong drink" instead of śkr (śakar) and, influenced by v. 20a, replaced ytr with yyn "wine" to make the phrase yyn wškr "wine and strong drink." The HebM reading is superior in avoiding not only "the offensive expression"[2] but also the uncharacteristic repetition of material in v. 20a. The various proposals by commentators[3] to deal with these difficulties are now obsolete.

V. 18b: The witnesses are quite similar for this stich. I read with Yadin´s[4] suggestion [śymh] lit. "what has been laid aside." This is reflected in the late Heb equivalent symh, which is found in HebBmg. HebB reads ´wṣr, which is the usual word behind the LXX thēsauros. The latter would normally be preferred, but HebM and HebBmg appear to reflect a vocabularly peculiarity of Ben Sira. In 41:14b we find the same MS readings: HebM _śymh_,[5] HebBmg _symh_, HebB _'wṣr_, Gr _thēsauros_. It seems reasonable to conclude that Ben Sira sometimes, at least, used the word _śymh_ to express the idea of "treasure" and that HebB substituted the more usual word _'wṣr_, perhaps under the influence of the Gr _thēsauros_, which almost always translates _'wṣr_ in the LXX.

V. 19a: The reading of HebB and HebM is superior to the Gr, which has an explanitory gloss[6] but still reflects the original, unlike Syr, which for the two subjects is independent.

V. 19bc: These stichs should be considered together, since together they are either accepted as genuine or rejected as a gloss. Both lines are missing in Gr but are found in HebB. Some, like Smend,[7] prefer to read with Gr, since line _c_ in HebB uncharacteristically repeats _šm_ "name" from line _a_. Others, like Box-Oesterley,[8] read with HebB but see the repetition of _šm_ as an internal Heb corruption. The reading of HebM now adds to the weight of the reading of HebB and to the genuineness of lines _bc_. However, HebM not only provides a witness to the early existence of lines _bc_, but it also clears up the problem of the repetition of _šm_. While line _c_ is largely mutilated, one word is certain. In the place where HebB has _šm_, HebM reads _š'r_. I would suggest a textual history as follows. HebM represents the original reading.[9] A very early, pre-Gr substitution accidently occurred in the text represented by HebB, which saw _šm_ from line _a_ replace _š'r_ in line _c_. This is the text that gave rise to Syr. It is also the text that served as _Vorlage_ for Gr, which deleted _bc_, because of homoioteleuton involving _sm_ in lines _a_ and _c_. Gr has, however, preserved the term _ḥkmh_ "wisdom" from line _b_, by using it in v. 20b (_sophia_).

V. 19d: I prefer the reading of HebB. Syr appears to have been influenced by the mention of "wisdom" in line _b_. Gr would seem to be a paraphrase.[10]

V. 20a: HebB provides the preferred reading. Gr or its Vorlage misread šyr "music" for škr "strong drink" and translated with mousika. A reference to music would be unexpected here, since it is the feature of v. 21a. The reading škr is further established because of its secondary insertion by HebB into v. 18a.[11] Syr consolidates the hendiadys phrase yyn wškr[12] "wine and strong drink" into the expression ḥmr' ʿtyq' "old wine."

V. 20b: I read with HebB. Syr equals Heb except for the singular opening formula "but better than that"[13] and the singular "friend." Gr reads sophias "wisdom" instead of "friends," under influence from v. 19b.

NOTES

Introduction

[1]Among the other important topics in Sirach are banquet manners, child discipline, honesty, the natural world, borrowing and lending, shame, education, sacrifices, a celebration of famous OT men, and especially wisdom.

[2]The commentaries that I have consulted for all or some of the texts considered in this study are (note the short forms to be used in subsequent citations): Edward Lee Beavin, "Ecclesiasticus or the Wisdom of Jesus the Son of Sirach," in The Interpreter's One-Volume Commentary on the Bible, ed. Charles M. Laymon (Nashville, Tennessee: Abingdon Press, 1971), pp. 550-76 (Beavin). George Herbert Box and William Oscar Emil Oesterley, "Sirach," in The Apocrypha and Pseudepigrapha of the Old Testament, ed. R. H. Charles (Oxford: Clarendon Press, 1913), 1:268-517 (Box-Oesterley). Hilaire Duesberg and Paul Auvray, Le Livre de L'Ecclésiastique, La Sainte Bible, (Paris: Les Éditions du Cerf, 1953) (Duesberg-Auvray). Andreas Eberharter, Das Buch Jesus Sirach oder Ecclesiasticus, vol. 6, pt. 5: Die Heilige Schrift des Alten Testaments, (Bonn: Peter Hanstein, 1925) (Eberharter). Alfred Edersheim, "Ecclesiasticus," in The Holy Bible According to the Authorized Version (A.D. 1911) . . . Apocrypha, ed. Henry Wace (London: John Murray Pub., 1888), 2:1-239 (Edersheim). Otto Fridolin Fritzsche, Die Weisheit Jesus Sirach's, vol. 5: Kurtzgefasstes exegetisches Handbuch zu den Apokryphen des Alten Testaments (Leipzig: S. Hirzel, 1859) (Fritzsche). Vinzenz Hamp, "Das Buch Sirach oder Ecclesiasticus," in Die Heilige Schrift (= Echter-Bibel), ed. Friedrich Nötscher (Wurzburg: Echter-Verlag, 1959), 4:569-717 (Hamp). Conleth Kearns, "Ecclesiasticus, or the Wisdom of Jesus the Son of Sirach," in A New Catholic Commentary on Holy Scripture, ed. Reginald C. Fuller (London: Thomas Nelson and Sons, 1969), pp. 541-62 (Kearns). Richard G. Moulton, The Modern Reader's Bible (New York: Macmillan Co., 1959) (Moulton). William Oscar Emil Oesterley, The Wisdom of Jesus the Son of Sirach or Ecclesiasticus (Cambridge: Cambridge University Press, 1912) (Oesterley). Norbert Peters, Das Buch Jesus Sirach oder Ecclesiasticus, vol. 25: Exegetisches Handbuch zum Alten Testament (Münster, i.W.: Aschendorffsche Verlagsbuchhandlung, 1913) (Peters, Jesus

Sirach). Victor Ryssel, "Die Sprüche Jesus', des Sohnes Sirachs," in Die Apokryphen und Pseudepigraphen des Alten Testaments, ed. E. Kautzsch (Tübingen: J. C. B. Mohr [Paul Siebeck], 1900), 1:230-475 (Ryssel). Othmar Schilling, Das Buch Jesus Sirach, vol. 7, pt. 2: Die Heilige Schrift (= Herders Bibelkommentar) (Freiburg, i.B.: Herder, 1956) (Schilling). N. Schmidt, Ecclesiasticus (= The Temple Bible) (London: J. M. Dent & Co., 1903) (Schmidt). Moses Hirsch Segal, Sēpher ben-Sîrā' ha-šālēm, 2nd ed. (Jerusalem: Bialik Institute, 1958) (Segal). Rudolf Smend, Die Weischeit des Jesus Sirach (Berlin: Georg Reimer, 1906) (Smend, Jesus Sirach). John G. Snaith, Ecclesiasticus or the Wisdom of Jesus Son of Sirach, The Cambridge Bible Commentary (London: Cambridge University Press, 1974) (Snaith, Ecclesiasticus). Ceslaus Spicq, "L'Ecclésiastique," in La Sainte Bible, ed. Louis Pirot and Albert Clamer (Paris: Letouzey et Ané, 1946-64), 6:529-841 (Spicq). Bruce Vawter, The Book of Sirach, Pamphlet Bible Series, vols. 40-41 (New York: Paulist Press, 1962) (Vawter). Thomas H. Weber, "Sirach," in The Jerome Biblical Commentary, ed. Raymond E. Brown, et al. (Englewood Cliffs, New Jersey: Prentice-Hall, 1968), 1:541-68 (Weber). Otto Zöckler, Die Apokryphen des Alten Testaments (Munich: C. H. Beck'sche Verlagsbuchhandlung, 1891), pp. 255-354 (Zöckler).

[3]Andrew Bruce Davidson, "Sirach's Judgment of Women," ET 6 (1894-95):402-04.

[4]Henry McKeating, "Jesus ben Sira's Attitude to Women," ET 85 (1973-74):85-87.

[5]"Women in Ben Sirach and in the New Testament," in For Me to Live: Essays in Honor of James Leon Kelso, ed. Robert A. Coughenour (Cleveland: Dillon/Liederbach Books, 1972). pp. 56-73.

[6]In addition to these studies we should note Schilling's (pp. 116-19) excursis on the topic of the wife in Sirach. This discussion occurs at the end of his comments on 25:1-26:27.

[7]The following are among the scholars who consider Ben Sira misogynistic, antifeminine, or personally biased against women: Edersheim, p. 203; A Dictionary of the Bible, s.v. "Sirach (Book of)," by Eberhard Nestle; Box-Oesterley, p. 471; Duncan Black MacDonald, The Hebrew Philosophical Genius (Princeton, New Jersey: Princeton University Press, 1936), p. 119; Robert H. Pfeiffer, History of New Testament Times: With an Introduction to the Apocrypha (New York: Harper & Bros., Pub., 1949), p. 367; Bruce Manning Metzger, An Introduction to the Apocrypha (New York: Oxford University Press, 1957), p. 85; Leonard Herbert Brockington, A Critical Introduction to the Apocrypha, Studies in Theology (London: Gerald Duckworth & Co., 1961), pp. 83-84; Snaith, Ecclesiasticus, p. 130.

[8]The most developed attempt to establish the balanced view of Ben Sira on women is by Joseph W. Gaspar, Social Ideas in the Wisdom Literature of the Old Testament, The Catholic University of America Studies in Sacred Theology, second series, no. 8 (Washington: Catholic University of America Press, 1947), pp. 57-62. Gaspar's approach is essentially limited to his assembly of positive material on women from Ben Sira to balance the negative. See also Davidson, p. 402; Weber, p. 549.

[9]See, e.g., Davidson, p. 404; Weber, p. 549; Bailey, p. 71; McKeating, pp. 85-87.

[10]I prefer to use this terminology rather than the expression misogynist, which contains connotations that cannot be determined or tested in a study of this nature.

[11]This is Smend's correction of HebB, which reads "Simon son of" before Joshua. Most scholars consider the reference to Simon to be secondary under influence of 50:1, 24. The Gr of 50:27 reads "Jesus the son of Sirach Eleazar." Cf. the Prologue, where the grandson refers to him as Jesus. Hence, he is often called Jesus the son of Sirach. He should not be called Ben Sirach, however, since that constitutes a mixing of Heb and Gr. For a concise discussion of the relevant items concerning his name, see IDB, s.v. "Ecclesiasticus," by T. Alec Burkill.

[12]This is the short form of the regular Gr title The Wisdom of Jesus the Son of Sirach. In La it was called Ecclesiasticus, a title which still enjoys wide usage.

[13]See 51:23. For a recent discussion, see Edmond Jacob, "Wisdom and Religion in Sirach," in Israelite Wisdom: Theological and Literary Essays in Honor of Samuel Terrien, ed. John G. Gammie et al. (Missoula, Montana: Scholars Press for Union Theological Seminary, New York, 1978), pp. 248-50.

[14]See Metzger, p. 78.

[15]For a good survey of the date question, see Burkill, p. 14. Some representative scholarly opinions on the date include the following: Burkill (p. 14)--between 195 and 171; Metzger (p. 78)--about 180; Jacob (p. 251)--between 190 and 180; Snaith (Ecclesiasticus, p. 1)--about 190; Box-Oesterley (p. 293)--180-175; Weber (p. 541)--about 180; Victor Tcherikover (Hellenistic Civilization and the Jews, tr. S. Applebaum [Philadelphia: Jewish Publication Society of America, 1959], pp. 142-43)--between 200 and 180; Martin Hengel (Judaism and Hellenism, tr. John Bowden, 2 vols. [Philadelphia: Fortress Press, 1974], 1:134)--just prior to Sept. 175. See also A. Haire Forster, "The Date of Ecclesiasticus," ATR 41 (1959):1-9.

[16]The translation was probably made about 116 B.C. See, e.g., Weber, p. 541. Cf. Tcherikover, p. 142.

[17]Robert Balgarnie Young Scott, The Way of Wisdom in the Old Testament (New York: Macmillan Co., 1971), p. 3.

[18]Ibid. For further discussion and lists of representative wisdom literature, see Scott, pp. 5-22, 192-201; John Coert Rylaarsdam, Revelation in Jewish Wisdom Literature (Chicago: University of Chicago Press, 1946), pp. 5-6; William A. Irwin, "Wisdom Literature" in The Interpreter's Bible, ed. George Arthur Buttrick (New York: Abingdon-Cokesbury Press, 1952), 1:212-19; IDB, s.v. "Wisdom," by Sheldon H. Blank.

[19]The most important work is Theophil Middendorp, Die Stellung Jesu Ben Siras zwischen Judentum und Hellenismus (Leiden: E. J. Brill, 1973). See p. 3. Cf. Jacob, pp. 249-50.

[20]Middendorp, pp. 32-33.

[21]P. 268.

[22]Middendorp, pp. 7-8.

[23]The most significant study of the detection and character of traditional material in Sirach is Werner Fuss, "Tradition und Komposition im Buche Jesus Sirach" (Th.D. Dissertation, University of Tübingen, 1963). See also Hengel, 1:131; Wolfgang W. M. Roth, "On the Gnomic-Discursive Wisdom of Jesus Ben Sirach," Semeia 17 (1980):59-79.

[24]For a discussion of Zahlensprüche or numerical sayings, see Appendix 1.

[25]The Gr of chaps. 30-36 has been disarranged. I have cited material from these chapters according to the correct order of Heb and Syr. The Gr references are always given in parentheses.

[26]Quotations from the Bible and Sirach are from the RSV unless otherwise indicated. The exception to this are the texts in each chap. which are the particular focus of this study and which are given according to my own translation.

[27]On the issue of the purpose behind Ben Sira's literary activities in relation to Hellenism, see the fine summary of recent discussion in Jacob, pp. 248-9.

[28]For these citations, see Arthur Ernest Cowley and Adolf Neubauer, The Original Hebrew of a Portion of Ecclesiasticus (Oxford: Clarendon Press, 1897).

[29]The original identification of Sirach materials included four MSS, designated A, B, C, and D. These were published in various forms as they were identified. The standard critical editions are: Hermann L. Strack, Die Sprüche

Jesus', des Sohnes Sirachs, Schriften des Institutum Judaicum in Berlin, no. 31 (Leipzig: A. Deichert [G. Böhme], 1903; Israel Lévi, The Hebrew Text of the Book of Ecclesiasticus, Semetic Study Series, no. 3 (Leiden: E. J. Brill, 1904); Norbert Peters, Liber Jesu filii Sirach sive Ecclesiasticus Hebraice (Freiburg, i.B.: Herdersche Verlagshandlung, 1905); Rudolf Smend, Die Weisheit des Jesus Sirach, hebraisch und deutsch (Berlin: Georg Reimer, 1906). While I have used or referred to all of these, I have generally depended on Smend. Some additional leaves of MSS B and C were published by Jefim Schirmann, "Dap ḥādāš mittôk sēper ben-Sîrā' ha-'ibri," Tarbiz 27 (1957-58):440-43. See also "Dappîm nôs^{e}pîm mittôk sēper 'ben-Sîrā'.'" Tarbiz 29 (1959-60):125-34. For the English publication, see Alexander A. Di Lella, "The Recently Identified Leaves of Sirach in Hebrew," Biblica 45 (1964):153-67.

[30]This MS has been designated E and was published by Joseph Marcus, The Newly Discovered Original Hebrew of Ben Sira (Ecclesiasticus xxxii, 16-xxxiv, 1): The Fifth Manuscript and a Prosodic Version of Ben Sira (Ecclesiasticus xxii, 22-xxiii, 9) (Philadelphia: Dropsie College for Hebrew and Cognate Learning, 1931).

[31]This MS has been designated M and was published by Yigael Yadin, The Ben Sira Scroll from Masada (Jerusalem: Israel Exploration Society, 1965).

[32]Yadin, p. 4.

[33]See James A. Sanders, The Psalms Scroll of Qumran Cave 11 (11QPs^{a}), vol. 4: Discoveries in the Judaean Desert of Jordan (Oxford: Clarendon Press, 1965), pp. 79-85.

[34]The standard text of Sirach in the LXX is now Joseph Zeigler, Sapientia Iesu Filii Sirach, vol. 12, pt. 2: Septuaginta Vetus Testamentum Graecum Auctoriatate Societatis Litterarum Gottingensis editum (Göttingen: Vandenhoeck & Ruprecht, 1965). I have used Zeigler consistently, though on occasion I have referred to Alfred Rahlfs, Septuaginta, 2 vols. (Stuttgart: Württembergische Bibelanstalt, 1935).

[35]For an excellent discussion of the text of Sirach and especially of GrII, see Kearns, pp. 542-47.

[36]For the Syr I have used Paul Anton de Lagarde, Libri veteris testamenti apocryphi Syriace (Osnabrück: Otto Zeller Verlag, 1972). See also Antonio Maria Ceriani, Translatio Syra Pescitto veteris testamenti ex codice Ambrosiano, 6 vols. (Milan: J. B. Pogliani et Sociorum, 1876-83).

[37]For the La, see Sapientia Salomonis, Liber Hiesu filii Sirach, vol 12: Biblia sacra iuxta Latinam vulgatam versionem (Rome: Typis Polyglottis Vaticanis, 1964).

38"The Wisdom of Ben Sirach," p. 60.

39In addition to standard biblical, linguistic, text critical, and exegetical abbreviations, I have employed the following abbreviations for reference works: BAG2--Bauer, Arndt, and Gingrich, 2nd ed. (see Bibliography); BHS--Biblia Hebraica Stuttgartensia; Jastrow--Marcus A. Jastrow, A Dictionary of the Targumim, the Talmud Babli and Yerushalmi, and the Midrachic Literature (see Bibliography); KB--Koehler and Baumgartner (see Bibliography); LSJ--Liddel, Scott, and Jones (see Bibliography).

Chapter I

1HebC 'šh ṭwbh 'šry b`lh (= b. Yebam. 63b, b. Sanh. 100b except for yph "beautiful" instead of ṭwbh, Syr). Cf. Gr gynaikos agathēs makarios ho anēr "blessed is the husband of a good wife."

2HebC ymym (= Gr). Syr reads dywmt' dḥywhy "of the days of his life."

3HebC 'št ḥyl. Cf. Gr gynē andreia "a worthy wife" (= Syr).

4Reading with Gr euphrainei ton andra autēs (= Syr). This flows more naturally from v. 1 than HebC tdšn lb`lh "makes fat her husband." The latter seems dependent on v. 13.

5Reading with Gr kai ta etē autou plērōsei en eirēnē. Cf. HebC as reconstructed by Di Lella ("Leaves of Sirach," p. 166) wšnwt [ḥyyw t]śmḥ "and the years of his life she will gladden." Syr wšny ḥywhy bḥdwt' nšlm "and the years of his life will be completed in joy" is a free rendition of the text represented by Gr. HebC appears to be based on Syr and influenced by the Gr of v. 2a.

6Reading with HebC as reconstructed by Di Lella ("Leaves of Sirach," p. 166) mnh [ṭwbh] (= Gr).

7HebC wbḥlq . . . tntn lit. "will be given in the share" (= Gr). B. Yebam. 63b; b. Sanh. 100b read bḥyq "in the bosom" instead of wbḥlq.

8HebC yr' yy. Cf. Tal. yr' 'lhym "him who fears God." Gr with its plur. part. seems contextually inconsistent phoboumenōn kyrion "of those who fear the Lord." Syr combines an abbreviated line a with line b 'ntt' ṭbt' ttyhb lgbr' ddḥl mn mry' ḥlp `bdwhy ṭb' "a good wife will be given to the man who fears the Lord for his good works."

[9]Reading with Di Lella's ("Leaves of Sirach," p. 166) reconstruction of HebC [ḥn] ʾšh. Cf. Gr charis gynaikos. The usual LXX translation of ḥn is charis. Cf. v. 15a; 42:1.

[10]HebC mṭyb bʿlh. Gr is equivalent with the gnomic fut. terpsei andra autēs. Syr is not extant for this verse.

[11]HebC śklh. Cf. Gr hē epistēmē autēs "her skill." While epistēmē stands for śkl in Neh 8:8, the usual LXX translation is synesis "knowledge." Cf. Sir 8:9.

[12]Reading with Di Lella's ("Leaves of Sirach," p. 166) reconstruction [ʿṣmyw] ydšn. Gr is equivalent with the gnomic fut. kai ta osta autou pianei.

[13]Gr gynē sigēra. Syr reads ʾnttʾ ṭbtʾ "a good wife." Heb is not extant for this verse.

[14]Gr dosis kyriou (= Syr). For a discussion of the text of vv. 14-15, see below.

[15]Reading with Smend's (Jesus Sirach, p. 237) emendation mysrt grwn. Cf. Syr lbṣyrwt ggrtʾ lit. "a lacking of throat." Gr reads pepaideumenēs psychēs "a disciplined soul."

[16]HebC as restored by Di Lella ("Leaves of Sirach," p. 166) ḥn ʿl ḥ[n] ʾšh byyšt (= Gr, Syr). See also n. 76.

[17]Reading with Gr kai ouk estin stathmos pas axios. Cf. HebC wʾyn mšql "and impossible to weigh (i.e., value)" (= Syr). As Smend (Jesus Sirach, p. 237) suggests, axios may be an addition.

[18]Reading with Gr egkratous psychēs. Cf. HebC lṣrwrt ph "a sealed mouth"; Syr lbṣyrwt pwmʾ lit. "a lacking of mouth."

[19]Reading with Gr hēlios antellōn en hypsistois kyriou with the comparative particle understood. Cf. ʾyk "as" in Syr. HebC is equivalent except for mʿl "above" instead of kyriou "of the Lord." Cf. Syr brqyʿʾ dsmyʾ "in the firmament of heaven."

[20]Reading with HebC as reconstructed by Di Lella ("Leaves of Sirach," p. 166) ypy ʾ[šh] with the comparative particle understood. Cf. Syr hknʾ "so." Gr shifts the emphasis slightly from the woman, the parallel to the sun, to beauty in the free rendering kai kallos agathēs gynaikos "and the beauty of a good wife" (= Syr except for hknʾ, noted above). The normal Heb word order would have been ʾšh yph. Cf. Deut 21:11; 2 Sam 14:27; Prov 11:22. However, this adj. sometimes precedes the noun. Cf. 1 Sam 16:12; Ps 48:3; Jer 11:16; Ezek 31:3; 33:32.

[21]Reading with Gr en kosmō oikias autēs. HebC is corrupt with bdbyd bḥwr "in the chosen shrine" or "in the shrine of a

young man." Syr is free with bmwtb byth "when she abides in her house." GrB reads autou "his" (= La), which is a secondary correction to indicate the actual owner of the home. See also n. 86.

[22]HebC nr śrp `l mnwrt qdš (= Gr, Syr). Syr has the comparative particle 'yk.

[23]Reading with Gr kai kallos prosōpou with the comparative particle understood. The word kallos is reflected in Syr šwprh d'ntt' "beauty of a woman" and the word prosōpou may be compared to HebC hwd pnym "splendor of a face." The term hwd is unlikely, in that it is never translated with kallos in the LXX. The usual translation is doxa. Furthermore, hwd is never used for a woman in the OT. The more likely Heb reading is ypy "beauty." Of its nineteen occurrences in the OT, fourteen are rendered by kallos in the LXX. Seven of these refer either lit. or figuratively to a woman. See Esth 1:1; Ps 45:11 (44:12); Prov 6:25; 31:30; Ezek 16:14, 15, 25. Cf. Sir 8:9.

[24]HebC `l qwmt twkn lit. "on the height of measurement" (= Gr). Syr reads bmqm byth "in keeping her house." Cf. v. 16b.

[25]Gr styloi chryseoi epi baseōs argyras with the comparative particle understood. Cf. Syr 'yk. Syr reverses the order of the objs. and the metals of which they are composed: 'yk ḥwmr' ddhb' `l 'sṭwn' ds'm' "as bases of gold upon a silver pillar." Heb is not extant for this verse.

[26]Gr kai podes hōraioi with the comparative particle understood. Cf. Syr y'yn `qbth "are her beautiful heels." I am taking podes lit. "feet" as "legs," or at least "feet with the legs." See LSJ. Heb was likely rglym "feet," for which KB lists ten instances where the meaning is "legs." The clearest examples where also the LXX employs a form of pous are: 2 Sam 9:13; Isa 7:20. For the image of columns (styloi) = legs (here knēmai) and the mention of bases (here baseis chrysas "golden bases," which probably influenced the Syr reversal in v. 18a), see Cant 5:15.

[27]Reading Gr as pternais eustathmois. The context supports some form of pternē. Cf. La plantas "sole of the foot." Edersheim's (p. 138) contention that the reading pternais "not only destroys the parallelism, but does not yield any good, scarcely an intelligible, meaning" is without foundation. The regular dat. plur. is, of course, pternais. Cf. Smend, Jesus Sirach, p. 238. Reading the adj. eustathmois best explains the existence of the other readings. Lit. it means "accurately measured" (LSJ) but may also be an unusual form of the adj. eustathēs "well built." See Ryssel, p. 365. Accordingly, I would suggest the following textual development. The reading pternais (attested to some extent by Gr613 pternēs)

eustathmois (GrS) first gave rise to pternois (GrS, 358, 545; Ziegler) eustathmois through the influence of the adj. form. Then pternois gave way to sternois (some form in the rest) through similar construction. Next eustathmois was changed to the more usual and expected eustathesi (Gr248-705, 46). Finally, eustathesi took the substantive form of the gen. sing. eustathous "(breasts) of a stable (woman)" (some form in the rest). This accounts for the TR reading sternois eustathous. Syr reads bmtqn byth "in the ordering of her house," which like v. 17b is dependent on v. 16b. For a consideration of Smend's suggested reconstruction of the Heb for v. 18b, see n. 94.

[28]Gottesfurcht bei Jesus Sirach, Analecta Biblica, no. 30 (Rome: E. Pontificio Instituto Biblico, 1967), pp. 170-72.

[29]Haspecker (pp. 19, 171) considers 26:19-27 (less v. 26cd, which restates 26:1) to be geniune. For a discussion of the status of this section, see below.

[30]He suggests a similar role for Gottesfurcht in the domestic passage, 3:1-16, and in the social passage, 6:16-17.

[31]For a rejection of the view that this element is the conclusion, see the discussion of 25:1.

[32]This is only one of three elements, 25:1d.

[33]25:8a. See the discussion of 25:8a for a consideration of v. 8b, a stich which is extant only in Heb and Syr.

[34]The present structure is given in Gr and Syr and is confirmed to some extent by HebC, where 26:2 follows 25:24 (25:25-26:1 is missing).

[35]Evil wife (fifteen distichs), good wife (four distichs), evil wife (six distichs), evil daughter (four distichs), and good wife (six distichs).

[36]Note HebC, which, though a MS of selections rather than a complete text, has this order. This order provides the best arrangement of material about the wife in relation to her husband and otherwise.

[37]25:12 is from GrII. For a summary of recent work on GrII, see Kearns, pp. 543-47.

[38]I would postulate a two stage disarrangement. Stage one: material was inserted between 25:11 and 26:1 in order to insulate the latter from the Zahlenspruch, to which it was only loosely related as an expansion of one of its ten elements. The inserted material, 25:13-26, was selected because it begins with what sounds like an introductory statement. Stage two: due to dissatisfaction with 26:12, the obscene ending to the whole

section on women, a scribe/editor created a new ending by relocating 26:13-18 at the end. The break would better have come between vv. 15 and 16. Nevertheless, this finished the section on a positive note.

[39]See 26:12; 16-18.

[40]P. 69.

[41]This is an opinion shared by Ryssel (p. 365), Peters (Jesus Sirach, pp. 217-18), Eberharter (p. 96), and Schilling (pp. 115-16).

[42]He suggests that the ten distichs (v. 26cd omitted) contain five distichs that give direct advice to a man about marriage and five distichs that contrast the good wife with the evil wife.

[43]Haspecker, p. 69.

[44]Ibid.

[45]Some important GrII witnesses do not contain the section (GrV and the Originistic recension).

[46]It is also cited by John of Damascus and Antonius Melissa.

[47]See Kearns, pp. 544-46.

[48]The distichs have positive and negative material as follows ("+" means positive and "-" means negative): v. 19 --, v. 20 ++, v. 21 ++, v. 22 --, v. 23 -+, v. 24 -+, v. 25 -+, v. 26 +-(++), v. 27 ----.

[49]P. 404.

[50]There are, e.g., only about twenty-five antithetical parallels in Sir 1-13, with no more than two in adjacent verses.

[51]If one includes v. 26cd.

[52]Northwest Semitic Philology and the Hebrew Fragments of Ben Sira, Biblica et orientalia, no. 28 (Rome: Biblical Institute Press, 1975), p. 47. For other examples, see also 26:3a, 15a; 3:26; 13:1; 44:7.

[53]Hamp, p. 638.

[54]I am reading this verse with Gr. See nn. 3-5. However, it is clear that gynē andreia = HebC ʾšt ḥyl. This phrase is from Prov 12:4, where LXX = Sir 26:2. Cf. Prov 31:10; Ruth 3:11.

[55] It is clear that Gr is here rendering the word *tśmḥ*, which HebC has misplaced in v. 2b. See Pss 45:8; 46:4; 90:15; 92:4; 104:15; Prov 10:1; 12:25; 15:20; 27:11; Jer 20:15; Hos 7:3. See also n. 5.

[56] For the *casus pendens* form, see the discussion of v. 1.

[57] Gr renders both *mnh* and *ḥlq* with *meris* "portion," in accordance with the usual LXX practice. See, e.g., 1 Sam 1:4, 5; 9:23; 2 Chr 31:19; Neh 8:10, 12; Esth 9:19, 22; Pss 16:5; 73:26; 119:57; 142:5; Eccl 2:10, 21; 3:22; 5:18-19; 9:6, 9; 11:2; Jer 13:25; Sir 41:21.

[58] For the relationship between a happy heart and a cheerful face, see 13:26a.

[59] P. 170.

[60] See above.

[61] The *Gottesfurcht* concept is particularly featured in wisdom literature and related genres, e.g., Deuteronomy, Job, Psalms, Proverbs, and Ecclesiastes. However, it is not limited to these. It is also established in the prophets, especially Isaiah.

[62] The observation by Snaith (*Ecclesiasticus*, p. 131) that this text compares with 3:1-16 as a family theme related to *Gottesfurcht* is valueless. First, this concept occurs in a wide variety of contexts in Sirach, certainly not limited to family themes. Second and more importantly, the mention of *Gottesfurcht* in 3:1-16 is secondary, since it is part of GrII. See the discussion of 3:1-16.

[63] P. 52.

[64] P. 94.

[65] P. 698.

[66] The Gr word *charis*, used here and generally in the LXX for *ḥn*, has a similar meaning.

[67] Hif. "make cheerful."

[68] For the former, see Ezra 8:18; Prov 12:8; 13:15. For the latter, see 2 Chr 2:11; 30:22.

[69] This metaphor is also found in Prov 15:30 MT.

[70] Cf. Box-Oesterley, p. 404; Eberharter, p. 96. It is interesting to note that the only OT use of *śkl* in relation to a woman is 1 Sam 25:3. There Abigail is said to be a woman of

good sense (ṭwbt śkl) and good looks (ypt t'r). She demonstrates her śkl by providing food for David and his men (25:18-22). Subsequently, she became David's wife (25:39-42). It is possible that this incident has influenced Ben Sira in our text. At least both share the elements of a wife who is śkl and who provides for the health of her husband or of one who was to become her husband.

71The usual pattern finds both lines of a distich reflecting related material. Cf. vv. 3, 4, 13, 16, 17, 18. Where an item is repeated or parallelled in a different distich, it is done so on the basis of line a of one distich being parallelled by line a of another distich and similarly for corresponding lines b. Cf. vv. 1-2. Furthermore, in the example cited both stichs of each distich are related so that in effect the distichs themselves are parallel to each other. The Syr of vv. 14-15 comes closest to this pattern, except that lines a and b of each distich are not easily related, especially in v. 15. The Gr repeats the element of v. 14b in v. 15b. Neither Syr nor Gr can be readily justified according to Ben Sira's style.

72Jesus Sirach, p. 237.

73The present textual condition of the extant witnesses probably resulted from a complex corruption. As Smend (Jesus Sirach, p. 237) has suggested, the Gr of v. 14b was no doubt influenced by v. 15b. It is unlikely, however, that mysrt was present in the Heb in both places. Its use in v. 14b may safely be granted, since some form of ysr is the usual Heb behind the LXX paideuō. This is true for Sirach also. Cf. 7:23; 10:1 (ywsd by mistake for ywsr); 30:13; 40:29 (HebBmg). However, mysrt would not be expected behind egkratous in v. 15b. While egkratēs does not occur in the LXX outside the Apoc., the verb forms egkrateō and egkrateuomai do. The usual word behind these is 'pq (only in hitp.) "to control oneself." Thus, it is reasonable to expect that in v. 15b the Heb read mt'pqt. In reverse, the Syr of v. 15b was probably independently influenced by v. 14b. Cf. Syr v. 14b lbṣyrwt ggrt' and v. 15b lbṣyrwt pwm'. Thus, the Gr moved a "modesty" element into the "silence" distich, while the Syr moved a "silence" element into the "modesty" distich. HebC completed the process by following Syr for v. 15.

74Smend (Jesus Sirach, p. 237) has conjectured the reading grwn "throat" here. The word, however, means "voice" in Pss 5:10; 69:4; 115:7; 149:6; Isa 58:1. This was probably the word used here by Ben Sira (cf. Syr grt' "throat") but with the meaning "voice."

75Cf. v. 3, where the good wife as a gift was introduced. Here the general statement of v. 3 is made specific in terms of her trait of silence.

[76]HebC reads *byyšt*, which occurs nowhere else. Di Lella ("Leaves of Sirach," p. 167) concludes that it means "modest." M. H. Segal ("'Dappîm nôs^{e}pîm mittôk sēper ben-Sîrā'' [H. Sirman . . .]," *Tarbiz* 29 [1959-1960]:322) conjectures the reading *bwšh* "shame." Gr reads *aischyntēra* "bashful, modest." This word also occurs in 32(35):10; 42:1, where in both instances HebB reads *bwš*. The gender for both is masc. However, in 42:1 HebM reads *bwyš*. For the form, see John Strugnell, "Notes and Queries on 'The Ben Sira Scroll from Masada,'" in *W. F. Albright Volume*, ed. A. Malamat, *Eretz-Israel*, vol. 9 (Jerusalem: Israel Exploration Society, 1969), p. 114. It appears certain that some form of *bwš* occurred in 26:15a behind the Gr *aischyntēra*. The reading which I have proposed, *bwyšt*, could be considered a fem. equivalent to *bwyš* in 42:1 (HebM). HebC *byyšt* could have easily have resulted from *bwyšt*.

[77]For *ḥn/charis*, see the discussion of v. 13. The phrase here is *ḥn `l ḥn/charis epi chariti*. The idea is clearly superlative, suggesting the highest kind of charm. Cf. Edersheim, p. 138; Smend, *Jesus Sirach*, p. 237; Peters, *Jesus Sirach*, p. 217.

[78]See n. 80 for a discussion of the question of sources behind this text.

[79]Note that Gr248 understood *aischyntēra* "modest" in terms of faithfulness by following it with the epexegetic expresion *kai pistē* "and faithful."

[80]We may compare vv. 14b and 15b to 6:15, where the subj. is a faithful friend. Both 6:15a and 26:14b contain the phrase *ouk estin entallagma* "there is no exchange for" or "priceless." Both 6:15b and 26:15b contain the phrase *ouk estin stathmos* "there is no weight (on a balance)" or "there is no price." The conjunction of these phrases in the single distich, 6:15, suggests that 26:14b, 15b originally formed one distich of traditional material taken over by Ben Sira. In that setting it would have been a simple, general statement. But when separated and attached to specific statements about women, they take on a meaning for Ben Sira that is related to the stichs that immediately precede them. We may further compare how Ben Sira uses these phrases for the friend and the wife. In 6:15 (cf. 6:14-17) the faithful friend is priceless to a person, but his excellence is his own. He is faithful in a purely voluntary way. However, the wife in 26:15 is valued as a piece of desirable property when she does not attempt to attract the lusts of men other than her husband. Such attraction would threaten his property rights over her. Fuss (p. 164) considers vv. 13, 15 to be Ben Sira's composition and v. 14 to be traditional.

[81]The form of these distichs is clearly that of the simile or, as Ryssel (p. 365) puts it, *emblematischen Spruchs*.

However, the comparative particles "like" and "so" are not present in HebC or Gr. The La has them only in v. 16. Syr also includes them in v. 16 but has only ʹyk "like" in vv. 17a, 18a. The original probably did not have the particles, but the simile form is implicit.

[82]Fuss (p. 164) takes v. 16 to be traditional and vv. 17-18 to be Ben Sira's composition.

[83]See n. 21 for a statement on the reading "his" in some witnesses. Edersheim (p. 138) is typical of those who prefer this reading: "The comparison is between the sun in the heights, or high places, of his lord, and woman in the house of her lord."

[84]As Smend (Jesus Sirach, p. 237) guessed, the reading here is zwrḥt "rising, shining forth." HebC appears to confirm this reading with [zwr]ḥt. However, Smend is not right in declaring that at this point the Gr misunderstood this word by rendering it with anatellōn. In each of the twelve OT uses of zrḥ with reference to the sun, the LXX translates with a form of anatellō. In fact, fifteen of the eighteen occurrences of zrḥ are rendered with anatellō by the LXX. Thus, its use here is regular and expected. In 42:16, however, where the Heb uses a form of this word, the LXX translates freely with phōtizōn.

[85]P. 138. For the comparison of the wife in her family to the sun in the sky, see Eberharter, p. 96; Spicq, p. 700.

[86]HebC here appears to be corrupt with bdbyr bḥwr "in the chosen shrine" or "in the shrine of a young man." The former is not very sensible in this context. The latter is unlikely, because bḥwr "young man" is never used of a married man, as this setting would require. According to Gr and Syr the last word should be byth "her home." The first word is more difficult to reconstruct. Gr reads en kosmō "in the order, arrangement" or "in the ornament." Syr reads bmwtb "when she abides." The latter appears to be a free interpretation. Gottfried Kuhn ("Beiträge zur Erklärung des Buches Jesus Sira, II," ZAW 48 [1930]:106) holds that the Gr is here translating what it takes to be bhdr "in the splendor." He proposes that the original read bḥdr "in the room" and thus gave rise to the Gr misunderstanding. The problem with this emendation is that nowhere does the LXX translate hdr or ḥdr with kosmos. So the translation kosmō here cannot have resulted from the confusion that Kuhn postulates. Ryssel (p. 365) has suggested the reading bsdr "in the order." This word, while absent from the OT, is at least used by Ben Sira in 10:1 (HebA) and 50:14 (HebD). The latter has a form of kosmeō in Gr. However, the word is postbiblical and probably secondary in these examples. Furthermore, this reading would not explain the existence of the HebC reading as well as what follows. Smend (Jesus Sirach, p. 237) suggests the reading btkwnt "arrangement" (from kwn). This word occurs in

Nah 2:10 and is rendered by the LXX as tou kosmou autēs. The word tkn pi. "to adjust, meet out" from a related root is found in Sir 42:21 and is translated in Gr by ekosmēsen. The most likely reading appears to be btkwnt. However, it was probably written defectively btknt. Thus, I take the reading here to have been btknt byth, which Gr faithfully translated and Syr freely translated. HebC represents it through a material corruption.

87We may note that kosmos also has the meaning "ornament" and is often so used of women. See LSJ.

88See Hamp, p. 640.

89See n. 82 for a statement on the sources for this section.

90The designation of the lampstand as mnwrh qdš (Gr lychnia hagia) "holy lampstand" would require the understanding of this as the lampstand in the temple Holy Place, despite the fact that such a phrase does not occur in the OT.

91HebC reads qwnt twkn lit. "stature of measurement, quantity." Hence, Gr reads hēlikia stasimē. Smend (Jesus Sirach, p. 238) was right in suggesting qwnt behind hēlikia but anticipated that nkwnh lay behind stasimē. While hēlikia can mean "age" (cf. Matt 6:27) as Edersheim (p. 138) maintains here, in this case it clearly means "stature" (cf. Luke 19:3), as the context and the Heb suggest. See also Peters, Jesus Sirach, p. 217.

92See Spicq, p. 700.

93The reference is certainly not to Jachin and Boaz, the free-standing bronze pillars in Solomon's temple (1 Kgs 7:15; 2 Kgs 25:13; Jer 52:17). The juxtaposition of this image with v. 17 suggests, but does not require, that these pillars were temple pillars. While we have no description of the columns of the Zerubbabel temple, 1 Mac 1:22, 23 attests the presence of gold and silver. It is possible, of course, that Sir 26:18a may be simply a piece of material from a nontemple context, edited by Ben Sira into this temple setting. See, e.g., Cant 5:10-16, especially v. 15. If this is the case, then the mention of gold and silver should be understood as a kind of hendiadys expression for high value and not a reflection of disparate values. Even if the latter were intended, the relative values for Ben Sira (or his source) could not now be determined. He is comfortable with either the order silver and gold (28:24; 29:10, 11; 51:28), reflecting the pre-Persian higher value of silver, or the order gold and silver (40:25; 47:18).

94Smend (Jesus Sirach, p. 238) holds that the reference is not to legs and heels but to feet and the floor of a house.

He conjectures for v. 18b the reading `qbwt in the sense of "place" or "floor" and suggests that eustathmois = mkwnth "her residence." The term podes = `qbyt "her heels" with the resultant word play. This emendation is untenable because (1) `qb, while translated topos "place" in 16:3 GrB (the rest have plēthos "multitude"), nowhere means "floor," (2) the context suggests that both items mentioned regarding the woman actually are parts of her body (cf. v. 17; v. 16, where such is not the case, is the general introduction to the section on beauty and is not tied to v. 18 as strongly as is v. 17), (3) eustathmos is never used to translate mkwnth (cf. 41:1; 44:6), and (4) the result would be a bad comparison--pillars with feet and bases with floor.

95 It is not necessary to see here a reference to the genitals, as is sometimes the case with the Heb circumlocution "feet." For the latter, see IDB, s.v. "Sex, Sexual Behavior," by Otto J. Baab.

96 Gaspar, p. 53.

97 Ibid.

98 HebB as reconstructed by Smend [k]l [z]kr (= Gr). Syr omits this verse, possibly due to the confusion evident in Heb, which places it after v. 18.

99 HebB as reconstructed by Smend tqbl ′[šh] (= Gr).

100 Reading with HebB as reconstructed by Smend ′k [yš ′šh m′šh] lit. "yet there is a woman more (pleasant) than a woman." Gr exhibits the same construction but uses thygatēr "daughter."

101 Reading with HebB as reconstructed by Smend [tn`]m. Cf. Gr kreissōn "better."

102 HebB has a var. beneath the line: ′k yš ′šh yph "yet there is a beautiful woman."

103 HebBC tw′r ′šh (= Gr, Syr).

104 Reading with Smend′s emendation yhlyl. Cf. Gr hilarynei "gladden"; Syr nšbḥ "glorifies." HebB is untenable with whlyl from the root yll "to howl." HebBmg restored the proper root with yhll but gave the pi. rather than the hif. Di Lella ("Leaves of Sirach," p. 166) restores HebC as [y′yr] "illuminates."

105 HebBC pnym (= Gr). Syr reads ′pyh "her face" (= John of Damascus). Gr307 adds andros "of (her) husband" (= Cos, La). Before pnym HebC reads mkl "above all."

[106]HebBC *w`l kl mḥmd `yn ygbr* (= Syr). Cf. 45:12; Ezek 24:16, 21. Gr is equivalent except for *epithymian anthrōpou* "human desire."

[107]Reading with HebBmgC *yš bh* lit. "there is in her." HebB reads *yš* only. Syr is not extant for this verse.

[108]HebBC *mrp´ lšwn*. Middendorp (pp. 43, 80) conjectures the Heb for this line as *´m blšwnh ḥsd w`nwh* "if on her tongue is kindness and humility" (= Gr). He considers HebB to be secondarily influenced by Prov 15:4. However, the Lucianic recension, by reading *kai iasis* "and healing" after "kindness and humility," may reflect the Heb *mrp´*, which may mean "healing." See Smend, *Jesus Sirach*, p. 325.

[109]HebB *´šh*, i.e., *´iššâ* (= HebC *´îšâ*, Gr).

[110]HebBC *mbny ´dm* lit. "like the sons of men" (= Gr).

[111]Reading with HebBmg *qwnh*, which is probably also reflected by HebD *q[ ]h* (= Gr). HebB and HebC as restored by Di Lella ("Leaves of Sirach," p. 166) read *qnh*, which is usually taken to be imper. See, e.g., Box-Oesterley, p. 443. Cf. Syr *qny*. See also Prov 4:7. However, *qnh* may also be understood as the part. defectively written. See KB. HebBmg probably read HebB *qnh* as imper., however, and noted the part. instead.

[112]HebBC *´šh* (= Gr). Syr reads *´ntt´ ṭbt´* "a good wife." In the Heb the verb is understood. Gr reads *enarchetai* "enters upon" (lit. "begins"). This may be due to a misunderstanding of the Heb *r´šyt*, which may mean "beginning" as well as "best."

[113]HebBC *r´šyt qnyn*. Cf. Syr *bryš qnynk* "at the head of your possession." Gr reads *ktēseōs* "possession."

[114]Reading with Smend's emendation *`zr kngdw* (= Gr, Syr). Cf. Gen 2:18, 20. Peters (*Jesus Sirach*, p. 299) prefers HebB *`zr wmbṣr* "a helper and a fortress." However, this appears to be a secondary substitution, which gave rise to the reading of HebBmgCD *`ry mbṣr* "a fortified city." Cf. Jer 1:18. This reading is supported by Middendorp (pp. 43, 69).

[115]HebBD *w`mwd mš`n*. Cf. HebC *mš`n h`myd*. Gr reads *stylon anapauseōs* "a pillar over against you."

[116]HebBCD *b´yn gdyr* (= HebCD *gdr*) *ybw`r krm* (= Syr). Gr is equivalent except for *ktēma* "property" instead of "vineyard."

[117]HebBCD *wb´yn ´šh n` wnd* (= Syr). Cf. Gr *kai hou ouk estin gynē, stenaxei planōmenos* "and where there is no wife, one sighs (gnomic fut.) and wanders."

[118]HebBD *my* *y'myn* *bgdwd* *ṣb'* (= HebC *bṣb'* *gdwd*). Cf. 1 Chr 7:4. This refers to a troop of soldiers, probably Greek units, which moved through the country, plundering as they went. Gr *euzōnō* *lēstē* "an active (lit. well girded) robber" is less likely, since the individual robber would not usually go from city to city. See Smend, *Jesus Sirach*, p. 326. For this expression Syr reads *lgdwd'* *ddm'* *lṭby'* "the youth like a gazelle."

[119]HebBCD *hmdlg* *m`yr* *'l* *`yr* (= Gr, Syr).

[120]HebB *kn* *'yš* *'šr* *l'* *qn* (= HebC *'yn* *lw* *qyn*, HebD *'yn* *lw* *qn*, Gr). Syr is equivalent except for *'ntt'* "wife" instead of "nest."

[121]HebBCD *hmrgy'* (= Gr). Syr reads *nmwt* "dies," an obvious mistake for *nbwt*, which = Heb.

[122]HebBD *b'šr* *y`rb* lit. "where evening occurs." Cf. Gr *hou* *ean* *opsisē* "wherever he happens to be late (at night)." Syr reads *b'tr* *dnštkḥ* "wherever he is found." HebC is corrupt with *k'šr* *ysbyb*.

[123]"Every . . ." / "But there is . . . ." Fuss (p. 213) considers these distichs (36:18, 21; 37:1, 7) to be traditional sentences, on which Ben Sira builds his discussion of their general content.

[124]*Jesus Sirach*, p. 323. Cf. Spicq, p. 748.

[125]This is the way Spicq (p. 748) summarizes the idea.

[126]Cf. Ryssel, p. 410.

[127]See 25:13-26; 26:5-12.

[128]See n. 123.

[129]36:18 *kl* *'wkl* . . . , / *'k* *yš* *'wkl* . . . .
36:21 *kl* *zkr* . . . , / *'k* *yš* *'šh* . . . .
37:1 *kl* *'whb* . . . , / *'k* *yš* *'whb* . . . .
37:7 *kl* *yw`ṣ* . . . , / *'k* *yš* *yw`ṣ* . . . .

[130]Smend (*Jesus Sirach*, p. 324) noticed that the form of v. 18, where the object of the sentence in v. 18a is treated in line *b*, is changed in v. 21. Here the subj. of line *a* is treated in line *b*.

[131]See the discussion of v. 24.

[132]Spicq, pp. 748-49. Cf. Ryssel, p. 410; Schilling, p. 151; Snaith, *Ecclesiasticus*, p. 177.

[133]The word is written defectively in MT and means "form, stately appearance." Its only OT use with regard to women is in Gen 29:17, where the context is purely neutral.

[134]Cf. 11:2, where the setting is negative, but the reference is to a man.

[135]In this negative sense cf. Prov 6:25; 31:30; Ezek 16:15, 25.

[136]In the OT yph is used mostly in a neutral sense. However, see Prov 11:22 for a negative use.

[137]Cf. 26:13.

[138]In the context of v. 23 the referenece is certainly to the husband's countenance. See n. 105 for the textual evidence. Cf. Ryssel, p. 410; Spicq, p. 749.

[139]P. 214.

[140]The point is not whether women were in fact subordinate to men in the society of the author of this statement but only that such subordination is not implied in the statement itself.

[141]P. 214.

[142]See Eberharter, pp. 122-23; Spicq, p. 749; Hamp, p. 666; Snaith, Ecclesiasticus, p. 177.

[143]Heb lit. "not from among the sons of men" ('yn . . . mbny 'dm).

[144]In the OT the verb is used twenty-seven times with reference to land. Note also its use with men (Gen 47:19), house (Lev 25:30), potter's flask (Jer 19:1), and ox (Isa 1:3). The part. means "a buyer," e.g., Deut 28:68; Isa 24:2. Note also the redeeming of slaves (Neh 5:8). Cf. Sir 37:11. Apart from these literal transactions, qnh is used metaphorically to refer to the acquistion of various spiritual and intellectual qualities and in settings where God is the subj. It may also mean "to obtain." Most of Ben Sira's uses fall into these metaphorical categories: friend (6:7), enemy (20:23), wisdom/understanding (51:20, 21, 25), silver/gold (51:28). Gaspar (pp. 6-7) denies that qnh here means "to get" in the sense of "to purchase." While admitting this to be the word's usual meaning, he points to its use in Proverbs with reference to wisdom and knowledge (1:5; 4:5, 7; 15:32; 16:16; 17:16; 18:15; 19:8; 23:23) as a precedent for its meaning "to acquire," without the element of purchase. However, these examples are all intangible qualities and related to qnh in a purely metaphorical way. When the word is used of tangible items the element of purchase is

clearly implied. We may further note that in Proverbs wisdom is personified as a wife, as one of the qnh references (4:1-9, the expression is found in vv. 5, 7) clearly indicates.

[145]The more frequent terms are ntn l'šh "to give to wife" and lqh l'šh "to take to wife."

[146]See Gen 31:18; 34:23; 36:6; Josh 14:4; Ezek 38:12-13. Note also Lev 22:11 (slave); Pss 104:24 (God's creatures); 105:21 (king's possessions); Prov 4:7 (wisdom).

[147]See, e.g., Exod 20:17; Jer 6:12.

[148]E.g., the transaction between Jacob and Laben (Gen 29:16-20).

[149]E.g., the transaction between Hamor (for Schechem) and Jacob (Gen 34:4-12).

[150]The noun mhr occurs in Gen 34:12; Exod 22:17(16); 1 Sam 18:25. In each case the recipient of the mhr is the father of the bride. The mhr may consist of money (Exod 22:16-17), a nonmonitory gift (1 Sam 18:25-27), service (Gen 29:16-20), or a special act (Josh 15:16-17; 1 Sam 17:25). For the verb, see Exod 22:16(15) and Ps 16:4. The latter is uncertain and, even if retained, is metaphorical.

[151]For a brief discussion, see IDB, s.v. "Marriage," by Otto J. Baab and IDB Sup, s.v. "Marriage," by Charles R. Taber

[152]For other types of marriage arrangements, see Baab, "Marriage."

[153]Elizabeth Mary MacDonald, The Position of Women As Reflected in Semitic Codes of Law, University of Toronto Studies: Oriental Series, no. 1 (Toronto: University of Toronto Press, 1931), pp. 7, 69; Johannes Pedersen, Israel, 4 vols. (London: Oxford University Press, 1926-40), 1:68; Roland de Vaux, Ancient Israel, trans. John McHugh (New York: McGraw-Hill Book Co., 1961), p. 27; Miller Burrows, The Basis of Israelite Marriage, American Oriental Series, no. 15 (New Haven, Connecticut: American Oriental Society, 1938), pp. 9-15; Baab, "Marriage." For the view that actual purchase was involved, see Henry Schaeffer, The Social Legislation of the Primitive Semites (New Haven, Connecticut: Yale University Press, 1915), p. 15-18; cf. Spicq, pp. 749-50.

[154]See MacDonald, p. 7; Pedersen, 1:68; de Vaux, p. 27; Baab, "Marriage."

[155]Note the use of mkr "to sell" in Gen 31:15.

156Baab ("Marriage") holds that the real basis of Hebrew marriage was not purchase but covenant. In this sense the mhr "seals the covenant between two families, establishes the prestige of the husband and his family and gives him authority, although not absolute control, over his wife." It is a "ratification of a covenant," where "a kind of purchase may be understood." He offers the testimony of Prov 2:17 and Mal 2:14. However, Prov 2:17 speaks of the "covenant of her God (bryt 'lhyh) in the general context of things the loose woman has abandoned. Mal 2:14 does refer to "your wife by covenant" ('št brytk), but the whole discussion about marriage and divorce in vv. 14-16 is figurative, as v. 11 clearly shows. It deals with the relatiohship of the Hebrews, especially their priests, to Yahweh. Furthermore, the idea of bryt is prominant in Malachi (2:4, 5, 8, 10, 14; 3:1) and refers to the divine-human relationship. These texts do not support the so-called covenant basis of Hebrew marriage in anything more than a remote way.

157See especially MacDonald, p. 69.

158As noted above, qnh is used for a wife only in Ruth 4:10, while qnyn is never used for a wife.

159r'šyt.

160As Snaith (Ecclesiasticus, p. 177) suggests, Ben Sira sees the mhr paid for a good wife as a good investment.

161`zr kngdw. The word `zr means a "helper" and is usually used of God. The term kngdw stands for "fitting, suiting him," i.e., his counterpart.

162Cf. 26:18, where a woman's beautiful legs are compared to the temple's golden pillars. The temple imagery is also present in 26:17.

163Cf. Tob 8:6, where Eve is called "a helper (boēthon as in Gen 2:18, 20 LXX; Sir 36:24) and support."

164See Middendorp, p. 60. He considers this to be an adaptation of rural references to urban life. Cf. Prov 24:30-31; Isa 5:5.

165I do not think it is legitimate to conclude, as does Ryssel (p. 411), that the fence of the property is the wife. Nor do I wish to exegete the meaning of the the fence with Spicq (p. 750) in terms of the wife's quality of thrift in managing the home.

166n` wnd. B. Yebam. 62b renders this freely: "Every man who has no wife, dwells without joy." See Cowley-Neubauer, p. xxvi.

[167]This comparison is tighter than that in v. 25 and may be Ben Sira's own creation for this purpose.

[168]See Smend, *Jesus Sirach*, p. 326; Snaith, *Ecclesiasticus*, p. 177; Middendorp, pp. 126, 168.

[169]The construction demands the repetition of the idea of the verb *y'myn* "to trust" in line *c* from line *a*.

[170]Cf. 15:26 Heb. Penar (p. 61) takes *qn* of HebB as a denominative qal from *qēn* "nest," giving the reading "who does not nest." The sense, of course, is the same as that of HebBmgCD and Smend, which I have followed.

[171]However, the Proverbs reference is to a man who strays from his home, while Ben Sira is describing a man who has no home.

[172]See Spicq, p. 750.

[173]The term *hmrgy'* "settles, rests" suggests the possibility of cohabitation.

[174]Cf. McKeating, p. 85.

[175]P. 151.

[176]While the wife of Prov 31 is described in relationship to her husband, she has an independent existence to at least a certain extent. See especially vv. 16-18, 20, 24, 26.

[177]HebA *'l tm's*. Gr *mē astochei* here has the sense of "do not depart from." See BAG[2]. This verb is used in the LXX only here and in 8:9, where in both cases the underlying Heb is *m's*. Syr reads *l' tḥlp* "do not exchange."

[178]HebA *'šh mśklt*, vocalized *maś-kelet*. If it is vocalized *m^ešakkelet*, it would be "barren, childless." However, the context suggests the former. Gr reads *gynaikos sophēs kai agathēs* "wise and good wife." This linking of *agathēs* with *sophēs* probably resulted from the translator's failure to understand the Heb phrase *wṭwbt ḥn* as a unit. He took *wṭwbt* to be part of a modifier of *'šh*, i.e., *'šh mśklt wṭwbt*. Syr reads *'ntt' ṭbt'* "a good wife."

[179]HebA *wṭwbt ḥn* with *'šh* understood from line *a* (= Syr). This phrase lit. means "(a wife) distinguished by grace" (KB). See Nah 3:4. Box-Oesterley (p. 34) understand the phrase to mean "well-favored." Gr reads *hē gar charis autēs* "for her charm."

[180]HebA mpnynym (= Syr). See 30:15 (cf. 31:6); Job 28:18; Prov 31:10. Gr hyper to chrysion "above gold" has probably been influenced by the mention of gold in v. 18b.

[181]Most begin with ʼl, the particle of immediate prohibition.

[182]Vv. 22-28 have certain formal characteristics of their own, which I will discuss below.

[183]The prohibition form dominates this section but is augmented by other forms as well. For a discussion of the formal characteristics of 7:1-36, see Haspecker, pp. 132-34.

[184]P. 35.

[185]In both these references the woman is actually Judah personified. The former (Isa 54:1-8) describes a barren, widowed, and temporarily forsaken and despised wife, who is to be fruitful and reunited with her husband (Yahweh). The latter mentions an unfaithful wife, who became despised by her "lovers."

[186]Cf. 8:9a "Do not reject the tradition of the aged." Here also the Heb is tmʼs and the Gr astochei (the only other use of astocheō in the LXX). The sense is clearly that of "disregard."

[187]For the silent wife, see 26:14. For the babbling and outspoken wife, see 25:20, 25. We have further confirmation that mśklt here implies the idea of restraint by noting the likely source of Ben Sira's phrase ʼšh mśklt. The expression is no doubt from Prov 19:14. In that setting the phrase implies a passive rather than an active characteristic. This is evident as we note that v. 13 speaks negatively of a "wife's quarreling." V. 14 then declares that an ʼšh mśklt "is from the Lord." Cf. Sir 25:8a; 26:14. Thus, she is "wise" in her restraint.

[188]See the discussion of 26:13 and 36:22.

[189]HebA ʼšh lk (= Gr, Syr). Gr adds kata psychēn "who pleases you" (RSV) or "(a) compatible (wife)." The translator may have added this to allow for the possibility of divorce when a wife did not meet this criterion. See Ryssel, p. 281; Smend, Jesus Sirach, pp. 70-71. Spicq (p. 608) gives the same function to kata psychēn but takes it to reflect the original and not an addition.

[190]HebA ʼl ttʽbh. Gr reads mē ekbalēs autēn "do not cast her our, divorce her." Syr reads lʼ tšbqyh "do not forsake her."

[191]For a discussion of the context, see above.

[192]Vv. 22-28.

[193]See Fuss, p. 71.

[194]Ben Sira appears to have edited this distich so that the second stich of the traditional distich actually now is v. 25b with v. 24b and v. 25a being Ben Sira's composition. For a fuller treatment, see the discussion of 7:24-25.

[195]See the discussion of 7:26b.

[196]See, e.g., Ryssel, p. 281; Smend, Jesus Sirach, pp. 70-71; Box-Oesterley, p. 341; Gaspar, p. 34; Spicq, p. 608; Snaith, Ecclesiasticus, p. 45.

[197]See n. 189.

[198]See above.

[199]Cf. 28:15, where ekballō implies divorce. However, there the Heb is not extant. This is also true for 25:26, but the Gr is a form of apotemnō "to cut off."

[200]He appears to have been similarly motivated in his redaction of vv. 24-25, which deal with daughters. See the discussion of these verses.

[201]HebA ʾl tqnʾ (= Gr, Syr).

[202]HebA ʾšt ḥyqk (= Gr). Syr reads bʾnttk "of your wife."

[203]The Heb is preferred for line b as closer to the formal pattern that characterizes five of the first six distichs of 9:1:-9. The form of HebA is ʾl . . . , / pn . . . . Gr (= Syr) reflects the coordinate pattern ʾl . . . , / wʾl . . . , which appears with some variations in the last five distichs.

[204]HebA tlmd (qal 3 fem.). Gr mistakes it for pi. 2 masc. and reads didaxēs "(nor) teach" (= Syr). The pattern of the traditional distichs represented by vv. 1, 3-6 (see below) favors the Heb over the Gr. In vv. 3-6 line b is always a negative motive clause that states an undesirable result to the reader who does not follow the advice of line a. Only the Heb of v. 1b fits this pattern. The Gr makes the suspected wife learn an evil lesson, which only indirectly reflects on the husband, the one addressed in line a. Thus, the Heb is to be preferred.

[205]HebA ʿlyk rʿh. Gr epi seauton paideian ponēran "an evil lesson against yourself" (Syr) is an expansion to make sense due to the way it reads tlmd. Alexander A. Di Lella (The Hebrew Text of Sirach, Studies in Classical Literature, no.

1 [The Hague: Mouton & Co., 1966], p. 146, n. 127) translates the Syr "a base scheme, plan."

[206]See Peters, Jesus Sirach, p. 81; Haspecker, p. 135.

[207]See above. Note that both 7:19 and 7:26a are part of the same section.

[208]P. 78.

[209]See n. 203.

[210]See chap. IV for the discussion of vv. 7-9.

[211]For the possibility that v. 2 contains a word play with v. 1, see the discussion of v. 2.

[212]For a recent discussion of this example, see William McKane, "Poison, Trial by Ordeal and the Cup of Wrath," VT 30 (1980):474-92. For a list of the relevant literature, see IDB Sup, s.v. "Ordeal, Judicial," by Tikva Simone Frymer. For parallels in other cultures, see Theador H. Gaster, Myth, Legend, and Custom in the Old Testament, 2 vols. (New York: Harper & Row, Pub., 1969), 1:280-300.

[213]"And her body shall swell, and her thigh shall fall away, and the woman shall become an execration among her people" (Num 5:27).

[214]For this term, see Deut 13:6 (7); 28:54; cf. 28:56.

[215]Cf. the similar expression ʾšt nʿwrym "wife of youth" in 15:2b. The full line reads: "And like the wife of youth she will receive him." This is part of the section, 14:20-15:10, which begins with a beatitude for the man who meditates on wisdom and describes the wise man's relationship to and benefits from wisdom. Wisdom is personified as a nurturing, supporting woman. In 15:2a she is compared to a mother and here to a young wife. The picture is that of a bride receiving her groom at the consummation of a marriage. For the expression "wife of youth," see Prov 5:18; Isa 54:6; Mal 2:14, 15; cf. Prov 2:17. The meaning of the term is the wife of one's first love, for whom he has increasing affection as life continues. Cf. Smend, Jesus Sirach, p. 139; Kearns, p. 553. The personification of Wisdom as a female figure is common in the wisdom tradition. See Prov 1:20-33; 3:13-20; 4:4-9; 7:4; 8:1-9:6; Sir 1:1-20; 4:11-19; 6:18-31; 14:20-15:10; 24:1-34; 51:13-22; Bar 3:9-4:4; Wis 6:12-25; 7:7-11:1. For language that implies Wisdom as a mother, see Prov 8:32; Sir 4:11; 15:2. For wife/lover language, see Prov 4:4-9; Sir 15:2; Wis 8:2, 9, 16.

[216]Box-Oesterley (p. 345) follows Edersheim (p. 67). Cf. Ryssel, p. 285; Eberharter, p. 42; Peters, Jesus Sirach, p. 81;

Spicq, p. 614. This is surprising for Box-Oesterley and Peters, since they actually read with the Heb here.

[217]See n. 204.

[218]Heb is not extant for 25:1. Thus, the translation is based on Gr, compared with Syr. However, for lines ab Gr appears to be corrupt:

> In three things I was beautiful (hōraisthēn),
> And I stood in beauty (hōraia) in the sight of the Lord and of men.

Instead of this, I have followed Ziegler's (Sirach, pp. 76-78, 242) conjectural emendation:

> en trisin ērasthē hē psychē mou,
> kai tauta estin hōraia enanti kyriou kai anthrōpōn.

This is based on Syr (cf. La), which reads:

> For three things my soul desires (ʼtrgrgt),
> And they are lovely (whnyn) in the sight of God and men.

For the recognition that Gr here is corrupt, see Smend, Jesus Sirach, p. 224; Peters, Jesus Sirach, p. 208; Box-Oesterley, p. 400. Spicq (p. 693), however, reads with Gr, considering a reading with Syr and La to be "easy" but "useless." He considers personified Wisdom of chap. 24 to be the speaker.

[219]Gr gynē kai anēr. These are transposed in GrV and the Lucianic and Origenistic recensions (= Syr, La, Cos, Eth).

[220]Gr heautois sympeheromenoi. Syr reads kd nhwwn šlmyn "if they are peaceful."

[221]For a fuller discussion of the context of 25:1, see the discussion of 26:1-4, 13-18.

[222]See Appendix 1 for a treatment of Zahlensprüche in general and their use by Ben Bira in particular.

[223]The mention of a wife in 25:1d (cf. v. 8a) is not a statement of the theme of 25:13-26:18. However, see Peters, Jesus Sirach, p. 207; Spicq, p. 693; Gaspar, p. 52; Haspecker, pp. 170-72. Nevertheless, 25:1d does give rise to Ben Sira's reflection on women in these verses. Also, the mention of an old man in 25:2d is related to the discussion of the aged in vv. 3-6.

[224]E.g., Edersheim, pp. 131-32; Peters, Jesus Sirach, p. 208; Gaspar, p. 52; Haspecker, pp. 170-72.

[225]P. 52.

[226]See Appendix 1.

[227]One may note that to Ben Sira the third elements of both vv. 1 and 2 serve to introduce longer discussions of their respective contents. But this does not make them climactic to either their author(s) or to Ben Sira.

[228]For the evidence, see n. 219.

[229]See, e.g., 7:26; 36:21.

[230]The part. _symperipheromenoi_ suggests a state where wife and husband maintain communication with each other and live in each other's society. Cf. Prov 5:19 LXX. Davidson (p. 404) suggests the translation "a woman and her husband that walk together in agreement." However, the translation by McKeating (p. 85) "man and his wife who are inseparable," is somewhat overstated. But to claim that this word reflects an intimacy and accord comparable to that of the trinity, as does Spicq (p. 694), is incredible.

[231]HebC [_'šry_] as restored by Smend (= Gr, Syr).

[232]HebC _b`l_. Syr with _lb`lh_ reads the Heb as _ba`al_ "husband." However, Gr reads the Heb as _bō`ēl_ "he who owns, rules, possesses" and translates it with _ho synoikōn_ "he who dwells with." In the LXX _synoikeō_ translates _b`l_ in Gen 20:3; Deut 24:1; Isa 62:5, where marriage is implied. Cf. _synoikizō_ for _b`l_ in Deut 21:13; 22:22; Isa 62:4. The Gr part. rendering is preferred (cf. Smend, _Jesus Sirach_, p. 226) since it best fits the pattern of the remaining elements of the _Zahlenspruch_. Only the first element (v. 7c) contains a noun as subj. of the expressed idea. The others use parts. or relative pronouns.

[233]Reading HebC according to Smend's reconstruction _'šh m[śklt]_ (= Gr). Syr reads _d'ntt' ṭbt'_ "of a good wife."

[234]The three _Zahlensprüche_ are 25:1; 25:2; 25:7-10, with v. 11 as a related editorial comment. For the role of these in the context, see the discussion of 25:1.

[235]For a full discussion of _Zahlensprüche_, including the question of climax, see Appendix 1.

[236]The Gr introductory formula itself calls for ten elements.

[237]Pp. 694-95.

[238]HebC _ḥwrš_. Smend (_Jesus Sirach_, p. 227) prefers _ḥrš_.

[239]Syr adds _'kḥd'_ "together." The line is defective at the end in HebC and may, as Smend (_Jesus Sirach_, p. 227) suggests, have followed Deut 22:10 with the equivalent expression _yḥdw_.

[240]E.g., Ryssel, p. 359; Smend, _Jesus Sirach_, p. 227; Peters, _Jesus Sirach_, p. 209; Box-Oesterley, p. 401; Snaith, _Ecclesiasticus_, p. 128. Haspecker (p. 107) holds that the stich would have seemed somewhat rustic to Ben Sira's grandson in his Hellenistic milieu and was thus deleted.

[241]For a similar interpretation of Deut 22:10, from which Sir 25:8b is taken, see Calum M. Carmichael, _The Laws of Deuteronomy_ (Ithaca, New York: Cornell University Press, 1974), pp. 159-62.

[242]See also Box-Oesterley, p. 401.

[243]Solomon Schechter, "A Further Fragment of Ben Sira," _JQR_ 12 (1900):464.

[244]Smend, _Jesus Sirach_, p. 227.

[245]Snaith, _Ecclesiasticus_, p. 128.

[246]We now have no idea what that element was, nor can we reconstruct it. As we have shown, it could not have been that which we now read in HebC and Syr. It is possible, of course, that it was not the fourth but some other element that fell from the archetype.

[247]Since we do not know what this element was, we cannot provide a reason for its deletion beyond that of simple scribal error.

[248]Middendorp (p. 41-42) prefers to read with Gr and wonders whether or not the original reading has been displaced by the OT quotation.

[249]See n. 232.

[250]See Deut 21:13; 24:1; Isa 62:5; Mal 2:11; 1 Chr 4:22. Cf. Gen 20:3; Deut 22:22; Isa 54:1, 5; 62:4; Sir 9:9.

[251]See the discussion of 36:24.

[252]For the phrase "a wise wife," see the discussion of 7:19.

[253]Gr _glōssa tritē_ (= Syr). Cf. v. 14a. Heb is not extant for this verse.

[254]Gr exebalen. Syr repeats v. 14a "the third tongue has taken many captive," which is a dittography due to the identically beginning lines.

[255]Gr gynaikes andreias.

[256]Gr esterēsen autas (= Syr).

[257]Gr ton ponon auton. Syr reads mn nksyhwn "of their wealth."

[258]For the OT words for divorce, see the discussion of 7:19 and 7:26a.

[259]7:19 does not contain ekballō; 7:26 does. However, in the latter the underlying Heb tʿb does not mean "to divorce" but "to abhor."

[260]E.g., Aristotle Politica 1277[b]; Poetica 1454[a].

[261]E.g., Lucian adversus Indoctum 3.

[262]See Ryssel, p. 374. Cf. Syr "wealth."

[263]If a husband divorced his wife he would probably forfeit the bride price, as stated in the Elephantine marriage deed, AP 15. See Arthur Ernest Cowley, Aramaic Papyri of the Fifth Century B.C. (Oxford: Clarendon Press, 1923), pp. 44-50. However, the situation at Elephantine may not reflect common Near Eastern practice, since, if divorced, the wife there could retain her property as well as receive the bride price, according to AP 14, AP 15, and BM 2. For the latter, see Emil G. Kraeling, The Brooklyn Museum Aramaic Papyri (New Haven, Connecticut: Yale University Press, 1953), pp. 53, 142-43.

[264]Both stichs begin with plēgē "a blow." Cf. the similar beginnings to stichs in vv. 19, 25.

[265]See the discussion of 25:26.

[266]For the discussion of the text of 40:18-20, see Appendix 2.

[267]HebB ʾšh nḥšqt. HebB follows with a reading in v. 20, which could be considered relevant to this discussion:

Wine and strong drink rejoice the heart,
But better than both is the love of friends.

The last phrase ʾhbt dwdym is rendered by Box-Oesterley (p. 463) "the affection of lovers." However, they also note that the above translation is tenable. Note Syr rḥmwth drhmʾ "the love of a friend." Cf. Spicq, p. 780; Beavin, p. 570. The word dwd is used extensively in Canticles for "beloved (one)." Elsewhere, it means "uncle," "cousin," and "love." The meaning "friend" is also possible. See the note to Isa 5:1 in JB. I prefer the meaning "friend" in this context, where the emphasis in the second stichs of these ten distichs is on very practical benefits. The love of friends, very close friends, is a tangible advantage that may have social and economic ramifications. The affection of lovers is but an emotional and sentimental phenomenon and out of place in this setting. Therefore, since I understand the phrase 'hbt dwdym to mean "the love of friends," there is no need to include v. 20 in this discussion of Ben Sira's view of women.

268 Reading with Box-Oesterley's (p. 464) reconstruction of the mutilated text of HebB ['whb wḥbr]. Cf. Gr philos kai hetairos and Syr rḥm' wḥbr'. Smend, however, reconstructs the phrase to read `[myt wr`], but the first `ayin is uncertain. With so little text extant any decision is arbitrary. The Box-Oesterley reading at least has the support of Gr and Syr.

269 HebB as reconstructed by Smend l[`t] ynhgw. Cf. Box-Oesterley, p. 464. Gr reads eis kairon apantōntes "meet at the right time." Syr reads b`dz' ntbrkwn "at the right time will receive greetings from one another."

270 HebB 'šh mśklt. Syr reads 'ntt' ṭbt' "a good wife." However, Gr gynē meta andros "a woman with (her) husband" would seem to be a free rendering, the complexity of which is uncharacteristic of the second stichs in these ten distichs.

271 Heb has ten distichs, while both Gr and Syr preserve only nine, though differing on the missing distich. See Appendix 2.

272 Line b in each distich begins with wmšnyhm.

273 Cf. Fuss, pp. 237-38.

274 The tenth distich proclaims the superiority of Gottesfurcht, the climax of the piece. Cf. Snaith, Ecclesiasticus, p. 200. Spicq (p. 780) reads with Gr and has only nine distichs but considers the last, dealing with Gottesfurcht, of such superiority that it in effect constitutes numbers nine and ten. Cf. his treatment of 25:7-11.

275 See Appendix 2.

276 This is the only occurrence of the nif. part. nḥšqt of the verb ḥšq "to be attached to, love" cited by KB. They suggest the meaning "devoted (wife)." Cf. Smend's (Jesus Sirach, p. 376-77) suggestion that the Gr amōmos "blameless" may have been a conjectural translation of nḥšqt meaning "faithful."

[277] See especially 36:24.

[278] See above.

[279] 7:26a; 9:1; 25:1; 25:8a; 28:15; 40:19, 23.

[280] 7:26a; 15:2; 25:1; 28:15; 40:23.

[281] 9:1; 25:8a; 40:19.

[282] An altered 7:26a is followed by a reconstructed 7:26b.

[283] 9:1 is softened by the addition of 9:2.

Chapter II

[1] Ben Sira frequently mentions father independently. See, e.g., 22:3, 5; 30:4; 34(31):20; 41:7; 42:9-10.

[2] His only other references to mother include the figurative application of the term in 15:2a and the expression "mother′s womb" in 40:1. See the discussions of these verses.

[3] The examples will all be considered in the discussion that follows.

[4] While the compound reference father/mother is well attested as a reference to parents, as we shall see, the plur. "fathers" is often used with the meaning "ancestors." Ben Sira reflects this in 8:9; 44:1; 47:23 Gr. See also Gen 15:15; 46:34; 1 Kgs 19:4; 21:3, 4; 2 Kgs 19:12; 20:17.

[5] My concern in this section is with vv. 2-4, 6, 9, 11, 16, since they alone mention mother. While my discussion will be limited largely to these verses, I have given them here, according to my own translation, within the context of the full section 3:1-16. The indented verses are from the RSV. Heb is not extant for vv. 1-6a and the first half of v. 6b.

[6] Gr edoxasen. Cf. Syr šbḥ "praised."

[7] Gr estereōsen (= Syr).

[8] Gr krisin (= Syr).

[9] Syr reads bny′ "sons" in line a and yldyh "her children" in line b. Gr is to be preferred as more difficult, wherein a mother has authority over her sons. Syr appears to be a softening of this. Furthermore, the juxtaposition of father and children in line a is a pattern already established in v. 1a.

[10] Gr ho timōn. Cf. Syr dmyqr "whoever esteems."

11Gr exilasketai (GrS*B exilasetai) hamartias. Syr reads mštbqyn ḥwbwhy "his sins are forgiven."

12Gr ho doxazōn. Syr reads dmyqr as in v. 3.

13Gr ho apothēsaurizōn (= Syr).

14Gr ho doxazōn. Syr reads dmyqr as in v. 3.

15Gr makroēmereusei (= Syr).

16Reading with Smend's emendation mnyḥ 'mw, which is supported also by Box-Oesterley (p. 324). Cf. Prov 29:17. Ryssel (p. 267) and Charles Cuttler Torrey (The Apocryphal Literature [New Haven, Connecticut: Yale University Press, 1946], p. 594) support the hif. imperf. ynyḥ. Smend (Jesus Sirach, p. 24) considers HebA mkbd "he who honors," which is supported by Peters (Jesus Sirach, p. 30) and Spicq (p. 577), to be secondary. It was probably influenced by Syr dmyqr l'mh "he who esteems his mother." Cf. vv. 3, 4, 6. One would expect mkbd to be the reading in vv. 3, 5a, where Gr reads ho timōn. Cf. v. 8. The usual word behind timaō in the LXX is some form of kbd. Here, however, Gr reads anapausei. The predominant LXX Vorlage behind anapauō is nwḥ. Cf. the use of anapausis for forms of nwḥ in Sir 6:28; 11:19; 30:17; 31(34):3, 4; 40:5. Thus, Smend's emendation seems to be justified. Other suggestions seem less likely. Kuhn (I, p. 290) suggests the reading mqyr "he who refreshes," lit. "he who keeps cool." He maintains that mqyr gave way to myqr "he who honors," lit. he who makes precious" (cf. Syr) and eventually to the synonym mkbd (HebA). Attractive as this may be from a material standpoint, it is unlikey, since the rare word qrr is never rendered by anapauō or any of its cognates. Di Lella (Hebrew Text, p. 41) offers the conjecture mnḥm "he who consoles." Cf. Jer 42(49):10, which is the only LXX example of anapauō translating nḥm (Gen 5:29 LXX has dianapausei). This rarity of relationship would speak against Di Lella's suggestion for our text.

17This reading is based on Syr rm' ḥwbl' ṭb' `l 'lh' "he lays up good rewards with God." Cf. Box-Oesterley, p. 324. Accordingly, Smend (Jesus Sirach, p. 24) reconstructs Heb as gml [`l] 'l. Peters (Jesus Sirach, p. 30) reads the last word as 'lhym. Both base their reconstructions on the relationship of the MT to Syr in Prov 11:17. As Smend notes, the Gr confused the subj. and pred. in a way that is uncharacteristic of the context and translated the expression with ho eisakouōn kyriou "he who obeys the Lord." For a discussion of v. 7, see below.

18The text for this verse differs widely in its major witnesses. While there is general agreement concerning the subj. in each stich, the Heb, Gr, and Syr record the pred. in the following different ways:

9a HebA . . . lays the foundation of a root (tysd šrš)
Gr . . . establishes the houses of his children (stērizei oikous teknōn)
Syr . . . shall establish his habitations (tqym mdyr')
9b HebA . . . uproots the plant (tntš nṭ`)
Gr . . . uproots the foundations (ekrizoi themelia)
Syr . . . roots up the root (t`qwr `qr')

The main problems for establishing the reading of this text are (1) the fact that the Gr terms are not used elsewhere to translate these Heb words with one exception, which we will subsequently note, and (2) the fact that ysd, which is usually associated with the laying of foundations, is never used with šrš "root." Adolph Büchler ("Ben Sira's Conception of Sin and Atonement," JQR, n.s. 13 [1922-23]:472) is among those who finds the juxtaposition of ysd with šrš to be impossible and the combination of tntš with nṭ` to be unnatural. Cf. Torrey (pp. 594-95), who holds that the Gr building figure was changed to planting in Heb. On the other hand, Louis F. Hartman ("Sirach in Hebrew and in Greek," CBQ 23 [1961]:449) concludes that Gr freely translated the Heb and thereby "moved the family from its Palestinian farm into an Alexandrian tenement house." Cf. Di Lella, Hebrew Text, pp. 41-42. Smend (Jesus Sirach, p. 25) and Box-Oesterley (p. 324) recognize the problems with the Heb but prefer to read with it. We may observe that, while ysd is predominantly used to convey the idea of foundation laying, it is also used metaphorically in 1 Chr 9:22 (the appointment of gatekeepers); Esth 1:8 (the orders given by a king); Ps 119:152 (the founding of Yahweh's testimonies). Though it may seem strange, it is possible that the verb could be used figuratively for establishing (or planting) a root. This is, after all, closer to the literal meaning of laying a foundation than the metaphorical uses just noted, since it also involves the ground as the place of founding. We may further note that šrš clearly conveys the notion of offspring, e.g., Isa 11:1; 14:29; Sir 47:22. Cf. Penar (p. 5), who finds this extended meaning also in Ugaritic, Phoenician, and Aramaic and sees in nṭ` the parallel to šrš, meaning "progeny." The difficulty of the expression tysd šrš would be evident to the LXX translators and would likely give rise to a clarification in Gr which would convey the same idea of offspring. Therefore, I prefer to read with HebA and to take Gr and Syr to be secondary. The Heb of v. 9b no doubt echoes the images of planting and uprooting which are common to Jeremiah. See 1:10; 24:6; 31:28; 42:10; 45:4. In each of these texts one finds tntš and the verb form of nṭ`. Note 1:10 in particular, where the LXX translates with ekrizoō, as in our text. Another influence on Ben Sira may have been Job 14:8, 9, where šrš and nṭ` are both used. The most likely textual history is as follows: Heb v. 9a gave rise to Gr v. 9a (by clarification), which gave rise to Syr v. 9a (a free rendering). Heb v. 9b was reproduced by Syr v. 9b, while Gr v. 9b retained the idea of the Heb verb but was internally 216 influenced by the building motif of v. 9a as well as by the foundation implication of ysd in Heb v. 9a.

[19]HebA wqllt 'm (= Gr, Syr)

[20]HebA kbwd (= Syr). Gr translates freely with ek timēs "(comes) from the honor." Cf. 45:12.

[21]Reading with Smend's emendation mqlh lit. "he who treats with contempt." This is followed by Box-Oesterley (p. 324). Cf. 10:29. HebA mqll "he who curses" is read by Peters (Jesus Sirach, p. 30) but is considered to be a mistake by Smend (Jesus Sirach, p. 25). Syr reads dmṣ`r "he who dishonors." Gr translates freely with mētēr en adoxia "a mother held in dishonor."

[22]Reading (w)mrbh ḥsd, after a suggestion by Smend (Jesus Sirach, p. 25). HebA reads (w)mrbh ḥṭ' "multiplies sin" (= Syr). The reading ḥṭ' is not in keeping with the honor/dishonor orientation of the two distich strophe (vv. 10-11). It is likely that the HebA reading, followed by Syr, arose when a scribe mistook ḥsd I "shame" for ḥsd II "loyalty" and, recognizing the obvious incongruity, changed it to ḥṭ' "sin." Gr freely translates the expression with oneidos teknois "(is) a disgrace to (her) children." However, this indirectly supports the reading ḥsd I. For the latter KB lists only Lev 20:17; Prov 14:34. It is significant that in Lev 20:17 the LXX reads oneidos. Thus, it seems reasonable that in our text Gr read ḥsd I.

[23]Reading with HebC h`wzb (= Gr). Cf. Hans Peter Rüger, Text und Textform im hebräischen Sirach, BZAW, no. 112 (Berlin: Walter de Gruyter, 1970), p. 29. HebA reads bwzh "he who despises" (= Syr). Hartman (pp. 449-50) argues against the reading h`wzb in favor of bwzh, because a man who "leaves" (`wzb) his parents does not automatically do wrong. Cf. Gen 2:24; 44:22. But one who "despises" (bwzh) them is a fool. Cf. Prov 15:20b. However, `zb is used very frequently in the negative sense of "to forsake, abandon" (cf. Deut 12:19; Prov 2:17) and can certainly have such a connotation here. Penar (pp. 6-7) prefers to read with HebA here and in line b (bwzh / mqll), because 1 Sam 17:42-43 contains the verbs bzh and qll in that order. This is not convincing for solving a textual problem in Sirach.

[24]Reading with HebC kmgdp (= Gr). Cf. Syr mṭl dmgdp "because of blasphemy." This is read also by Rüger (p. 29) and Hartman (p. 450). HebA reads ky mzyd "for one who acts presumptuously." Penar (p. 6) prefers HebA as the harder reading. Before the discovery of this portion of HebC, Smend conjectured the reading kmzyd "like one who acts presumptuously." Cf. Box-Oesterley. p. 325. Peters (Jesus Sirach, p. 31) considers mzyd

to be the equivalent of blasphēmos, despite the lack of LXX support.

[25]Reading with Rüger's (p. 29) emendation mk'ys, which is based on Gr ho parorgizōn. He considers HebC yshwb (from sḥb "to drag") to be a secondary transmission in Mishnaic Heb. His reading is supported by the fact that k's is the usual Heb word behind parorgizō in the LXX. Segal (Ben-Sîrā') emends HebC to ysḥwp (from sḥp I "to despise" in Jewish Aramaic according to Jastrow). Cf. Hartman p. 450. This reading may account for the transition to the present reading of HebC, but it does not seem adequate to explain Gr. HebA reads mqll "he who curses" (= Syr) and is preferred by Peters as in v. 11 (see n. 21), Box-Oesterley (p. 325), and Penar (see n. 23). This reading was probably influenced by Exod 21:17; Lev 20:9. As in v. 11 Smend emends mqll to mqlh "he who lightly esteems" and is followed by Hartman (p. 450).

[26]Reading with HebC as corrected wz'wm instead of wzw'm "and cursing (God)." See Segal, Ben-Sîrā'; Rüger, p. 29; and Ernesto Vogt, "Novum folium Hebr. Sir 15,1-16,7 MS B," Biblica 40 (1959):1060-62. Hartman (p. 449, n. 13) notes the needed correction but considers HebC to be corrupt for this line. Cf. Gr kai kekatēramenos and Syr wlyṭ, which both mean "and cursed." HebA reads wmk'ys "and (like) one who provokes." Cf. Hartman, pp. 449-50.

[27]HebC 'l. Cf. Gr kyriou "(by the) Lord." However, HebA reads bwr'w "his creator" (= Syr). The reading of HebA is preferred by Hartman (p. 449). A word on the textual history of v. 16 is in order. HebC best gives rise to the Gr, which, in turn, is the basic source of Syr. HebA is a secondary text, which is influenced by its own mistaken reading in v. 11 (mqll) and the transposition of the parts. in v. 16b. Syr has also been influenced by HebA in v. 16a. The God orientation, which is unanimous in line b, is best paralleled in line a by the "blaspheme" expression in HebC.

[28]The pattern is 1 + 4 + 4 + 4 + 1. For a discussion of the deletion of v. 7, see below.

[29]For Ben Sira's treatment of parents' responsibilities to their children, see 30:1-13.

[30]P. 126.

[31]V. 13 assumes 'b/patēr as the subj. of the verbs. V. 15 continues the benefits resulting from "kindness to a father," noted in v. 14.

[32]Vv. 2-4, 6, 16 are synonymously parallel distichs, where 'b/patēr in line a combines with 'm/mētēr in line b to equal parents. The same may be said for vv. 9, 11, even though

the parallelism is antithetical. Cf. the father and mother parallel in Job 17:14; 31:18; Prov 1:8; 4:3; 6:20; 10:1; 15:20; 19:26; 23:22; 30:11, 17; Jer 16:7; Ezek 16:45; Mic 7:6.

[33]P. 58. Cf. Hartman, p. 448.

[34]E.g., Ryssel, p. 267; Smend, Jesus Sirach, p. 24; Peters, Jesus Sirach, p. 30; Box-Oesterley, p. 324; Spicq, p. 577; Hartman, p. 448.

[35]Pp. 58-60.

[36]For a similar problem of genuineness and a similarly motivated conclusion by Haspecker, see the discussion of 26:19-27 in chap. I.

[37]This expression, the related phrase "father or mother," and separated references to father and mother, as in Deut 21:18 ("the voice of his father or the voice of his mother"), occur about sixty times in the OT with the general meaning parents. A typical example is found in Judg 14:2-16.

[38]The only LXX use of this part. for parents is in Tob 10:13, for which the Heb, even if original, is not extant. In Zech 13:3 it is used twice along with "his father and his mother." Cf. Jer 16:3, which uses it with "fathers" ("mothers" is mentioned with the part. tōn tetokuiōn "who bore"), and Prov 23:22 ("father who begat"). In Sir 22:4 it stands for "fathers." Its only other related use is in Deut 32:18 with reference to God. We may note that the noun goneis "parents" is found only in Esth 2:7 (Heb "father and mother"), Prov 29:15 (Heb "mother"), and parts of the Apoc. that were originally written in Gr.

[39]Fuss, p. 47. This is especially true if one reads v. 1a with Syr and La: "Hearken, children, to the judgment of your father." This reading certainly fits the pattern of the section better than Gr, which has father = Ben Sira himself. However, this textual decision is not necessary for the present investigation.

[40]Exod 20:12; Deut 5:16.

[41]Eph 6:2.

[42]Cf. Snaith, Ecclesiasticus, p. 21.

[43]See n. 32 for a list of similar OT distichs where the parallel involving father and mother means parents.

[44]See Deut 10:18; 27:19; Ps 140:12; Jer 5:28. For a discussion, see TDNT, s.v. "Krisis," by Friedrich Buchsel, and s.v. "Krinō," by Volkmar Herntrich.

[45]For a discussion of the relationship between honor to God and honor to parents, see Spicq, p. 576. Note also that 2:1-18, which precedes this section, concerns one's duty to God.

[46]Both Gr and Syr (Heb is missing) arrange these units as follows ABC / CAB.

[47]The Gr word used here is the pres. part. of apothēsaurizō "to store, hoard up." This is its only occurrence in the LXX. It is equally rare in the NT, where it is found only in 1 Tim 6:19. Its use there is also metaphorical for the laying up of liberal and genereous deeds, whereby one may make eternal life secure. A more frequently found word is the synonym thēsaurizō. Cf. the reading of Gr155. Note especially the metaphorical use in Tob 4:9. The context of vv. 7-11 declares that through almsgiving one lays up treasure "against the day of necessity" (v. 9) and delivers him "from death" and keeps him "from entering the darkness" (v. 10). Cf. Matt 6:20. For the negative equivalent, see Prov 1:18 LXX; Jas 5:3; and particularly Rom 2:5. The word is used with other metaphorical meanings in Prov 2:7; 16:27 LXX; Amos 3:10; Mic 6:10.

[48]Box-Oesterley, p. 324.

[49]Ben Sira also notes specifically that almsgiving atones for sin (v. 30; cf. Tob 4:9, 10) and generally that keeping the law "makes many offerings" (35[32]:1; cf. Prov 16:6). For the doctrine of sin and atonement in Ben Sira, see Buchler, "Sin and Atonement."

[50]For a discussion of self-interest in Sirach, see Pfeiffer, pp. 387-88.

[51]The Syr for line b is a somewhat tighter parallel. See n. 17.

[52]This recalls Exod 20:12; Deut 5:16. Cf. Sir 1:12, 20 for long life in relationship to Gottesfurcht.

[53]See n. 16.

[54]2 Chr 14:6; 15:15 (the element involving no war is in v. 19).

[55]Deut 12:10; 25:19; Josh 21:44; 23:1; 2 Sam 7:1, 11; 1 Chr 22:9. This implication is also found in many other places, e.g., Deut 3:20; 1 Chr 23:25.

[56]1 Kgs 5:4 (18 Heb).

[57]Isa 14:3. For the idea of freedom from pain, see also Sir 38:7.

[58]Spicq, p. 577.

[59]See n. 17.

[60]Note especially Deut 32:5, 15-18.

[61]See n. 17.

[62]For the establishment of the reading, see n. 18.

[63]See Spicq, p. 577.

[64]The blessings and curses of Deut 27-28 are pronounced on positive and negative behavior respectively.

[65]See vv. 12-13.

[66]Note, e.g., Isaac and Jacob (Gen 27:27), Jacob and his sons (Gen 49), and Moses and Israel (Deut 33).

[67]Cf. Ps 1:3; Prov 12:3; Jer 12:2. see Spicq, p. 577.

[68]To appreciate the relationship between these distichs it will be helpful to see them together and in their relative word order, at least in terms of subj. and pred. Unlike the translation of v. 10 given at the head of our treatment of this section, this one is based on the Heb. Gr offers a reading for v. 10b which is expansive for the purposes of clarification.

10 Do not glorify yourself in the dishonor of your father,
For that is no glory to you.
11 A man's glory is the glory of his father,
But he multiplies shame who dishonors his mother.

[69]See Spicq, p. 578.

[70]For a discussion of the important textual problems of this distich, see nn. 23-27.

[71]Cf. Deut 27:16.

[72]See vv. 8-9. V. 9 refers to a mother's (= parental) curse. However, as a motive, this is not as strong as a divine curse.

[73]Presumably Ben Sira considers this to be blasphemy against God, since it disregards his direct command (Exod 20:12) and his establishment of parental honor (Sir 3:2). Cf. a similar idea in Prov 14:31; 17:5, where mistreating the poor insults (<u>ḥrp</u>) one's maker.

[74]When we compare this, Ben Sira's fullest treatment of parents, to the evidence of Proverbs we find that the latter has

a similar ratio of father to father/mother constructions (eleven to twelve in Proverbs and six to six in Sirach). Proverbs, however, refers to mother independently of father (29:15; 31:1). Sir 3:1-16 contains no such reference. In fact, the only independent reference to mother in Sirach, apart from conception and birth language, is 15:2a. But this is a simile, which refers to personified Wisdom, and not a reflection of the role of mother.

[75]These verses are not extant in Heb. The omission is perhaps due to the similarity of the beginning of vv. 27a and 29a, bkl lkb "with all your heart." See Smend, Jesus Sirach, p. 71; Peters, Jesus Sirach, p. 73; Box-Oesterley, p. 341. Cf. v. 30a bkl m'wdk "with all your strength." Gr reads en holē kardia doxason ton patera sou (= Syr, La).

[76]Reading with Syr wl'mk dyldtk, which preserves what appears to be a tight parallel involving father and mother with the meaning parents. For Ben Sira's style, see the discussion of 3:1-16. Gr reads mētros ōdinas "(your) mother's birth-pains." Cf. La. This reading puts the emphasis on birth-pains and loses the tightness of the parallel.

[77]Reading with Syr 'tdkr dkw l' hnwn l' 'ytyk (= La). Cf. Peters (Jesus Sirach, p. 73), who reads with Syr in his reconstruction of the Heb. This has a cryptic ring, which most likely was smoothed out by the Gr free rendering mnēsthēti hoti di autōn egenēthēs "remember that through them you were born." Smend (Jesus Sirach, p. 71) considers it possible that Gr has here corrected Syr. The Syr reading best fits the comparison form of line b.

[78]Reading with Gr kai ti antapodōseis autois kathōs autoi soi lit. "and what shall you bive back to them as they to you?" Cf. La. See also Peter's (Jesus Sirach, p. 73) reconstruction of the Heb. Syr loses the comparison by concluding with drbywk "who have reared you" after the word "them."

[79]For a discussion of the larger context and the formal relationship of some of these verses, see the discussions of 7:19; 7:24-25; 7:26a.

[80]For a consideration of this expression, see the discussion of 3:1-16.

[81]We may compare Ben Sira's treatment to the counsel of Tobit to his son Tobias: "My son when I die, bury me,and do not neglect your mother. Honor her all the days of your life; do what is pleasing to her, and do not grieve her. Remember, my son, that she faced many dangers for you while you were yet unborn. When she dies, bury her beside me in the same grave" (Tob 4:3-4). Here the mother is specifically identified for parental honor. Cf. b. Ketub. 103a.

[82]Reading with Gr *mnēsthēti patros kai mētros sou*. Syr *'tdkr d'b' w'm' 'yt lk* "remember that you have a father and a mother" orients the verse differently by treating one's relationship to parents in isolation.

[83]As Smend (*Jesus Sirach*, p. 208) noted, Gr *gar* "for" is probably due to a mistranslation of the Heb *ky* "when." The latter makes better sense in the context and is also read by Box-Oesterley (p. 394). Cf. *RSV*, *NEB*, *JB*, and Goodspeed.

[84]Gr *synedreueis*.

[85]With this line the Gr orients the verse to one's behavior and reputation in public life, with the parents before one's eyes as a deterrent to shameful words and deeds. Syr, however, continues the focus on parents by reading *wmn 'yd' dḥlt' ttplṭ* "and you will be preserved from fear of them."

[86]Reading with Syr *ttql*. Gr *epilathē* "(lest) you forget" is weak in the context, unless it can be extended to "forget yourself." But even that is too passive. The active expression in Syr fits the setting better. See Smend, *Jesus Sirach*, p. 209; Box-Oesterley, p. 394.

[87]Gr *mōranthēs*. Syr reads *tṣṭ`r* "you be despised."

[88]Gr *tō ethismō sou*. Cf. Syr *wbywlpnk* "and in your manner."

[89]Gr *kai thelēseis ei mē egennēthēs*. Syr gives direct speech *wt'mr dlw l' 'tbryt* "and say, 'O that I had not been created!'"

[90]The arrangement of the stichs in vv. 1-5 appears to be out of order in Gr. For various reconstructions, see Smend, *Jesus Sirach*, pp. 203-5; Box-Oesterley, p. 393.

[91]The prayer not only contains material on words and ideas which relates to the instruction in vv. 7-15 but also introduces the subj. of desires in anticipation of vv. 16-27. Cf. Weber, p. 548.

[92]Some scholars have concluded that vv. 12-15 are referring to two distinct types of speech abuse, one milder than the other. In order to establish this contention they have resorted to a reordering of the text, in order to group these two elements together. Smend (*Jesus Sirach*, p. 208) and Box-Oesterley (p. 394) arrange the verses as follows: 12, 14, 13, 15. The latter two are considered less severe than the former. However, such a rearrangement is unnecessary for two reasons. First, the form of the subsection as it stands parallels that of the preceding subsection. See n. 94. Secondly, the content of vv. 12-15 may be understood as homogeneously referring to the same

type of speech abuse. These verses contain four references to the problem. In v. 13a it is called apaideusian asyrē "lewd insolence." The word apaideusia is found in the LXX outside of Sirach only in Hos 7:16, where it tranlates z`m "curse" and clearly means "insolence." Cf. RSV, NASV, NIV. In Sir 4:25 (Gr represents a different text than Heb) and 21:24 (no Heb extant) the word means "ignorance," with the idea of "ill-mannered" in the latter. The term asyrēs, an LXX hapaxlegomenon and rare elsewhere, means "lewd, filthy." Smend (Jesus Sirach, p. 209) considers it a translator's ornamenation or a gloss. If this is so, then the insolence which Ben Sira originally described may not have been obscene in nature. In v. 13b Gr contains the phrase logos hamartias, which would appear to further describe the speech abuse. It may be translated "sinful speech" (RSV). But Deut 23:14 (Heb 15); 24:1 contain a phrase that may be analogous to our text: `rwt dbr (cf. postbiblical dbr r` and dbr sl) "something detrimental." If this pattern is followed, the expression logos hamartias would mean "something sinful." Cf. NEB. However, Joseph Ziegler ("Ursprüngliche Lesarten im griechischen Sirach," in Mélanges Eugène Tisserant, 7 vols., Studi e testi, nos. 231-37 [Vatican: Biblioteca Apostolica Vaticana, 1964], 1:470) has suggested the reading logismos instead of logos on the basis of 27:7; 42:3, where logismos is supported by Heb. This would have the line read, "for by it is the reckoning of sin." Thus, whether we read logos hamartias "something sinful" or follow Ziegler, v. 13b does not provide an actual description of the speech abuse under consideration. In v. 15a the problem is called logois oneidismou lit. "words of reproach." The term oneidismos is used extensively in the LXX as a translation of ḥrph "reproach, disgrace." Like the Heb word, it may have either an active (insult, insolence) or a passive (disgrace) meaning. However, the expression logos oneidismou is unique to Sirach, occurring in 31(34):31; 41:22 in addition to 23:15. In both 31(34):31 and 41:22 the Heb reads ḥrph, and the context would suggest an active meaning. It is reasonable to assume that such is also the case in 23:15. That oneidismos my have an active meaning for Ben Sira is evident from 22:22; 27:28 29:23, 28. For the passive meaning, see 6:9; 42:14; 47:4. We have seen that both apaideusian asyrē and logois oneidismou may refer to insolent speech. Accordingly, they may reasonably be grouped together as Smend and Box-Oesterley have sggested. However, to justify rearranging the order of the text it is necessary to show that v. 14 is dealing with another kind of speech abuse. But a look at v. 14 does not offer such justification. This verse makes only a veiled reference to speech, not at all precise enough for one to determine that it is different from vv. 13 and 15. The reader is advised to remember his parents when he sits in the council, lest he be "regarded as a fool because of [his] manner." The latter expresion (tō ethismō) is correctly recognized by Box-Oesterley (p. 394) to mean "manner (of speech)." However, even this is apparant only because the context deals with speech abuse. It is not necessary with Fuss (p. 148) to see this material as only superficially related to vv. 7-15. But its meaning is not obvious apart from vv. 13-15. Thus, vv. 13-15 need not be reorderd. To do so on grounds that they represent two different kinds of speech abuse is mistaken. This leaves the matter of v. 12. There the problem is termed lexis antiparabeblēmenē thanatō "speech compared to death." This is the reading of the Origenistic recension, which is followed by Rahlfs, Ziegler, Smend, and Box-Oesterley. Cf. Syr "and if there is another thing that is like it." The reading of GrAB is antiperibeblēmenē thanatō "clothed about with death." Both Smend and Box-Oesterley (cf. Weber, p. 548) consider this to be a reference to blasphemy and its penalty of death. See Lev 24:16. However, if one reads antiparableblēmenē, the idea is clearly one of comparison and not one of penalty. Such speech is like death. It does not result in death. Thus, v. 12 may be taken to refer to the kind of speech abuse explicitly descibed in vv. 13, 15 and assumed in v. 14, i.e., insolent speech. It is deathlike in the general sense that it is sin (vv. 12d, 13b) and in the specific sense that it dishonors one's parents (v. 14a). This nullifies the life promise of the decalogue and causes one to abhor his birth (v. 14ef). Accordingly, it is preferable to retain the standard order of vv. 12-15 and to see these verses as a unit counselling against the use of insolent language.

[93]Vv. 7-11 contain eight distichs compared to seven in v. 12-15.

[94]The arrangement is as follows:

	Oath-taking	Insolent speech
Introduction:	2 distichs (vv. 7-8)	2 distichs (v. 12)
Imperative:	1 distich (v. 9)	1 distich (v. 13)
Illustration:	2 distichs (v. 10)	3 distichs (v. 14)
Motivation:	3 distichs (v. 11)	1 distich (v. 15)

[95]See the discussion of 3:1-16.

[96]Smend (Jesus Sirach, pp. 208-9) takes the megistanes lit. "great men" to be heathen kings, before whom one may be in danger of renouncing Judaism through godless speech. The LXX uses megistan to refer predominantly to "prince," and Ben Sira echoes this in 8:8; 10:24; 20:27, 28; 28:14. However, the verb synedreuō "to sit in council" suggests that in 23:14 megistanes refers instead to members of a local council. Ben Sira reflects this use elsewhere (note the parallel expressions): 4:7 (great man / congregation); 32(35):9 (great men / elders [Heb]); 33:18 (30:27) (great among the people / leaders of the congregation). He also speaks of various persons who will be found among the great: the humble (11:1), the physician (38:3), and the student of the law (39:4).

[97]For the expression "curse the day of your birth," cf. Job 3:1-10, especially v. 1; Jer 20:14-18, especially v. 14.

[98]HebBM bwš (= Gr). Syr does not include this verse.

[99]HebBM `l (= Gr). For a discussion, see the treatment of context and form below.

[100]Reading pḥz with HebBmgM. HebB reads znwt "fornication" (= Gr). The reading pḥz is more likely, due, in part, to the resultant word play with kḥš "lying," as Middendorp (p. 94) observes. Yadin (p. 20) takes znwt to be both popular and corrupt. Furthermore, as we shall see, the context of vv. 17-19a notes a series of negative acts done to a particular person or group. Accordingly, the act of insolence better fits the context than the act of fornication. It is inconceivable that the latter would be directed toward or even in the presence of one's parents.

[101]HebBM m-. Cf. Gr apo. For a discussion, see the treatment of context and form below.

[102]The second subsection (42:1-8) is a contrast, dealing with things for which one should not be ashamed. Vv. 14-16 are introductory.

[103]The construction for this indication is m- + the context or obj.

[104]Here the construction is `l + the act.

[105]The text mentions mother. However, see the discussion of 3:1-16, which demonstrates that mother is part of a literary convention including father, which together = parents.

[106]See chap. I

[107]Cf. the picture of Yahweh in Isa 49:14, 15; 66:13.

[108]For a discussion of the identification of wisdom with yeṣer tob, the inherent tendency to good, see Box-Oesterley, p. 319.

[109]The term in the text is a related mother expression: "until the day of his returning to the mother of all living" (ʹl ʹm kl ḥy). Just as "mother's womb" symbolizes birth, "mother of all living" refers to man's final resting place. Cf. Job 1:21. These are the parameters of life--birth and death. For a discussion of the concept of Mother Earth, see Gaster 2:786-87.

[110]Cf. Jer 1:5.

[111]Cf. Pss 29:8; 97:4.

112 The line reads lit. "and like the heart of a woman with birth pains imagines." Box-Oesterley (pp. 433-34), following Smend and the suggestion of Syr ("he that trusts in them his heart is there") emends the line to read: "Even as thou hopest (so) seeth thy heart." Whether or not this is to be preferred as yielding "an excellent sense" is irrelevant to our present concerns. I have merely listed the text as reflecting the word ōdinō. The figure of a woman in labor is common in the OT, though it is usually constructed from yld. See, e.g., Ps 48:6; Jer 6:24; Isa 26:17.

113 For similar uses of this metaphor, see Job 15:35; Ps 7:14.

114 See 2 Kgs 18:13-15; 2 Chr 32:1-3; Isa 36:1-3.

115 The same idea is expressed even more vividly in 19:10:

Have you heard a word? Let it die with you.
Be brave! It will not make you burst!

116 HebA ytwmym (= Gr, Syr).

117 HebA wtmwr b`l (= Gr, Syr).

118 HebA ʼlmnwt (= Syr). Gr reads tē mētri autōn "to their mother." Smend (Jesus Sirach, p. 38) suggests that Gr has beautified the passage to read like Isa 49:15; 66:13. Whatever motivated the change, Gr is clearly secondary. The juxtaposition of widows and orphans is very common in the OT, occurring some twenty-nine times. This is about half the total number of references to widow. See also the same juxtaposition in 35(32):14, where the same order prevails. Furthermore, the section 4:1-10 is largely composed of parallel distichs where each line contains a term that describes a desparate member of society. The exceptions are vv. 5, 6, 7, 8. However, v. 5 is incomplete in Heb. V. 7 seems out of place with its different topic, though it does present a parallel. See n. 122. Accordingly, Heb best fits this model. The Gr expresses the same idea in more colorful language. For a similar Gr free rendition, see Job 24:21.

119 Reading with HebA wʼl yqrʼk bn. This is a little tighter parallel than Gr, which reads kai esē hōs huios hypsistou "and you will be like a son of the Most High." The idea of comparison which is expressed by Gr is somewhat out of place with the definite metaphor in v. 11. Even though it introduces a new section, the mention there of "Wisdom's son" seems to consciously relate to the idea of "God's son" in our text. Penar (p. 15) prefers Heb but suggests that the waw of wyḥnk "and he will be gracious to you" from line d should be added to the last word of line c, making bnw "his son."

[120]Reading with HebA wyḥnk. The verss. are virtually synonymous: Gr "and he will love (agapēsei) you"; Syr "and he will have pity (mnrḥm) on you."

[121]HebA wyṣylk mšḥt. Gr continues the thought in the first half of the line with mallon ē mētēr sou "more than your mother." This resultant paraphrase was likely inluenced by the Gr of line b. Such a reading disregards the function of v. 10cd as the conclusion of the entire section. Syr does not contain this half of the line.

[122]The categories include: ʿny "poor" (vv. 1, 3, 8), mr rwḥ "bitter of spirit" (vv. 1, 6), npš ḥsyrh "needy soul" (v. 2), dk "wretched" (v. 2), mskyn (Smend) "needy one" (v. 3), dl "weak" (v. 4), mdkdk npš "afflicted soul" (v. 4), deomenos (no Heb extant) "one who is needy" (v. 5), mwṣq "oppressed one" (v. 9), ytwmym "orphans" (v. 10), ʾlmnwt "widows" (v. 10). V. 7 seems out of place with its parallel that involves the assembly and the ruler of the city.

[123]See n. 115.

[124]See n. 118.

[125]For a review of the ancient Near Eastern material, see Charles F. Fensham, "Widow, Orphan, and the Poor in Ancient Near Eastern Legal and Wisdom Literature," JNES 21 (1962):129-39. Hebrew wisdom was not above its Near Eastern counterparts (Spicq, p. 288) in this respect.

[126]For legal material, see, e.g., Deut 10:18; 14:29; 16:11; 24:17, 19; 26:12-13; 27:19. For wisdom literature, see, e.g., Job 22:9; 24:3, 21; 29:13; 31:16. For prophetic literature, see, e.g., Isa 1:17, 23; 10:2. Note also the law of the levirate.

[127]E.g., Fensham, p. 136.

[128]See EJ, s.v. "Widow: Biblical Period," by Chayim Cohen, which is followed by John H. Otwell, And Sarah Laughed: The Status of Women in the Old Testament (Philadelphia: Westminster Press, 1977), pp. 123-31.

[129]See, e.g., Gen 38:11; Lev 21:14; 22:13; Num 30:9; 2 Sam 14:5; Ezek 44:22.

[130]P. 130. Of course, the Israelite woman sold into slavery had an even worse condition. For more on the widow in the OT, see IDB, s.v. "Widow," by Otto J. Baab.

[131]See 4:11.

[132]See especially Ps 68:5. Cf. Deut 10:18; Ps 146:9; Prov 15:25; Jer 49:11; Mal 3:5. The king is to be the supreme human protector of widows. See 2 Sam 14. Cf. the role of the king in Mesopotamia, Egypt, and Ugarit discussed by Fensham (pp. 130-37).

[133]See 4:6; 35:14.

[134]Otwell, p. 130.

[135]This assumes, of course, that by definition a widow is so deprived. But, as we have observed, this definition is not necessary. However, such deprivation may be expected for a widow who is classed with aliens and orphans, since she no doubt experienced a severe social condition.

[136]It is not so much that widows are elevated to equality with the class of resident aliens who would contain men, but the reverse. Resident aliens were classed with the lowly condition of certain widows and orphans. But even among these there would be different levels of status as economics and position would demand. The real significance of the threefold grouping is more likely in its function as a standard literary convention, expressing society's responsibility to its oppressed members. The earliest appearance of the grouping is Exod 22:21, 22 in the order alien, widow, orphan. Cf. Ps 146:9. The most frequent order is alien, orphan, widow. See Deut 10:18; 14:29; 16:11; 24:17, 19; 26:12-13; 27:19; Jer 7:6; 22:3; Ezek 22:7. Other orders include: widow, alien, orphan in Ps 94:6 and widow, orphan, alien in Zech 7:10; Mal 3:5.

[137]It may be argued that Ben Sira has deliberately deleted reference to resident aliens here in order to avoid the possibility of their classification with women and children. But we have no evidence to support such a view. We may observe, however, that even here Ben does not depart from his careful handling of material dealing with women.

[138]Reading with HebBmg _ʼnqt_ (= Syr). HebB _sʽqt_ "cry," which is retained by Smend, was probably influenced by Exod 22:22, 23. Cf. Middendorp, p. 42. Gr reads _hiketeian_ "supplication." This word occurs only in the Apoc. in original Gr compositions except here and 51:9. In the latter it translates _qwl_. The choice between _ʼnqt_ and _sʽqt_ is difficult, since they are virtual synonyms and since both are used with reference to oppressed classes. For _ʼnqt_, see Job 34:28; Ps 9:12. For _sʽqt_, see Pss 12:5; 79:11; 102:20. I have allowed the external convergence of HebBmg and Syr to tip the balance slightly in favor of _ʼnqt_.

[139]Heb _ytwm_ (= Gr, Syr).

[140]Heb _'lmnh_ (= Gr). Syr renders this line freely: "and the prayer of widows (_d'rmlt'_) he hears."

[141]Reading with Gr _ekcheē_. HebB reads _trbh_ "multiplies." HebBmg, which Smend follows, reads _tḥbṭ_ "beats out." Cf. Box-Oesterley, p. 438. Neither of these Heb readings seems satisfactory, since they nowhere stand behind _ekcheō_ in the LXX, nor are either associated elsewhere with the word _śyḥ_, which follows here. The predominant _Vorlage_ for _ekcheō_ in the OT is _špk_ "to pour out." This combination is also common in Sirach. See 20:13; 30:18; 32(35):4; 36(33):7; 37:29. The reading of 32(35):4 is particularly interesting, since there we find the identical phrase in Gr, appearing as a negative command: _mē ekcheēs lalian_ (cf. 35[32]:14 _ekcheē lalian_) "do not pour out talk." This is a literal translation of the Heb _'l tšpk śyḥ_. With the same Heb and Gr direct objs. and the same Gr verbs we would be justified in expecting the same Heb verbs. And since the Gr translator regularly employed _ekcheō_ to translate _špk_, as we have seen, I suggest that the phrase in 35(32):14b originally contained the verb _špk_. For a similar association of _špk_ and _śyḥ_, see Pss 102:1 (Heb); 142:2; 1 Sam 1:15, 16. It is possible that HebB resulted from a mistaken reading of _trd_ in v. 15a and that HebBmg was an attempted correction.

[142]HebB _śyḥ_. Cf. Gr _lalian_. The Heb term is often used in the OT with the meaning "complaint," especially in Job and Psalms. See Job 7:13; 9:27; 10:1; 21:4; 23:2; Pss 64:1; 102:1 (Heb); 142:2. However, its extended meaning "empty talk" is also present in 2 Kgs 9:11. See KB. It is with this latter meaning that Ben Sira uses the word. See 13:11; 32(35):4. We may also note that in addition to these texts the Gr _lalia_ is found with a negative meaning in 5:13 (from _bṭ'_ "to talk idly"); 19:6; 20:5; 27:14; 42:11 (from _dbh_ "evil report). Hence, the meaning of _śyḥ_ here is not the positive "complaint" (_NEB_) nor the neutral "story" (_RSV_, _JB_, Goodspeed) but the negative "chatter."

[143]HebB _dm'h_. Gr reads the equivalent with _dakrya_ but adds _chēras_ "of the widow." This reading was influenced by the mention of widow in v. 14b and the assumption that vv. 14 and 15 were to be read together. See Smend, _Jesus Sirach_, p. 314. This would give the following distich pattern for the section (vv. 12-20): 2 + 3 + 3 + 5 + 1. The pattern in Heb is 2 + 2 + 2 + 2 + 5 + 1. See Box-Oesterley, p. 438. They also observe that the question in v. 15 indicates that the widow is no longer the subj. The entire verse is missing in Syr.

[144]HebB _'l lḥy trd_ (= Gr).

[145]Reading HebB _'nḥh_ as a verb _'anᵉḥāh_ and not as a noun _'anāḥāh_ "sighing." This loosely = Gr _hē kataboēsis_ "out cry." The subj. is _dm'h_ in line a.

[146]Reading with Box-Oesterley's (p. 438) emendation mwrydh (= Gr). HebB reads mrwdyh "her wanderings." Smend reads mwrdyh "her descents." The "her" in these readings refers to the fem. dm`h, a sing. word which may also have the plur. meaning "tears." In this line the translation would have to be "their wanderings, flowings." The term in HebB, which is from rwd "to roam," is unlikely, since it makes little sense in the context and since katagō never translates rwd in the LXX. On the other hand, the emendations of both Box-Oesterley and Smend derive from yrd "to go down," which is the predominant word behind the LXX katagō. Of these two emendations, the hif. of Box-Oesterley is preferable as the one most likely to have given rise to Gr and as the most sensible in the context. HebB resulted from consonant transposition.

[147]For the distich pattern, see n. 140.

[148]dl "weak" (vv. 13, 17), mwṣq "oppressed one" (v. 13), ytwm "orphan" (v. 14), ʾlmnh "widow" (v. 14).

[149]See n. 119.

[150]See n. 115 and the discussion above.

[151]See above.

[152]See n. 139.

[153]Ryssel (p. 406) admits this much but does not see the widow described with contempt and blame.

[154]Edersheim (p. 174) understands this to mean "prattle" --a negative word.

[155]See n. 140.

[156]Some who support the Heb reading of v. 15 have suggested that the subj. changes here from oppressed social classes to oppressed Israel. See Smend, Jesus Sirach, p. 314; Box-Oesterley, p. 439. This may be true for vv. 18-20 (cf. Weber, p. 551), but it is unlikely that this is already the case in v. 15. In v. 13a Ben Sira mentions the dl "weak," a term used in v. 17a with no apparent shift in meaning. Therefore, it is more likely that, despite what may happen in vv. 18-20 with regard to Israel, vv. 13-17 concern specific and general references to the socially oppressed classes.

[157]For the evidence from Proverbs, see n. 71. See also Gen 3:20; Judg 5:7; Pss 35:14; 113:9. In Isa 50:1-3; Ezek 19:1-14 Israel and Judah are symbolized by a mother. The OT often describes mothers in child training, advising their monarch sons, directing marriage plans for their children, etc. See the surveys by Otto J. Baab (IDB, s.v. "Family" and s.v. "Woman")

and Otwell (pp. 49-66). The latter is useful despite the gross overstatement in its conclusion: "No higher status could be given anyone than was given the mother in ancient Israel" (p. 66). Note also the equally unsupportable statement by Isaac Mendelsohn ("The Family in the Ancient Near East," *BA* 11 (May 1948):24-40, reprinted in *The Biblical Archaeologist Reader*, 3 vols., ed. Edward F. Campbell, Jr. and David Noel Freedman [Garden City, New York: Doubleday & Co., 1970], 3:157): "As mother, the woman's position was equal to that of father." Mendelsohn is more realistic in his summary: "A woman attains the highest station in life when she becomes a mother; while the father represents power and authority, the mother personifies love and affection" (p. 160).

Chapter III

[1]Reading with GrSAB *kardia*. Cf. Syr. Lucianic recension reads *psychē* "soul." Heb is not extant for 26:5-9.

[2]Reading with Syr *wmn ʹrb`*. Gr is certainly corrupt with *epi tō tetartō prosōpō* "before the fourth face." This has produced various suggestions by commentators. Edersheim (p. 137) suggests that Gr read *pn* as "face" instead of "lest" and restores as follows: "and over a fourth, lest it befall me." Ryssel (p. 363) holds that Gr must have read *pnym* for *mpny* "with my face." Cf. Smend, *Jesus Sirach*, p. 234. Peters (*Jesus Sirach*, p. 216) offers *epi tō prosōpō tetartou* = *`l pny rby`y* "before my face a fourth." The simple Syr reading is preferable to any of these suggestions and much less problematic. Gr may be accounted for on the basis of influence from 26:17a (*pnym*/ *prosōpou*). In the arrangement of 25:7-26:18 that I have proposed (see chap. I) 26:17a comes just five stichs ahead of 26:5b.

[3]Gr *ephobēthēn*. There are many vars. which are also to be taken in a gnomic sense: B, 46, 336 *edeēthēn* "I ask"; S* *edothēn* "I am given"; 679 *edeiliase* "it is afraid"; the emendation of Kuhn (I, p. 105) *edediein* "I am afraid." The reading *ephobēthēn* is read by Zeigler and confirmed by Syr with some expansion *sgy dḥlt* "I am sore afraid." The latter is preferred by Ryssel (p. 363).

[4]Smend (*Jesus Sirach*, p. 234) suggests that this line was = 42:11c, where he emends HebB to read *dbt `yr wqhlt `m*. This reading is now confirmed by HebM. See the discussion of 42:11. Cf. Peters, *Jesus Sirach*, p. 216. Gr for 26:5c reads *diabolēn poleōs kai ekklēsian ochlou* "the slander of a city and the assembly of a crowd." Cf. 42:11c *lalian en polei kai ekklēton laou* "a rumor in the city and summoned by (or an assembly of) the people." I have read 26:5c according to Smend's suggestion that behind Gr lay a Heb text = 42:11c. It is reasonable that the contrasting Gr of 26:5c and 42:11c may be taken to have

resulted from the same Heb text. We may demonstrate this by grouping the two Gr lines into four word pairs, each with a parallel word from the two lines. The first pair, diabolē / lalia, may traced to dbh. This is the reading in 42:11c (lalia) as well as in 51:2 (diabolē). The expressions poleōs / en polei are obviously from ʿyr. Both ekklēsia and ekklēton translate qhl, as evidenced by 42:11c (ekklēton--the only LXX use) and the usual situation for ekklēsia (e.g., 15:5; 46:7). The final pair, ochlos / laos, may render ʿm. This is the overwhelming case for laos, many examples of which are found in Sirach. For ochlos resulting from ʿm, see Num 20:20; Jer 38(45):1 (S*; laos ABS2); 48(31):42. Syr translates both lines freely but gives some indication of their common Heb text: rṭwnyʾ dknwštʾ bswgʾʾ dʿmʾ "the murmur of the assembly in the multitude of the people" (26:5c); wšwʿytʾ wrṭwnyʾ bʿmʾ "and a rumor and a murmuring among the people" (42:11c).

[5]Gr katapseusmon. Syr is missing for this line. Smend (Jesus Sirach, p. 234) finds this third element of the Zahlenspruch inadequate by the pattern set in the first two. He wants to see a legal proceeding that includes a gen. expression and suggests the reading for the line: "the accusation (śṭnh) of one who rebukes (mwkyḥ) wrong (ʿml)." Smend postulates that mwkyḥ was corrupted to mmwt "than death" and was so read by Gr. But he is certain that an expression like "all are worse than death" could not follow the third element, since he is convinced that it is the fourth element in v. 6 which is the worst. But, as we shall see below, such a conclusion is unnecessary. Furthermore, by Smend's own identification of line c with 42:11c, we are not compelled to require that each element of the Zahlenspruch contain a gen. construction. Kuhn (I, p. 105) represents another emendation of the third element by reading kai katapsēphismon hyper thanatou "the vote concerning a death (sentence)." But this is far too grave for the company of the previous elements. It is also unclear how Kuhn understands the expression panta mochthēra.

[6]Gr mochthēra. 543, Cos ponēra "(more) evil"; John of Damascus reads lypēra "(more) painful"; 673 + ponēra.

[7]Gr hyper thanaton. See n. 5 for the treatments of this phrase by Smend and Kuhn. Fuss (p. 162) rejects Smend's conclusion that this phrase is false.

[8]Gr algos kardias. 248 reads achthos "burden"; 679 reads salos "perplexity." Syr is missing for this line.

[9]Gr penthos. 542* reads ponos "pain."

[10]Gr gynē antizēlos epi gynaiki. Smend (Jesus Sirach, p. 235) and Peters (Jesus Sirach, p. 216) consider epi gynaiki an addition of the translator that overloads the line. However, antizelōs is a technical term for a rival wife. See 37:11,

where the Heb is *ṣrh*, as in 1 Sam 1:6. The sense requires the indication of a relationship, whether implied or explicit. Cf. *T. Jos*. 7:5. The retention of *epi gynaiki* is further strengthened by the analogy of Lev 18:18 LXX: *gynaika epi adelphē* . . . *antizēlon*. Behind *antizēlon* Heb uses the verb *ṣrr* "to be a rival wife."

[11]Gr *mastix glōssēs*, probably from *šwṭ lšwn*. Cf. Job 5:21. Syr reads *mḥwt' dlšn'* "blow of the tongue."

[12]Gr *pasin epikoinōnousa*. Gr limits the mention of the tongue action to this element of the *Zahlenspruch*, i.e., the wife who has a rival shares her hostility with everyone through her speech. Reading with Gr are Peters (*Jesus Sirach*, p. 216; cf. *RSV*, Goodspeed) and Edersheim (p. 137; he understands the tongue-lashing to fall equally on everyone; cf. *NEB*). Syr reads *kwlhyn 'kḥd'* "(are they) all together." This gives a reading for the line: "and the blow of the tongue are they all together," i.e., all the elements of the *Zahlenspruch* (even though Syr gives only one confused element in v. 5c) constitute blows of the tongue. Following Syr are Smend (*Jesus Sirach*, p. 235) and Box-Oesterley (p. 403; cf. *JB*). This reading, however, appears to be a free, interpretive rendition, since not all the elements necessarily involve the negative action of the tongue, e.g., the assembly of the people (v. 5c). Kuhn (I, p. 105) offers an emendation: "The lash of the tongue is (worse) than any flood." But this is highly conjectural and unlikely, since it requires not only reconstructing the Heb *štp* but also postulating that this was a misprint for *šṭp* "flood," producing a word play *šwṭ* / *šṭp*.

[13]Gr *gynē ponēra* (= Syr).

[14]Supplied because of the clear comparison and the analogy of line *b*. Cf. La and the reconstruction by Box-Oesterley (p. 403).

[15]Gr *boozygion saleuomenon* lit. "an ox yoke being shaken to and fro." This is the basis for the readings of Edersheim (p. 137), Peters (*Jesus Sirach*, p. 216), and Eberharter (p. 95). Cf. Hamp, p. 639, *RSV*, *NEB*, *JB*, Goodspeed. While *saleuomenon* may not be "senseless," as Smend (*Jesus Sirach*, p. 235) observes, it is unusual in combination with a word for yoke. No such combination occurs in the LXX or in the MT for the words that would lie behind them. Ryssel (p. 363) offers the suggestion that the expression "bars of a yoke" may have been originally present here, as in Lev 26:13 and Ezek 34:27. He is followed by Smend (*Jesus Sirach*, p. 235) and Box-Oesterley (p. 403). The emendation is reasonable, and I have read with it. While the LXX uses *saleuō* to translate twenty-three different Heb words, the most frequent *Vorlage* is *mwṭ*. Cf. Sir 13:21. The emendation is based on the assumption that Gr mistook *mṭwt*

(from mṭh in the phrase mṭwt ʿl) for a form of the verb mwṭ "totter," resulting in boozygion saleuomenon.

[16]Gr ho kratōn autēs. The Heb was probably a form of tmk "lay hold of," as in 4:13 and 38:25. Cf. Ryssel, p. 363; Peters, Jesus Sirach, p. 216. Smend (Jesus Sirach, p. 235) suggests that the Heb was nś' "take a wife" and was mistranslated by Syr with msybr "he who tolerates." But there is no LXX rendition of nś' with krateō, making such a Heb reading unlikely.

[17]Gr ho drassomenos skorpiou (= Syr).

[18]Gr gynē methysos. 248 + kai rhembas "and roving". Cf. Syr 'ntt' rwyt' wphy' "a drunken and roving wife." With Smend (Jesus Sirach, p. 235) I take the longer reading of Gr248 and Syr to be secondary.

[19]Gr orgē megalē (=Syr).

[20]Gr sygkalypsei (=Syr).

[21]Gr aschēmosynēn (=Syr).

[22]I have included this verse here for the sake of completeness in this section on the bad wife. However, since it deals with adultery, I have chosen to discuss it in chap. IV, where that topic is fully explored.

[23]HebC kl mkh (= Gr). The pattern in this and the next verse (not extant in Heb) is: any "A," but not the "A" of "B." The form is followed twice in each distich. Syr presents the variation: all "A's," but not like the "A" of "B." This may be freely translated: there are many "A's," but none is so bad as the "A" of "B." Cf. Smend, Jesus Sirach, p. 228.

[24]Reading [mkt] lb according to Smend's reconstruction of HebC on the basis of b. Šabb. 11a and Gr. HebC reads k[ ] lb, presumably k[mkt] lb "like a wound of the heart." Cf. Syr 'yk mḥwt' dlb'. The rabbinic citation according to Cowley-Neubauer (p. xxiv) is:

Rab said:
any sickness, but not sickness of the bowels;
any pain (kl k'b), but not the pain of the heart (k'b lb);
any ache, but not the aching of the head;
any evil (kl rʿh), but not an evil woman ('šh rʿh).

[25]HebC kl mkh (= Gr).

[26]Reading r[ʿt 'šh] with Smend's reconstruction, which is based on his reading of b. Šabb. 11a. Cf. Gr ponērian gynaikos and Cowley-Neubauer's reading of b. Šabb. 11a ('šh rʿh). HebC

reads k̲r̲[   ], presumably k̲r̲[`t ′šh] "like the wickedness of a woman." Cf. Syr.

[27]Gr p̲a̲s̲a̲n̲ e̲p̲a̲g̲ō̲g̲ē̲n̲. Syr reads k̲w̲l̲ ′wl̲ṣ̲n̲y̲n̲ "all oppressions." Heb is not extant for vv. 14-16.

[28]Gr e̲p̲a̲g̲ō̲g̲ē̲n̲ m̲i̲s̲o̲u̲n̲t̲ō̲n̲. Syr reads ′wl̲ṣ̲n̲′ d̲s̲n̲′′ "an oppression of (or caused by) one who hates."

[29]Gr p̲a̲s̲a̲n̲ e̲k̲d̲i̲k̲ē̲s̲i̲n̲. Cf. Syr, which is plur.

[30]Gr e̲k̲d̲i̲k̲ē̲s̲i̲n̲ e̲c̲h̲t̲h̲r̲ō̲n̲. Gr 149, 260, 534, 606 reads e̲k̲d̲i̲k̲ē̲s̲i̲n̲ e̲c̲h̲t̲r̲o̲u̲ (= Syr). See below for a discussion of Smend's conjectural reconstruction of the Heb behind m̲i̲s̲o̲u̲n̲t̲ō̲n̲ and e̲c̲h̲t̲h̲r̲ō̲n̲.

[31]Gr k̲e̲p̲h̲a̲l̲ē̲. Cf. Syr r̲š̲′. Scholars have overwhelmingly taken the Gr, followed by the Syr, to be a misunderstanding of the Heb. See Edersheim, p. 134; Ryssel, p. 360; Smend, Jesus Sirach, p. 229; Peters, Jesus Sirach, p. 214; Box-Oesterley, p. 401; Spicq, p. 696. This theory suggests that r̲′š̲ II "poison" was read by Gr (and Syr) as r̲′š̲ I "head." Cf. such a possible misunderstanding in the loose LXX translation of Lam 3:5. To support the association of r̲′š̲ II with snakes, those who take this position offer the analogy of Deut 32:33 and Job 20:16. However, the case for Gr (and Syr) musunderstanding is more a convenient assumption than a reasoned conclusion, based on the evidence of LXX translation practices. The word r̲′š̲ II is used with regard to snakes only in Deut 32:33 and Job 20:16. However, in both texts the associated word is p̲t̲n̲ "cobra," a word never translated in the LXX by o̲p̲h̲i̲s̲ "snake"--the word used in our text. Furthermore, the words translated by o̲p̲h̲i̲s̲ (ś̲r̲p̲, n̲ḥ̲š̲, ′p̲`h̲) are, with one exception, never used in connection with a direct statement about poison. The exception, Ps 58:4, mentions "the venom of a serpent (n̲ḥ̲š̲)," but here the word for venom is ḥ̲m̲h̲ not r̲′š̲ II. We seem faced with several possible solutions. If we presuppose that r̲′š̲ II stood in our text and was misread by Gr (and Syr), then we may suggest that o̲p̲h̲i̲s̲ is a loose, uncharacteristic translation of p̲t̲n̲ and that, following LXX practice, it should have read a̲s̲p̲i̲s̲ (cf. Deut 32:33), d̲r̲a̲k̲ō̲n̲ (cf. Job 20:16, though unlikely because of Sir 25:16), or e̲c̲h̲i̲s̲ (cf. Ben Sira's own use in 39:30). It is also possible that Ben Sira is using a unique expresion r̲′š̲ II n̲ḥ̲š̲. The third possibility is that the Heb read r̲′š̲ I and was translated correctly by both Gr and Syr. Of these alternatives, the last appears most likely. The argument in favor of a misunderstanding by Gr (and Syr) seems logical and convincing not so much because of the identity of the Heb roots involved but particularly because of the commonality of associating snakes with poison. However, the transparency of such an assocition would have been just as certain to the translators as to us. We may expect, then, that their departure from such a natural idea to a much more obscure one was done deliberately. The reason for such a choice of

words, "head of a snake," probably can be traced to the influence of the story of man's fall in Gen 3. That our text (cf. also v. 24) is an allusion to this Genesis story, particularly the fall of Eve, has been noted by others. Cf. Edersheim, p. 134; Ryssel, p. 360. The general content of v. 15, referring to both a snake and a woman, would seem to confirm such influence. However, the case is strengthened by the recognition that of the variety of potential words the LXX consistently uses the word ophis (for nḥš) throughout Gen 3. Furthermore, in Gen 3:15 the judgment upon the ophis includes the declaration that the woman's seed will bruise the serpent's head (r'š I/kephalē). Under this apparent influence it seems reasonable to take the Gr and Syr readings as accurate reflections of the underlying Heb, which probably read: r'š I . . . r'š I nhs "head . . . head of a snake."

[32]Gr opheōs (= Syr). See also n. 31.

[33]Gr thymos. Syr reads b`ldbbwt' "enmity."

[34]Reading gynaikos with Gr795. Cf. the edited text by Ziegler, Syr, La, Arm. The remaining Gr witnesses read echthrou "of an enemy," as does Rahlfs. This majority reading no doubt resulted from vertical dittography, as recognized by Peters (Jesus Sirach, p. 214). Cf. also Smend, Jesus Sirach, p. 229; Box-Oesterley, p. 401.

[35]Reading with Syr pqḥ lm`mr "better to dwell." This = the Heb of Prov 21:9 twb lšbt (cf. 21:19; 25:24), which seems likely to have influenced Ben Sira. The LXX rendering of these is kreisson/kreitton oikein. However, in Sir 25:16 Gr appears to render the Heb freely with synoikēsai . . . eudokēsō "I would prefer to dwell." The verb eudokēsō is read by both Rahlfs and Ziegler. For the large number of vars. see Ziegler, Sirach, p. 244. The reading of Antiochus Monachus ameinon "better" is closest to the conjectured Heb and probably resulted from an attempt to correct the Gr.

[36]Gr leoni kai drakonti (= Syr).

[37]Following Rahlfs and Ziegler in reading with $GrS^{c}A$ synoikēsai (= Syr). The var. enoikēsai "to dwell in (a house)," found in $S^{*}B$ is preferred by Smend (Jesus Sirach, p. 229) and Box-Oesterley (p. 401). The latter translates the expression "keep house." The remaining Gr readings are not significant.

[38]Gr ponēras. Cf. Syr byšt'. Gr46 reads pornēs "prostitute."

[39]Gr gynaikos (= Syr). Syr has the added phrase bgw byt' "in the midst of a house."

[40]HebC r` ´šh. Cf. Gr ponēria gynaikos. Syr reads byšwth d´ntt´ byšt´ "the wickedness of a wicked wife."

[41]Reading with HebC yšḥyr. The verb šḥr I occurs in the MT only in Job 30:30, where the LXX translates with eskotōtai. Cf. line b of our text for skotoō as the translation of the Heb qdr. See also Jer 8:21; 14:2. Here, however, Gr renders the rare šḥr I by alloioi "changes." The verb alloioō is common in Sirach (nine times) as the translation of šhn or its equivalent šn´. Note its use with prosōpon (a word used in line b) in 12:18; 13:25. The present translation of šḥr I by alloioi instead of by skotoi is no doubt due to the preference for using skotoō for qdr in line b. Syr reads twrq "makes pale," as in Jer 30:6.

[42]Reading mr´h with Smend. Cf. Gr tēn horasin autēs. HebC reads mr´h ´yš "the appearance of (her) husband." Cf. Syr ´pwhy db`lh "the face of her husband." Smend (Jesus Sirach, p. 230) successfully argues that ´yš is a bad gloss. Cf. Peters, Jesus Sirach, p. 214; Box-Oesterley, p. 401.

[43]HebC wyqdyr. Cf. Gr skotoi; Syr wtwkm.

[44]Reading pnyh with Smend. Cf. Gr to prosōpon autēs. HebC here continues the reference to the woman´s husband from line a with pnyw "his face." Cf. Syr, which merely reads the pronoun here, but which, as noted above, reads with HebC in line a: "and makes it black." That it is the wife´s appearance which is here described is clear from the context and the logic of the idea.

[45]Reading kdwb with Smend. Cf. HebC ldwb "to (that of) a bear"; GrSAVOL hōs arkos (= 311, 705* arktos). The major competing reading is reflected in Syr ´yk gwn´ dsq´ "like the color of a sack." Cf. GrB hōs sakkon "like a sack/sackcloth." La has the conflation "like a bear and like sackcloth." It is generally recognized that the readings arkos and sakkon represent internal Gr variation. However, Ryssel (p. 360) represents those who prefer sakkon, with arkos resulting from the mention of other animals in v. 16. See also David Samuel Margoliouth ("Note on Ecclus. vii.25," ET, 23 [1911-12], 234), who considers HebC to have been influenced by the Gr arkos which he understands to be secondary. The opposite position is championed by Box-Oesterley (p. 276; cf. 401), who argues that dwb "bear" (HebC and Gr) and śq "sackcloth" (Syr) may represent two different recensions of the Heb, with the former being original. The "bear" reading is also supported by Smend (Jesus Sirach, p. 230) and Peters (Jesus Sirach, p. 214). As Box-Oesterley recognizes, the context of animal comparisons in vv. 15-16 and the idea of fierceness rather than sadness speak in favor of the "bear" reading. This would mean that Syr is here influenced by Gr which, as Smend observed, is a more likely situation than for

the Heb to have been influenced by Gr. The suggestion by Box-Oesterley that two Heb recensions lie behind these readings is unacceptable, since the variation is clearly an internal Gr corruption. Further support for the "bear" reading may be seen in the rather widespread use of the "bear" comparison in the OT: 2 Sam 17:8 "enraged like a bear (kdb)"; Isa 59:11 "growl like bears (kdbym)"; Hos 13:8 "fall upon them like a bear (kdb)." In each instance LXX translates with hōs arkos. The reading of HebC (ldwb) is reflected in Dan 7:5, where the Aram reads dmyh ldb "resembling a bear." There Gr reads homoiōsin echon arkou "having the likeness of a bear" (LXX) and homoion arkō "like a bear" (Th.). However, unlike the kdb examples, which are clear comparisons, this Daniel text is merely giving a description of the second beast seen in vision. Thus, Smend's correction of HebC ldwb to kdwb seems justified. On the other hand, śq "sackcloth" is not used in the OT in comparisons. Even in Isa 50:3, where LXX reads hōs sakkon, there is no comparison, and MT merely reads śq.

[46]HebC b`lh (= Gr). Syr reads b`lh dsklt' "the husband (lit. her husband) of the foolish one."

[47]HebC yšb (= Syr). Gr reads anapeseitai "will take meals (lit. will recline at table)."

[48]HebC byn r`ym (= Gr, Syr).

[49]Reading with Smend wbl' ṭ`m lit. "and without sensing." This = Gr248 akousiōs, which is read by Ziegler and Rahlfs and Syr wdl' bṣbynh. HebC reads wbl' ṭ`mw "and without his sensing." Smend (Jesus Sirach, p. 230) argues that the suffix w- is wrong, suggesting instead the reading ṭ`m mr (see n. 51). He is followed by Box-Oesterley (p. 401). Peters (Jesus Sirach, p. 214), however, reads with HebC. If Smend's argument holds, as Gr would imply, then the HebC reading may have arisen from a confusion of consonants. Most Gr MSS read akousas "(he) having heard," which is a clear corruption. The ṭ`m reading may be strengthened by a possible play on words with m`ṭ in v. 19a.

[50]HebC yt'nḥ (= Gr anestenaxen, taken gnomically, and Syr).

[51]Reading with Smend mr. See n. 49. While this is not reflected in Syr, it is suggested by Gr pikra "bitterly" (lit. "bitter things"). Cf. the Lucianic recension pikrōs. Peters (Jesus Sirach, p. 214) rejects pikra as an addition through dittography with mikra in v. 19a. While this may be true for the reading meikra in S*, it is unlikely for pikra.

[52]HebC m`ṭ r`h. As Smend (Jesus Sirach, pp. 230-31) and Box-Oesterley (p. 402) recognize, Gr and Syr render the line,

especially this part, freely: Gr mikra pasa kakia "any wickedness is small"; Syr sg´´ byšt´ "many are the kinds of wickedness." Of these, Gr is closer to Heb, with mikron a frequent LXX rendition of m`ṭ (cf. 11:3) and kakia the usual expression for r`h.

[53]HebC kr`t ´šh (= Gr with pros "compared to" rendering k- "like"). Syr is free with wl´ ´yk z`wrwt byšwth d´ntt´ "but not like the slightest wickedness of a wife."

[54]HebC gwrl hwṭ´ ypwl `lyh (= Gr). Syr is also equivalent except for the plur. "sinners."

[55]The text of HebC for this line is largely mutilated and has been restored by various editors with reference to Gr and Syr. However, the first word of HebC is clearly visible. It contains the preformative k- "like" (= Syr). Cf. the Gr Lucianic recension hōs, which is missing from Gr. With or without the particle, comparison is certain.

[56]Gr ammōdēs. Cf. Syr dḥl´ "(an ascent) of sand." From this we may reconstruct the Heb to read ḥwl lit. "(an ascent) of sand" or "(a sandy) ascent." Cf. Lévi, Hebrew Text, p. 27; Peters, Liber Jesu, p. 365. Smend´s reading (Jesus Sirach hebraisch, p. 22) ḥl is the defective equivalent. However, the full form with w is to be preferred as the consistent MT spelling. Since the Gr ammōdēs is an LXX hapaxlegomenon, we must reconstruct the Heb from the noun ammos "sand," as suggested by Syr. The usual Heb word behind the LXX ammos is ḥwl. We may presume that hwl stood in the Heb of Sir 1:2; 18:10; 22:15, where Gr reads ammos. Note especially the comparison hōs . . . ammou / houtōs . . . in 18:10.

[57]HebC km`lh (= Gr, Syr). For k- see n. 55. This is the only word clearly visible for this line in HebC.

[58]Gr en posin. Cf. Syr brglwhy "to the feet." From Gr and Syr and from LXX practice it is clear that a form of rgl "foot" stood here in Heb. Smend reads brgly "to the feet" after the analogy of Syr. Cf. Lévi (Hebrew Text, p. 27), who reads the sing. brgl. However, Peters (Liber Jesu, p. 365) has a more likely reconstruction with lrgly "to the feet." Gr en is regularly used in the LXX for b-. Also the expression en tois posin always has a form of brgl behind it. In the LXX the anarthrous en posin is unique to Sirach. Besides our text, see 21:19; 38:29. Unfortunately, no Heb is extant for either of these. However, both these texts, like the instances of en tois posin in the rest of the LXX, clearly involve a loc. (e.g., "on your feet") or instr. (e.g., "with his feet") idea and not the dat. idea evident in our text. The latter is best expressed by l-. The closest example is Lam 1:13, where lrgly (du. with 1 sing. suffix, unlike our du. c.s.) is rendered by the Gr dat. tois posin mou, both meaning "for my feet." Cf. Jer 18:22 Heb.

We may also note that the parallel expression in line b is reconstructed by Smend, Lévi, and Peters as l'yš "to a man." Cf. Gr andri and Syr lwt gbr'. Though the choice between b- and l- remains somewhat unclear, I cautiously favor the reading lrgly for the reasons stated.

[59]Gr presbyterou. Cf. Syr dgbr' qšyš' "of an aged man." Reconstructions of the mutilated HebC at this point include the following: Smend and Box-Oesterley (p. 402) read yšyš "aged"; Lévi (Hebrew Text, p. 27) and Peters (Liber Jesu, p. 365) read zqn "old"; I suggest the reading śb "aged." The reading yšyš would seem to be supported by the Syr qšyš'. Smend has also pointed to its use in 8:6a and 42:8. However, while the former is likely in the damaged HebA, the latter is untenable. Smend himself reads 42:8 with HebBmg kwšl (now confirmed by HebM) against HebB wyšyš. Even in 8:6a, Gr translates with gēras "old age" and not presbyteros as here. Not only does Gr not translate yšyš with presbyteros in Sirach, but it does so only once in the entire LXX (Job 32:6). Cf. the related yšš in 2 Chr 36:17 and yšyš, which is translated presbytēs "old man" in Job 29:8. The expression yšyš is therefore unlikely to have stood in the Heb of our text. Lévi and Peters have no doubt been influenced by the usual LXX translation of zqn with presbyteros. Of the 174 uses of this Heb adj. in the OT, over 130 are translated with presbyteros and almost 30 with presbytēs. This tendency is impressive. However, the adj. zqn is never translated by presbyteros in Sirach. The one clear use of the adj. zqn is in 32(35):9a, but there Gr translates with megistanōn. In 8:6b Smend seems justified in reading mzqynym, a hif. part. which is reflected by Gr gēraskousin. HebA, followed by Box-Oesterley (p. 343), reads mzqnym "among the aged." Cf. Syr s'byn "elders." However, the MS reading is unlikely, since the LXX regularly translates the verb zqn with gēraskō, but never the adj. zqn. The hif. tzqyn is also found in 30:24b, translated with gēras agei. Conversely, the term presbyteros (presbytēs is not used) in Sirach is used to translate a variety of Heb words, but never zqn. In 4:7 (according to S^c, whereas the preferred reading is megistani) Heb reads šltwm "mastery"; in 7:14 Heb reads śrym "princes"; and in 32(35):3 Heb reads śb "aged (one)." For the other uses of presbyteros (6:34; 25:4, 20) the Heb is either not extant or mutilated. Thus, as attractive as the adj. zqn may appear behind presbyterou in our text based on the common practice of th LXX, the tendency of Ben Sira would suggest otherwise. My suggestion of the reading śb is based on its use in 32(35):3, which Gr translates presbytere. The sing. is also found in 42:8 but is there translated eschatogērōs. For the plur., translated gerontōn, see 8:9. Cf. the related noun śybh, translated gērous in 46:9. It is clear that this word group is well represented in Sirach, and that in one instance outside our text the term śb is translated by Gr with a form of presbyteros. While we can point to no such LXX translation of śb outside Sirach, we should note that the LXX translates the related Aram śb with presbyteros in Ezra 5:9;

6:7-8, 14. See also Job 15:10, where śb is translated with presbytēs. Even though there is no unassailable evidence in support of śb for our text, it is at least plausible on the basis of Ben Sira's usage and the Gr translation of 32(35):3. This is at least more than can be claimed for the other suggested readings.

60Reading with Gr houtōs. Cf. Syr hkn' hy. This is clearly the sense of HebC with k- in line a. However, the expected kn is not present, though it is restored by Lévi (Hebrew Text, p. 27) and Peters (Liber Jesu, p. 365).

61Reading with Smend's reconstruction of the mutilated HebC 'št [lšwn]. Only the first word of the line, 'št, is clearly visible. For the same reading, see Lévi, Hebrew Text, p. 27; Peters, Liber Jesu, p. 365; Box-Oesterley, p. 402. Cf. Gr gynē glōssōdēs "a garrulous wife." Syr is free with 'ntt' dlšnh 'ryk "a woman whose tongue is long." The reading 'št lšwn is established on the basis of the analogous Heb idiom 'yš lšwn "a talkative man (lit. a man of tongue)," which KB renders a "big talker." This expression is translated by the LXX with anēr glōssōdēs. See Ps 140:11 (Heb 12); Sir 8:3 (anthrōpou glōssōdous); 9:18. The occurrence of glōssōdēs in Prov 21:19 is an addition behind which there is no Heb.

62I have reconstructed the mutilated Heb here to read l'yš ʿny. This is a conjectural emendation with a low degree of certainty. Gr reads andri hēsychō. While 'yš may be confidently seen behind andri, the Heb Vorlage of hēsychō is not so apparent. The word hēsychos occurs in the LXX only in Isa 66:2 (for nkh rwḥ), Wis 18:14 (no Heb), and in our text. Smend (Jesus Sirach, p. 231) follows Lévi (Hebrew Text, p. 27) in identifying a letter with a raised horizontal line at the end, which, according to Syr mkyk' (lwt gbr' mkyk' "to a meek man"), must represent mk (from mwk "to be depressed, grow poor"). This identification is challenged by Peters (Jesus Sirach, p. 214), who claims that the letter remains are inconclusive and may be w from the word ʿnw "poor, humble, meek." The problem of reconstructing the Heb here is that, while both words are used by Ben Sira (12:5; 3:20), neither mk nor ʿnw or any related forms (including ʿny) lie behind the LXX hēsychos or any of its cognates. While mk seems reflected in Syr, it does not totally satisfy the context and appears strange as a modifier. Lev 27:8 may be a remote example. The same may be said of ʿnw, though it is contextually superior. For this reason, then, I would prefer to read ʿny. It is well represented in Sir (4:1, 3, 8; 10:14; 31(34):4) and, though usually employed as a substantive, is found also as a modifier (Ps 18:27 (Heb 28) = 2 Sam 22:28). The term fits the present context when understood in the sense of "humble." Cf. the similar meaning in Sir 10:14, where it contrasts g'ym "the proud."

[63]HebC _'l_ _tpwl_. Syr _l'_ _tštdl_ "do not be enticed" is a free translation. However, Gr _mē_ _prospesēs_ "do not throw yourself" is a misunderstanding of the Heb, by reading _npl_ in the sense of "to prostrate" (intentional) rather than "to fall" (unintentional).

[64]Reading with Smend's restoration of HebC [_`l_]. This seems to be the intent of Syr _l_- (_lšwprh_). Smend (_Jesus Sirach_, p. 231) takes _`l_ in line _b_ to be a reminiscence of its use here. For the expression _npl_ _`l_ in the sense of "to fall because of," see Isa 54:15. Lévi (_Hebrew Text_, p. 27) offers the reading _b_- (_bypy_). Gr _epi_ continues the misunderstanding noted above, giving "do not throw yourself upon." This no doubt gave rise to the vars. _pros_ (Origenistic recension) and _eis_ (248).

[65]Reading with Smend's restoration of HebC [_ypy_ _'š_]_h_. Cf. Gr _kallos_ (_kallous_ S^{c}) _gynaikos_. Syr (_l_)_šwprh_ _d'ntt'_ _byšt'_ "(because of) the beauty of a wicked woman" is a softening qualification.

[66]Reading with Smend's restoration of HebC [_'l_ _tlk_]_d_. This reading is supported by the parallel of falling (_npl_) into a trap and getting caught (_lkd_), which is used regarding evil women in 9:3, 4. For the same parallel in a different context, see Isa 24:18. Lévi (_Hebrew Text_, p. 27) reads [_'l_ _tḥm_]_d_ "do not desire (her)." Cf. Strack, _Sohnes Sirachs_, p. 21. However, this depends on Gr, which is clearly secondary, and Syr, which at this point is a free translation that tones down the rather dark picture of the Heb. See Smend, _Jesus Sirach_, p. 231. Apparently, the Gr of this line was lost or mutilated quite early and was restored with the general and contextually inappropriate _kai_ _gynaika_ _mē_ _epipothesēs_ "and do not yearn after a woman." The MSS show various attempts to fill out this short stich. After _gynaika_, SA etc. + _en_ _kallei_ "in beauty" (cf. line _a_) and after _epipothesēs_, the Lucianic recension + _eis_ _tryen_ "for indulgence." The Gr may have been influenced by Syr _w'pn_ _'yt_ _lh_ _nks'_ _'l_ _ttrgrg_ _lh_ "and even if she has wealth do not desire her." It is also possible, of course, that Syr was influenced by the general Gr stich to tone down the Heb, while retaining the basic Heb structure.

[67]HebC (_w_)_`l_ _yš_ _lh_. For Gr and Syr, see note 66.

[68]Reading with Smend's reconstruction of HebC [_qšh_] (= Syr _qšy'_). Cf. Box-Oesterley, p. 402. For the expression _`bdh_ _qšh_, see Exod 1:14; 6:9; Deut 26:6. Gr may have read _qš'_ "stubbornness" and translated with _anaideia_ "impudence." This resulted in three coordinates rather than the two present in Heb and Syr: _orgē_ _kai_ _anaideia_ _kai_ _aischynē_ _megalē_ "(there is) wrath and impudence and great shame." Strack (_Sohnes Sirachs_, p. 21) fills the lacuna with [_wqlwn_] "and dishonor."

[69]Reading with Smend `bdh (= Syr). Cf. Peters, Jesus Sirach, p. 214; Box-Oesterley, p. 402. HebC b`dh "through/behind her" is clearly the result of letter transposition. However, both Strack (Sohnes Sirachs, p. 21) and Lévi (Hebrew Text, p. 27) read with HebC. Gr read `brh and translated with orgē "wrath" but by doing so confirmed `bdh.

[70]HebC wbwšt. Both Gr and Syr contain unwarranted additions. Gr reads kai aischynē megalē "and great shame." The translator tends to ornament the text by adding megas. Cf. 41:12; 44:19; 50:1. The expression aischynē megalē is unique in the LXX. Syr reads wbhtt' byšt' "evil shame." Cf. Antonius Melissa, p. 1156.

[71]HebC 'šh mklklt (= Gr gynē ean epichorēgē with the addition of ean). Gr46 reads epichōrē "goes against" for epichorēgē and thereby echoes Syr 'ntt' dsrḥ' `l "a woman who commits an offense against." La + contraria est "is contrary (to)."

[72]HebC b`lh (= Gr, Syr).

[73]Gr and Syr include v. 23ab as follows:

Gr A dejected heart and a gloomy face
And a wound of the heart is an evil wife.

Syr And she covers the heart which is in her.
Darkness and a wound of the heart is an evil wife.

It is possible that the deletion of this distich in HebC may be due to the fact that it occurs at the division between the recto and verso sides of the MS, folio 4. The similar content of lines ab to cd may have facilitated this deletion. However, this similarity itself represents an awkward repetition, that is uncharacteristic of the section. This awkwardness is especially evident in Gr, where references to "heart" are clumsily made in both lines a and b. This "heart" orientation is no doubt influenced by v. 13a. In fact, the expression plēgē kardias is found in both vv. 13a and 23b. Syr is no better, since line a is attached to and a continuation of v. 22. This negative evidence against the genuineness of v. 23ab is balanced by the positive support of the distich pattern for this part of the section when v. 23ab is omitted. For vv. 13-26 the pattern without v. 23ab is: 2 + 1 + 1 + 2 + 1 + 1 + 2 + 1 + 1 + 2. The inclusion of v. 23ab would conclude with the uncharacteristic pattern 2 + 2 + 1 + 2. Accordingly, I consider v. 23ab to be secondary and have not included it in the section. I note with interest that Box-Oesterley (p. 402) reached a similar conclusion but chose to include the distich in the text anyway. Those who assume the genuineness of v. 23ab include Smend (Jesus Sirach, p. 232) and Peters (Jesus Sirach, p. 213). Fuss (p.

160) sees v. 23abcd as representative of Ben Sira's compositional technique, in which ideas are gathered from previous elements in the text and from the OT. Some of his particular identifications, however, are questionable. Others, such a the "wound of the heart" notion can be argued equally as a secondary influence, as I have done.

[74]HebC rpywn ydym (= Gr, Syr).

[75]HebC wkšlwn brkym (= Gr). Cf. Syr wtbr' dbwrk' "and broken knees."

[76]So HebC (= Syr). Gr merely contains hētis.

[77]HebC bʽlh (= Gr, Syr).

[78]Or "does not call (her husband) blessed." Either is possible with HebC l' t'šr (= Gr ou makariei, here a gnomic fut.). Gr248 reads parakalesei, with en stenōsei at the end of the line giving "does not comfort (her husband) in anguish." Syr also is free with (d)l' myqr' wmšbḥ' "does not honor and praise." Gottfried Kuhn ("Beiträge zur Erklärung des Buches Jesus Sira, II," ZAW 48 [1930]:105) suggests the deletion of l' and reads tr'š "who makes (her husband) poor," thus providing a contrast to v. 22. However, this must be rejected as without textual foundation in light of the universal witness to the presence of the negative particle.

[79]HebC m'šh (= Gr, Syr).

[80]HebC tḥlt ʽwn (= Gr, Syr).

[81]HebC wbgllh gwʽnw yḥd (= Gr, Syr). Several Gr minuscules, John of Damascus, Antonius Melissa, and Antiochus Monachus read di autēs "through her."

[82]Heb is not extant for vv. 25-26. Gr mē dōs hydati diexodon (= Syr).

[83]Gr parrēsian. Cf. GrB exousian "authority" (probably under the influence of 33:19); John of Damascus and Antonius Melissa anesin "indulgence" (from 26:10); 248 + exodou "(boldness) of exit" (to tighten the parallel with line a; 443 + tou lalein "(boldness) to speak" (by way of explanation). La reads veniam prodeundi "permission to appear." Syr 'p' wšwlṭn' "face and rule" is either a free translation or, more likely, a misreading of the Heb. The reading parrēsian best fits the context.

[84]Gr gynaiki ponēra (= Syr). Syr includes an additional distich here, which Smend (Jesus Sirach, p. 233) attributes to a Heb gloss. It reads according to Box-Oesterley's (p. 402) rendering:

For as the bursting forth of water goes on and increases,
So does an evil wife continue to sin more and more.

[85]Gr ei mē poreuetai. Cf. Syr w'm l' 'ytyh 'ty' "and if she does not come."

[86]Gr kata cheiras sou lit. "according to your hands." This is the reading of S and several minuscules. and is preferred by Rahlfs and Ziegler. Cf. 14:25. The reading of the rest is cheira "hand." Syr reads btrk "after you."

[87]Gr apo tōn sarkōn (404, 493 sarkos) sou apoteme autēn. Cf. Syr bsrk qṣṣ "cut off your flesh." Gr248 + didou kai apolyson "give and send (her) away" to explain the figurative expression. Syr apparently knew this reading and extended it even further: hb lh wšryh mn bytk "give to her and send her from your house."

[88]See chap. I, including nn. 34-39.

[89]See chap. I, including nn. 40-51).

[90]Vv. 22b, 23a, 25b, 27.

[91]Peters, Jesus Sirach, p. 213. Cf. Box-Oesterley, p. 403. The second of these elements could be 1 + 1 + 1, since each distich has its own subj. But 3 is more likely since the three distichs appear to represent a developing thought, as I shall argue below.

[92]See n. 73.

[93]This is similar to the arrangement by Box-Oesterley (p. 401) except for their inclusion of v. 23ab. Peters (Jesus Sirach, p. 213) also includes v. 23ab but employs a different distich scheme.

[94]For a treatment of Zahlensprüche in general and their use by Ben Sira in particular, see Appendix 1.

[95]See Fuss, p. 162. See also my discussion in chap. I.

[96]On the surface, "the assembly of the people" might appear quite neutral and hence strange in this setting. However, the expression no doubt refers to the assembly (qhl) as it meets to consider legal matters and to pass judgment, making it something to be feared. For more on the phrase, see on 42:11c.

[97]Cf. 25:1-2. This would make the Zahlenspruch a single number type (X).

[98]For this view, see Fuss, pp. 161-62.

[99]See chap. I for a discussion of the function of Zahlensprüche in Sir 25-26.

[100]See Appendix 1.

[101]The climactic nature of the rival wife element has often been recognized by scholars, though generally for reasons different than my own. See Smend, Jesus Sirach, p. 234; Peters, Jesus Sirach, p. 216; Eberharter, p. 95; Spicq, p. 698; Weber, p. 549; Snaith, Ecclesiasticus, p. 133.

[102]Not all scholars hold the view that Ben Sira is referring to a situation of polygamy. Snaith (Ecclesiasticus, p. 133) thinks the subj. may be either a rival wife or simply another woman seeking a man's affections. Ryssel (p. 363) holds that the woman is another man's wife. Gaspar (p. 6, n. 16) follows Peters (Jesus Sirach, p. 304) in taking the Gr term in the general sense of jealousy. For my discussion of antizēlos and the Heb ṣrh (cf. 37:11) as technical terms for a rival wife, see n. 10. Cf. Box-Oesterley, p. 403.

[103]Besides our text, see 37:11 and probably also 28:15.

[104]Outside of Sirach antizēlos is found in the LXX only in Lev 18:18, where it translates ṣrr II "to be a rival wife." This is the only use of ṣrr II in this sense. Apart from Sir 37:11, the Heb noun ṣrh II "rival wife" is used only in 1 Sam 1:6.

[105]Cf. 25:13a. However, there the heart wound is not necessarily caused by a wife.

[106]P. 164.

[107]One distich (v. 7) involves comparison. One distich (v. 9) centers on a prostitute's eyes (mentioned in both stichs). One distich (v. 8) combines a note on reaction to a drunken woman, with mention of her conduct as a type of cause and effect statement.

[108]This is the reading of HebB, which is reflected in Gr gynaiki ponēra. We may take this as the probable Heb expression behind the Gr phrase wherever it occurs. For 42:6a, however, the reading, as restored from HebM and partly reflected in HebBmg, should probably be 'šh mṭšt "a wife who plays the fool." See on 42:6 for a discussion.

[109]Gr 25:23ab (gynē ponēra) emphasizes depression. However, I do not consider this distich to have been part of the original text. See n. 73.

[110]r`t 'šh. See 25:13, 17 (r` 'šh), 19.

[111]See 2:16; 5:20; 7:5. For the more general parallel of zr with nkry, see 5:10; 20:16; 27:13 (the BHS conjecture of nkrym is more likely here than MT nkryh.). In fact, outside of 6:24 and 23:27, where BHS offers the conjecture zrh, the term nkryh with reference to women occurs only in parallel with zrh.

[112]P. 116.

[113]Edersheim, p. 137.

[114]Peters, Jesus Sirach, p. 216.

[115]Schilling, p. 116.

[116]Eberharter, p. 95; Hamp, p. 639.

[117]Box-Oesterley, p. 403.

[118]Cf. Sir 30:13 Heb.

[119]For more evidence of the influence of this 1 Kings material on Sirach, see the discussion of 25:22.

[120]So Smend, Jesus Sirach, p. 235.

[121]I have argued above (n. 16) that the Heb probably contained a form of tmk "to lay hold of."

[122]For a similar assessment, see Box-Oesterley, p. 403; Snaith, Ecclesiasticus, p. 133; McKeating, p. 85. The latter sees control of a wife as characteristic of Ben Sira′s attitude toward women.

[123]E.g., Peters, Jesus Sirach, p. 216; Eberharter, p. 95. Box-Oesterley (p. 403) has a similar view but notes that the evil wife′s retaliation against assertions of authority over her involves "some bitter slander or false accusation."

[124]Deut 8:15; Ezek 2:6. Cf. Luke 10:19; 11:12.

[125]Cf. Rev 9:3, 5, 10.

[126]Ryssel (p. 363) sees the mention of a scorpion to be very harsh, since according to popular belief its sting was fatal.

[127]The Gr gynē methysos may have translated ′šh sb′h. Cf. 18:33a Heb. It is also possible that the Heb read škrh, as in 1 Sam 1:13, which LXX translates with methyousan.

[128]The closest biblical analogy to Sir 26:8 is Rev 17:6, where the great harlot (cf. Sir 26:9) is said to be drunk with

the blood of saints and martyrs. However, this is not a picture of reality but of symbolic apocalypticism.

[129]For other references by Ben Sira to women and wine, see 9:9 and 19:2.

[130]Eberharter, p. 95.

[131]Box-Oesterley, p. 403.

[132]Cf. the allusion to his embarrassment in v. 6b.

[133]While aschēmosynē can mean "disgraceful conduct" in general, it no doubt here translates `rwh. Such is the case in its predominate LXX use in Lev 18 and 20. There the meaning is clearly "nakedness," referring to the genitals. Cf. Sir 29:21 (no Heb extant). The Gr term is also used in 30:13. But there the Heb reads 'wlt "foolishness." The expected translation would have been aphrosynē, as in 8:15 and 47:23. It is likely, therefore, that aschēmosynē in 30:13 resulted from an early internal Gr corruption.

[134]Cf. Tal. "pain of the heart" (k'b lb) and "wickedness of a wife" (r`t 'šh) with Ben Sira's "wound of the heart" ([mkt] lb) and "wickedness of a wife" (r`t 'šh).

[135]Cowley-Neubauer present this material within an extensive comparative printing of "Ben Sira's Proverbs" and their quotations and/or allusions in rabbinic writings. Smend has reconstructed portions of the Heb text of v. 13 based on the Tal. material. Cf. Ryssel, p. 360; Box-Oesterley, p. 401.

[136]See Cowley-Neubauer.

[137]P. 158.

[138]Reading r`t 'šh with Smend. See n. 26. The reading 'šh r`h "an evil wife" does not fit the pattern evident in the last half of each stich and is no doubt secondary. It may have resulted from the general influence of Ben Sira on rabbinic material.

[139]There is no way of knowing for certain the size or arrangement of the original material. However, from the six lines that we have it may be possible to reconstruct part of the pattern. Three lines refer to maladies involving parts of the body and would naturally fall together. Let us identify them as A, B, and C. One line considers a wife's wickedness. We will call it D. The two lines which deal with adversaries will be E and F. It is possible to treat these as two tristichs, one dealing with body illnesses (A:B:C), the other with negative social relationships (D:E:F). However, given the relative rarity of tristichs in this kind of literature, it is more

likely that the original was constructed on the distich model. This offers several possibilities. One would be the arrangement of the six extant stichs as follows: A:B, C:D, E:F. While the first and last distichs are justifiable, the second is untenable. A more likely distich arrangement is based on the premise that the original contained material which neither Ben Sira nor the rabbis quoted. We can then postulate the following arrangement: A:B, C:?, ?:D, E:F.

[140]Smend, *Jesus Sirach*, p. 229. Cf. Box-Oesterley, p. 401.

[141]Smend reads instead with a form of *qwṣ* "to loathe." This is preferable in the context and has the support of Ben Sira's use elsewhere, e.g., 4:9 (not certain); 6:25; 50:25. Either reading, however, illustrates my point.

[142]Smend, *Jesus Sirach*, p. 392.

[143]Yadin, p. 24.

[144]When one combines all the unique topics treated in Ben Sira's quotation and the rabbinic quotation the subj. of women represents only one of six topics.

[145]6:1, 4, 9, 13; 12:8, 9, 10; 18:31.

[146]12:16; 36:7, 10mg (33:9, 12); 46:1; 49:9.

[147]12:16; 47:7.

[148]See the discussion on 26:6, where Gr reads *antizēlos* and the Heb (not extant) is likely *ṣrh*.

[149]Lev 26:17; Num 10:35; Deut 30:7; 2 Sam 22:18, 41; Pss 18:17, 40; 21:8; 25:19; 35:19; 38:19; 55:12; 68:1; 83:2.

[150]Pss 69:4; 106:10; 106:41-42 (the terms do not occur in the same distich); 139:22.

[151]Ps 44:7 contains the parallel in Heb, but the LXX translates *ṣr* with a form of *thlibō*.

[152]See, e.g., Peters, *Jesus Sirach*, p. 213. Those who consider the lines to be part of the original text point to the "dejected heart" and "wound of the heart" being "caused by an evil wife" of v. 23ab as evidence of this relationship. However, as I have argued, this distich does not appear to be genuine. See n. 73. Thus, it has no control over the meaning of v. 13a.

[153]Smend, *Jesus Sirach*, p. 229.

[154]Another element that betrays Ben Sira's efforts is the shift from the sing. of v. 13b to the plur. of both terms in v. 14. The disparity was clear to Syr, which made the terms in v. 14 sing. Cf. NEB, JB.

[155]This is against Fuss (p. 158), who sees vv. 15-16 as traditional.

[156]See n. 31. Ben Sira has another allusion to the snake and the Genesis story in 21:2.

[157]Or is "head" a reference to the snake's craftiness (Gen 3:1)?

[158]It is possible that even the reference to anger (thymos) may reflect the idea of enmity ('ybh) from Gen 3:15. This must be considered no more than a loose reference at best, since thymos never translates 'ybh in the LXX. Nevertheless, the ideas are not unrelated.

[159]See on 26:7.

[160]See n. 85.

[161]Cf. Middendorp, p. 83.

[162]Prov 21:9; 25:24. In Prov 21:19 we find the extended expression "a contentious and fretful wife."

[163]Prov 21:9; 25:24.

[164]Prov 21:19.

[165]Cf. Fritzsche, p. 140.

[166]See n. 35.

[167]P. 158.

[168]The term "bears" is found in 47:3 but not in a comparison. It is merely one of several kinds of animals with which David is said to have played.

[169]See also v. 19.

[170]In vv. 13, 19 the Heb reads r`t 'šh.

[171]Cf. also the only other OT hif. use in Ezek 31:15, where Lebanon will be made dark in a context of mourning. For qal uses that involve the luminaries, see Jer 4:28; Joel 2:10; 4:15; Mic 3:6.

[172]Cf. Box-Oesterley, p. 401.

[173]The term used here is r`ym. The word r` is the predominant term for neighbor in the OT. It can also mean "friend." The LXX plēsion "neighbor" usually has r` as its Vorlage. The situation is also true in Sirach. There plēsion occurs about twenty-five times. Where the Heb exists and represents a related reading (eight places) the Vorlage is always r` or its equivalent ry`. In these eight instances the RSV translates the term with "neighbor." This seems preferable to Box-Oesterley's practice of alternating between "neighbor" and "friend." There is no evidence to support the contention of Edersheim (p. 134), followed by Ryssel (p. 360), that those here described as neighbors were actually near relatives.

[174]See chap. V, n. 265.

[175]For the sorrow idea, see Lam 1:4, 8, 21; Isa 24:7; Jer 22:23; Ezek 9:4; 21:6, 7. For the frustration idea, see Exod 2:23; Lam 1:11; Prov 29:2 (this may also fit the sorrow idea). Cf. Sus 22, which reads anastenazō, as in our text.

[176]Eberharter (p. 93) suggests that this outburst of sighing is caused by the contrast of the man's home trouble with the merriment of his friends. But the text says nothing about the activities of his neighbors. It merely describes him as sitting among them. Spicq (p. 696) is even more fanciful by suggesting that the husband sighs when he compares the good wives of his friends to his own.

[177]P. 158.

[178]See the above discussion of these verses for my assessment of their origin.

[179]The form of our text is also like v. 15, which I consider Ben Sira's composition. It might be argued on the strength of that comparison that v. 19 is also from Ben Sira. However, the presence of r`t 'šh in our text (cf. v. 17) links it more to the traditional vv. 13-14 than to the composed v. 15.

[180]E.g., Num 36:3.

[181]E.g., Ps 16:5; Dan 12:13.

[182]Gen 13:13; Num 16:38; 1 Sam 15:18; Ps 26:9; Isa 1:28.

[183]Ps 1:5-6; Isa 13:9; 33:14.

[184]Cf. Smend (Jesus Sirach, p. 231), who sees the sinner's lot as the fate which sinners may expect and from which the pious are exempt. This is certainly preferable to Eberharter's (p. 93) contention that her lot is to fall under the control of an evil husband, who will deal with her evil accordingly.

[185]In discussing this verse Gaspar (p. xii) argues that Ben Sira does not here display misogynistic characteristics. He suggests that it is wrong to take "a single detail" and view it "separately from the rest of the picture," where womanhood is seen to be "beautiful and noble." Gaspar's contention would be valid if the total picture were as positive as he assumes it to be. But this particular verse is merely typical of Ben Sira's negative bias against women, which lies behind his treatment of women within every category.

[186]P. 159.

[187]For other references to sand in Sirach, see 1:2; 18:10; 22:15.

[188]Cf. Box-Oesterley, p. 402.

[189]Cf. Snaith, Ecclesiasticus, p. 130.

[190]For this reading of the text, see n. 61.

[191]The expression is rather ambiguous in 8:3, as reflected in the various translations: "chatterer" (RSV); "long-winded man" (NEB); "man of quick tongue" (JB); "garrulous man" (Goodspeed); "loud-mouthed man" (Box-Oesterley). In 9:18 the phrase is paralleled by the mention of one reckless in speech. Ps 140:11 is generally translated with the idea of slander.

[192]See Box-Oesterley, p. 402.

1933P. 159.

[194]Cf. Eccl 7:26.

[195]11:2; 40:22; 43:9, 18.

[196]26:16-17; 36:22 (24 Heb, 27 Gr).

[197]9:8; 25:21; 42:12. Cf. Prov 6:25; 11:22; 31:30.

[198]At least in the case of line a.

[199]Exod 1:14; 6:9; Deut 26:6.

[200]1 Kgs 12:4; 2 Chr 10:4. We have already detected influence from this material in Sir 26:7. See the discussion there. It is possible that Ben Sira is more conscious of the "hard slavery" associated with the Solomonic oppression than the other OT examples. Yet it is hard to imagine tht he is not aware of the expression in relationship to the Egyptian slavery.

[201]Isa 14:3.

[202]Middendorp (p. 57) considers Ben Sira soft on the notion of hard slavery in Egypt (see chap. 45 on Moses) and Babylon because of the political situation of his day, when foreigners ruled in Palestine.

[203]The meaning of the Heb word which Gr translated with a form of aischyneō is unclear.

[204]Cf. Spicq, p. 697.

[205]Cf. Gaspar, pp. 20, 31. He understands this to imply that the husband has lost his dignity as baʿal.

[206]See, e.g., 9:2; 33:19-20. It is interesting to note that when Ben Sira fantacizes about Wisdom as an ideal wife, he is quite content to have her support him and to do so without shame. See 15:5; 24:22; 51:18. But the emphasis in these passages is on his assessment of Wisdom and not on the ideal wife. He did not originate this personification but merely adopted it from his wisdom sources, in which the metaphor abounded as a literary convention. For a discussion of this personification and its place in Sirach and elsewhere, see chap. I, n. 215. In reality, Ben Sira's glowing regard for dame Wisdom stands in astounding contrast to his reflections on women in the flesh.

[207]See n. 73 for the textual status of v. 23ab.

[208]The structure of v. 22 in Heb and Syr is lit.:

For hard slavery and a disgrace (Syr evil shame)--
A wife who supports (Syr commits an offense against) her husband.

For line b Gr reads: "if a wife supports her husband." The structure of v. 23cd in Heb, Gr, and Syr is lit.:

Drooping hands and tottering (Syr broken) knees--
A wife who does not make her husband happy (Syr honor and praise her husband).

[209]For a discussion, see Fuss, pp. 159-60.

[210]See n. 73 for the distich pattern.

[211]Ben Sira makes a similar assertion in 4:18 but has Wisdom gladdening the possessor.

[212]Gen 30:13.

[213]Cant 6:9. In this and the above instances those who call the women blessed/happy are other women.

[214]The metaphor is used at least thirteen times. See, e.g., Jer 6:24; 38:4; 47:3; 50:43.

[215]Isa 35:3; Ezek 7:17; 21:7; Job 4:3-4.

[216]Note, e.g.:

RSV Drooping hands and weak knees
are caused by the wife who does not make her husband happy.

NEB Slack of hand and weak of knee
is the man whose wife fails to make him happy.

[217]The verbal form kšl is sometimes used with knees. One example is Isa 35:3, which contains the same double metaphor as our text but with the words reversed in each unit: ydym rpwt wbrkym kšlwt. Another difference lies in Isaiah's use of rpwt where Ben Sira has rpywn, found elsewhere only in Jer 47:3. The latter has the identical Heb expression rpywn ydym, except with the preformative m-. In the other example, Ps 109:24, the expression is literal.

[218]See BDB, s.v. kšlwn.

[219]Box-Oesterley (p. 402) consider the metaphors to be a description of the wife whose lot is "fearfulness and calamity." Cf. the translation in JB:

Slack hands and sagging knees
indicate a wife who makes her husband wretched.

[220]P. 160.

[221]For later reflections and developments of this idea, see Adam and Eve 3, 5, 16, 18; Apoc. Mos. 24:1-3; 2 Enoch 30:16-18; 31:6; Tg. Ps.-J. Gen 3:19; 1 Tim 2:14. Cf. 2 Cor 11:3. All these are dated in the first century A.D. or later.

[222]Bruce J. Malina, "Some Observations on the Origin of Sin in Judaism and St. Paul," CBQ 31 (1969):22-24.

[223]See 1 Enoch 6:1-6; 7:1-6; 15:2-16:1; Jub. 5:1-6; 10:1, 5-9, 11; CD II.16-18.

[224]See, e.g., Midr. Bemidbar Rab. 13. Cf. 2 Apoc. Bar. 54:15-19; 56:6; Rom 5:12-21; 1 Cor 15:22.

[225]P. 697. Cf. Gen 3:20.

[226]Gerhard von Rad, Wisdom in Israel, trans. James D. Martin (London: SCM Press, 1972), p. 262.

[227]See Fritzsche, p. 141; Weber, p. 549.

[228]H. Maldwyn Hughes, The Ethics of Jewish Apocryphal Literature (London: Robert Culley, [1909]), p. 148. For a similar argument, see Tiburtius Gallus, "'A muliere initium peccati et per illam omnes morimur,'" Verbum domini 23 (1943):273. Cf. Spicq, p. 697.

[229]Frederick Robert Tennant, "The Teaching of Ecclesiasticus and Wisdom on the Introduction of Sin and Death," JTS 2 (1901-2):210. However, Tennant still considers the verse "ambiguous as a guide to its writer's teaching on the introduction of general sinfulness."

[230]Gallus (p. 273) seems troubled that the text is ambiguous. He inquires whether sin refers to Eve's sin, Adam's sin, or original sin.

[231]Note 24:22, where Wisdom as the ideal wife keeps her adherents from sinning.

[232]Gallus (pp. 274-75) is also concerned with the sense in which Eve's sin caused death to pass to all. He considers several possibilities.

[233]Ben Sira is aware of the relationship of death to the decree in the Genesis story, as we see in 8:7 and 14:17.

[234]P. 160.

[235]See the discussion on 26:7 and 25:16.

[236]Cf. Smend, Jesus Sirach, p. 232.

[237]Jesus Sirach, p. 215.

[238]See n. 87, where it is evident that the longer readings of Gr248 and Syr understood the distich as a reference to divorce. For further discussion of this theme in Sirach, see on 7:19; 7:26; 28:15.

[239]The verb apotemnō is found only in Judg 5:26 (GrA) and Jer 36:23, neither of which is related to divorce.

[240]At least according to my survey of LSJ.

[241]See 40:17; 41:11; 44:18, 20; 50:24.

[242]According to KB, s.v. krt, the verb in postbiblical Heb meant "to cut off, divorce." Cf. Jastrow, s.v. k^{e}rat.

[243]E.g., Ryssel, p. 362; Smend, Jesus Sirach, p. 233; Peters, Jesus Sirach, p. 215; Box-Oesterley, p. 402; Gaspar, p. 35; Snaith, Ecclesiasticus, p. 130.

[244]See BAG², s.v. sarx.

[245]For bśr, see 8:19; 13:15-16; 14:17-18; 30:14; 37:11; 39:19; 41:4; 44:18, 20; 48:12-13; 50:17; 51:2. For š'r, see 7:24; 38:16; 40:19; 41:21.

[246]13:16; 14:17; 39:19; 41:4; 44:18, 20.

[247]See KB, BDB.

[248]Ps 78(77):27; Mic 3:2-3. For the sing. sarx, see Ps 73(72):26.

[249]31(34):1

[250]My check of the divorce material from Elephantine does not reveal any use there of this particular metaphor relative to divorce.

[251]P. 35.

[252]Ecclesiasticus, p. 130.

[253]Deut 24:1, 3; Isa 50:1; Jer 3:8. The latter two texts use the term figure of Israel (and/or Judah) in a condition of apostasy. The Jeremiah material is particularly interesting, because in 3:1 it reflects Deut 24:1-4. But then as the text explores the faithless condition of Israel and Judah in vv. 2-10, it is clear that the reason for the "divorce" is because Yahweh's "wives" have "committed adultery."

[254]The second marriage may be dissolved either by divorce or by the death of the husband.

[255]The unit of casuistic legislation is 24:1-4, with vv. 1-3 providing the case conditions, or protasis, and v. 4 containing the legislation itself, or apodosis. The divorce(s) is/are part of the conditions. Thus, this is not legislation that governs divorce but case law that prohibits remarriage under certain circumstances. For a discussion of this unit, see the standard commentaries such as: Samuel Rolles Driver, A Critical and Exegetical Commentary on Deuteronomy, The International Critical Commentary (Edinburgh: T. & T. Clark, 1901), pp. 269-73; Gerhard von Rod, Deuteronomy, trans. Dorothea Barton, The Old Testament Library (Philadelphia: Westminster Press, 1966), pp. 149-50; Anthony Phillips, Deuteronomy, The Cambridge Bible Commentary (Cambridge: Cambridge University Press, 1973), pp. 159-60; Peter C. Craigie, The Book of Deuteronomy, The New International Commentary on the Old Testament (Grand Rapids, Michigan: William B. Eerdmans Pub. Co., 1976), pp. 304-6; Andrew D. H. Mayes, Deuteronomy, New Century Bible (London: Oliphants, 1979), pp. 322-23. See also Carmichael, p. 206.

256The literal uses include Gen 9:22-23; Exod 28:42; Lev 18:6-19; 20:11, 17-21; Ezek 22:10. Most of these deal with unacceptable sexual behavior. The figurative uses include Ezek 16:8, 36-37; 23:10, 18, 29; Isa 47:3; Lam 1:8; Hos 2:11.

257In Deut 24:3 the wife is divorced by her second husband because he distains (śn' lit. "hates") her. The context would suggest that his displeasure toward her is similar to that of the first husband and so he reacts in the same way. The verb śn' is widely used in reference to wives. See Gen 29:31, 33; Deut 21:15-17; 22:13, 16; Judg 14:16; 15:2; Prov 30:23; Isa 60:15 (figurative). However, the use that seems most helpful in elucidating its meaning in Deut 24:3 is Deut 22:13, 16, where a new bride is distained because of alleged lack of virginity at marriage. Thus, I take 24:3 to be a reference to a woman being divorced by her second husband for the same reason that she was divorced by her first husband, i.e., unacceptable sexual behavior.

258The commentators are in general agreement that this behavior does not involve actual adultery, since in deuteronomic law (22:22) such behavior merited death for both participants. S. R. Driver, p. 271; Phillips, p. 159; Craigie, p. 305; Mayes, p. 322. However, they understand the term ʿrwt dbr differently. Phillips (pp. 159-60) sees it as anything distasteful in the wife. Mayes (p. 322) does not take it to be a "particular act of indecency" but "some state of impurity in general." For Craigie (p. 305) the expression may refer to some physical deficiency, such as the inability to bear children. But in light of the widespread genital and sexual connotations of the root ʿrh and the word ʿrwt in particular, these interpretations seem inadequate. Von Rad (p. 150) merely observes that the expression "must have been clear in the time of Deuteronomy." However, S. R. Driver (pp. 270-71) is more likely to be correct when he says that ʿrwt dbr "signifies most probably some improper or indecent behavior," but short of adultery. We may also note that the LXX translation of this expression, aschēmon pragma "an indecent thing," may be understood in view of the use of aschēmōn in Gen 34:7. There Jacob's sons consider Shechem's rape of Dinah as an indecent act.

259The same contrast exists when one compares our verse to the OT verb grš when it is used with the meaning "to divorce." See Lev 21:7, 14; 22:13; Num 30:9 (Heb 10); Ezek 44:22, where divorce is assumed but with no conditions laid down.

260Cf. Snaith (Ecclesiasticus, p. 130), who sees the length of this section as a reflection of Ben Sira's "personal prejudice against women." In contrast, Peters (Jesus Sirach, p. 213) denies that one can generalize from this section to establish Ben Sira's enmity against women. Cf. Gaspar (p. 58), who rejects the notion that Ben Sira is a misogynist but admits that he does express this view "rather strongly."

[261]Reading with Smend's emendation ttn, which is reflected in Gr and Syr. Cf. Israel Lévi, "Notes sur les ch. VII.29-XII.1 de Ben Sira edites par M. Elkan N. Adler," JQR 13 (1900-1):6; Box-Oesterley, p. 345. HebA reads tqn' "(do not) be jealous." Smend, Lévi, and Box-Oesterley take this to be the result of vertical dittography with v. 1, where the same verb occurs. Penar (p. 27), however, sees no need to emend the reading to ttn. Instead, he suggests that npšk "your soul" (= "yourself") should be seen as the subj. and not the obj. Thus, his reading is: "Let not your soul be filled with passion for a woman." He offers the analogy of 4:9b. I consider Penar's case to be defective and must reject it. The evidence for dittography between vv. 1 and 2 seems more than adequate. It is recognized not only by those who read ttn but also by those who read some form of tqnh (see below). Penar's reference to 4:9b is weak in comparison to the contrary analogy of 9:6a and 47:19a, which support the reading ttn.

9:2a	'l	ttn	l'šh	npšk
9:6a	'l	ttn	lzwnh	npšk
47:19a		wttn	lnšym	kslyk

9:2a	do not	give yourself	to a woman.
9:6a	do not	give yourself	to a prostitute.
47:19a	but you	gave your loins to	women.

Vv. 9:6a and 47:19a compare with 9:2a by offering a structural parallel involving ttn in combination with l- attached to the word for woman and concluding with the obj., to which is attached the possessive suffix -k. We find that 9:6a is a particularly tight parallel. Furthermore, 9:2a and 47:19a are also parallel in subj. matter, since both deal with the topic of wives (women) who rule their husbands. Shilling (p. 54) also reads tgn' in 9:2a but sees it as a word play with 9:1a. He vocalizes the latter as t^{e}qannē' "(do not) be jealous" and the form in 9:2a as taqne' "(do not) sell." He appears to presuppose the verb to be tqh "to acquire," used in the nif. reflexive. But taqne' suggests the root tq' "to be jealous." The form of tqh that one would expect here would not be taqne' (cf. Aram tiqnē' in Ezra 7:17) but tiqqāneh (nif.) or taqneh (hif.). This is, in fact, the reading suggested by Peters (Jesus Sirach, p. 81), with the contention that this caused the scribal error based on dittography. Cf. Gaspar, p. 67. While this may easily account for the dittography, it is not unique in doing so. The reading ttn is not dissimilar in appearance to tqn'. The evidence from 9:6a and 47:19a, as well as the extensive use of ntn translated by didōmi in Sirach, lead me to prefer the reading ttn here.

[262]HebA npšk lit. "your soul" (= Gr, Syr.)

[263]HebA l'šh (= Gr, Syr).

[264]HebA lhdrykh (= Gr as in 46:9c). Syr lmšlṭwth "to give her power" is an interpretation of the original metaphor.

[265]HebA `l bmwtyk. Gr reads epi tēn ischyn sou "upon your strength." Here Gr interprets the metaphor. But this is not unique, as attested by the relationship between bmwt and ischys in Deut 32:13a. Smend (Jesus Sirach, p. 82) takes this as evidence that bmwt had lost its original meaning. Cf. Box-Oesterley, p. 345. Penar (pp. 27-28) understands bmwtyk to mean "your back," since in Ugaritic bmt means "back (of an animal or person)." Since such a meaning is not clearly attested in the OT in contrast to the extensive use of bmh as "high place," I am not persuaded by Penar's interpretation. He is right, however, in seeing the expression as a metaphor of subjugation. This is true no matter how we translate it. Syr `l kl m' d'yt lk "over all that you have" completes the line by continuing the interpretation of the metaphor.

[266]See the discussion of 9:1.

[267]Cf. Fuss, p. 78.

[268]Gen 30:4; 38:14; 1 Sam 18:19; 1 Kgs 2:21.

[269]See nn. 264-65.

[270]Cf. Peters, Jesus Sirach, p. 81; Spicq, p. 614; Gaspar, p. 67. Edersheim (p. 67) quotes a single number Zahlenspruch from Beṣa 32b, which includes one element of life that is not life at all: "of him over whom his wife holds rule."

[271]Cf. Box-Oesterley, p. 345; Spicq, p. 614; Weber, p. 545.

[272]HebE bn w'šh (= Gr, Syr). In HebE this is v. 20ab.

[273]Reading 'ḥ. This = Gr, Syr and is suggested by Marcus (p. 18), the publisher of HebE. HebE reads 'hb "friend," which, as Marcus observes, is synonymous with r`.

[274]HebE wr` (= Gr, Syr).

[275]HebE 'l tmšyl. Cf. Gr mē dōs exousian epi se "do not give power over you" and Syr l' tšlṭ bk "do not let have power over you." While bk might be expected to follow tmšyl on the basis of Gr and Syr and on the analogy of v. 20b (21b Heb), it is not likely to have stood in the original here. The construction mšl II b- b- is very unlikely, whereas mšl II b- is well attested. See Gen 1:18; 3:16; 4:7; 24:2; 45:8, 26; Isa 3:12. We also find mšl II b- in Sir 9:17; 37:18; 45:17; 47:19; 48:12. Cf. 30:11, where b- means "in." Thus, I prefer to read with

HebE, taking Gr and Syr *epi se*/*bk* to be explanitory interpolations.

[276]HebE *bḥyyk*. Cf. Gr *en zōē sou* (= Syr) "in your life." See n. 275 for Gr and Syr interpolation *epi se*/*bk* "over you."

[277]In Heb and some current translations these verses are numbered 20-24. In Gr this section is 30:28-32.

[278]The arrangement of the first four of these six distichs varies with the witnesses. The verse numbering system in the *RSV* follows a sequence based on Gr: 19abcd, 20, 21. HebE and Syr present the order: 19ab, 20, 19cd, 21. The latter is more logical, since it groups related material into a 2 + 2 distich pattern.

[279]The superiority of the advisee is certified or at least suggested by v. 22a, which in Box-Oesterley's translation reads: "In all thy works remain uppermost" (p. 431).

[280]See also 47:19-20 and my treatment of 26:7.

[281]Especially 30:11.

[282]HebB *wttn* (= Syr). Gr reads *paraneklinas* "laid . . . beside." This word is not only an LXX hapaxlegomenon, but LSJ gives our text as the only reference in Gr literature.

[283]HebB *kslyk* (= Gr). Syr reads *twqpk* "your strength," possibly under the influence of Prov 31:3a.

[284]HebB *lnšym* (= Gr, Syr).

[285]HebB *wtmšylm* (= Syr). Cf. Gr free translation *enexousiasthēs* "you were brought into subjection." Note, however, that the LXX sometimes translates *mšl* with the related *exousiazō*, e.g., Neh 9:37; Eccl 9:17; 10:4.

[286]HebB *bgwytk* (= Syr). Cf. Gr *en tō sōmati sou* "by your body."

[287]We should note that the 1 Kings material characterizes the women who caused Solomon his problems as *nšym nkrywt* "foreign women." Such women were always assessed negatively. The same phrase is found several times in Ezra 10:2-11. See also Prov 2:16; 5:20; 6:24; 7:5; 23:27. For the related expression *ʾšh zrh* "strange woman," see Sir 9:3; Prov 2:16; 5:3, 20; 7:5. For the classic study of the Proverbs materal, see Boström. See also Oliver Shaw Rankin, *Israel's Wisdom Literature* (Edinburgh: T. & T. Clark, 1936), pp. 259-64. These "foreign women" were either directly or connotatively associated with the alien fertility cults and their related idolatry. To condemn Solomon for consorting with such women would have been understandable

and in line with the biblical material. Ben Sira, however, condemns him for his relationships to women without further qualification. Thus, he exceeds his biblical source and betrays his negative bias against women.

[288]This fact is recognized by Smend (*Jesus Sirach*, p. 455), Box-Oesterley (p. 498), Weber (p. 554), and Snaith (*Ecclesiasticus*, p. 236). However, Smend feels that Ben Sira indirectly condemns Solomon's idolatry, and Box-Oesterley see such a reference to it in v. 21a. This latter contention is groundless.

[289]This *RSV* translation (cf. Goodspeed, *NEB*) correctly interprets the metaphor in the Gr *exeporneusen* lit. "(did not) indulge in immorality." The context makes it clear that what is meant is apostasy from Israel's God into idolatry. Ben Sira also reflects the lifelessness of idols in 30:18-19.

[290]Even Ben Sira seems to be aware of Solomon's departure from Yahweh when he declares in 49:4 that all Judah's kings except David, Hezekiah, and Josiah "sinned greatly" and "forsook the law of the Most High."

[291]Snaith (*Ecclesiasticus*, p. 236) notes that "lack of self-control with women seems to be Solomon's chief sin!"

[292]For a consideration of these terms, see the discussion of 9:2 and 33:19ab (30:28ab).

[293]So Heb and Syr. Gr reads *sperma* "seed."

[294]This reading with Heb means that not only did Solomon's offspring experience divine wrath (line *c*) but he himself suffered the consequences of his actions. Gr reads *aphrosynē* "folly."

[295]See Snaith, *Ecclesiasticus*, p. 236.

[296]HebA *'l t'mn* (= Syr). Gr reads *mē empisteusēs seauton* "do not entrust yourself." Smend (*Jesus Sirach*, p. 71) considers *seauton* to be a later addition, based on the analogy of other uses of *empisteuō* in Sirach, such as 2:10; 4:17; 6:7. If this is valid and the original Gr read *mē empisteusēs* then Gr would = Heb.

[297]HebA *(w)śnw'h . . . bh*. The antecedent is *'šh* "wife" in line *a*. Cf. Gr *misoumenē* "to one who is hated." Here also the fem. part. relates to *gynē* in line *a*. Syr reads *(w)'n `wl' hy . . . bh* "in her if she is ungodly."

[298]Gen 29:31, 33; Deut 21:15-17; Prov 30:23; Isa 60:15. The last reference is a metaphorical use in which Israel is

hated. The verb śn' is also used with the meaning "to distain one's wife" (KB). See Deut 22:13, 16; 24:3; Judg 14:16; 15:2.

299Gen 29:31, 33; Deut 21:15-17. Spicq (p. 608) sees our text as having a possible allusion to bigamy.

300Prov 30:23 and the uses of śn' noted above.

301Peters, Jesus Sirach, p. 73.

302Louis Ginzberg, "Randglossen zum hebräischen Ben Sira," in Orientalische Studien: Theodor Nöldeke zum siebzigsten geburtstag (2. März 1906) gewidmet, 2 vols., ed. Carl Bezold (Giesgen: Alfred Töpelmann, 1906), 2:617.

303It may be, as Smend (Jesus Sirach, p. 71) suggests, that this wife is hated because of circumstances beyond her control. But since the text is not specific, it is best to interpret it in a general sense.

304See chap. I.

305HebBD 'l tw`ṣ (= Gr, Syr).

306HebBD `m 'šh (= Gr, Syr).

307HebB `l ṣrth (= Gr). HebBmgD reads 'l "with regard to" instead of `l. In what Box-Oesterley (p. 445) think is an attempt to avoid the sanction of polygamy, Syr reads d'l tgwryh "lest you commit adultery with her."

308For more on the larger context and the opening formula, see the discussion of 36:21-26.

309P. 558.

310See the discussion of 26:6. Cf. 28:15.

311Gaspar (p. 6) admits that "second wife" is a possible translation of ṣrh but, with Peters (Jesus Sirach, p. 304) considers this meaning here to be more general. He thinks it strange that, if this implies polygamy, the reference is so isolated. Ben Sira usually lashes out repeatedly against the evils of his day. However, if Ben Sira was not opposed to polygamy as such, and there is no evidence that he was, then it would not be strange to find him almost silent on the subj. Here and in 26:6 (and possibly 28:15) he merely implies that because of problems with certain wives, polygamy has a negative side.

312Smend, Jesus Sirach, p. 330; Box-Oesterley, p. 445.

313Weber, p. 551; Snaith, Ecclesiasticus, p. 180.

314HebBBmg (and HebM as restored by Yadin [p. 23] and Strugnell [p. 115]) 'l 'šh (= Gr). Syr is not extant for this distich.

315Reading with HebM as restored by Strugnell (p. 115) [mṭp]št. Other restorations include those by Yadin (p. 23) [r'h t]št "(upon) an evil (wife) set (a seal)" and Middendorp (p. 104) [b]št "(a wife) of shame." HebB reads r'h "an evil (wife)." The margin of HebB contains two readings. One, which I shall designate HebBmg[1], reads ṭpšh "foolish." The other, which I shall term HebBmg2 reads like HebB text, except for the deletion of ḥkm at the end of the line. The Gr ponēra = HebB. Yadin's restoration places a verb in the line. But this is uncharacteristic not only of line b but also of both stichs in v. 7, where there are no verbs stated. In fact, Strugnell (p. 115) argues that v. 5bc also originally contained two stichs without verbs. Furthermore, none of the witnesses contains a verb in this line. This makes Yadin's suggestion untenable. Middendorp's restoration avoids the verb problem and is, in fact, plausible. However, given the reading ṭpšh in HebBmg[1], Strugnell's mṭpšt seems preferable. Gr represents a free translation, using an expression not uncommon to Ben Sira. See on 26:7. The Gr accordingly influenced HebBmg[2].

316HebBBmgM ḥwtm. Cf. Gr kalon sphragis "a seal is good." This free translation is echoed in HebB, which after a sôp pāsûq at the end of the line adds ḥkm "wise."

317HebBM wmqwm lit. "and a place." Cf. Gr kai hopou "and where."

318HebM rbwt (= Gr). HebB reads rpwt "slack." The full phrase, ydym rpwt "slack hands," (cf. Job 4:3; Isa 35:3) has been recognized by editors and commentators to be a mistake for rbwt. See, e.g., Ryssel, p. 440; Smend, Jesus Sirach, p. 390; Peters, Jesus Sirach, p. 354; Box-Oesterley, p. 469.

319HebBM ydym (= Gr).

320HebM mptḥ. This is reflected in the free Gr translation kleison "lock up." HebBBmg reads tptḥ "may you open." All the editors and commentators listed in n. 318 took this reading to be a mistake for mptḥ, as demanded by the context and the suggestion of the Gr.

321In Heb and Gr the section is 42:1e-8.

322V. 8b is an exception.

323P. 115. By including v. 5bc in the second pattern, I am following Strugnell's suggestion that originally vv. 5b-7 constituted a unit involving the same form.

[324]So Fuss, p. 244.

[325]It is possible that this expression may be the equivalent of *'št ksylwt* "a foolish woman" in Prov 9:13, where the meaning, according to the context (vv. 13-18), is clearly that of a prostitute.

[326]These are the predominant OT meanings of the term.

[327]The equivalent Gr term *sphragis* is used in this way in 22:27 (no Heb extant). Cf. the use of the verb *ḥtm* in the sense of "to put a seal around" in Deut 32:34; Job 9:7; 14:17; 37:7; Cant 4:12.

[328]It is possible, though less likely, that this line should be taken lit. In that case, the seal would be placed on the husband's personal property to prevent his wife's unauthorized use. This is the implication of the translations in *RSV*, *NEB*, *JB*, in contrast to Goodspeed (cf. Strugnell, p. 115). The contention of Peters (*Jesus Sirach*, p. 354) that the line refers to the seal for a bill of divorce (Deut 24:1-3) is without foundation.

[329]See 9:2; 25:26; 26:7; 33:19; 47:19.

[330]E.g., evil wife.

[331]E.g., drunken wife, a religious curse on a wicked wife, a wife not calling her husband blessed, divorce for a wife whom a husband cannot control, and a woman being responsible for sin and death.

Chapter IV

[1]Gr *houtōs kai gynē* (= Syr). Heb is not extant for this section.

[2]Gr *katalipousa ton andra*. Syr reads *dsrh' `l b`lh* "who sins against (lit. hurts) her husband."

[3]Gr *kai paristōsa*. Cf. Syr *wmqym'* "and brings into existence."

[4]Gr *klēronomon* (= Syr). Gr248 reads *klēronomian* "inheritance" (= La).

[5]Gr *ex allotriou*. Cf. Gr248 and the Origenistic recension *ex allou* "by another" (= Syr). La reads *ex alieno matrimonio* "from a strange marriage."

[6]Gr *ēpeithēsen*. Syr reads *ddglt b-* "she was unfaithful to."

[7]Gr en nomō hypsistou. Cf. Syr nmws' dlm' "the law of God."

[8]Gr eplēmmelēsen. Syr has no verb in this line. So the verb of line a is understood in line b.

[9]Gr eis andra autēs. Syr reads bb`l ṭlywth "(unfaithful) to the husband of her youth." Cf. Joel 1:8.

[10]Gr en porneia emoicheutē. Cf. Syr bznywt' dgwr' "in the fornication of adultery."

[11]Gr parestēsen. Cf. Syr 'qymt "brought into existence."

[12]Gr tekna. Syr reads sing.

[13]Gr ex allotriou andros. Cf. Syr (d)mn nwkry' "by a stranger."

[14]Gr exachthēsetai. Syr reads tpwq "thrust out."

[15]Gr eis ekklēsian. Syr reads mn knwšt' "from the assembly."

[16]Gr episkopē estai lit. "there will be a visitation." Syr translates freely with ḥṭhyh ntdkrwn "her sins will be remembered."

[17]Gr epi ta tekna autēs (= Syr).

[18]Gr ta tekna autēs (= Syr). Gr248 reads huioi autōn "their sons," no doubt under influence from the scenario of vv. 22b, 23d.

[19]Gr ou diadōsousin (= Syr).

[20]Gr eis rhizan lit. "as a root." Cf. Syr `qr' b'r`' "a root in the earth." Cf. Dan 4:15 (12 Aram).

[21]Gr hoi kladoi autēs (= Syr).

[22]Gr ouk oisousin karpon. Cf. Syr l' n`bdn p'r' "will not produce fruit."

[23]Gr kataleipsei (= Syr).

[24]Gr eis kataran to mnēmosynon autēs (= Syr).

[25]Gr kai to oneidos autēs. Syr loses the parallel with line a in its reading wḥwbyh "and her debts/sins." Cf. Smend, Jesus Sirach, p. 214.

[26]Gr ouk exaleiphthēsetai (= Syr).

[27]For a discussion of Zahlensprüche in Sirach, see Appendix 1.

[28]Weber (p. 549) considers v. 27 to be the conclusion to the first part of the book or at least to the section beginning in 16:22. For a similar sounding statement, see 46:10.

[29]Pp. 166-67.

[30]It is rare for a Zahlenspruch to be set in parallelism. One example is Prov 30:24-28. Most Zahlensprüche contain simple lists that comprise the enumerated elements. See 25:1; 25:2; 25:7-11; 26:5-6 (I have argued that v. 6 was added by Ben Sira); 26:28 (Line f is probably an addition; 50:25-26; Prov 6:16-19; 30:7-8; 15-16; 18-19; 21-23; 29-31; Job 5:19-22; Ps 62:11-12a. It would seem likely that the Zahlenspruch in this section originally contained a simple list as well. The elements were probably brief identifications of the particular types of sinners involved. See Moulton, p. 1539. Cf. Duesberg-Auvray (p. 102) who consider the present form of the Zahlenspruch to represent an alteration of the original. Ben Sira apparantly expanded the simple list of elements through parallelism to fit his composition scheme.

[31]Many scholars hold that the expression en sōmati sarkos autou "in the body of his flesh" refers to masturbation. See, e.g., Eberharter, p. 85; Schilling, p. 104; Hamp, p. 631; Spicq, p. 682; Weber, pp. 548-49. However, I identify with those who see behind this phrase the Heb expression š'r bśrw, which, as in Lev 18:6; 25:49, means "near relative." Accordingly, I understand the offense in 26:16e to be incest. Cf. Fritzsche, pp. 120-21; Smend, Jesus Sirach, p. 210; Zochler, p. 301; Kearns, p. 555. See 41:21a, where š'rk in HebM "your kinsman."

[32]Two other topics often considered as candidates for the three elements of this Zahlenspruch are: (4) the adulterer and (5) the adulteress. Most scholars hold that the three elements involve numbers 2, 3, and 4. Others have suggested different groups. It is beyond the scope of this study to fully engage in this debate. Rather than reviewing the many weaknesses of the 2-3-4 view and several other positions, let me merely note the points that favor the 1-2-3 view. This position is most consistent with the pattern of Zahlensprüche. Of the six examples in Sirach, four (25:1; 25:2; 26:28; 50:25-26) clearly list each element as a short phrase or clause. Of the remaining two, 25:7-11 is defective in Gr, with some elements missing (Syr has all ten elements). But the extant elements are short clauses. 26:5-6 contains three original short phrases and one full distich, added by Ben Sira. Sirach provides no analogy to a Zahlenspruch in which one element involves an extended discussion, let alone a two-faceted exposition like that of 23:18-27. A comparison with the Zahlensprüche listed in n. 30 yields similar results. We may conclude that Zahlensprüche do not

contain extended discussions. After all, this would defeat their mnemonic purpose. Thus, the Zahlenspruch in 23:16-17 is best interpreted to contain the elements 1-2-3.

[33]Cf. the offense of Reuben, mentioned in similar terms in Gen 49:4; 1 Chr 5:1. "Bed" stands for marriage bed or marriage itself.

[34]Von Rad, p. 265.

[35]See below on v. 24.

[36]Pp. 149-51.

[37]The linking formula, houtōs kai, in v. 22a can be variously interpreted. I prefer to see it used here in a very general sense. The topic of vv. 18-21, adultery, is generally similar to that of vv. 22-27. The details of each section are quite different.

[38]"Sin and Atonement," p. 466.

[39]I am not aware of any general use of klēronomos in the sense of "son" or "child." Hence, the term certainly means "heir" in v. 22b and strongly implies that the couple was heirless. It is possible, of course, that the couple had other children, and this illegitimate one was merely added as another heir. If that is the case, then our text contains no hint as to the woman's motivation for her act. I prefer to see kai paristōsa as equivalent to stating the purpose of katalipousa, i.e., she left her husband in order to provide an heir.

[40]"Ueber Abfassungs-Ort und -Zeit, sowie Art und Inhalt von prov. I-IX," ZAW 15 (1895):121. Cf. Schmidt, p. 158.

[41]Frankenberg, p. 122. Whether she was disfavored or not, still she felt unfulfilled and inferior to woman who were mothers. See 1 Sam 1:1-8. The importance of an heir is seen in the experience of Abraham, Sarah, and Hagar in Gen 16:1-6. This is the reverse of the situation in Sir 23, where the wife's solution is to have herself impregnated by another man. Furthermore, the whole concept of levirate marriage (Gen 38:8; Deut 25:5-10) highlights the significance of an heir.

[42]The use of this general term instead of the masc. klēronomos as in v. 22b is probably influenced by Num 27:1-11, where daughters were to be heirs in case there were no sons. This precedent apparently allowed a more liberal interpretation of the laws of inheritance. Cf. Job 42:15, where both sons and daughters were heirs; Philo Spec. Leg. 2. 124; Matt 22:24, a loose quotation of Deut 25:5ff with tekna used in place of bn. Deut 25:5 LXX has already moved away from bn by using sperma.

[43]Pp. 73, 79-80.

[44]'šh zrh or zrh/nkryh.

[45]See Böstrom. Cf. Rankin, pp. 259-61.

[46]The latter is part of GrII only.

[47]The LXX in Proverbs renders the Heb quite freely. In several places where the Heb reads "strange woman" the LXX reads either something entirely different (e.g., 2:16) or does not translate lit. (e.g., gynaikos pornēs for zrh in 5:3). When the sense is retained (e.g., 5:20; 6:24), the LXX usually uses allotria "the strange" (fem.). In one case, 7:5, the LXX renders 'šh zrh as gynaikos allotrias kai ponēras "strange and evil woman." There is no fem. form of the adj. allotrios in Sir 23:22-26. The masc. form occurs in vv. 22b, 23d, having reference to the woman's consort in adultery. In the latter the full term is allotriou andros "another man." This compares with the Heb 'yš zr in Deut 25:5, where it means a nonrelative. It is used elsewhere for a non-Aaronic Israelite in Num 16:40 (17:5 Heb) and for a non-Israelite in Lev 22:12.

[48]2:16; 6:24; 7:5.

[49]7:5; 23:27; possibly 6:24.

[50]2:16; 5:3; 6:24; 7:5; 22:14.

[51]"The Inheritance of Illegitimate Children According to Jewish Law," in Jewish Studies in Memory of Israel Abrahams, ed. George Alexander Kohut (New York: Jewish Institute of Religion, 1927), p. 402.

[52]Cf. Gen 15:3.

[53]Cf. Gen 21:1. Judg 11:2 represents an individual act of injustice, not legal status.

[54]B. Yebam. 44a.

[55]Tschernowitz, pp. 406-7. However, Tschernowitz (p. 407) draws the following conclusion:

> Thus the Halachah only applied the stigma of bastardy to the offspring of an adulterous wife or of one, who had committed incest within the degrees of kinship, forbidden in Leviticus. In no other system of ecclesiastical or civil law has there been such a humane provision.

Unfortunately he does not discuss "the offspring of an adulterous wife." He does not even support his claim that such children were indeed bastards. All his cases of extraordinary inheritance deal with the father in situations of adoption, polygamy, adultery, etc. In all such instances any son the father accepted was considered a full heir. He makes no mention of a wife having any such right.

56 Büchler ("Sin and Atonement," p. 466) declares without any elaboration that such children brought "into her husband's house . . . will inherit her husband's property and name."

57 P. 402.

58 V. 11 contains a similar three part form. However, unlike v. 23, this does not enumerate the three aspects of a particular offense but lists the consequences of three possible courses of action. Nevertheless, there does seem to have been some correlation between these verses in the author's scheme, as we have seen. Not only does each contain three elements, but each also contains the verb plēmmeleō "to err."

59 Exod 20:14; Deut 5:18. Ben Sira may have also had in mind Lev 20:10; Deut 22:22, but only in a general way, since these speak of adultery primarily from the point of view of the male offender.

60 The verb used here is a form of plēmmeleō, which lit. means "to make a false musical note." By extension, it came to mean "to err, make a mistake." From its passive use we have the meaning "to mistreat, insult." It occurs also in 9:13; 10:7 (var.); 19:4; 23:11.

61 See the discussion of 26:11.

62 The first two charges of v. 23 sound like those laid against the "strange woman" in Prov 2:17. However, as we have seen, these two women are not to be identified with each other.

63 Duesberg-Auvray, p. 103.

64 Davidson, p. 403.

65 Eberharter, p. 85.

66 "Sin and Atonement," pp. 466-67.

67 P. 549.

68 P. 683.

69 P. 396.

70 Pp. 148-49, 160.

71 4:7; 10:2.

[72]9:13 <u>l'yš šlyṭ lhrg</u>.

[73]Exod 20:14; Deut 5:18.

[74]In some instances, result may be more accurate than punishment.

[75]Cf. John 8:3-11, where the account of an accused adulteress includes a reference to proposed stoning. This material is generally regarded to be authentic Jesus tradition, despite its textual problems.

[76]Gen 20:3.

[77]Gen 26:11. Here and in Gen 20:6 the verb <u>ng'</u> "to touch" has a sexual connotation. Cf. Prov 6:29.

[78]Cf. 2:18; 5:5; 9:18.

[79]5:6

[80]2:19.

[81]The discussion in v. 21 shifts from the specific consideration of sexual relations with a "loose woman" to the detection and results of undisciplined behavior.

[82]Vv. 33-35. Some commentators, e.g., Hamp, p. 631; Weber, p. 549, have pointed to Prov 5:11-14; 6:32-35 as evidence that execution was not employed in adultery cases.

[83]One other "death" related text must be noted. Jer 29:21-23 refers to two men who were executed by the king of Babylon. Part of their offense was "adultery with their neighbor's wives." The relationship of their death to their adultery is unclear. It does seem certain, however, that the king was not executing Jewish law. This event does not contribute to an understanding of the Jewish punishment for adultery.

[84]Gen 20:18; possibly Num 5:27.

[85]Gen 39:20.

[86]Prov 6:33.

[87]Prov 5:9; 6:33.

[88]This is the possible meaning of Num 5:27. For a recent treatment of this material which takes this view, see McKane.

[89]Deut 24:1-4.

[90]Mal 2:13-16.

[91]Prov 6:34-35.

[92]Job 31:9-12; Prov 5:8-14; 6:29.

[93]Jer 5:7-9; 23:9-15 (?); Ezek 18:10-13; Mal 3:5.

[94]Ezek 16:1-62; 23:1-49. The figure of adultery is used here and in the following group for Israel's and/or Judah's apostasy. These chapters contain both literal and figurative consequences.

[95]Jer 3:6-10; 13:26-27; Ezek 16:1-62; 23:1-49.

[96]Cf. v. 22. In Semitic languages, like many others, shame is a euphemism for nakedness, which is itself a euphemism for the genitals. Note the following Heb words: bšt "shame" used in construct with ʿryh "nakedness" in Mic 1:11; qlwn "shame" found in parallel with mʿr "nakedness" in Nah 3:5 and used alone for "genitals" in Jer 13:26; ʿrwh "nakedness" used in Isa 20:4 in the sense of "shame" associated with "nakedness." The last word occurs in conjunction with š'r bśrw in Lev 18:6: "none of you shall approach any one near of kin (kl š'r bśrw) to uncover nakedness (lglwt ʿrwh)." In Lev 18:6-19; 20:1-21 ʿrwh occurs some thirty times referring to genitals.

[97]The stripping in Ezek 23:26 is probably a literal humiliation associated with the captivity.

[98]Pfeiffer, p. 449.

[99]The RSV "assembly" in vv. 41, 60 is unwarranted, since the Gr reads synagōgē, which is generally a translation of ʿdh "congregation" in distinction from qhl/ekklēsia, for which "assembly" would be proper.

[100]This view was first advanced by N. Brüll, "Das apokryphische Susanna Buch," Jahrbuch für Jüdische Geschichte und Literature 3 (1877) :1-69.

[101]Pp. 453-54. Pfeiffer discusses the added details without reference to the "death" material, which he apparently sees as part of the core story.

[102]Adolph Büchler ("Die Strafe der Ehebrecher in der nachexilischen Zeit," Monatsschrift für Geschichte und Wissenschaft des Judentums 55 (1911):196-219) argues that the penalty for adultery was death, but that it was seldom enforced in this period. Louis M. Epstein (Sex Laws and Customs in Judaism (New York: Bloch Pub. Co., 1948), p. 199) concludes that execution for adultery must have been rare in biblical times, since no a single case is reported. For the rabbis this kind of punishment was meant to be theoretical (p. 209). This is probably also the case with Philo. See Spec. Leg. 3. 52. Some see a reference to

execution for adultery in 9:9. See my discussion of this text for reasons why I reject this view.

[103]See our discussion of 42:11.

[104]P. 158.

[105]Here the adulterer feels ruined in the assembly and in the congregation (qhl w'dh). With both terms used, the reference would not likely be to a judicial examination.

[106]See e.g., 5:7; 12:6; 35(32):23; 48:7.

[107]Jesus Sirach, p. 213. Cf. Oesterley, p. 156.

[108]Eberharter (p. 86) holds that the children's punishment is isolation from the husband's family.

[109]The same figures are used in the more highly developed treatment of such children in Wis 3:16-19; 4:3-6. See also the contrasting use of these figures in Sir 24:12, 16.

[110]P. 683.

[111]HebA h'lym (= Tal.; see below). Cf. Gr apostrepson "turn away."; Syr l'nḥwrn "let not (your face) look upon." Parts of this section of Sirach are quoted in b. Sanh. 100b and b. Yebam. 63b. The text and translation according to Cowley-Neubauer (p. xxi) are as follows:

(8a) h'lm 'ynyk m'št ḥn
pn tlkd bmṣwdth
(9a) 'l tṭ 'ṣlh
(9b) lmswk 'mh yyn wškr
(8c) ky btw'r 'šh yph rbym hwšḥtw
w'ṣwmym kl hrwgyh

(8a) Hide thine eyes from a comely woman,
lest thou be caught in her snares;
(9a) turn not aside to her,
(9b) to mingle wine and strong drink with her:
(8c) for through the beauty of a fair woman many have been destroyed,
and "all her slain are a mighty host." (Prov 7:26)

The second line is constructed from parts of vv. 3b and 4b, which read:

pn tpwl bmṣwdtyh
pn tlkd blqwtyh.

[112]HebA 'yn lit. "eye" (= Gr). Cf. Tal. 'ynyk "your eyes." Syr renders the expression freely with 'pyk "your face."

(= La). For a discussion of the possible du. meaning of the sing. ʿyn, see Penar, p. 28.

113 HebA mʾšt ḫn (= Tal.). Cf. Syr bʾntt' dšpyr "upon a fair woman." Gr reads apo gynaikos eumorphou "from a shapely woman."

114 HebA wʾl tbyt̮ ʿl. Cf. Gr kai mē katamanthane "and do not look intently at"; Syr wlʾ ttbqʾ b- "and do not consider."

115 HebA ypy lʾ lk (= Syr). Gr reads kallos allotrion, which is lit. "strange beauty" but may be translated "beauty belonging to another."

116 Reading with Smend's emendation of HebA btʾr ʾšh (= Gr, Syr, La). Cf. Box-Oesterley, p. 346. HebA reads bʿd ʾšh "through a woman." The Tal. reading ky btwʾr ʾšh yph "for through of a fair woman" contains what Smend (Jesus Sirach, p. 85) characterizes as a "superfluous" addition. Lévi ("Notes," p. 8) prefers btwʾr ʾšh.

117 Reading HebA with Smend's restoration [h]šḫtw rbym (= Tal. rbym hwšḫtw). Cf. Gr polloi eplanēthēsan "many have been led astray"; Syr sgʾʾ ʾbdw "many have perished" (= La). Penar's translation of the Heb as "many have been pitted" (from šḫt "pit") is unconvincing.

118 Reading with Smend's emendation of HebA wkn ʾhbh. See also Box-Oesterley, p. 346. Cf. Gr kai ek toutou philia "and by it (beauty) love"; Syr wrḫmth "and her love." HebA reads wkn ʾhbyh "her lovers." Hamp (p. 593) accepts this reading. Cf. Penar, p. 29. This would require the verb tlht̮ to mean "she consumes," giving "she consumes her lovers." Kuhn (I:293) suggests the reading whn ʾhbh (ʾahubâ) "and the charm of a lovely ([woman] is like a burning fire)." But it is not Ben Sira's practice to leave the word "woman" understood, as this reading would require.

119 HebA tlht̮ (= Gr, Syr, La). However, unlike HebA, which would require the subj. to be "she," I understand the subj. to be ʾhbh "love," according to Smend's emendation. See n. 118.

120 Reading with Smend's emendation of HebA kʾš (= Gr, Syr, La). Cf. Box-Oesterley, p. 346. HebA reads bʾš "by a fire."

121 Reading with Smend's emendation of HebA ʾl tt̮ ʾṣyl. Cf. Box-Oesterley's (p. 346) reading ʾṣlk "your elbow." However, the cryptic expression unencumbered by the pronominal suffix is preferable. For the same expression, see 41:19c (mt̮h ʾṣyl). This reading is reflected in Syr^{1} (see below) with lʾ tsmwk yṣylk "do not prop your elbows." Cf. the reading of GrL,

694, 672 which stands before this line kai mē kataklithēs ep agkona (ep agkalōn "elbows" 248) "and do not lie down at table upon elbows." A similar reading is found after this line in Clement of Alexandria. HebA reads ʼl tṭʽm "do not eat (lit. taste)." Kuhn (I:293) emends this to conform to Smend's reading of the Heb: mē katathes ōlenen "do not lay down the elbow." The evidence from the Tal. is complicated. Cowley-Neubauer reflect the older editions with ʼl tṭ ʼṣlh, which they translate "turn not aside to her." They also note the var. reading ʼṣl bʽlh "beside her husband." Here the term bʽlh must be read as baʽalâ "her husband," as confirmed by the fact that this alternate reading later includes the expression ʽmw "with him," and not bᵉʽulâ "a married woman" or baʽalâ "a mistress." In addition to these vars., Smend notes that some MSS read ʼṣlh ʽm bʽlh "beside her with her husband." Syr includes a form of v. 9 both before and after v. 8. We will designate the former Syr[1] and the latter Syr[2]. The first two lines of Syr[1] together with lines c and d of Syr[2] appear to most nearly reflect the Heb and Gr. These two forms of v. 9 in Syr are as follows:

9[1] ʽm mrt bytʼ lʼ tsmwk yṣylk
wlʼ tmzwg ʽmh ḥmrʼ ʽtyqʼ
dlmʼ nsṭʼ btrh lbk
wḥyb mwtʼ tḥwt lšywl

9[2] ʽn ʼntt gbrʼ lʼ tsgʼ mmllʼ
wlʼ tgr ʽmh šwʽytʼ
dlmʼ nsṭʼ btrh lbk
wbdmʼ ḥybʼ tḥwt lšywl

9[1] With the mistress of a household do not prop your elbow,
And do not mix old wine with her,
Lest your heart turn aside after her,
And condemned to death you descend to Sheol.

9[2] With a married woman do not multiply talk,
And do not conduct conversation with her,
Lest your heart turn aside after her,
And in guilty blood you descend to Sheol.

122 HebA ʽm bʽlh (= Gr). Cf. Syr[1] ʽm mrt bytʼ "with the mistress of a house." For vars. in the Tal. reading, see n. 121.

123 Reading with Box-Oesterley's (p. 346) emendation of HebA wʼl tmsk (= Syr[1]). This is also reflected in the Tal. lmswk "(turn not aside to her) to mix." HebA reads wʼl [ ]sb, which Smend restores as wʼl [t]sb "and do not sit down." Kuhn's (I:293) restoration includes the emendation wʼl [t]sbʼ "and do not drink." Gr kai mē symbolokopēsēs "and do not be given to feasting" is a free translation. Smend is no doubt right in

restoring HebA to read [t]sb. But HebA probably represents a material corruption involving b and k.

[124]Reading with Tal. ʿmh yyn. This is also the emendation of HebA by Box-Oesterley (p. 346). Cf. Syr[1] ʿmh ḥmrʾ ʿtyqʾ "old wine with her"; Gr met autēs en oinō "with her at wine." HebA reads ʿmh škwr "drunk with her." Cf. Smend. The Tal. reading is actually ʿmh yyn wškr "wine and strong drink with her." Cf. Kuhn's (I:293) suggestion ʿmh škr "strong drink with her." The double expression yyn wškr would probably overload the line and can be easily accounted for as a natural expansion. Of the two terms yyn is preferable, because it is the regular Vorlage behind both Gr oinos and Syr ḥmrʾ in Sirach. See e.g., 19:2; 31(34):25-29; 32(35):5-6; 49:1. There is no such clear case for škr. The reading škwr seems unnatural in this setting. The counsel is against eating and drinking with a married woman, not sitting down drunk with her.

[125]HebA pn . . . lb lit. "heart." Cf. Syr[1,2] lbk "your heart" (= Gr-Clement of Alexandria, La, Cos, Arm). Cf. Gr mēpote . . . hē psychē sou "lest your soul."

[126]Reading with Smend's reconstruction of HebA tṭh [ʾ]lyh (= Gr). Cf. Syr[1,2] nsṭʾ btrh "turn aside after her."

[127]HebA wbdmym. Cf. Syr[2] wbdmʾ hybʾ "and in guilty blood." Zeigler reads Gr with Clement of Alexandria kai tō haimati sou "and by your blood" (= La). Rahlfs reads with the rest of Gr kai tō pneumati sou "by/in your spirit."

[128]Reading with Smend's suggestion tḥt (= Syr[2]). Cf. Box-Oesterley, p. 347. For a similar use of nḥt involving šʾwl "Sheol," see Job 21:13. HebA reads tṭh "you decline." Smend (Jesus Sirach, p. 86) considers this to be an intrusion from line c. Cf. Box-Oesterley, p. 347. Gr reads olisthēs "you slip into."

[129]HebA ʾl šḥt. Cf. Syr[2] lšywl "to Sheol." Gr reads eis apōleian "into destruction" (= La).

[130]See on 9:1.

[131]P. 79.

[132]V. 9 is clearly concerned with a married woman, as the use of bʿlh in line a attests. Although no such specific identification is found in v. 8, the same kind of woman appears to be intended. This is reflected in v. 8b, where the "charming woman" of line a is described in terms of "beauty that is not yours." Thus, vv. 8-9 may be taken to refer to married women.

[133]This represents a restoration of the Heb. See the discussion of the verse.

[134]Prov 11:16.

[135]Prov 31:30; Nah 3:4.

[136]For the textual evidence, see the discussion of these verses. See also the related adj. yph "beautiful," used in 26:16.

[137]Esth 1:11; Ps 45:11 (12 Heb); Isa 3:24.

[138]Prov 6:25; 31:30.

[139]Gen 29:17; Deut 21:11; 1 Sam 25:3; Esth 2:7.

[140]Cf. the hif. "to spoil, ruin, pervert, corrupt."

[141]For the use of the word ʼhbh in the sense of sexual desire, see 2 Sam 13:15; Cont 2:5; 5:8, its use in this setting with the mention of fire confirms this meaning here.

[142]See, e.g., Charles Taylor, "The Wisdom of Ben Sira," JQR 15 (1902-3):456; Penar, p. 29. Cf. Job 31:9-12. Ben Sira has a similar play on words between ʼyš "man" and yš in 8:3.

[143]Box-Oesterley (p. 346) note that the husband is probably present.

[144]See, e.g., 31(34):12-24; 31(34):31-32(35):2; 32(35):4-6; 49:1.

[145]41:17-23 RSV.

[146]HebM wmmṭh ʼṣyl ʽl lḥm.

[147]Oesterley (p. 65) reflects this when he considers the text to be counsel "against sitting at table in an unseemly manner when a married woman is present." However, his notion that "leaning on the elbow would denote undue familiarity" is without foundation. How else could one recline on a dining couch so as to eat? We may gain some insight into the activity intended here by noting the scene in Philo. Vita Cont. 45. Philo describes some banquet guests who become drunk, "throw the left elbow forward (ton euōnymon agkōna probalontes), turn the neck at a right angle, belch into the cups and sink into a profound sleep." This is probably not what Ben Sira has in mind, but it does suggest that stretching out the elbow may refer to a kind of uncultured reclining at the table.

[148]Smend (Jesus Sirach, p. 85) argues that stretching out the elbow would be usual at a banquet of wine (mšth hyyn. See 31(34):31; 32(35):5-6; 49:1) but indecent at a regular banquet. The difference is that women would be present at the latter but not at the former. This would make both 9:9a and 41:19c reflect

such a regular banquet. However, this distinction breaks down, since according Esth 5:6; 7:2, 7-8 a woman, in this case the queen, was present at a mšth hyyn. In fact, 7:8 specifically mentions the queen on her couch.

[149]He recognizes both the positive and negative characteristics of wine in his major statement on wine in 31(34):25-31. The rest of his incidental remarks on wine are positive. See 9:10; 32(35):5-6; 40:20; 49:1.

[150]See 19:2; 26:8.

[151]In addition to Prov 7:25, see Num 5:12, 19-20, 29.

[152]The reference to "heart" (lb) in line c should not be interpreted to mean that the man has merely been sexually aroused. That the result which Ben Sira expected is illicit sexual intercourse is confirmed by the grave nature of the second element of consequence indicated in line d. Cf. Prov 7:25.

[153]See, e.g., Ps 16:10. Note also the Syr for this line (n. 121).

[154]For the use of blood and Sheol in reference to violent death, see 1 Kgs 2:9.

[155]See, e.g., Zöchler, p. 277; Spicq, p. 615; Kearns, p. 553.

[156]See, e.g., Smend, Jesus Sirach, p. 86; Oesterley, p. 65; Box-Oesterley, p. 347; Schilling, p. 54; Hamp, p. 592.

[157]See the discussion of 23:24.

[158]In the consideration of 23:24.

[159]Prov 6:26, 32; 7:23, 26-27.

[160]Prov 6:31, 33-35.

[161]Prov 6:33; Sir 23:21.

[162]Prov 6:31, 34-35.

[163]Sir 23:19-20.

[164]Gr porneia gynaikos (= Syr). Heb is not extant for this distich.

[165]Verb supplied, since none is present in Gr or Syr.

[166]Gr en meteōrismois ophthalmōn. Cf. Syr bmrmwt ʿynyh "in the haughtiness of her eyes."

[167]Gr kai en tois blepharois autēs. Cf. Syr wmn gbynyh "and with her eyebrows."

[168]Gr gnōsthēsetai (= Syr).

[169]See the introduction to the discussion of 26:1-4; 13-18.

[170]P. 164.

[171]See the discussion of 26:7-8.

[172]Fuss apparently sees the sense of treating the whole subsection together in terms of the question of composition.

[173]See 23:23; 42:8.

[174]For this expression, see 23:4. In addition to this, we may note that Ben Sira uses the word ophthalmos some thirty-eight times. Two of these relate to women (9:8; 26:11). The latter is particularly significant, because it is a Ben Sira composition that describes a daughter's sexual interests in terms of "her shameless eye." See the discussion on this verse.

[175]The only exception to this is the section that deals with daughters (26:10-12).

[176]emoicheuthē.

[177]See the discussion of 23:22-26.

[178]See e.g. ydʿ/ginōskō in Gen 4:1, 17; I Sam 1:19.

[179]Jesus Sirach, p. 235.

[180]P. 639.

[181]P. 83.

[182]"Greek Lexicographical Notes: Fifth Series," Glotta 50 (1972):57.

[183]See Pss 42(41):7 (8 Heb); 88(87):7 (8 Heb); 93(92):4; Jonah 2:3 (4 Heb, Gr). See also 2 Sam 22:5 Heb.

[184]See LSJ.

[185]Jesus Sirach, p. 235.

[186]Cf. the suggestion of Renehan noted above.

[187]The OT reflects the relationship between a woman's eyes and her sexual desire. See Gen 39:7; Prov 6:25; Isa 3:16. See also Ben Sira's description of a daughter in Sir 26:11 and our discussion of the verse.

[188]Those who understand the mention of eyelids to possibly mean the use of eye cosmetics include: Spicq, p. 699; Weber, p. 549.

[189]See the discussion of this verse.

[190]Reading *'l tgrh* with Smend's (*Jesus Sirach*, p. 82) suggestion (= Gr). HebA reads *'l tgrb 'l* "do not draw near to." This no doubt represents an *easy* scribal accommodation to a common expression used as a euphemism for sexual intercourse. Ben Sira uses it this way in the metaphorical invitation to cohabit with dame Wisdom in 6:19. (The sexual imagery is confirmed by the figurative reference to plowing, sowing, and harvesting, which is used here in a way much like Philo. *Vita Cont*. 62.) However, there the Gr reads *proselthe autē*. In *five* of the eight OT uses of *'l grb 'l* with a sexual meaning, the LXX translates with a form of *proserchomai* (Lev 18:6, 19; 20:16; Deut 22:14; Isa 8:3). Once the LXX has the related *eiserchomai* (Lev 18:14). The other have *haptō* (Gen 20:4) and *proseggizō* (Ezek 18:6). On the basis of *both* the analogy of Sirach and that of the OT, we could expect the Gr to contain a form of *proserchomai* here, if the Heb read *'l tqrb 'l*. Smend has argued against this reading, also because *line a* cannot reflect sexual intercourse in the light of the consequence stated in line *b*. The verb *qrh* is the regular word behind the LXX *hypantaō*, which is used *here*. A synonym of *qrh*, the verb *qr'*, lies behind *hypantaō* in 12:17. Either *qrh* or *qr'* would fit the context of this distich better than the reading of HebA. Syr is loose with *l' t`n' `m* "do not be occupied with."

[191]HebA *'šh zrh*. Cf. Gr *gynaiki hetairizomenē* "a woman who is a prostitute; Syr *znyt'* "a prostitute." Smend (*Jesus Sirach*, p. 82) suggests that the original may have read simply *zrh*, as he suspected also in 41:20b. See also Peter Walters, *The Text of the Septuagint* (New York: Cambridge University Press, 1973), pp. 214-15. The reading *zrh* is now confirmed by HebM. In the light of the HebM reading for 41:20b, *zrh* is certainly not impossible in our text. The term *zrh* is used alone in Prov 5:3, 20; 22:14. But the expression *'šh zrh* is also represented in Prov 2:16; 7:5.

[192]HebA *pn tpwl* (= Gr). Syr has the same verb but changes the line from consequences to purpose: *dl' tpl* "so that you do not fall." The Tal. reads *pn tlkd* "lest you be caught." The Tal. reading for this line combines elements of v. 3b and v. 4b. See n. 111.

[193]HebA bmṣwdtyh (= Syr). Cf. Tal. bmṣwdth "in her net." Gr reads eis tas pagidas autēs "into her snares."

[194]HebA contains a doublet variant form of v. 4 along with v. 4 itself. The two distichs are as follows:

4^1 ʿm zwnh ʾl tstyyd
pn tlkd blqwtyh
4^2 ʿm mngynt ʾl tdmwk
pn yśrpk bpypytm

4^1 Do not consort with a prostitute,
Lest you be caught in her punishments.
4^2 Do not sleep with female musicians,
Lest they (masc.!) burn you with their mouths.

It is clear that line b of v. 4^2 is corrupt. The reference to zwnh in v. 4^1 is undoubtedly secondary, since that is the focus of v. 6. On the basis of evidence from the verses, it seems that the original Heb is now most likely reflected in parts of both these distichs. With Smend and Box-Oesterley (p. 345) I have here read with HebA v. 4^1 ʾl tstyyd (= Syr). Gr reads mē endelechize "do not continue." Note HebA v. 4^2 ʾl tdmwk "do not sleep."

[195]Reading with HebA v. 4^2 ʿm mngynt. However, the second word should be vocalized m^{e}naggênet (cf. Smend, Jesus Sirach, p. 82; Box-Oesterley, p. 345), rather than the vocalization provided in the MS m^{e}nagg^{e}ynōt "female musicians." Cf. Gr meta psallousēs "female singer" (= Syr).

[196]Reading with HebA v. 4^1 (= Tal., Gr). Cf. Smend, Box-Oesterley, p. 345; Peters, Jesus Sirach, p. 82; Levi, "Notes," p. 6. HebA v. 4^2 reads pn yśrpk "lest they burn you." The verb is masc. plur. Cf. Syr dlmʾ twdbk "lest she destroy you."

[197]Reading bḥlqwtyh with Lévi, "Notes," p. 3. The reading of HebA v. 4^1 blqwtyh "in her punishments" seems out of place in this setting. Several scholars share this assessment and have offered various emendations. Peters (Jesus Sirach, p. 82), followed by Box-Oesterley (p. 345), reads btqlwtyh "in her snares." Smend (Jesus Sirach, p. 83) suggests blqḫwtyh "by her tricks." Cf. Kuhn, I:293. Hamp (p. 593) offers the reading bqlwtyh "by her sounds." HebA v. 4^2 reads bpypytm "with their mouths." Cf. Syr bšwʿyth "by her utterances." Godfrey Rolles Driver ("Hebrew Notes on the 'Wisdom of Jesus Ben Sirach,'" JBL 53 [1934]:275) considers the strange Heb expression to be a diminutive formation from ph "mouth" with the meaning "kisses." Gr reads en tois epicheirēmasin autēs "in her attempts." For further discussion of the text of v. 4, see Rüger, p. 16.

[198]HebA ʾl ttn . . . npšk (= Gr, Syr).

[199]HebA lzwnh (= Syr). Gr reads plur.

[200]Reading with Smend's emendation of HebA pn tsyb lit. "lest you turn over." Cf. Gr hina mē apolesēs "lest you lose" (= Syr). HebA reads pn tswb "lest you change." Peters (Jesus Sirach, p. 83) retains HebA and considers it an Aramaism for nsb "to take away," giving "lest she take away." This is unlikely, since the verbs in line b of vv. 3, 4, 5 are 2 masc. not 3 fem. Box-Oesterley (p. 346) suggest the reading pn tʾbd with the sense of "lest you lose." This is the Heb behind apollymi in 8:12; 41:2; 49:7. However, it is less satisfactory here than tsyb, which more easily accounts for the reading of HebA tswb on material grounds.

[201]HebA nḥlth (= Gr). Syr is expansive with ywrtnʾ dnksyk "the inheritance of your assets." GrS* reads in place of this line hina mē atimazōntai hoi progonoi sou "lest your ancestors be disgraced." This comes from 8:46.

[202]Reading with Gr mē periblepou. It is from this that Smend reconstructs the Heb to read ʾl ttnbṭ "do not look around." Cf. Peters, Jesus Sirach, p. 83; Box-Oesterley, p. 346. HebA is corrupt for this distich.

lhtnbl bmrʾh ʿynyk
wlšwmm ʾḥr byth

To be despised in the sight of your eyes,
And to be amazed behind her house.

The expression lhtnbl "to be despised" is retained by Lévi ("Notes," pp. 7-8). Cf. Syr wtsṭʿr "and you will be despised."

[203]Reading with Gr en rhymais (= Syr). Smend follows Lévi ("Notes," pp. 7-8) in suggesting bmbwʾy but also approves (Jesus Sirach, p. 84) bmbwʾwt. For the latter, cf. Peters, Jesus Sirach, p. 83. The OT term mbwʾ means "entrance," but it came to also mean "alley, lane" in postbiblical Heb. See Jastrow, s.v. mbwy. Ben Sira seems to mean "path," while in 42:11f it clearly means "entrance." Even though the LXX never elsewhere translated mbwʾ with rhymē, it seems probable that it did so here. Either bmbwʾy or bmbwʾwt could have stood in the original. Cf. Ezek 26:10; 27:3 for both in plur. c.s. This reading is also detectable in the material remains of HebA. See n. 202.

[204]Reading with Gr poleōs (= Syr). Accordingly, Smend has reconstructed HebA to read ʿyr "(of a) city." Cf. Peters, Jesus Sirach, p. 83; Lévi, "Notes," pp. 7-8.

[205]Reading with Gr kai . . . mē planō. From this Smend has reconstructed HebA to read wʾl tšwṭṭ "and do not rove

about." Cf. Peters, Jesus Sirach, p. 83. This is also reflected in Lévi's ("Notes," pp. 7-8) reading wlšwṭṭ "and to rove about," which is made to parallel his reading of line a. See n. 202. Syr for this line is unlike the other witnesses: wttktb bgwr' dḥwb' "and you will be inscribed in the book of sins."

206Reading with Gr en tais erēmois autēs. The Heb probably originally read bḥrbwtyh "in its desolate places." Cf. Peters, Jesus Sirach, p. 83. Smend (Jesus Sirach, p. 84) suggests Gr here mistook brḥbwtyh "in its open places" to be bḥrbwtyh. Cf. Lévi, "Notes," pp. 7-8. Clearly Gr intended to be translating bḥrbwtyh, as common LXX practice would attest. See, e.g., Lev 26:31, 33; Isa 44:26; 48:21; 49:19, etc. See also Sir 43:21. However, it does not seem necessary to postulate that Gr misread Heb here. It is more likely that bḥrbwtyh actually stood in the text. Not only would this allow us to account for Gr, but it would provide the most logical reading from which the corrupt text of HebA could have resulted. Note that HebA reads 'ḥr byth which contains the sequence of consonants ḥ + r + b. G. R. Driver (p. 275) tries to retain the reading of HebA for this line, with the understanding "to play the fool behind her (i.e., the prostitute's) house."

207See the discussion of 9:1.

208P. 78.

209For more on the matter of form in relation to the question of tradition and composition in 9:1-9, see the discussion of 9:1.

210See the discussion of 23:22. I have included the references from Proverbs there.

211Some scholars consider her merely a prostitute. See Box-Oesterley, p. 345; Spicq, p. 614.

212See n. 190.

213Cf. Smend, Jesus Sirach, p. 82.

214One of several references to Jewish female musicians in antiquity mentioned in IDB, s.v. "Music," by Eric Werner, is The Acts of Thomas, 5-9, where a Jewish piper girl comforts the sad apostle after his arrival in India.

215Davidson, p. 402.

216This involves the figurative description of Tyre as a prostitute, who will play the harp and sing sweet songs as part of her seduction. See also Spicq, p. 614; IDB, s.v. "Prostitution," by Otto J. Baab.

217 See n. 197.

218 See Prov 5:3; 6:24; 7:21.

219 See the discussion of 9:2.

220 Cf. Prov 5:9-10, 14; 6:31.

221 Cf. Ryssel, p. 285; Box-Oesterley, p. 346; Snaith, Ecclesiasticus, p. 51.

222 See Prov 7:8-9, 27.

223 Gen 38:12-23.

224 HebC yyn wnšym (= Gr, Syr).

225 HebC restored by Smend [ypḥ]yzw lb (= Syr mpḥzyn lb′). Gr reads apostēsousin synetous "will mislead intelligent men." Box-Oesterley (p. 382) suggest that Gr tones down the more direct Heb. The "heart" element of Heb and Syr is reflected in Basilius Magnus kardias sophōn "hearts of the wise" and Antiochus Monachus kardias synetōn "hearts of the intelligent."

226 Gr kai ho kollōmenos (= Syr). HebC contains vv. 2a and 3b only.

227 Gr pornais. Syr reads lznyt′ "to a prostitute."

228 Syr n′bd. Gr reads tolmēroteros estai "shall be very reckless." The Gr reading seems unlikely and was apparently troublesome to the scribes. See Zeigler (Sirach) on this text for the vars. in the MSS. Edersheim (p. 104) suspected that the "reckless" idea was a marginal gloss that came first into v. 3b and then in this line. Syr is more understandable and leads naturally into v. 3. Cf. Smend, Jesus Sirach, p. 173.

229 Gr sēpē. This is the reading of both Zeigler and Rahlfs. GrS*, 130 read sēpes "putrifying sores." For the other vars., see Zeigler (Sirach) on this text. Syr does not include this line.

230 Gr kai skōlēkes.

231 Gr klēronomēsousin auton.

232 HebC wnpš ʿzh (= Syr). Cf. Gr kai psychē tolmēra "and a reckless soul."

233 HebC as reconstructed by Smend [t]šḥyt bʿlyh (= Syr). Gr reads exarthēsetai "will be carried off." The Lucianic recension and 243 + en paradeigmatisō meizoni "in a greater spectacle of shame." Cf. La.

[234]P. 125.

[235]6:4a reads ky npš ʿzh tšḥt bʿlyh.

[236]We find a similar double use of a traditional line in 26:10a and 42:11a, as well as in 26:5c and 42:11c. See the discussions of these verses.

[237]See the discussion of 9:9.

[238]Prov 23:27-35; 31:3-5; Hos 4:11.

[239]I am not suggesting that v. 36, which I have concluded is traditional, originally had anything to do with the idea of punishment for or consequences of illicit sexual conduct. The line is used with a totally different meaning in 6:4. However, Ben Sira has added v. 3 to the traditional v. 2 in our text as his expansion of the concept of perishing because of prostitutes, which is expressed in v. 2b. In the process, the traditional line (v. 3b), which he included in his expansion, is now made to serve this new setting. The insolent soul is one who clings to prostitutes. He will be destroyed.

[240]Following the reading sēpes (see n. 229), NEB here reads "sores." Snaith (Ecclesiasticus, p. 97) suggests that this means venereal disease that may cause death. Such an interpretation is both textually unlikely and exegetically fanciful.

[241]See 10:11. Cf. 7:17.

[242]P. 547.

[243]For similar long term implications involving the verb kallaō (or proskallaō), see 2:3; 6:34; 13:16.

[244]See also the discussion of death and adultery in our considerations of 23:24 and 9:9 earlier in this chapter.

[245]The imper. advice that is presupposed throughout vv. 1-8 is actually stated in 42:1e (RSV 42:1a). The reading of HebBM is ʾl tbwš.

[246]HebB ʿl mwsr (= Gr). Cf. Smend, Jesus Sirach, p. 391. HebBmg reads mrdwt "rebellion" instead of mwsr. This would imply either rebellion against the simple and foolish or the correction of the rebellion, with "correction" understood, but not stated. Unfortunately, HebM does not solve the problem with its reading m[ ]. Yadin (p. 23) considers the gap too large for m[wsr] and therefore reads m[rdwt]. Cf. Middendorp (p. 96), who, with Jastrow, claims a meaning "correction." However, mrdwt does not fit the context and never elsewhere stands behind

paideia. The gap is not so large as to invalidate mwsr. Syr does not contain this text.

[247] HebB pwth. This reading = Yadin's (p. 23) reconstruction of HebM [p]wth. Strugnell (p. 115) reads the defective equivalent pth. Cf. Gr anoetou "of the senseless."

[248] HebBM wksyl (= Gr).

[249] Reading with Yadin's (p. 23) reconstruction of HebM [ś]b kwšl. Cf. HebBmg wśb kwšl "or of a tottering old man," which is read by Smend and Box-Oesterley (p. 469). HebB reads wśb wyšyš "or of a gray haired and old man." Gr reads kai eschatogērōs "or of a very old man." This is Ziegler's reading according to GrB, 339. He lists several vars. which reflect no essential change in meaning.

[250] HebM `nh (= Smend's emendation of HebBmg `wnh). HebBmg reads w`wnh. HebB reads wnwṭl `ṣh "and one who (or who) weighs advice." The w- would seem to introduce either a new subj. or an added assertion about the old man. The MS contains the word wšw'l "and one who (or who) asks" beneath wnwṭl. Cf. Gr krinomenou "who quarrels (or disputes)."

[251] HebBBmgM bznwt. I take this to be zōnôt, the defective plur. of zwnh "prostitute," rather than z^{e}nût "prostitution." Gr read the latter, which it reflects with peri porneias "concerning prostitution (or fornication)." This is Ziegler's reading, based on the Origenistic recension and the Lucianic recension minus 248. Most MSS read pros neous "with youth." Cf. Rahlfs.

[252] See the discussion of 42:6.

[253] E.g., 42:6.

[254] Cf. Box-Oesterley, p. 469.

[255] HebM 'yš kšl; HebB 'yš kwšl.

[256] The verb `nh II is not elsewhere used in a context related to sex. See 11:18; 13:3; 33:31 (30:40); 49:7.

[257] One of the elements of a negative Zahlenspruch in 25:2 that refers to "three types of men my soul hates" is "an adulterous old man (geronta moichon) lacking intelligence." A form of this Zahlenspruch appears in b. Pesaḥ. 113b, in which this line reads wzqn mn'p "and an old man who is an adulterer." See Cowley-Neubauer, p. xxiv. Smend includes the line in this text but adds ḥsr md` "lacking understanding" to both fill out the line and account for Gr.

[258]Cf. Snaith, *Ecclesiasticus*, p. 206. An example of a call for respect and forbearance regarding an aged father, even an irrational one, is found in 3:12-13.

[259]The verb that governs the exhortations in 41:17-23 is found in 41:17a, HebBm *bwš*. It is generally recognized that Gr reflects the wrong order of lines in vv. 20-21. See, e.g., Smend, *Jesus Sirach*, p. 387; Box-Oesterley, p. 468. La has followed the same order. On the basis of Heb, especially HebM, the original and contextually preferable order may be restored. I have reflected this order in the two distichs that constitute our text. The Gr order represents a simple dislocation of the two stichs following v. 19d. These stichs (v. 21ab) were relocated after v. 20b. It is possible, of course, that v. 20ab was the unit dislocated. The effect is same. Syr does not contain this material and is therefore of no help in reconstructing the order. The problem is further complicated by both the mutilated state of the Heb MSS, especially HebB, and their textual characteristics. HebB reflects the original order but only includes vv. 20b and 22b as one distich. Vv. 21c and 22a have fallen out. The reason for this omission no doubt lies in the material similarity of vv. 21c and 22b. We may compare these lines as follows, according to my reading

21c *wmhtbwnn* *'l* *b`wlh*
22b *wmhtgwmn* *`l* *bṣ`yh*

A scribe could easily pass from v. 20b directly to v. 22b. The sense is not particularly disturbed by such a resultant distich. Because HebM reads *zrh* at the end of the second line of the first distich and because *zrh* corresponds to *gynaikos* *hetairas* in v. 20b, Yadin (pp. 21-22) considers the order reflected in HebM to be: 21c, 20b, 22a, 22b. He further argues that this order is reflected in the resultant Heb/Gr verb correspondences. But Strugnell (p. 114) notes that, based on LXX usage, the verbs correspond best when the order that I have reflected is maintained. See also KB and LSJ. Strugnell suggests that the objs. of the first and second lines have become exchanged. For the transposition of words within two parallel hemistichs, see Strugnell, pp. 114, 116. Another point in favor of considering *zrh* in HebM as mistakenly occurring in the second line is the fact that the reading of v. 21c, which I have given above with the word *b`wlh*, best explains the accidental deletion of vv. 21c and 22a from HebB. Let me make one final observation in favor of the order that I have provided. The fact that Gr reads *autou* in v. 22a necessitates v. 21c coming immediately before it. The antecedent must be the man presupposed in v. 21 (*hypandrou*). The order in which I have listed these lines seems secure. The disarrangement in Gr is a matter of simple interchange involving vv. 20ab and 21ab. This is much easier to conceive than the two stage disarrangement that Yadin's order would require.

[260]HebBM mhbyṯ ʹ[l] (= Gr). Cf. 42:25, wherein lhbyṯ in HebBmgM is translated by horōn.

[261]Reading [z]rh with Smend's restoration of HebB. He claims to see the upper edges of the word. Smend also includes the word ʹšh from HebBmg. Cf. 9:3. See n. 191 for a review of the evidence from Proverbs. Both zrh and ʹšh zrh mean "strange woman." Gr reads gynaikos hetairas "a woman who is a courtesan." Note also GrSAC etc. gynaikos heteras "another woman."

[262]HebM wmhtbwnn ʹl (= Gr kai apo katanoēseōs). Cf. katanoeō for byn in 23:19; 33:17 (30:26).

[263]Reading bʽwlh with Smend (Jesus Sirach, p. 387). This = Gr. It is also possible that the defective bʽlh stood here, as in 9:9. However, bʽwlh may be somewhat preferred as more easily accounting for the accidental omission of vv. 21c and 22a represented in HebB. See n. 259. HebM reads zrh "strange woman," but as we saw in n. 259 this must be rejected.

[264]HebM mhtʽśq ʽ[m] (= Gr).

[265]Reading with Segal's suggestion špḥtk. This is preferable to HebM, which Yadin (p. 22) restores to read [šp]ḥh lk "a maidservant of yours." The expressions špḥtk and ʹmtk are common OT synonyms for "your maidservant." For the former, see Gen 16:6; Ruth 2:13; for the latter, see Exod 20:10; 23:12, etc. Gr reads with the corresponding noun but has the pronoun "his" (paidiskēs autou). See n. 259.

[266]HebM wmhtgwmm ʽl. Cf. Smend's restoration of HebB wmhtq[wmm]. Gr reads mē epistēs epi "do not approach."

[267]HebM yṣʽyh (= Gr tēn koitēn autēs). Smend thought he saw the upper edges of mškbh "bed," which is the usual Heb behind the LXX koitē.

[268]In Heb and Gr the verses are numbered 41:17-42:1d.

[269]See the discussion of 41:17a.

[270]P. 242.

[271]I might have treated 9:1-9 as a whole here also were it not for the fact that it is even more variegated than our text. It seemed best to deal with good wife, bad wife, prostitute, etc. in the chapters devoted to these topics.

[272]See the discussion of 9:3.

[273]See the discussion of 9:8. For the word byn, see the discussion of 9:5.

[274]"Bed" often has sexual connotations in the OT. See Gen 49:4; 1 Chr 5:1; Ezek 23:17; Cant 3:1. The first two texts involve a violation of someone's bed. The Ezekiel text is also negative.

[275]There the Gr uses the more neutral term klinē, rather than koitē, which sometimes has the special sense of "marriage bed" or at least a sexual connotation, as in our text. E.g., Gen 49:4; Heb 13:4. These terms are used elsewhere in Sirach in an ordinary sense as follows: koitē in 31(34):19; 40:5; klinē in 48:6.

[276]Jesus Sirach, p. 388.

[277]Among these is 9:5, which I have discussed. He also notes 30:20 and Deut 22:18.

[278]See BDB, s.v. špḥh.

[279]Ps 123:2; Isa 24:2.

[280]Gen 16:1; Prov 30:23.

[281]Ruth 2:13.

[282]Gen 29:24, 29.

[283]Gen 30:4-5, 9-10.

[284]Lev 19:20.

[285]I am indebted to Elizabeth Platt for this suggestion.

[286]For slaves marrying while remaining slaves, see Exod 21:1-6.

Chapter V

[1]HebA bnwt lk (= Gr, Syr). HebC by vertical dittography reads bnym lk "do you have sons?" See Ruger, p. 47.

[2]HebAC nṣwr. Cf. Gr proseche "be concernerd about" and Syr tr "keep."

[3]HebA š'rm (=Gr, Syr). HebC reads š'r without the suffix, though it is clearly to be understood.

[4]HebA w'l t'yr . . . pnym (= Gr, Syr). Instead of the hif., HebC reads the qal t'r, but the meaning is not changed. For the qal with the same meaning, see 13:26.

[5]HebA 'lhm (= HebC lhm, Gr, Syr).

[6]HebA hwṣʹ (= HebC hwṣyʹ, Gr, Syr). The hif. of yṣʹ means lit. "cause to go forth" but is used here in the sense of "hand over." That the meaning here is "hand over (in marriage)" is confirmed by line b. See KB. Cf. Ezra 10:3, 19, where the verb is used for the expulsion of foreign wives.

[7]HebAC ʿsq. Cf. Gr ergon mega "a great work." The term mega is no doubt an addition (cf. Smend, Jesus Sirach, p. 70), which extends the Gr misreading of the Heb. Syr ʿšwqyʹ "oppression" indirectly supports the Heb, since it apparently read ʿšq "oppression" for ʿśq (the biblical equivalent of the postbiblical ʿsq, lit. "business"). Gr read the term with its later meaning, as in 40:1, where ʿsq gdwl means "much labor." Cf. 3:22; 11:10; 38:24. Di Lella (Hebrew Text, p. 58) understands the expression this way also. He translates the clause: "and an important task is done with." However, ʿsq should be understood here more in the sense of "trouble." Both Smend (Jesus Sirach, p. 70) and Peters (Jesus Sirach, p. 72) take it in this sense (Plage), while Box-Oesterley (p. 341) translate the term with the word "sorrow." This understanding conforms more to the biblical ʿśq "quarrel" and is likely in view of the verb yṣʹ "will depart," of which ʿsq is the subj. Cf. the order in Prov 22:10.

[8]HebAC wyṣʹ (= Syr). Gr kai esē tetelekōs "and you will have completed." See the above note on the Gr misunderstanding of the Heb in the second half of this line.

[9]HebC zbdh (= Gr dōrēsai autē, Syr). HebA ḥbrh "join her." The Gr verb dōreomai translates zbd in Gen 30:20 (the only use of zbd in the OT) but never translates ḥbr. This makes the reading of HebC more likely in our text. Cf. Di Lella, Hebrew Text, p. 58; Rüger, p. 47.

[10]Reading with Smend's reconstruction of HebC (w)ʹl g[br] nbwm (= Gr andri syneto, Syr). HebA wʹl nbwn gbr merely represents a transposition with equivalent meaning. Di Lella (Hebrew Text, p. 58), however, offers the translation for HebA as: "one who is understanding, among men." The order gbr nbwn is substantiated by the analogy of 33(36):3 ʹyš nbwm (Gr anthrōpos synetos). Cf. 25:8; 26:28.

[11]For more on these contextual matters, see the discussions of 7:19, 7:26a, and 7:26b.

[12]7:26a contains a modified form of this pattern dealing with a wife. I have argued that the modification represents Ben Sira's redaction of the traditional line.

[13]P. 71.

[14]Actually, the traditional material contained the additional distich now represented by v. 26. However, as we have

seen, Ben Sira reconstructed that distich rather radically. See the discussions of 7:26a and 7:26b.

[15]V. 24b also begins with w-. However, the content of the line in relationship to v. 24a is clearly adversative, requiring the translation "but."

[16]The original form of the two traditional distichs represented by vv. [23], [24a, 25b] was probably:

23 bnym lk ysyr 'wtm
wš' lhm nšym bn'wryhm
24a bnwt lk nṣwr š'rm
25b w'l gbrym nbwn zbdn

23 Do you have sons? Discipline them,
And give them wives in their youth.
24a Do you have daughters? Protect their body,
25b And bestow them to men of understanding.

[17]Smend, Jesus Sirach, p. 70.

[18]Spicq, p. 608. Cf. Ryssel, p. 281.

[19]Vv. 23b, 25-26 focus on marriage.

[20]This statement is dependent on the suggestion that vv. 24a, 25b originally constituted a distich in Ben Sira's source.

[21]See Num 6:25; Pss 31:16; 67:1; 80:3, 7, 19; 119:135; Dan 9:17.

[22]13:26 speaks of "a happy heart" and "a cheerful face." Like our text, 35(32):9 uses a hif. form of 'wr with pnym along with the parallel bśśwn "with rejoicing."

[23]Peters (Jesus Sirach, p. 72) understands this line to mean that a father must take care that his daughter retains her fear of him. Cf. Spicq, p. 608.

[24]See n. 6. For a discussion of the transactions involved in a father giving a daughter in marriage, see chap. I.

[25]Spicq, p. 608.

[26]The play on words is preserved in Syr 'pq . . . wnpwq.

[27]See n. 7 for other translations.

[28]P. 17.

[29]Jesus Sirach, p. 70.

[30]See the discussion of 42:9-14.

[31]*Jesus Sirach*, pp. 72-73.

[32]See the discussion of 22:3-5.

[33]In addition to the daughter material of vv. 24-25, he has altered the wife distich (v. 26).

[34]Gr *aischynē patros*, lit. "disgrace of a father." Cf. Syr *bhtt′ hw l′b′* "there is shame to a father." Heb is not extant for these verses.

[35]Gr *en gennēsei*. There is no equivalent in Syr. However, the line length and parallel with line *b* would support the reading of Gr. Smend (*Jesus Sirach*, p. 196) feels that *en gennēsei* may have been written because of *ginetai* in line *b*. Ryssel (p. 341) suggests that Gr may be reflecting a Heb reading *yōlēd* k^{e}*sil* "who begets a foolish son" (cf. Prov 17:21), which Syr read as *yeled* k^{e}*sîl* "a foolish son."

[36]Gr *apaideutou*. This substantive adj. could be understood as fem. and thus related to the daughter material in the next five lines. However, with *de* in line *b* introducing an apparent contrast, *apaideutos* in line *a* should be seen in contrast to *thygatēr* in line *b*. The term clearly refers to a son. Syr is more specific with *br′ skl′* "foolish son."

[37]Gr *thygatēr*. Syr translates loosely with *(w)nqbt′* "female." The context favors the more specific Gr. Some witnesses add various adjs. to qualify *thygatēr*. Gr613, 743 + *mora* "foolish"; cf. Eth; La171 + *inprudens* "imprudent"; Cos + "evil."

[38]Gr *ginetai* (= Syr).

[39]Gr *ep elattōsei*. Cf. Syr *lḫwsrn′* "to his loss." Smend (*Jesus Sirach*, p. 196) holds that both Gr and Syr may have mistakenly read a form of *ḫsr* "to decrease" instead of a form of *ḫsd* I "to disgrace." Cf. Peters, *Jesus Sirach*, p. 179. However, I consider the Gr and Syr readings justified. The idea of "disgrace" is present in each of the three distichs of this strophe. Note the forms *aischynē* (v. 3a), *kataischynousa* (v. 4b), and *kataischynei* (v. 5a). However, this idea is found in only one line of each distich. With its presence in v. 3a, it would be unlikely to find it again in line *b*. Also, *ḫsd* I is not unquestionably reflected in Sirach. It contrast, forms of *ḫsr* are found in 31(34):4 and 40:26, both translated by *elattōsis*. Cf. other uses in 3:13; 51:24. The one possible Sirach reading of *ḫsd* I is in 14:2, where Heb reads *ḫsrtw*, which Box-Oesterley (p. 366), e.g., emends to *ḫsdtw*.

[40]Gr *thygatēr phronimē*. This verse is missing in Syr.

[41]Gr klēronomēsei andra autēs. The verb, which lit. means "to inherit," is often used both metaphorically and in the general sense of "to acquire, obtain, receive." See LSJ and BAG[2]. Most commentators, however, take the verb in the more lit. sense and therefore find untenable the social idea which it conveys. It was similarly understood by some ancient scribes, as evidenced by 443, which read timēsei "will honor" instead of klēronomēsei, and by 248, which read andros autēs "from her husband" in place of andra autēs. Cf. La hereditas viro suo "an inheritance for her husband." Cf. JB. Ryssel (p. 341) tries to account for the Gr by positing that it had falsely read yāršāh "she will inherit" instead of y^erûsat "treasure." Cf. Box-Oesterley, p. 390; Spicq, p. 675. Smend (Jesus Sirach, p. 197) reasons that if a form of nḥl stood behind klēronomēsei, as is often the case for klēronomeō in the LXX, then it could mean: she helps him receive an inheritance (nḥlh). However, he notes that, since Gr translates hnḥyl with kataklēronomeō in 15:6 and 46:1, one should read our text: klēronomia andros/andri "an inheritance for/to (her) husband." I consider these attempts to solve the problem by positing various textual readings or by supplying a nonexistent Heb and then arguing for a Gr misreading to be unnecessary. The verb klēronomeō may easily be understood to convey the simple, nontechnical meaning "to receive." I would suggest that the underlying Heb may have been a form of mṣʼ. This verb is frequently used by Ben Sira with the meaning "to find." See 3:18, 31; 6:14, 28; 11:19; 12:2, 16-17; 15:6; 31(34):8; 40:18; 42:1; 44:17, 20, 23; 51:16, 20, 26-27, where Gr translates with euriskō. The term is also used in 6:10, 27; 31(34):21. The most significant use of mṣʼ for our purposes is 4:13, where Gr reads klēronomēsei "he will obtain (glory)."

[42]Gr hē kataischynousa.

[43]Gr eis lypēn.

[44]Gr gennēsantos.

[45]Gr hē thraseia lit. "the insolent woman." But the context demands the idea of "daughter." For the substantive use of thrasys, see 3 Macc 2:14. Prov 9:13 uses the term as a modifier of gynē in the phrase gynē aphrōn kai thraseia "a foolish and insolent woman." For the expression thrasys en glōssē sou "insolent in your speech," see Sir 4:29. Syr reads skltʼ lit. "a foolish woman." But here also the context requires "daughter."

[46]Gr kataischynei (= Syr).

[47]Gr patera (= Syr). Gr493, 578 read mētera "mother."

[48]Gr andra. Syr (w)ʼmh "(and) her mother" (= La^x, Arm). The Syr reading no doubt resulted from a shift to the conventional Heb expression for parents, "father and mother."

For a discussion, see chap. II. The Gr reading is required by the occurrence of anēr in v. 4a. Between lines a and b La + et ab impiis non minorabitur "and she will not be menaced by the ungodly."

49Gr kai hypo amphoterōn atimasthēsetai (= Syr).

50This is not the only parenthesis in the section. See also 21:1-10, which discusses the nature of sin.

51The connection of v. 6 to vv. 3-5 is not through a direct link to the topic of daughters or even of sons. In fact, it does not even mention children, though the idea is implicit. The point of contact between v. 6 and vv. 3-5 appears to be the word paideia "discipline" in v. 6b. Note the contrasting term apaideutos in v. 3a.

52Fuss, p. 140.

53See n. 37.

54E.g., Smend, Jesus Sirach, p. 196; Box-Oesterley, p. 390.

55The LXX for this verse is as follows:

A father does not rejoice over a ignorant son (huiō apaideutō),
But a wise son (phronimos) gladdens his mother.

56It is also understood that way in today's standard translations, e.g., RSV, NEB (implied), and JB.

57See n. 75.

58It is found only in Ps 119:28; Prov 10:1; 14:13; 17:21.

59In 14:1; 30:21, 23; 37:2; 38:18 the Heb MSS read dn (dîn) "judgment," which Smend emends to read dwn (dāwōn) "sorrow." On the reading of this nonbiblical word, see also Box-Oesterley on the above texts.

60See, e.g., Prov 8:5; Wis 17:1; Sir 6:20; 20:24; 51:23.

61See, e.g., Prov 5:23; Sir 10:3; Zeph 2:1.

62See n. 37.

63P. 117. Edersheim does identify a progression from an undisciplined son to an undisciplined daughter.

[64]P. 675. Spicq also views such a daughter as worse than a son both in terms of dishonor to parents and in the difficulty in arranging a marriage for her.

[65]P. 548.

[66]Jesus Sirach, p. 178.

[67]Jesus Sirach, p. 197. Smend also notes some of the qualifying textual variations. He concludes with a classic statement, worthy of Ben Sira himself: "Was beim Sohne möglich ist, ist bei der Tochter Regel."

[68]P. 548. Cf. Spicq, p. 675.

[69]Pp. 79-80.

[70]7:24a; 22:4a; 42:9c, 10ac.

[71]22:5; 42:9d, 10bd.

[72]7:25a.

[73]26:10-12; 42:11.

[74]42:14b.

[75]See Snaith, Ecclesiasticus, p. 110.

[76]In 21:24 phronimos is used in contrast to the term apaideusia. Note also phronimos used in 21:11-28 as the opposite of mōros "foolish (person)" (21:17, 21, 24-26). Prov 17:21 LXX also uses phronimos in contrast to apaideutos. See n. 53.

[77]See the discussions of 25:8a, 26:3; 36:24.

[78]The term used is gennēsantos, which is undoubtedly the translation of yld and which clearly refers to the daughter's father. Cf. Goodspeed, RSV, NEB, and JB. This oblique reference to father is strange standing alone in the distich. One might rather expect that a simple reference to father would be expressed by ʼb/patēr and that the use of yld/gennēsas would represent a second reference, using the part. for purposes of stylistic variation. See Prov 23:24 (ʼb / ywld) and 17:21, where the terms are reversed (yld / ʼb). However, while gennēsantos may appear unusual standing alone in v. 4, it is accompanied by the use of patēr in vv. 3a and 5a and, in the context of the whole strophe, should not be unexpected.

[79]P. 390.

[80]P. 458.

[81]Fuss (p. 140) sees the verse as a summary of vv. 3-4. It is more likely, however, that v. 3, particulary line b, is the statement of the theme, with vv. 4-5 forming similar expositions of that theme.

[82]The underlying Heb probably read zdh "insolent (woman)." The adj. zd is translated in the LXX by thrasys in Prov 21:24. The word group is well represented in Sirach. For zd, see 11:9; 12:5. The noun zdwn is found in 7:6; 9:12; 10:13, 18; 12:14; 13:24; 15:7; 16:3, 10; 35(32):23.

[83]See 7:26b; 25:16, 18, 22, 23cd, 25-26; 26:6, 8.

[84]Heb is not extant for this section. However, I have reconstructed it for this line based on 42:11a. That line according to Yadin's (p. 24) restored reading of HebM reads [bny] `l bt ḥzq mšmr. The clue to its duplication here without bny "my son" lies in the Gr, which reads epi thygatri adiatreptō stereōson phylakēn "keep a firm watch over a headstrong daughter." This reading is identical to the Gr of 42:11a. We have already seen that Ben Sira appears to have used other material verbatum in both chaps. 26 and 42. See the discussion of 26:5. It is reasonable to assume that the Heb of 26:10a and 42:11a were identical with the exception of bny. If this is the case, then Syr translated 26:10a loosely (cf. Smend, Jesus Sirach, p. 235) with `l hsypt' 'sg' nṭwr' "firmly place a guard over a wanton woman," in contrast to 42:11a, where it translated lit. Syr treats this entire section as a continuation of the material on the evil wife which is found in the preceding verses. I will deal below with the issue of whether the focus of this section is daughters or wives.

[85]Gr hina mē. Cf. Syr mṭl "because."

[86]Gr heurousa anesin. Syr reads dlyt lh nyḥ' "she has no rest."

[87]Gr heautē chrēsētai. Cf. Syr 'l' 'n gnbt "except she steal it." I am taking heautē to be used here as the equivalent of autē, a dat. whose antecedent is anesin. Cf. Smend, Jesus Sirach, p. 236. Ryssel (p. 364) takes this verb in the passive sense ("lest. . . she be abused") and thus considers heautē to be a latter addition. This is unlikely.

[88]Gr phylaxai. Syr hrṭ "run." Gr is preferred, since it continues the theme of guarding, which was introduced in v. 10a (stereōson phylakēn).

[89]Gr opisō anaidous ophthalmou. Cf. Syr btr ḥsypt `yn' "after her wanton eyes."

[90]Gr kai mē thaumasēs. Syr wl' tštwḥr "and do not tarry." Smend (Jesus Sirach, p. 236) suggests that kai mē

should be understood as "lest." However, this is not convincing.

[91]Gr ean eis se plēmmelēsē. Syr dlmʹ tdgl bk "lest she deceive you." Box-Oesterley (p. 404) cautiously prefer Syr for this line. But Syr reads as it does, because it develops the entire section around the theme of a wanton woman, not a daughter.

[92]Gr hōs dipsōn hodoiporos. Cf. Syr ʹyk ṣhyʹ "like a thirsty man." Syr has a free version of this line and actually scatters the phrases represented by Gr along with additional material over two lines. Here it + dʿʹl mn ʹwrḥʹ "who comes in from the road."

[93]Gr anoixei (gnomic). Cf. Syr btyḥ "(his mouth) is open." The pres. anoigei found in GrBS* and some of the vers. is preferred by Smend (Jesus Sirach, p. 236).

[94]Gr stoma (= Syr). Gr613 and some of the vers. + autēs "her," but this is influenced by the female orientation of the section. Before its word for stoma La inserts ad fontem "at a fountain." At the end of the line Gr248 + eurōn plēgēn "finding running water." Cf. the extra material of Syr lmyʹ gryrʹ "to cold water." The second of the two Syr lines that reflects this single Gr line reads: "and his mouth is open to cold water."

[95]Gr pietai (gnomic) (= Syr).

[96]Gr (kai) apo pantos hydatos tou syneggys. Cf. Syr (w)mn kl myn "from any water."

[97]Gr kathēsetai (gnomic). Cf. Syr mstmk "rests." Syr erroneously continues the vehicle element of the simile involving the thirsty man into lines c and d. Cf. Smend, Jesus Sirach, p. 236. The reading of Gr578 kauthēsetai "will burn" is a visual error, that was probably reinforced by 23:16c.

[98]Gr katenanti pantos passalou. Cf. Syr (w)ʿl kl qys "on every piece of wood."

[99]Gr anoixei (gnomic) (= Syr). Gr679, 705 anypsoi "raises up."

[100]Gr pharetran. Cf. Syr qṭrqh "his quiver." While Gr does not contain the pronoun "her," it is implied by the fact that lines cd represent the tenor element in the simile that constitutes v. 12. This element must refer to the subj. matter of the section, i.e., a daughter.

[101]Gr (kai) enanti belous lit. "before an arrow." Cf. Syr (w)qdm kl gʹrʹ "before every arrow." Cf. Peters, Jesus

Sirach, p. 217. After this line Syr + the explicit tenor element of the simile in two lines as follows:

hkn' hy 'ntt' ǵrt'
dlkl 'nš ptyḥ rhmh

So is an adulterous wife,
Who opens her womb to every man.

[102]See chap. I.

[103]42:14 in the section 42:9-14.

[104]P. 164.

[105]This distich, 42:11cd, itself contains traditional material from a different source. See the discussion of this verse.

[106]The traditional line in 42:11a does not stand at the head of the whole daughter section, as it does here. However, it introduces the second part of the daughter material in 42:9-14. That part, 42:11-14, deals with the negative behavior of daughters in contrast to the first part, 42:9-10, which reflects the anxiety of the father of a daughter. A further indication of the start of a new subsection at this point is the appearance of bny "my son" at the beginning of 42:11a.

[107]Jesus Sirach, p. 235. Cf. Peters, Jesus Sirach, p. 216; Eberharter, p. 95.

[108]26:5-9.

[109]26:13-18.

[110]As I have suggested earlier, this original placement of 26:10-12, with its obscene images, at the end of the material on women probably contributed to the disarrangement of the material into its present arrangement. See chap. I, n. 38.

[111]In addition to these sections that deal with daughters, Gr uses the term thygatēr twice in 36:21b (Gr 26b, Heb 23b). However, in our consideration of the section, 36:21-26, I have read 'šh "woman" with the Heb, as reconstructed by Smend, according to a scribal reading beneath the mutilated line of HebB. See my discussion of this section.

[112]The view that this section deals with daughters is stated or implied by Box-Oesterley (p. 404) and Snaith (Ecclesiasticus, p. 133). Some scholars see v. 10 as a reference to daughters, but vv. 11-12 as a return to the theme of the bad wife. See Edersheim, p. 138; Ryssel, p. 364; Fuss, p. 164. This view is untenable. Elsewhere Ben Sira mentions daughters

only in multi-distich units, 7:24-25; 22:3-5; 42:9-14. A single distich here would be unusual. It would be even stranger as an island in the midst of a sea of bad wife material. On the other hand, it is perfectly natural that a multi-distich daughter unit would appear at the end of this lengthy section on women.

[113]P. 364.

[114]Jesus Sirach, p. 236. His understanding of heautē in the sense of "at will" is unlikely.

[115]The Heb for these terms would be mšmr in v. 10a, as I have read the line according to the equivalent in 42:11a (HebM), and a form of šmr in v. 11a. The latter is the usual Heb verb underlying phylassōn in the LXX. Cf. 32(35):22; 37:8.

[116]See Deut 28:50; Prov 7:13; 25:23; Eccl 8:1; Dan 8:23 LXX, Th.

[117]The noun aidōs sometimes refers to a woman's modesty. See Diodorus Siculus 13. 55. 4; 1 Tim 2:9.

[118]9:13; 10:7; 19:4; 23:11, 23; 26:11; 49:4.

[119]The lit. meaning is "to make a false note in music." See LSJ.

[120]For a discussion, see on 23:22-26.

[121]The word thygatēr is not found in this distich. However, the subj. of the 3rd sing. verbs is clearly the daughter who is featured in vv. 10-11.

[122]These metaphors were clearly identified by Peters (Jesus Sirach, p. 217). Cf. Hamp, p. 640; Snaith, Ecclesiasticus, p. 134. For similar uses of passalos and belos in Gr literature, see the references in LSJ. Ben Sira's idea source for arrow and quiver may have been Ps 127:3-5, where sons are described as arrows. The quiver there, however, seems to be merely the father's household.

[123]HebB bt (= Gr, Syr). Cf. Tal. material quoted below. This is probably also the intent of HebM, where according to Yadin (p. 24) a b may be faintly visible as an attempt to correct the first letter in the reading []š[]. Some lines of vv. 9-10 appear to be quoted in b. Sanh. 100b. The text and translation according to Cowley-Neubauer (p. xxvii) are as follows:

(9a) bt l'byh mtmwnt šw'
(9b) mpḥdh l' yyšn

(10a) bqṭnwth šm′ ttpth
(9c) bn`rwth šm′ tznh
bgrh šm′ l′ tnś′
(10d) nś′t šm′ l′ yhyw lh bhym
hzqynh šm′ t`sh kšpym

(9a) A daughter is a vain treasure to her father:
(9b) for fear about her, her does not sleep;
(10a) in her youth, lest she be seduced;
(9c) in her maidenhood, lest she play the harlot;
when she is marriageable, lest she be not married;
(10d) when she is married, lest she have no sons;
when she is old, lest she practice sorcery.

124Reading with a restoration of HebM mṭmwn šq[d] (= Gr). For the first word cf. HebBmg1. Smend read the second word in his correction of HebB. Other readings include: HebB mṭmnt (= mṭmwn) sqr "a treasure of deceit"; Tal. mṭmnt šw′ "a treasure of vanity." Syr is free with yqyr′ sgy "very heavy."

125HebBM l′b (= Gr). Cf. Tal. l′byh "to her father"; Syr `l ′bwh "upon her father."

126HebBmg1 wd′gth (= Gr, Syr). Cf. HebB d′gh "anxiety." Tal. reads mpḥdh "for fear about her."

127Reading with HebM [tn]yd as restored by Joseph M. Baumgarten, "Some Notes on the Ben Sira Scroll from Masada," JQR 58 (1967-68):326. The same restorations are made by Patrick William Skehan (review of The Ben Sira Scroll from Masada, by Yigael Yadin, in JBL 85 [1966]:260) and Strugnell (p. 115). This reading (= Gr, Syr). Yadin (p. 24) restores HebM [tpr]yd "separates from." Smend restores HebB tp[ry`] "causes a loss."

128HebM nwmh. Cf. Smend′s reconstruction of HebB [šnh] (= Gr). Cf. Syr šnth "his sleep." Tal. reads l′ yyšn "he does not sleep."

129HebBM bn`wryh (= Tal. bn`rwth, Gr, Syr).

130HebM pn tm′s. Cf. Syr dl′ tṣṭh′ "lest she be despised." The HebM reading with its echo of Isa 54:6 seems preferable to those of the other witnesses. Cf. Yadin, p. 24. HebB reads pn tgwr "lest she commit adultery." Tal. reads šm′ tznh "lest she play the harlot." Box-Oesterley offers the reading pn tbgr "lest she pass the flower of her age." Cf. Middendorp (pp. 36, 96), who also suggests pn tgr` "lest she diminish." Gr reads like pn tbgr with mēpote parakmasē "lest she be past her prime."

131Reading wb`lyh with the restoration of HebM by Strugnell (p. 115) This = Smend′s correction of HebB wb`wlh, Gr, Syr. Yadin (p. 24) reads HebM as wbymyh "and in her maturity," but this is disputed by Strugnell. HebB wbbtwlyh "and in her virginity" is a mistake from v. 10a.

[132]HebBmg[1] pn tnšh. This = Yadin's restoration of HebM ṗṅ ṫ[nš]ḣ (p. 24). He offers the alternative ṗṅ ṫ[šk]ḣ "lest she be forgotten/forsaken." Strugnell (p. 115) suggests the reading t[`ṣ]r, due to "an interchange among parallel words in adjacent hemistichs." See v. 10d. I do not consider his case convincing. Smend restores HebB as pn [tśn'] "lest she be hated" (= Gr, Syr).

[133]HebBM bbtwlyh (= Gr 542, 795, Syr). Cf. Gr en parthenia lit. "in virginity." Tal. reads bqṭnwth "in her youth."

[134]HebM pn tḥl (= Gr, Syr). Cf. Middendorp, p. 96. HebB pn tpwth "lest she be seduced" (= HebBmg[1] pn ttpth, Tal. šm' ttpth).

[135]HebM w`l 'yšh (= Gr meta andros ousa, Syr w`l b`lh). HebB restored by Smend reads wbbyt [b`]lh "and in the house of her husband" (= HebBmg[2]). Cf. HebBmg[1] wbbyt 'yšh. If we use the Gr verse order as the numbering standard, as is usually the case, this line and the next should be designated v. 10cb. This order, which is the reverse of the Gr, is confirmed by HebBM. Syr has three lines in v. 10. The first = v. 10a. However, the second and third lines merely constitute an extended v. 10c. Thus, it too reflects the Heb order. The order b, c, a, d is reflected in HebBmg[1]Bmg[2].

[136]HebM restored by Yadin (p. 24) [pn] tśṭh (= HebBmg[1], Gr mēpote parabē). This is also Smend's emendation of HebB, whereas it was no doubt originally l[' tśṭ]h "she will not be unfaithful." HebBmg[2] reads pn tnšh "lest she be forgotten" from v. 9d. Syr extends the content of this line in a loose translation over two lines. In addition to the part cited in n. 135 it reads: dlm' tšṭ' bmd`h / wt'zl btr gbr' 'ḥrn' "lest she be foolish in her understanding / and go after another man." For the Gr, cf. Num 5:12,19-20, 29.

[137]HebM byt 'byh (= HebB bbyt 'byh). Cf. Gr en tois patrikois autēs "among her father's possessions." Syr does not include this or the following line.

[138]HebM pn tzry`. Cf. HebB as restored by Smend pn [thrh] "lest she become pregnant" (= Gr). Ryssel (p. 441) suggested that the original read pn tznh "lest she commit fornication." However, he was content to read HebB like Smend.

[139]Here HebM reads wb`l[ ]. I am following the restoration and vocalization of Strugnell (p. 115) ûba`lāh. With this reading byt from line b is understood, implying "the house of her husband." Cf. Smend's restoration of HebB wbbyt '[yš]h (=

HebBmg^{2}). Yadin (p. 24) restores and vocalizes HebM as ûbeʿûlah "when she is married" (= Tal. nś´t, Gr).

[140]HebB restored by Smend [pn tʿ]ṣr (= HebBmg^{2}, Gr). This is also the restoration of HebM by Yadin (p. 24) [pn tʿ]ṩ[r]. However, since only the top tips of ṣ are visible, Strugnell (p. 115) offers the reconstruction [pn tśn´/tnšh] "lest she be hated/forgotten." The Tal. reading šm´ l´ yhyw lh bnym "lest she have no sons" and the evidence from Gr support the restoration by Smend and Yadin.

[141]HebBBmg^{2} bny (= Syr). Cf. Yadin´s restoration of HebM [bny] (p. 24). This address is not found in Gr. Peters (Jesus Sirach, p. 356) considers bny as overloading the line. However, there is clearly room for its inclusion in HebM.

[142]HebM ḥzq mšmr (= Gr, Syr). Smend restores HebB using the hif. [hḥz]q mšmr (= HebBmg^{2}). The Gr for this line is identical to 26:10a. See n. 84.

[143]HebM ʿl bt. Cf. HebBmg^{1} ʿl btk "over your daughter" (= Syr). Gr epi thygatri adiatreptō "over a headstrong daughter" is the basis of Smend´s restoration of HebB to read either ʿl b[t ʿw]l[h] "over a wicked daughter" or ʿl b[t nb]l[h] "over a senseless daughter."

[144]I am reading this line with the restored HebBmg^{2} p[n] tʿ[śk] ś[mḥh] l´[wybym]. Before noting the wide variety of suggested readings for this line, it may be helpful to list the remains of the MSS along with Gr and Syr.

HebB	[ ]n [ ] šm srh
HebBmg^{1}	srḥ
HebBmg^{2}	p[ ] tʿ[ ] m[ ] l´[ ]
HebM	[ ]ṅ ṫ[ ]
Gr	mēpote poiēsē se epicharma echthrois
Syr	dlm´ tʿbdk šm´ byš´

All editors read the first word as pn "lest." It is also clear that the next expression must be either tʿśk (Smend; Box-Oesterley [p. 470] in restoration of HebBmg^{2}; Lévi, Hebrew Text, p. 54) or tʿśh lk (Box-Oesterley; Yadin, p. 25). Both mean essentially "(lest) she make you" (= Gr, Syr). The choice would be determined by what follows. The third word in HebBmg^{2} is m[ ]. Lévi reads this as m[šl] "a byword." Smend considers m to be a mistake for ś and restores the reading ś[mḥh] "fun." Similarly, Box-Oesterley reads š[mṣh] "a wispering, laughing stock." (= Gr). Smend completes HebBmg^{2} by reading l´[wyb] "to your enemy," while Box-Oesterley follows Gr with l´[wybym] "to your enemies." Lévi, however, reads l´[ḥrym] "to strangers." Some read the last two words with HebB šm srh "a name of rebellion" (Yadin) or with the var. in HebBmg^{1} šm srḥ "a putrefying name" (Box-Oesterley). Cf. Syr šm' byš' "a bad name."

145HebBBmg[2]M dbt `yr. Cf. Gr lalian en polei "a rumor (lit. report) in the city." See chap. III, n. 4 for a discussion of the identity of the Heb of 26:5c and 42:11c. Syr for this and the next lines represents a free, extended translation:

wšw`yt' wrṭwny' b`m'
wbknš' dqrytk tbhtk brṭwny' d`m'

And a rumor and a murmuring among the people,
And in the assembly of the city she put you to shame in the murmuring of the people.

146HebM wqhlt `m (= Gr kai ekklēton laou, which may also be translated "and summoned by the people"). Smend had anticipated this reading in his correction of HebB, which reads wqllt `m "and accursed by the people."

147HebBmg[1] whwbyštk (= Gr, Syr). Cf. HebBmg[2] whbšt "and shame." HebB has transposed some letters with whwšbtk "and cause you to sit."

148Reading HebB [b`]dt š`r, which Smend, Box-Oesterley (p. 470), and Yadin (p. 25) restored according to HebBmg[2] b`dt. HebM has only r extant at the end of the line. Gr en plēthei pollōn "in the multitude of the great" must be an early internal Gr corruption involving pollon for pylon "of the gates."

149HebM mqwm tgwr. This is the obvious restoration of HebB [m]qwm tqwr. The second word is a form of gwr I "to dwell." Cf. the same phrase in 41:19a. For Strugnell's reading of tgwr as a form of gwr II, see n. 150. HebBmg[1] reads the synonym [t]šb. Cf. Syr 'tr d'mr' "from the place where she dwells." Gr does not include this or the next line. As Peters (Jesus Sirach, p. 356) observes, this may have been due to vertical dittography with wbyt in vv. 11f and 12b.

150HebB 'l yhy 'šnb. HebM reads 'l yhy "let there not be." Yadin (p. 25) considers this "incomprehensible" and suggests that the scribe forgot to copy the last word. This seems more plausible than the attempt by Strugnell (p. 116) to make sense of the present line in HebM. He postulates that tgwr is a form of gwr II, which in postbiblical Heb could mean "to commit adultery." Thus, he translates the line: "Let there not be an opportunity for her to have illegitimate intercourse." Cf. the term used in this way in 42:9c (HebB). But both HebB and HebM read gwr I in the phrase mqwm tgwr in 41:19a. Syr reads l' tšbqyh npq' "let her not go forth."

[151]HebB *wbyt mbyṯ*. For the second word Smend conjectures the reading *tbwt*, providing a combination which he understands to mean "the place where she spends the night." This suggestion is not convincing. Syr reads *wbbt'* "and in houses."

[152]HebB *wbw' sbyb*. Cf. HebBmg[1] *msbyb* "from round about." HebM has only *b* remaining at the end of the line. Syr reads *l' thw' ḥdr'* "let her not go about."

[153]HebM *'l tbn t'r*. While the predominant meaning of *byn* is "to understand," Yadin (p. 25) takes it here to mean "to expose, show, reveal." The context requires such a meaning. The strangeness of *tbn* with this sense may have given rise to the reading of HebB *'l ttn t'r* "let her not give/expose her beauty." Strugnell (p. 116) is reluctant to retain *tbn* and conjectures *tpn* "(let) her (not) turn." However, the reading of HebM is far from impossible and should be retained. Both Gr and Syr misread the verbs as 2nd masc. sing. The former reads *mē emblepe en kallie* "do not look at beauty," while the latter reads *l' tgl' m' dblbk* "do not reveal what is in your heart."

[154]HebBM *lkl zkr*. Cf. Gr *panti anthrōpō* "in any man/person"; Syr *lkl gbr* "to every man." As for the reading of HebBmg[1] *mwzkry[m]*, Smend (*Jesus Sirach*, p. 393) confesses, "There is nothing I can do with [it]."

[155]Reading with Smend's orthographic emendation *'l tstyyd*, which is based on the analogy of 8:17; 9:4, 14. This hit. is spelled *tstwyd* in HebB and *tstyd* in HebBmg[1]. Cf. Gr *mē synedreue* "do not sit in council"; Syr *l' tšpr šw`yt'* "do not talk much." HebM does not have this line extant.

[156]Reading with Smend's emendation *wbyn* "(and) among (= Gr, Syr). Cf. Box-Oesterley, p. 471. HebB reads *wbyt* "in the house/place." Peters (*Jesus Sirach*, p. 357) considers this a mistake through vertical dittography with v. 11f.

[157]HebB *nšym* (= Gr, Syr).

[158]HebBM *ky mbgd*. Cf. Gr *apo gar himatiōn* "for from garments"; Syr *mṭl d'ykn' dblbwš'* "for as upon a garment."

[159]HebM *yṣ' ss* (= HebB *yṣ' `š*, Gr). Syr reads *npl ss'* "falls the moth."

[160]HebB *wm'šh* (= Gr). HebM has only the last letter of the word extant [ ]*h*. Syr has a free translation for this line: *hk' ṭnn' d'ntt' mn byšwth dḥbrth* "so the jealousy of a woman from the wickedness of her fellow."

[161]HebB *r`t 'šh* (= HebM *r`t [']šh*, Gr).

[162]HebBmg[1]M _ṭwb_ (= Gr). HebB is corrupt with _mṭwb_ "from goodness." Syr does not include v. 14.

[163]HebBmg[1]M _r` 'yš_ (= HebB _rw` 'yš_, Gr).

[164]HebBmg[1] _mṭwb 'šh_. Cf. Smend; Ryssel, p. 441; Box-Oesterley, p. 471; Strugnell, p. 116. HebB reads _mṭyb 'šh_ "than a woman who does good" (= Gr). Yadin (p. 25) is certain that "though it is sometimes difficult to differentiate between _yod_ and _waw_ in the Scroll, the copyist here emphasized the _yod_." Strugnell (p. 116) disputes this and contends that the letter formation allows for _waw_.

[165]HebM _wbt_. Cf. Smend; Ryssel, p. 442; Box-Oesterley, p. 471. Gr reads _kai gynē_ "and a woman." HebB is corrupt for this line. For this word it reads _wbyt_ "and a house." Peters (_Jesus Sirach_, p. 357) suggests that this resulted from vertical dittography with vv. 11f and 12b. Though HebBmg[1] attempts to correct the line, it repeats the erroneous _wbyt_.

[166]HebM _mpḥdt_. Cf. Strugnell, p. 116; Baumgarten, p. 327 (one of two suggestions). Smend prefers the reading of HebBmg[2] _mḥprt_ "who causes shame" (= Gr). Cf. Ryssel, p. 442; Box-Oesterley, p. 471. HebBBmg[1] reads _mḥrpt_ "(house) which disgraces." Strugnell translates the expression _bt mpḥdt_ as either "a religious daughter" or "a daughter of a religious wife," with _w-_ understood as "but." One could not quarrel with this in isolation. However, given the present context, such an implication is highly unlikely. This line is not a corrective of line _a_ but a continuation and culmination of it. Hence, it serves to bind off the entire daughter discussion that began in v. 9. In fact, it resounds the same theme as v. 9ab. Note that the Tal. rendition of v. 9b includes the word _mpḥdh_. Thus, it is more natural to render this line as I have done. Cf. Baumgarten.

[167]Reading _mbn lḥrph_ with the emendation of HebM by Baumgarten (p. 327) and Strugnell (p. 116). The scroll itself reads _mkwl ḥrph_ "more than any disgrace." Both Baumgarten and Strugnell agree that the fully written _kwl_ is never elsewhere found in the scroll, while _kl_ is frequent. Both also suggest the need to obtain the _'yš_ / _'šh_ : _bn_ / _bt_ parallelism between lines _a_ and _b_. Actually the parallel is chiastic (_'yš_ / _'šh_ : _bt_ / _bn_), but the point is well taken. Furthermore, the reading of HebBmg[1] (_tby` ḥrph_ "pours forth disgrace") may provide additional support for the Baumgarten-Strugnell reading. If written without spaces the two readings would appear as follows:

mbnlḥrph
tby`ḥrph

The confusion of the materially similar _bn_ and _by_ and a poorly written or preserved _m_ taken to be _t_ may have led to the reading of HebBmg[1] and the first word of HebB (see below). If this is the case, than HebM and HebBmg[1] (and to some extent HebB) represent two independent material corruptions of the original. HebB only partially reflects this with tby′ ′šh "pours forth a woman." The last word is by dittography with line a. Gr eis oneidismon "unto disgrace."

168For a discussion of the arrangement of this material, see on 41:17a.

169Spicq (p. 789) considers the daughter section to be an appendix to the shame material. He suggests that protection of a daughter′s honor is a kind of virtuous shame. However, it is unlikely that this was Ben Sira′s intention.

170See, e.g., Moulton, p. 1634. Cf. Schilling, p. 177; Hamp, p. 684.

171I will treat the question of tradition and composition when discussing each portion of the text.

172The way I have read v. 14b, bt is placed in contrast to bn "son" and must mean "daughter" in the literal sense. See n. 167.

173Because of the required link between vv. 12 and 13, this pattern seems preferable to those suggested by Box-Oesterley (p. 470), 4 + 2 + 2 + 2, or Peters (Jesus Sirach, p. 355), 2 + 2 + 2 + 2 + 2. The attempt to force vv. 13 and 14 into a two distich strophe strains the content of these distichs.

174P. 244. Fuss provides several examples of places where he considers Ben Sira′s pattern to be characterized by opening a thought unit with a traditional statement, followed by his own details of circumstances.

175We may find support for Fuss′ contention in the fact that v. 9ab represents a different formal structure than vv. 9cd-10. The former is designed as a synonymous parallel. The latter, however, contain references to two circumstantial settings, each described three times in alternation. See the discussion below.

176The unmarried setting is described in three ways: in her youth (bn`wryh); in her virginity (bbtwlyh); in the house of her father (byt ′byh). The married setting is also described in three ways: when she is married (b`lyh); when she is married (`l ′yšh); (in the house) of her husband (b`lh). For a contrast between women viewed as unmarried and married, see Num 30. This may have been Ben Sira′s source for some of the terminology used here. In Num 30:3, 16 an unmarried woman is described as bbyt ′byh and bn`ryh. A married woman is said to be byt ′yšh.

[177]E.g., Isa 54:6.

[178]Jer 4:30f: "Your lovers despise (m'sw) you."

[179]See n. 132.

[180]For the technical use of the root śn' for a hated wife, see Gen 29:31; Deut 21:15.

[181]In Lev 21:15 among the women whom a priest may not marry is one defiled. Gen 49:4 uses the expression "to defile one's father's bed" as a circumlocution for illicit sexual activity. Cf. 1 Chr 5:1. For our purposes Lev 19:29 and 21:9 are of particular interest. In the former one is counseled not to defile his daughter by making her a harlot. The latter declares that a priest's daughter who defiles herself by playing the harlot actually defiles her father.

[182]For a discussion of the order of the lines in v. 10, see n. 135.

[183]The use unrelated to our discussion is in Prov 4:15.

[184]Prov 7:25.

[185]The four uses are found in vv. 12, 19-20, 29.

[186]Cf. Smend, Jesus Sirach, p. 392.

[187]See Lev 12:2; Num 5:28.

[188]See Gen 16:2; 20:18; Isa 66:9 (metaphorical). Cf. the noun `ṣr in Prov 30:16.

[189]Even if it was the husband who was actually sterile, the wife, of course, would be the one considered barren by the ancients.

[190]P. 403.

[191]See above.

[192]See also n. 106.

[193]P. 245.

[194]See above. The voc. formula bny was added by Ben Sira.

[195]See chap. III, n. 4.

[196]Fuss, p. 162. See also my discussion in chap. III.

[197]This is obvious, since v. 11c comes from the Zahlenspruch, which now appears in an edited form in 26:5-6. For a discussion, see chap. III.

[198]See above.

[199]The simple reading of HebM `l bt "over a daughter" is more universal than the readings with the qualifying adjs. found in Gr ("headstrong") or Smend´s reconstruction of HebB ("wicked" or "senseless"). See n. 143. These qualified readings were no doubt an attempt to soften the universal impact of the original. But it is precisely this universal implication that Ben Sira appears to have wanted when he used this statement.

[200]See Box-Oesterley, p. 334. Also the word for enemy in Heb (śn´) is different from the one used in 42:11b (´wybym).

[201]The comparative Gr texts are as follows:

6:4b	kai			epicharma		echthrōn	poiēsei auton
18:31b		poiēsei	se	epicharma	tōn	echthrōn	sou
42:11b	mēpote	poiēsē	se	epicharma		echthrois	

[202]This, of course, is the meaning of the behavior of one´s soul.

[203]See also the texts on daughters covered previously in this chapter. The section 26:10-12 is especially significant.

[204]See Gen 37:2; Num 13:32; 14:36-37; 25:10.

[205]See Ps 31:13 (14 Heb); Jer 20:10; Ezek 36:3.

[206]46:7 (evil report); 51:2 (undeserved evil report).

[207]The introductory formula of the Zahlenspruch refers to things that cause the heart concern and make one afraid.

[208]Besides our text, qhlh occurs only in 7:7.

[209]31(34):11; 39:10; 44:15. These are not actually legal decisions but statements of praise concerning various people or groups.

[210]23:24. This is a negative scene involving an adulteress and is accompanied by punishment upon her children. See my discussion of this text.

[211]P. 790.

[212]P. 158.

[213]2 Kgs 7:1, 18.

[214]Neh 8:1, 3.

[215]Gen 23:10, 18; Ruth 4:1-11.

[216]Deut 21:18-21; 22:13-21.

[217]For the expression <u>`dt</u> <u>š`r</u>, see 7:7.

[218]General populace--16:6; 45:18; 46:7, 14; constituted body--7:14; 41:18; 44:15; undetermined--4:7; 7:7.

[219]This is the view of Peters (<u>Jesus Sirach</u>, p. 356).

[220]In Sirach the <u>`dh</u>, like the <u>qhl</u>, develops opinions about persons or groups. Positive opinions are reflected in 4:7; 44:15 and a negative opinion in 7:7.

[221]P. 245.

[222]Cf. Fuss, p. 245. It is possible that the garment/moth line (v. 13a) is traditional. Ben Sira may have used it to set up his second line, which he applies to woman's wickedness. This is unclear, however, and one may equally argue that Ben Sira has composed the entire distich.

[223]For a discussion of this understanding of the expression <u>'l</u> <u>tbn</u>, see n. 153.

[224]The Heb words that Ben Sira uses for a woman's beauty include: <u>ḥn</u>, <u>yph</u>, <u>ypy</u>, <u>t'r</u>.

[225]7:19b; 26:13a, 16b, 17b, 18b; 36:22 (24 Heb, 27 Gr).

[226]9:8abc; 25:21.

[227]2 Sam 11:1-5. In v. 2 she is described as <u>ṭwbt</u> <u>mr'h</u> lit. "good of form." Cf. the Susanna incident.

[228]See Ryssel, p. 441; Smend, <u>Jesus Sirach</u>, p. 394; Box-Oesterley, p. 471; Spicq, p. 790; Kearns, p. 559. The word <u>nšym</u> may be translated "wives."

[229]See Job 4:19; 13:28; Ps 39:11; Isa 50:9; 51:8. Job 27:18 Heb speaks of building a house like the moth. The use of <u>`š</u> in Hos 5:12 may be <u>`š</u> II "putrefaction" rather than <u>`š</u> I "moth."

[230]Donald J. Borror, Dwight M. DeLong, and Charles A. Triplehorn, <u>An Introduction to the Study of Insects</u>, 4th ed. (New York: Holt, Rinehart and Winston, 1976), p. 509.

[231]See 26:7; 25:13,16,17,19.

[232]See our discussion of 26:7.

[233]See also 37:11a.

[234]9:2; 33:19ab; 47:19.

[235]42:6.

[236]23:22-23.

[237]See Box-Oesterley, p. 471.

[238]See n. 160.

[239]Gr547.

[240]See, e.g., Peters, Jesus Sirach, p. 357; Gaspar, pp. 60-61. See also my review of several scholars' views of v. 14a below.

[241]P. 245.

[242]Pp. 441-42.

[243]Jesus Sirach, p. 357.

[244]Pp. 60-61.

[245]P. 177.

[246]P. 685.

[247]P. 559.

[248]P. 790.

[249]Pp. 60-61.

[250]See our discussion of the texts listed in n. 231.

[251]P. 203.

[252]Ecclesiasticus, p. 207.

[253]See n. 167.

[254]Besides our text, see 7:23-25; 22:3-5.

[255]HebA ʼl ttbwnn (= Gr, Syr).

[256]HebA bbtwlh (= Gr, Syr).

[257]HebA pn twqš. Cf. Gr mēpote skandalisthēs "lest you stumble" (as in 32(35):15); Syr dlm' ttḥyb "lest you be indebted." For several var. forms of Gr skandalizō, see Zeigler, Sirach, p. 165.

[258]HebA bʿwnšyh lit. "in her fines" (= Gr). Syr translates the expression interpretatively, bprnyth 'ʿp' "with her dowry doubly," probably following Deut 22:28-29.

[259]See on 9:1.

[260]P. 78.

[261]See Smend, Jesus Sirach, p. 83; Gaspar, p. 69; Middendorp, p. 77.

[262]42:21c. See the discussion of this text.

[263]P. 54.

[264]P. 593.

[265]In addition to this text, we may note that Ben Sira mentions virgins and maidens in two other places. Both of these are similes involving eunuchs. In 20:4 we find the following distich:

> Like a eunuch (kn'mn) who spends the night with a virgin (btwlh),
> So is one who does justice by force.

In 30:20 Ben Sira refers to one who is afflicted by the Lord in this way:

> He sees with his eyes and sighs,
> As a eunuch (srys) who embraces a maiden (nʿrh).

Neither of these texts contributes to the issue with which we are concerned.

[266]7:25a (cf. 7:23b); 22:3; 42:14b.

[267]7:25a; 22:3b; 42:9-10.

[268]22:4-5; 26:11b; 42:9-11d.

[269]7:24; 26:10-11; 42:11-12.

[270]7:25; 22:4-5; 42:9-10.

[271]22:4-5; 26:10-12; 42:9-14.

[272]Contrast the daughter in 42:11b.

[273]Incidental references to daughters are found in Job 1:2, 13, 18; 42:13, 15; Prov 30:15 (metaphorical); 31:29; Eccl 12:4. None of these are discussions of daughters as such, and none are pejorative.

[274]E.g., the difference in privileges between sons and daughters sold into slavery reflected in Exod 21:7-11.

[275]E.g., the injunction in Deut 23:17 against allowing either sons or daughters to become cult prostitutes.

[276]E.g., the provision in Num 27:8 that daughters may inherit if there are no sons.

[277]This is especially prevalent in Isaiah, Jeremiah, Lamentations, and Micah.

Appendix 1

[1]E.g., Prov 26:25.

[2]E.g., Judg 5:30.

[3]The translation is by Roth ("The Wisdom of Ben Sirach," p. 69). The arrangement of the text has been conformed to my pattern of citation.

[4]Prov 9:1; 26:25 may represent remnants of fully developed X type Zahlensprüche.

[5]The translation is from the RSV; the arrangement is mine.

[6]Prov 30:11-14 may be an X/X+1 Zahlenspruch, which has lost its introduction. For a discussion and a possible reconstruction, see Wolfgang M. W. Roth, Numerical Sayings in the Old Testament, Supplements to Vetus Testamentum, vol. 13 (Leiden: E. J. Brill, 1965), p. 38.

[7]The studies of this material include: Hans Bauer, "Die Gottheiten von Ras Shamra," ZAW 53 (1935):54-59; Augustin Bea, "Der Zahlenspruch in Hebräischen und Ugaritischen," Biblica 21 (1940):196-98.

[8]The text is the translation of H. L. Ginsberg (ANET, p. 132) quoted by Roth (Numerical Sayings, p. 80). Roth discusses it on pp. 80-82. See also Wolfgang M. W. Roth, "The Numerical Sequence X/X+1 in the Old Testament," VT 12 (1962):306; Georg Sauer, Die Sprüche Agurs, Beiträge zur Wissenschaft vom Alten und Neuen Testament, no 84 (Stuttgart: W. Kohlhammer Verlag, (1963), pp. 64-65.

[9]See Roth, "The Numerical Sequence X/X+1," pp. 304-6. On p. 307 he also gives an example of an X/X+1 Zahlenspruch with a list among the fifth century Elephantine papyri.

[10]"A Mnemonic Use of Numbers in Proverbs and Ben Sira," Glasgow University Oriental Society, Transactions 9 (1938-39): 26-38.

[11]Stevenson, p. 30.

[12]Stevenson, pp. 29-30.

[13]Numerical Sayings, p. 99.

[14]Ibid.

[15]Ibid., p. 100.

[16]See Prov 30:24-28; Sir 23:16-17.

[17]Sometimes they appear to have expanded only one or two items in the list into a parallel distich. See Prov 30:29-31; Sir 26:28.

[18]The extended discussions are vv. 18-21 (the adulterer) and vv. 22-26 (the adulteress).

[19]The extended discussion is v. 6 (the rival wife).

[20]23:16-17 originally contained a list of three items: a heated person, an incestuous person, a fornicator. For 26:5, see my discussion of the text.

[21]Cf. the Ugaritic example quoted earlier. This is also true of the example from Elephantine. The one exception is Job 33:14-30, which in its present form contains two lengthy items (one is vv. 15-18, the other is vv. 19-30). For a discussion, see Roth, Numerical Sayings, pp. 58-59.

[22]Some who use this argument concerning 23:16-17 are, e.g., Fritzsche, pp. 120-21; Edersheim, p. 123; Ryssel, p. 350; Schilling, p. 104.

[23]Sir 25:1; 37:17-18. Sir 25:2 is inconclusive and could be argued either way. The only possible exception among the OT examples listed above is Isa 47:9.

[24]However, see the discussion of 25:1.

[25]23:16-17; 26:5; 50:25-26.

[26]25:7-11; 26:28.

[27]Job 5:19-22; Ps 62:11-12a; Prov 6:16-19; 30:15b-16; 21-23.

[28]Prov 30:18-19; 29-31.

Appendix 2

[1]See Yadin, p. 20.

[2]Box-Oesterley, p. 463.

[3]E.g., Ibid.

[4]Yadin, p. 15.

[5]This is where Yadin finds the suggestion for his reading in 40:18b. Cf. also his restoration in 41:12b, where the witnesses have the same readings only in the plur.

[6]Cf. Smend, Jesus Sirach, p. 377.

[7]Ibid.

[8]P. 463.

[9]For a contemporary rejection of lines bc despite HebM, see Otto Rickenbacher, Weisheitsperikopen bei Ben Sira, Orbis biblicus et orientalis, no. 1 (Freiburg, Switzerland: Universitätsverlag, 1973), p. 17. Rickenbacher argues that lines bc represent an expansion of the Vorlage of Gr. He dismisses the witness of HebM with the view that this expansion occurred at an early date.

[10]See Smend, Jesus Sirach, p. 377.

[11]Box-Oesterley (p. 463) hold that the word škr was secondarily inserted by HebB into v. 20a under influence from v. 18a. But this is rendered obsolete if one reads v. 18 with HebM. The influence is then clearly the reverse.

[12]Middendorp (p. 44) takes this expression to have resulted from the later influence of Lev 10:9. He prefers instead to read with Gr, because of its connection with v. 21. But it is more likely that šyr in v. 21a influenced the misreading of v. 20a.

[13]This is to agree with the simple subj. that Syr has in v. 20a.

BIBLIOGRAPHY

A. Reference Works

Barthélemy, Dominique and Rickenbacher, Otto. Konkordanz zum hebräischen Sirach: Mit syrisch-hebräischem Index. Göttingen: Vandenhoeck & Ruprecht, 1973.

Bauer, Walter. A Greek-English Lexicon of the New Testament and Other Early Christian Literature. Translated and adapted by William F. Arndt and F. Wilbur Gingrich. 2nd ed. by F. Wilbur Gingrich and Frederich W. Danker. Chicago: University of Chicago Press, 1979.

Gensenius, William. A Hebrew and English Lexicon of the Old Testament. Edited by Francis Brown, S. R. Driver, and Charles A. Briggs. Boston: Houghton Mifflin Co., 1906.

Jastrow, Marcus A. A Dictionary of the Targumim, the Talmud Babli and Yerushalmi, and the Midrashic Literature. 3 vols. Brooklyn, N.Y.: P. Shalom, 1967.

Koehler, Ludwig and Baumgartner, Walter, eds. Lexicon in veteris testamenti libros. Leiden: E. J. Brill, 1958.

Liddell, Henry George and Scott, Robert. A Greek-English Lexicon. 9th ed. by Henry Stuart Jones. Oxford: Clarendon Press, 1953.

Rickenbacher, Otto. Nachtraege zum "griechisch-syrisch- hebräischen Index zur Weisheit des Jesus Sirach von Rudolf Smend." Werthenstein, Switzerland: Sendboten-Verlag, 1970.

Smend, Rudolf. Griechisch-syrisch-hebräischen Index zur Weisheit des Jesus Sirach. Berlin: Georg Reimer, 1907.

Smith, Jessie Payne, A Compendious Syriac Dictionary. Oxford: Clarendon Press, 1903.

Winter, Michael M. A Concordance to the Peshitta Version of Ben Sira. Monographs of the Peshitta Institute, Leiden, vol. 2. Leiden: E. J. Brill, 1976.

B. Texts and Versions of Sirach

1. Hebrew

Baillet, M., Milik, Josef Tadeusz, and Vaux, Roland de. Les 'petites grottes' de Qumrân. Vol. 3: Discoveries in the Judaean Desert of Jordan. Oxford: Clarendon Press, 1962.

Cowley, Arthur Ernest, and Neubauer, Adolf. The Original Hebrew of a Portion of Ecclesiasticus. Oxford: Clarendon Press, 1897.

Di Lella, Alexander A. "The Recently Identified Leaves of Sirach in Hebrew." Biblica 45 (1964):153-67.

Lévi, Israel. The Hebrew Text of the Book of Ecclesiasticus. Semetic Study Series, no. 3. Leiden, E. J. Brill, 1904.

Marcus, Joseph. The Newly Discovered Original Hebrew of Ben Sira (Ecclesiasticus xxxii, 16-xxxiv, 1): The Fifth Manuscript and a Prosodic Version of Ben Sira (Ecclesiasticus xxii, 22-xxiii, 9). Philadelphia: Dropsie College for Hebrew and Cognate Learning, 1931.

Peters, Norbert. Liber Jesu filii Sirach sive Ecclesiasticus Hebraice. Freiburg, i.B.: Herdersche Verlagshandlung, 1905.

Sanders, James A. The Psalms Scroll of Qumrân Cave 11 (11QPs^{a}). Vol. 4: Discoveries in the Judaean Desert of Jordan. Oxford: Clarendon Press, 1965.

Schechter, Solomon. "A Further Fragment of Ben Sira." Jewish Quarterly Review 12 (1900):456-65.

Schechter, Solomon, and Taylor, Charles. The Wisdom of Ben Sira. Cambridge: Cambridge University Press, 1899.

Schirmann, Jefim. "Dap ḥădāš mittôk sēper ben-Sîrā' ha-`ibrî." Tarbiz 27 (1957-58):440-43.

________. "Dappîm nôs^{e}pîm mittôk sēper 'ben-Sîrā'.'" Tarbiz 29 (1959-60):125-34.

Smend, Rudolf. Die Weisheit des Jesus Sirach, hebraisch und deutsch. Berlin: Georg Reimer, 1906.

Strack, Hermann L. Die Sprüche Jesus', des Sohnes Sirachs. Schriften des Institutum Judaicum in Berlin, no. 31. Leipzig: A. Deichert (G. Böhme), 1903.

Vattioni, Francesco. Ecclesiastico. Pubblicazioni del Seminario di Semitistica, no. 1. Naples: Istituto Orientale di Napoli, 1968.

_______. "Nuovi fogli ebraici dell'Ecclesiastico." Rivista Biblica 8 (1960):169-79.

Vogt, Ernesto. "Novi textus Hebraici libri Sira." Biblica 41 (1960):184-90.

_______. "Novum folium Hebr. Sir 15,1-16,7 MS B." Biblica 40 (1959):1060-62.

Yadin, Yigael. The Ben Sira Scroll from Masada. Jerusalem, Israel Exploration Society, 1965.

2. Greek

Rahlfs, Alfred. Septuaginta. 2 vols. Stuttgart: Württembergische Bibelanstalt, 1935.

Ziegler, Joseph. Sapientia Iesu Filii Sirach. Vol. 12, pt. 2: Septuaginta Vetus Testamentum Graecum Auctoritate Societatis Litterarum Gottingensis editum. Göttingen: Vandenhoeck & Ruprecht, 1965.

3. Syriac

Ceriani, Antonio Maria. Translatio Syra Pescitto veteris testamenti ex codice Ambrosiano. 6 vols. Milan: J. B. Pogliani et Sociorum, 1876-83.

Lagarde, Paul Anton de. Libri veteris testamenti apocryphi Syriace. Osnabrück: Otto Zeller Verlag, 1972.

4. Latin

Sapientia Salomonis, Liber Hiesu filii Sirach. Vol 12: Biblia sacra iuxta Latinam vulgatam versionem. Rome: Typis Polyglottis Vaticanis, 1964.

Herkenne, Heinrich. De veteris Latinae Ecclesiastici. Leipzig: J. C. Hinrichs'sche Buchhandlung, 1899.

C. Commentaries on Sirach

Beavin, Edward Lee. "Ecclesiasticus or the Wisdom of Jesus the Son of Sirach." In The Interpreter's One-Volume Commentary on the Bible, pp. 550-76. Edited by Charles M. Laymon. Nashville, Tennessee: Abingdon Press, 1971.

Box, George Herbert, and Oesterley, William Oscar Emil. "Sirach." In The Apocrypha and Pseudepigrapha of the Old Testament, 1:268-517. Edited by R. H. Charles. Oxford: Clarendon Press, 1913.

Duesberg, Hilaire, and Auvray, Paul. Le Livre de L'Ecclésiastique. La Sainte Bible. Paris: Les Éditions du Cerf, 1953.

Duesberg, Hilaire, and Fransen, Irénée. Ecclesiastico. La Sacra Bibbia. Rome: Marietti, 1966.

Eberharter, Andreas. Das Buch Jesus Sirach oder Ecclesiasticus. Vol. 6, pt. 5: Die Heilige Schrift des Alten Testaments. Bonn: Peter Hanstein, 1925.

Edersheim, Alfred. "Ecclesiasticus." In The Holy Bible According to the Authorized Version (A.D. 1611) . . . Apocrypha, 2:1-239. Edited by Henry Wace. London: John Murray Pub., 1888.

Fritzsche, Otto Fridolin. Die Weisheit Jesus-Sirach's. Vol. 5: Kurzgefasstes exegetisches Handbuch zu den Apokryphen des Alten Testaments. Leigzig: S. Hirzel, 1859.

Hamp, Vinzenz. "Das Buch Sirach oder Ecclesiasticus." In Die Heilige Schrift (= Echter-Bibel), 4:569-717. Edited by Friedrich Nötscher. Würzburg: Echter-Verlag, 1959.

Kearns, Conleth. "Ecclesiasticus, or the Wisdom of Jesus the Son of Sirach." In A New Catholic Commentary on Holy Scripture, pp. 541-62. Edited by Reginald C. Fuller. London, Thomas Nelson and Sons, 1969.

Lévi, Israel. L'Ecclésiastique; ou la sagesse de Jesus, fils de Sira. 2 vols. Paris: E. Leroux, 1898-1901.

Moulton, Richard G. The Modern Reader's Bible. New York: Macmillan Co., 1959.

Oesterley, William Oscar Emil. The Wisdom of Jesus the Son of Sirach or Ecclesiasticus. Cambridge: Cambridge University Press, 1912.

Peters, Norbert. Das Buch Jesus Sirach oder Ecclesiasticus. Vol. 25: Exegetisches Handbuch zum Alten Testament. Münster, i.W.: Aschendorffsche Verlagsbuchhandlung, 1913.

Ryssel, Victor. "Die Sprüche Jesus', des Sohnes Sirachs." In Die Apokryphen und Pseudepigraphen des Alten Testament, 1:230-475. Edited by E. Kautzsch. Tübingen: J. C. B. Mohr (Paul Siebeck), 1900.

Schilling, Othmar. Das Buch Jesus Sirach. Vol. 7., pt. 2: Die Heilige Schrift (= Herders Bibelkommentar). Freiburg, i.B.: Herder, 1956.

Schmidt, N. Ecclesiasticus (= The Temple Bible). London: J. M. Dent & Co., 1903.

Segal, Moses Hirsch. Sēpher ben-Sîrā' ha-šālēm. 2nd ed. Jerusalem: Bialik Institute, 1958.

Smend, Rudolf. Die Weisheit des Jesus Sirach. Berlin: Georg Reimer, 1906.

Snaith, John G. Ecclesiasticus or the Wisdom of Jesus Son of Sirach. The Cambridge Bible Commentary. London: Cambridge University Press, 1974.

Spicq, Ceslaus. "L'Ecclésiastique." In La Sainte Bible, 6:529-841. Edited by Louis Pirot and Albert Clamer. Paris: Letouzey et Ané, 1946-64.

Vawter, Bruce. The Book of Sirach. Pamphlet Bible Series, vols. 40-41. New York: Paulist Press, 1962.

Weber, Thomas H. "Sirach." In The Jerome Biblical Commentary, 1:541-68. Edited by Raymond E. Brown, Joseph A. Fitzmyer, and Roland E. Murphy. Englewood Cliffs, New Jersey: Prentice-Hall, 1968.

Zöckler, Otto. Die Apokryphen des Alten Testaments. Munich: C. H. Beck'sche Verlagsbuchhandlung, 1891.

D. Monographs, Articles, etc. on Sirach

Bailey, Kenneth. "Women in Ben Sirach and in the New Testament." In For Me to Live: Essays in Honor of James Leon Kelso, pp. 56-73. Edited by Robert A. Coughenour. Cleveland: Dillon/Liederbach Books, 1972.

Bauckmann, Ernst Günter. "Die Proverbien und die Sprüche des Jesus Sirach: Eine Untersuchung zum Struckturwandel der israelitischen Weisheitslehre." Zeitschrift für die alttestamentliche Wissenschaft 72 (1960):33-63.

Bauer, J. "Des Vaters Segen . . . , der Fluch der Mutter . . . ." Bibel und Liturgie 23 (1955-56):295-96.

Baumgarten, Joseph M. "Some Notes on the Ben Sira Scroll from Masada." Jewish Quarterly Review 58 (1967-68):323-27.

Baumgartner, Walter. "Die literarischen Gattungen in der Weisheit des Jesus Sirach." Zeitschrift für die alttestamentliche Wissenschaft 34 (1914):161-98.

Büchler, Adolph. "Ben Sira's Conception of Sin and Atonement." Jewish Quarterly Review, n.s. 13 (1922-23):303-35, 461-502; 14 (1923-24):53-83.

Cadbury, Henry J. "The Grandson of Ben Sira." Harvard Theological Review 48 (1955):219-25.

Carmignac, Jean. "Les rapports entre l'Ecclésiastique et Qumrân." Revue de Qumran 3 (1961-62):209-18.

Davidson, Andrew Bruce. "Sirach's Judgment of Women." Expository Times 6 (1894-95):402-4.

Delcor, Mathias. "Le texte hébreu du cantique de Siracide LI,13 et ss. et les anciennes versions." Textus 6 (1968):27-47.

A Dictionary of the Bible. S.v. "Sirach (Book of)," by Eberhard Nestle.

Dictionnaire de spiritualité. S.v. "Ecclésiastique (Livre de l')," by Hilaire Duesberg.

Dictionnaire de theólogie catholique. S.v. "Livre de l'Ecclésiastique," by L. Bigot.

Di Lella, Alexander A. The Hebrew Text of Sirach. Studies in Classical Literature, no. 1. The Hague: Mouton & Co., 1966.

Driver, Godfrey Rolles. "Hebrew Notes on the 'Wisdom of Jesus Ben Sirach.'" Journal of Biblical Literature 53 (1934):273-90.

Encyclopaedia Biblica. S.v. "Ecclesiasticus," by Crawford Howell Toy.

________. S.v. "Sirach," by Crawford Howell Toy.

Forster, A. Haire. "The Date of Ecclesiasticus." Anglican Theological Review 41 (1959):1-9.

Fuss, Werner. "Tradition und Komposition im Buche Jesus Sirach." Th.D. dissertation, University of Tübingen, 1963.

Gallus, Tiburtius. "'A muliere initium peccati et per illam omnes morimur.'" Verbum domini 23 (1943):272-77.

Gasser, Johannes Konrad. Die Bedeutung der Sprüche Jesu Ben Sira für die Datierung des althebräischen Spruchbuches. Gutersloh: C. Bertelsmann, 1904.

Ginzberg, Louis. "Randglossen zum hebräischen Ben Sira." In Orientalische Studien: Theodor Nöldeke zum seibzigsten geburtstag (2. März 1906) gewidmet, 2:609-25. Edited by Carl Bezold. Giesgen: Alfred Töpelmann, 1906.

Hartman, Louis F. "Sirach in Hebrew and in Greek." Catholic Biblical Quarterly 23 (1961):443-51.

Haspecker, Josef. Gottesfurcht bei Jesus Sirach. Analecta Biblica, no. 30. Rome: E. Pontificio Instituto Biblico, 1967.

The International Standard Bible Encyclopaedia. S.v. "Sirach (Book of)," by T. Witton Davis.

Interpreter's Dictionary of the Bible. S.v. "Ecclesiasticus," by T. Alec Burkill.

Interpreter's Dictionary of the Bible, Supplementary volume. S.v. "Ecclesiasticus," by Patrick William Skehan.

Jacob, Edmond. "Wisdom and Religion in Sirach." In Israelite Widsom: Theological and Literary Essays in Honor of Samuel Terrien, pp. 247-60. Edited by John G. Gammie, Walter A. Brueggemann, W. Lee Humphreys, and James M. Ward. Missoula, Montana: Scholars Press for Union Theological Seminary, New York, 1978.

The Jewish Encyclopedia. S.v. "Sirach, The Wisdom of Jesus the Son of," by Israel Lévi.

Kilpatrick, George Dunbar. "Prosanoikodomēthēsetai Ecclus. iii. 14." Journal of Theological Studies 44 (1943):147-48.

Kolle, J. L. "Die Bibel des Ben-Sira." Oudtestamentische Studiën 14 (1965):374-96.

Kuhn, Gottfried. "Beiträge zur Erklärung des Buches Jesus Sira, I." Zeitschrift für die alttestamentliche Wissenschaft 47 (1929):289-96.

________. "Beiträge zur Erklärung des Buches Jesus Sira, II." Zeitschrift für die alttestamentliche Wissenschaft 48 (1930):100-21.

Lang, Bernhard. Anweisungen gegen die Torheit: Sprichwörter Jesus Sirach. Vol. 19: Stuttgarter kleiner Kommentar: Altes Testament. Stuttgart: KBW Verlag, 1973.

Lehmann, Manfred R. "Ben Sira and the Qumran Literature." Revue de Qumran 3 (1961-62):103-16.

Lévi, Israel. "Notes sur les ch. VII.29-XII.1 de Ben Sira édités par M. Elkan N. Adler." Jewish Quarterly Review 13 (1900-1):1-17.

________. "Un nouveau fragment de Ben Sira." Revue des études juives 92 (1932):136-45.

McKeating, Henry. "Jesus ben Sira's Attitude to Women." Expository Times 85 (1973-74):85-87.

McRae, Calvin Alexander. "The Hebrew Text of Ben Sira." Ph.D. dissertation, University of Toronto, 1910.

Marböck, Johannes. "Sirachliteratur seit 1966: Ein Überblick." Theologische Revue 71 (1975):177-84.

________. Weisheit im Wandel: Untersuchungen zur Weisheitstheologie bei Ben Sira. Bonner biblische Beiträge, no. 37. Bonn: Peter Hanstein Verlag, 1971.

Margoliouth, David Samuel. "The Date of Ben-Sira." In Occident and Orient: [M.] Gaster Anniversary Volume, pp. 403-8. London: Taylor's Foreign Press, 1936.

________. "Note on Ecclus. vii.25." Expository Times 23 (1911-12):234-35.

Middendorp, Theophil. Die Stellung Jesu Ben Siras zwischen Judentum und Hellenismus. Leiden: E. J. Brill, 1973.

Muraoka, T. "Sir. 51, 13-30: An Erotic Hymn to Wisdom?" Journal for the Study of Judaism 10 (1979):166-78.

Patterson, Roy Kinneer, Jr. "A Study of the Hebrew Text of Sirach 39:27- 41:24." Ph.D. dissertation, Duke University, 1967.

Pautrel, Raymond. "Ben Sira et le Stoïcisme." Recherches de science religieuse 51 (1963):535-49.

Penar, Tadeusz. Northwest Semitic Philology and the Hebrew Fragments of Ben Sira. Biblica et orientalia, no. 28. Rome: Biblical Institute Press, 1975.

Peters, Norbert. "Ekklesiastes und Ekklesiastikus." Biblische Zeitschrift 1 (1903):47-54, 129-50.

Rabinowitz, Isaac "The Qumran Hebrew Original of Ben Sira's Concluding Acrostic on Wisdom." Hebrew Union College Annual 42 (1971):173-84.

Rad, Gerhard von. "Die Weisheit des Jesus Sirach." Evangelische Theologie 29 (1969):113-33.

Die Religion in Geschichte und Gegenwart, 2nd ed. S.v. "Jesus Sirach," by Walter Baumgartner.

Die Religion in Geschichte und Gegenwart, 3rd ed. S.v. "Jesus Sirach," by Ernst Jenni.

Rickenbacher, Otto. Weisheitsperikopen bei Ben Sira. Orbis biblicus et orientalis, no. 1. Freiburg, Switzerland: Universitätsverlag, 1973.

Roth, Wolfgang M. W. "On the Gnomic-Discursive Wisdom of Jesus Ben Sirach." Semeia 17 (1980):59-79.

Rüger, Hans Peter. Text und Textform im hebräischen Sirach. Beihefte zur Zeitschrift für die alttestamentliche Wissenschaft, no. 112. Berlin: Walter de Gruyter, 1970.

Sanders, Jack T. "Ben Sira's Ethics of Caution." Hebrew Union College Annual 50 (1979):73-106.

Schechter, Solomon. "A Glimpse of the Social Life of the Jews in the Age of Jesus the Son of Sirach." In Studies in Judaism, Second Series, pp. 55-101. Philadelphia: Jewish Publication Society of America, 1908.

Seligmann, Caesar. Das Buch der Weisheit des Jesus Sirach (Josua ben Sira) in seinem Verhaltness zu den solomonischen Sprüchen und seiner historischen Bedeutung. Breslau: Pruss & Jünger, 1883.

Skehan, Patrick William. Review of The Ben Sira Scroll from Masada, by Yigael Yadin. Journal of Biblical Literature 85 (1966):260-62.

Snaith, John G. "Biblical Quotations in the Hebrew of Ecclesiasticus." Journal of Theological Studies, n.s. 18 (1967):1-12.

________. "The Importance of Ecclesiasticus (The Wisdom of Ben Sira)." Expository Times 75 (1963):66-69.

Stevenson, William Barron. "A Mnemonic Use of Numbers in Proverbs and Ben Sira." Glasgow University Oriental Society, Transactions 9 (1938-39):26-38.

Strugnell, John. "Notes and Queries on 'The Ben Sira Scroll from Masada.'" In W. F. Albright Volume. Edited by A. Malamat. Eretz-Israel, vol. 9. Jerusalem: Israel Exploration Society, 1969.

Taylor, Arthur F. The Wisdom of Jesus Ben Sira. New York: Doubleday, Doran & Co., [1928].

Taylor, Charles. "Studies in Ben Sira." Jewish Quarterly Review 10 (1897-98):470-88.

________. "The Wisdom of Ben Sira." Journal of Theological Studies 1 (1899-1900):571-83.

________. "The Wisdom of Ben Sira." Jewish Quarterly Review 15 (1902-3):440-74, 604-26.

Tennant, Frederick Robert. "The Teaching of Ecclesiasticus and Wisdom on the Introduction of Sin and Death." Journal of Theological Studies 2 (1901-2):207-23.

Ziegler, Joseph. "Ursprüngliche Lesarten im griechischen Sirach." In Mélanges Eugène Tisserant, 1:461-87. Studi e testi, no. 231. Vatican: Biblioteca Apostolica Vaticana, 1964.

________. "Vokabel-Varianten der O-Rezension in griechischen Sirach." In Hebrew and Semitic Studies Presented to Godfrey Rolles Driver, pp. 172-90. Edited by D. Winton Thomas. Oxford: Clarendon Press, 1963.

________. "Zum Wortschatz des griechischen Sirach." In Von Ugarit nach Qumran: Beiträge zur alttestamentlichen und altorientalischen Forschung (Festschrift für Otto Eissfeldt), pp. 274-87. Edited by Johannes Hempel and Leonhard Rost. Beihefte zur Zeitschrift für die alttestamentliche Wissenschaft, no 77. Berlin: Walter de Gruyter, 1958.

Zorell, F. "Canticum Ecclesiastici (Sir 36)." Verbum domini 7 (1927): 169-71.

E. Other Monographs, Articles, etc.

Allegro, John M. "'The Wiles of the Wicked Woman' A Spiential Work from Qumran's Fourth Cave." Palestine Exploration Quarterly 96 (1964): 53-55.

Bauer, Hans. "Die Gottheiten von Ras Shamra." Zeitschrift für die alttestamentliche Wissenschaft 53 (1935):54-59.

Bea, Augustin. "Der Zahlenspruch im Hebräischen und Ugaritischen." Biblica 21 (1940):196-98.

Beer, Georg. Die soziale und religiöse Stellung der Frau im israelitischen Altertum. Tübingen: J. C. B. Mohr, 1919.

Bird, P. "Images of Women in the OT." In Religion and Sexism, pp. 41-88. Edited by R. Reuther. New York: Simon & Schuster, 1974.

Birnbaum, Solomon A. The Bar Menasheh Marriage Deed. Uitgaven van het Nederlands Historisch-Archaeologish Instituut te Istanbul, no. 13. Istanbul: Nederlands Historisch-Archaeologisch Instituut in het Nebije Oosten, 1962.

Blinzler, Joseph. "Die Strafe für Ehebruch in Bibel und Halacha zur Auslegung von Joh. VII.5." New Testament Studies 4 (1957-58):32-47.

Boer, Pieter Arie Hendrik de. Fatherhood and Motherhood in Israelite and Judean Piety. Leiden: E. J. Brill, 1974.

Bonsirven, Joseph. Le Judaïsme Palestinien. 2 vols. Paris: Gabriel Beauchesne et ses fils, 1934.

Boström, Gustav. Proverbiastudien: Die Weisheit und das fremde Weib in Spr. 1-9. Lund: G. W. K. Gleerup, 1935.

Bousset, D. Wilhelm. Die Religion des Judentums im späthellenistischen Zeitalter. 3rd ed. Handbuch zum Neuen Testament, no. 21. Tübingen: J. C. B. Mohr (Paul Siebeck), 1926.

Brockington, Leonard Herbert. A Critical Introduction to the Apocrypha. Studies in Theology. London: Gerald Duckworth & Co., 1961.

Büchler, Adolph. "The Jewish Bethrothal and the Position of a Woman Betrothed to a Priest in the First and Second Centuries." In Studies in Jewish History, pp. 126-59. Edited by I. Brodie and J. Rabbinowitz. London: Oxford University Press, 1956.

________. "Die Strafe der Ehebrecher in der nachexilischen Zeit." Monatsschrift für Geschichte und Wissenschaft des Judentums 55 (1911):196-219.

________. "Die Todesstrafen der Bibel un der jüdisch-nachbiblischen Zeit." Monatsschrift für Geschichte und Wissenschaft des Judentums 50 (1906):539-62, 664-702.

________. Types of Jewish-Palestinian Piety. Jews' College Publication, no. 8. London: Jews' College, 1922.

Burrows, Miller. The Basis of Israelite Marriage. American Oriental Series, no. 15. New Haven, Connecticut: American Oriental Society, 1938.

Carmichael, Calum M. The Laws of Deuteronomy. Ithaca, New York: Cornell University Press, 1974.

________. Women, Law, and the Genesis Traditions. Edinburgh: Edinburgh University Press, 1979.

Causse, A. "La Sagesse et la propangande juive à l'époque perse et hellénistique." In Werden und Wesen des alten Testaments, pp. 148-54. Edited by Paul Volz, Friedrich Stummer, and Johannes Hempel. Beihefte zur Zeitschrift für die alttestamentliche Wissenschaft, no. 66. Berlin: Alfred Töpelmann, 1936.

Cowley, Arthur Ernest. Aramaic Papyri of the Fifth Century B.C. Oxford: Clarendon Press, 1923.

Craigie, Peter C. The Book of Deuteronomy. The New International Commentary on the Old Testament. Grand Rapids, Michigan: William B. Eerdmans Pub. Co., 1976.

Cronbach, Abraham. "The Social Ideals of the Apocrypha and the Pseudepigrapha." Hebrew Union College Annual 18 (1943-44):119-56.

Cross, Earle Bennett. The Hebrew Family: A Study in Historical Sociology. Chicago: University of Chicago Press, 1927.

Driver, Samuel Rolles. A Critical and Exegetical Commentary on Deuteronomy. The International Critical Commentary. Edinburgh: T. & T. Clark, 1901.

Duesberg, Hilaire. Les Scribes Inspirés. 2 vols. Paris: Desclée, de Brouwer, 1938-39.

Eberharter, Andreas. Das Ehe- und Familienrecht der Hebraer. Alttestamentliche Abhandlungen, vol. 5, pts. 1-2. Münster: Aschendorffsche Verlagsbuchhandlung, 1914.

Elmslie, William Alexander Leslie. Studies in Life from Jewish Proverbs. London: James Clarke & Co., [1917].

Encyclopaedia Judaica. S.v. "Widow: Biblical Period," by Chayim Cohen.

Epstein, Louis M. The Jewish Marriage Contract. New York: Jewish Theological Seminary of America, 1927.

________. Marriage Laws in the Bible and the Talmud. Cambridge: Harvard University Press, 1942.

________. Sex Laws and Customs in Judaism. New York: Bloch Pub. Co., 1948.

Fensham, Charles F. "Widow, Orphan, and the Poor in Ancient Near Eastern Legal and Wisdom Literature." Journal of Near Eastern Studies 21 (1962):129-39.

Fitzmyer, Joseph A. "A Re-Study of an Elephantine Aramaic Marriage Contract (AP15)." In Near Eastern Studies in Honor of William Foxwell Albright, pp. 137-68. Edited by Hans Goedicke. Baltimore: Johns Hopkins Press, 1971.

Frankenberg, W. "Ueber Abfassungs-Ort und -Zeit, sowie Art und Inhalt von prov. I-IX." Zeitschrift für die alttestamentlic he Wissenschaft 15 (1895):104-32.

Gaspar, Joseph W. Social Ideas in the Wisdom Literature of the Old Testament. The Catholic University of America Studies in Sacred Theology, second series, no. 8. Washington: Catholic University of America Press, 1947.

Gaster, Theodor H. Myth, Legend, and Custom in the Old Testament. 2 vols. New York: Harper & Row, Pub., 1969.

Gazov-Ginzberg, Anatole M. "Double Meaning in a Qumran Work ('The Wiles of the Wicked Woman')." Revue de Qumran 6 (1967-69):279-85.

Gordis, Robert. "The Social Background of Wisdom Literature." Hebrew Union College Annual 18 (1943-44):77-118.

Hengel, Martin. Judaism and Hellenism. Translated by John Bowden. 2 vols. Philadelphia: Fortress Press, 1974.

Herford, Robert Travers. Talmud and Apocrypha. London: Soncino Press, 1933.

Higgins, Jean M. "The Myth of Eve: The Temptress." Journal of the American Academy of Religion 44 (1976):639-47.

Hughes, H. Maldwyn. The Ethics of Jewish Apocryphal Literature. London: Robert Culley, [1909].

________. "The Social Teaching of the Hebrew Apocrypha." In The Social Teaching of the Bible, pp. 129-45. Edited by Samuel Edward Keeble. New York: Eaton & Mains, [1909].

Interpreter's Dictionary of the Bible. S.v. "Adultery," by Otto J. Baab.

________. S.v. "Beauty," by G. Henton Davies.

________. S.v. "Bill," by Otto J. Baab.

________. S.v. "Concubine," by Otto J. Baab.

________. S.v. "Crimes and Punishments," by Moshe Greenberg.

________. S.v. "Dancing," by G. Henton Davies.

________. S.v. "Daughter-in-law," by Otto J. Baab.

________. S.v. "Divorce," by Otto J. Baab.

________. S.v. "Dress and Ornaments," by Jacob M. Myers.

________. S.v. "Family," by Otto J. Baab.

________. S.v. "Fornication," by Otto J. Baab.

________. S.v. "Immorality," by Burton H. Throckmorton.

________. S.v. "Incest," by Otto J. Baab.

________. S.v. "Jealousy," by Edwin M. Good.

________. S.v. "Jealousy, Ordeal of," by Otto J. Baab.

________. S.v. "Marriage," by Otto J. Baab.

________. S.v. "Music," by Eric Werner.

________. S.v. "Prostitution," by Otto J. Baab.

________. S.v. "Sex, Sexual Behavior," by Otto J. Baab.

________. S.v. "Shame," by Simon J. De Vries.

________. S.v. "Virgin," by Otto J. Baab.

________. S.v. "Water of Bitterness," by Lawrence E. Toombs.

________. S.v. "Widow," by Otto J. Baab.

________. S.v. "Wisdom," by Sheldon H. Blank.

________. S.v. "Woman," by Otto J. Baab.

Interpreter's Dictionary of the Bible, Supplementary volume. "Divorce," by Charles R. Taber.

________. "Kinship and Family," by Charles R. Taber.

________. "Marriage," by Charles R. Taber.

________. "Ordeal, Judicial," by Tikva Simone Frymer.

________. "Sex, Sexual Behavior," by Charles R. Taber.

________. "Virgin," by Harry M. Orlinsky.

________. "Woman in the Ancient Near East," by Rivkah Harris.

________. "Woman in the OT," by Phyllis Trible.

Irwin, William A. "Wisdom Literature." In The Interpreter's Bible, 1: 212-19. Edited by George Arthur Buttrick. New York: Abingdon-Cokesbury Press, 1952.

Jellicoe, Sidney. The Septuagint and Modern Study. Oxford: Clarendon Press, 1968.

Jeremias, Joachim. Jerusalem in the Time of Jesus. Translated by F. H. Cave and C. H. Cave. Philadelphia: Fortress Press, 1969.

The Jewish Encyclopedia. S.v. "Marriage: Biblical Data," by J. F. McLaughlin.

________. S.v. "Marriage Laws," by Julius H. Greenstone.

Kahana, Kopel. The Theory of Marriage in Jewish Law. Leiden: E. J. Brill, 1966.

Kennett, Robert Hatch. Ancient Hebrew Social Life and Custom As Indicated in Law, Narrative, and Metaphor. London: Humphrey Milford, 1933.

Kraeling, Emil G. The Brooklyn Museum Aramaic Papyri. New Haven, Connecticut: Yale University Press, 1953.

Lebram, Jürgen C. H. "Nachbiblische Weisheitstraditionen." Vetus Testamentum 15 (1965):167-237.

MacDonald, Elizabeth Mary. The Position of Women As Reflected in Semitic Codes of Law. University of Toronto Studies: Oriental Series, no. 1. Toronto: University of Toronto Press, 1931.

McKane, William. "Poison, Trial by Ordeal and the Cup of Wrath." Vetus Testamentum 30 (1980):474-92.

Malina, Bruce J. "Some Observations on the Origin of Sin in Judaism and St. Paul." Catholic Biblical Quarterly 31 (1969):18-34.

Mayes, Andrew D. H. Deuteronomy. New Century Bible. London: Oliphants, 1979.

Mendolsohn, Isaac. "The Family in the Ancient Near East." Biblical Archaeologist 11 (May 1948):24-40. Reprinted in The Biblical Archaeologist Reader, 3:144-60. Edited by Edward F. Campbell, Jr. and David Noel Freedman. Garden City, New York: Doubleday & Co., 1970.

Metzger, Bruce Manning. An Introduction to the Apocrypha. New York: Oxford University Press, 1957.

Meyers, Carol. "The Roots of Restriction: Women in Early Israel." Biblical Archeologist 41 (September 1978):91-103.

Moore, George Foot. Judaism. 3 vols. Cambridge: Harvard University Press, 1927.

Muffs, Yochanan. Studies in the Aramaic Legal Papyri from Elephantine. Studia et documenta ad iura orientis antiqui pertinentia, vol. 8. Leiden: E. J. Brill, 1969.

Murphy, Roland E. Seven Books of Wisdom. Milwaukee: Bruce Pub. Co., 1960.

Nembach, Ulrich. "Ehescheidung nach alttestamentlichem und jüdischem Recht." Theologische Zeitschrift 26 (1970):161-71.

Oesterley, William Oscar Emil. An Introduction to the Books of the Apocrypha. New York: Macmillan Co, 1935.

Otwell, John H. And Sarah Laughed: The Status of Woman in the Old Testament. Philadelphia: Westminster Press, 1977.

Pedersen, Johannes. Israel. 4 vols. London: Oxford University Press, 1926-40.

Pfeiffer, Robert H. History of New Testament Times: With an Introduction to the Apocrypha. New York: Harper & Bros., Pub., 1949.

Phillips, Anthony. Deuteronomy. The Cambridge Bible Commentary. Cambridge: Cambridge University Press, 1973.

________. "Some Aspects of Family Law in Pre-Exilic Israel." Vetus Testamentum 23 (1973):349-61.

Prusak, Bernard P. "Woman: Seductive Siren and Source of Sin." In Religion and Sexism, pp. 89-116. Edited by R. Ruether. New York: Simon & Schuster, 1974.

Rad, Gerhard von. Deuteronomy. Translated by Dorothea Barton. The Old Testament Library. Philadelphia: Westminster Press, 1966.

________. Wisdom in Israel. Translated by James D. Martin. London: SCM Press, 1972.

Rankin, Oliver Shaw. Israel's Wisdom Literature. Edinburgh: T. & T. Clark, 1936.

Renehan, Robert. "Greek Lexicographical Notes: Fifth Series." Glotta 50 (1972):38-60.

Rost, Leonhard. Einleitung in die alttestamentlichen Apokryphen und Pseudepigraphen. Heidelberg: Quelle & Meyer, 1971.

Roth, Wolfgang M. W. Numerical Sayings in the Old Testament. Supplements to Vetus Testamentum, vol. 13. Leiden: E. J. Brill, 1965.

________. "The Numerical Sequence X/X+1 in the Old Testament." Vetus Testamentum 12 (1962):300-11.

Rylaarsdam, John Coert. Revelation in Jewish Wisdom Literature. Chicago: University of Chicago Press, 1946.

Sauer, Alfred von Rohr. "Wisdom and Law in Old Testament Wisdom Literature." Concordia Theological Monthly 43 (1972):600-9.

Sauer, Georg. Die Sprüche Agurs. Beiträge zur Wissenschaft vom Alten und Neuen Testament, no. 84. Stuttgart: W. Kohlhammer Verlag, 1963.

Schaeffer, Henry. The Social Legislation of the Primitive Semites. New Haven, Connecticut: Yale University Press, 1915.

Scott, Robert Balgarnie Young. The Way of Wisdom in the Old Testament. New York: Macmillian Co., 1971.

Smith C. Ryder. "The Social Teaching of the Apocryphal and Apocalyptic Books." Expository Times 37 (1925-26):505-8.

Swete, Henry Barclay. An Introduction to the Old Testament in Greek. 2nd ed., rev. Richard Rusden Ottley. Cambridge: Cambridge University Press, 1902.

Swidler, Leonard. Women in Judaism: The Status of Women in Formative Judaism. Metuchen, New Jersey: Scarecrow Press, 1976.

Tcherikover, Victor. Hellenistic Civilization and the Jews. Translated by S. Applebaum. Philadelphia: Jewish Publication Society of America, 1959.

Terrien, Samuel "The Omphalos Myth and Hebrew Religion." Vetus Testamentum 20 (1970):315-38.

________. "Toward a Biblical Theology of Womanhood." Religion in Life 42 (1973):322-33.

Theological Dictionary of the New Testament. S.v. "Krino," by Volkmar Herntrich.

________. S.v. "Krisis," by Friedrich Buchsel.

Torrey, Charles Cutler. The Apocryphal Literature. New Haven, Connecticut: Yale University Press, 1946.

Tschernowitz, Chaim. "The Inheritance of Illegitimate Children According to Jewish Law." In Jewish Studies in Memory of Israel Abrahams, pp. 402-15. Edited by George Alexander Kohut. New York: Jewish Institute of Religion, 1927.

Vaux, Roland de. Ancient Israel. Translated by John McHugh. New York: McGraw-Hill Book Co., 1961.

Wagner, Walter H. "The Demonization of Women." Religion in Life 42 (1973):56-74.

Walters, Peter. The Text of the Septuagint. New York: Cambridge University Press, 1973.

Wolff, Hans Walter. Anthropology of the Old Testament. Translated by Margaret Kohl. Philadelphia: Fortress Press, 1974.

Wood, James. Wisdom Literature. Studies in Theology. London: Gerald Duckworth & Co., 1967.

Yaron, Reuven. Introduction to the Law of the Aramaic Papyri. Oxford: Clarendon Press, 1961.

INDEX OF SUBJECTS

Abigail 193
Adam 82, 255
adoption 269
adulterer . . 95-97, 99, 102
106, 108, 126, 170
adulteress . . chap. IV, 170
angels' fall 81
anger 66, 72, 250
assembly . . 59, 103, 107-8
154, 245, 271-72
atonement 43

banquet . . . 111-13, 276-77
bastard 101, 268
Bathsheba 156
bear . . 73-74, 237-38, 250
beauty . . 17-18, 21, 78-79
109-11, 114, 156, 168
273, 275-76, 308
bed 90, 97, 126
267, 288, 306
Ben Sira's name . . 2-3, 185
birth pain . . 51, 221, 226
blasphemy . . . 46, 220, 224
blessing 45-46, 220
body 131, 198, 248
bride price . . . 23, 162-63
brothers 31

Cain 24
charm 14, 110, 195
chatter 54-55
children . . . 99-103, 107-8
218
columns 18, 197
concubine 126-27
congregation . . 107, 153-55
271-72
control 64-65, 88-90
93-94, 247

council 49-50, 223
curse 45-46, 220

Daniel 106
daughter . . chap. V, 170-71
David 156, 194, 250
death . . 60, 80-81, 86, 107
108, 113, 123-24, 170, 224
255-57, 270-71, 277, 284
dining couch . . . 112, 276
disgrace . . 98, 107-8, 114
136-40, 144, 149-51, 153
155, 158, 160-62, 223, 291
divorce 6, 28, 35-36
83-85, 103, 105, 108
150-51, 161, 205-6
211, 255-57, 264
dragon 72-73

elbow . . 111-12, 273-74, 276
enemies 67-79, 152-53
248
eunuch 75, 310
Eve 81, 255
evil report . . . 59, 153-54
execution 98, 103-7
110-11, 113-14
123, 270-72
exposure . . . 156, 158, 161
eyes 116-17, 143-44
278-79

fathers . . . . chaps. II, V
169-70
fecundity 150
feet 18, 198, 239
female musician 120
fence 203
flattery 120
flesh 83-85

fornication . . . 96, 115-17, 225
freedom 143-44, 146
friend(s) 195, 211-12, 251

garment 157
gate 153-55
genitals . . 85, 105, 145-46, 198, 248, 271
gold 18, 197
<u>Gottesfurcht</u> . . . 10-12, 14, 37, 41, 82, 191, 193, 212, 219
grief 135, 139-40

hands, doooping 80-81, 254
head 235-36, 250
heels 18, 197
heir 99-102, 107, 267, 269
husband . . . chaps. I, III-V, 168

idolatry 90-91, 261
incest 96, 101, 266
inheritance 121
insolence 49-50, 139, 223-25, 284

Jachin and Boaz 197
Jacob 126
jealousy 29-30, 61
Judah 113
judgment 43, 114

knees
  tottering 80-81
  weak 254

Laban 126
lampstand 17, 197
law 102, 104, 106-8, 268, 270
legs 18, 197, 203
levirate . . . 53, 227, 267
lion 72-73
loss 136-37, 149

magistrate 104
maiden 310
maidservant . . . 126-27, 287

man's wickedness . . 158-60
marriage . . . 21-23, 87-88, 127, 132-34, 137-38, 144, 149-51, 203, 267, 290, 294
masturbation 266
mercenaries 25, 200
misogynist . . 167, 172, 185, 252, 258
mistress 126
modesty . . 15, 16, 195, 298
moth 157
mother . . . . chap. II, 169
Mother Earth 225
mother of all living . . 225

nakedness 66, 85, 118, 248, 271
neighbor(s) . . . 31, 74, 251
nets 119

obscenity 141, 143, 145-46, 223, 297
old man . . . 124-25, 240-41, 285
orphans 52-54, 226-30
outspokenness 83

parents . . . . chap. II, 169
  honor to 42-47, 219, 294
  dishonor to 42-47, 219, 294
Pharisees 106
Pit 113
planting 45
poison 235
polygamy 61, 91, 101, 246, 262, 269
prostitute . . chap. IV, 170
prudence 15
punishment . . . 98-99, 101, 103-7, 110-14, 123, 154, 162, 270-72, 280, 284, 307

rape 156
respect 80-81
rest 44
robber 200
room(s) 155-57, 161

Sadducees 106
sand 77, 239
scorpion . . 64-66, 86, 247

seal 93, 264
seduction 144, 156
self control 15-16
sex appeal . . . 18, 22, 114
sexual activity . . . 109-13
116, 119-21, 124-27
139, 143-44, 146, 150
154, 156, 158, 162
277, 279, 284, 306
sexual desire 99, 101
109-11, 116, 118, 123
145-46, 161-62, 276-79
shame . . . 49, 79, 93, 112
124-27, 147, 154-55
222, 271, 305
Sheol 274-75, 277
silence . . . 15-16, 22, 168
194
silver 18, 197
sin 81-82, 86, 97-98
162, 170, 223, 255, 293
sinner's lot 76, 251
Sirach
as textbook 3
compilation 3-4
date 3, 185
organization 5
text and versions . . 4-5
186-87
slavery, hard . . 79, 252-53
sleeplessness . . . 148, 150
151, 158, 161
snake 71-72, 235-36
250
Solomon . . . 79, 89-90, 252
260-61
son(s) . . 129, 133, 135-37
140, 158, 160-61
164, 170, 227
speech 22, 222-24
sterility 150, 161
stoning 270
sun 17
Susanna 106

Tamar 113, 121
temple 17-18
thirsty traveler 145
throat 194
Tobias 221
Tobit 221
tongue-lashing . . . 61, 233
trouble 133-34

uprooting 45

virgin . . 126, 162-63, 310
virginity . . . 132, 144, 149
153, 161, 305
voice 194
watch . . . 141, 143-44, 151
152-55, 157, 161-62
water 83
widow . . . . . chap. II, 169
wife
as helper 24, 203
as property . . 22-23, 35
168
as supporter . . . 79, 86
babbling 77
bad . . . chap. III, 169
compatible 32, 205
devoted 37
drunken 62, 65-66
115, 118, 172, 246
envious 59-60
evil 62-66, 69-70
72-76, 83, 86
157-58, 245, 248
good . . . . chap. I, 168
hated . . 91, 261-62, 306
of bosom 30
of youth 207
rival . . . 36, 59-62, 68
83, 92-93, 232-33, 246
wickedness of . . . 70-76
157-58, 161
wise . . 26-27, 35-38, 168
wine 111-12, 122-23
274-77
Wisdom . . . 50-51, 53, 80
207-8, 226, 253, 279
wisdom literature . . 3, 186
woman (women)
courageous 35
goodness of . . 158, 160
loose 104-05
married . . . chaps. I-IV
slander of 35-36
strange . . . 63, 100-101
120, 125-27, 260
268, 287
wickedness of 308
womb 51, 213, 225
worry . . . 147-51, 158, 161
wound 69-70

yoke 63-65, 86, 234

Zahlensprüche . . . 4, 10-11
31-35, 59-62, 86, 94, 95
96, 98, 107, 151-54, 171
175-78, 191, 208-9, 232-33
245, 246, 259, 266-67, 285
307, 311-13

INDEX OF SIRACH PASSAGES

1:1-20 207
1:2 252
1:12, 20 219
1:14 51

2:3 284
2:10 261
2:12 80

3:1-16 . . . . . 40-47, 193
3:13 291
3:18, 31 292
3:20 241
3:30 219

4:1-10 . . . 52, 54, 226-27
4:1, 3, 8 241
4:7 . . . . 224, 240, 308
4:9 249
4:9b 258
4:10 52-55
4:11-19 207
4:11 207
4:13 . . . . 234, 292
4:17 261
4:18 253
4:20 211
4:29 292

5:13 229

6:1, 4, 9, 13 249
6:2 153
6:4 284
6:4b 152-53
6:7 . . . . 201, 261
6:9 223
6:10, 27 292
6:14, 28 292
6:15 195
6:18-31 207
6:19 279
6:20 293
6:25 249
6:34 . . . . 240, 284

7:1-9:16 . . . . 29, 129
7:1-21 26
7:6 295
7:7 307-8
7:14 . . . . 240, 308
7:19 . . . . 26-27, 110
7:22-28 . . . . . 26, 47, 129
7:24-25 . . 129-34, 142, 298
7:24 256
7:26a . . . 27-29, 91-92, 289
7:26b 28, 91-92
7:27-28 47-48

8:1-19 29
8:3 . . . . 77, 241, 252, 276
8:6 240
8:7 255
8:8 224
8:9 . . . . 204, 213, 240
8:12 281
8:15 248
8:18 51
8:19 256

9:1-9 . . . . . 29, 109, 125
162, 287
9:1 . . . . 29-30, 87
9:2 . . . 29, 87-89, 120, 253
9:3-4 . . . . 78, 118-20, 242
9:3 . . . . 260, 287
9:5 162-63
9:6-7 120-21
9:6a 258
9:8-9 108-15

9:8 . . . . 21, 252
9:9 . . . . 122-23, 248
9:12 295
9:13 269
9:17 259
9:18 . . . . . 77, 241, 252

10:1 196
10:3 293
10:7 269
10:13, 18 295
10:14 241
10:18 51
10:24 224

11:1 224
11:2 . . . . 201, 252
11:10 289
11:19 292

12:2, 6-17 292
12:5 241
12:8, 9, 10, 16 249
12:12 75
12:14 295

13:4-7 79
13:11 229
13:15-16 256
13:16 284
13:24 295
13:26 . . . . . 132, 288, 290
13:26a 193

14:1 293
14:2 291
14:17-18 256
14:17 255
14:20-15:10 207

15:2a 50-51, 207
15:2b 207
15:5 . . . . 232, 253
15:6 292
15:17 295

16:3, 10 295
16:6 308
16:22 266

18:10 . . . . 239, 252
18:30-33 122
18:31 249
18:31b 152-53
18:33a 247

19:1-3 122
19:2-3 122-23
19:2 . . . . 248, 275
19:4 269
19:6 229
19:10 226
19:11 51

20:1-22:18 134
20:4 310
20:5 229
20:13 229
20:23 201
20:24 293
20:27-28 224

21:1-10 293
21:2 250
21:18-28 294
21:24 294

22:3-6 134
22:3-5 . . . 134-40, 160-61
298
22:4 218
22:15 . . . . 239, 252
22:22 223
22:27-23:6 . . . . . . 48, 117
22:27 264

23:7-27 96
23:7-15 48
23:11 269
23:12-15 222-24
23:14 48-49
23:16-27 113-14
23:16-17 . . . . 95-96, 312
23:18-21 95-98
23:18a 126
23:22-26 . . . . 95-105, 138
23:23 . . . . 116, 144
23:24 307

24:1-34 207
24:12, 16 272
24:22 253

25:1-26:27 10

25:1-11 . . . . 10, 31
25:1 . . . . 10, 31-32, 209
266, 312
25:1d 208
25:2 . . . 31, 209, 266, 312
25:2b 208
25:3-6 208
25:4, 20 240
25:7-26:18 231
25:7-11 . . . . 266, 312
25:7-10 209
28:8 289
25:8a 33-35, 73
25:8b 33-34
25:13-32:13 31
25:13-26:18 208
25:13-26 . . 59, 67-87, 157
25:13a 246
25:21 . . . . 110, 252
25:23ab . . 243-44, 246, 249
25:26 206

26:1-4 12-14
26:5-9 . . . . . 59-66, 175
26:5-6 . . . . 266, 307
26:5 312
26:5c 284
26:6 262
26:7-9 115
26:9 115-18
26:10-12 . . . . 140-46, 278
26:10a 151-52, 284
26:11 . . . . 102, 279
26:13-18 . . . . . 14-18, 21
26:13 110
26:16-17 252
26:16 276
26:17 110
26:19-27 12
26:19-24 101
26:28 . . . . . 266, 289, 312

27:14 229
27:28 223

28:13-26 35-36
28:14 224
28:15 . . . . 35-36, 206, 262

29:21 248
29:23, 28 223

30:1-13 89

30:11 259-60
30:13 248
30:14 256
30:18-19 261
30:18 229
30:20 . . . . 75, 310
30:21, 23 293
30:24b 240

31(34):4 . . . 137, 241, 291
31(34):8 292
31(34):11 307
31(34):12-24 276
31(34):19 288
31(34):21 292
31(34):25-31 277
31(34):25-29 275
31(34):31-32(35):2 . . . 276
31(34):31 223

32(35):3 240-41
32(35):4-6 276
32(35):4 229
32(35):5-6 . . . . 275, 277
32(35):9 224
32(35):9a 240
32(35):15 310
32(35):22 298

33(36):3 289
33:18 (30:27) 224
33:19-23 (30:28-32) . . . 88
33:19-20 (30:28-29) . . . 253
33:19 (30:28) 244
33:19ab (30:28ab) . . . 88-89
90

34(31):5 51
34(31):18-26 54

35(32):1-11 54
35(32):9 . . . . . . 132, 290
35(32):12-20 54
35(32):14-15 54-55
35(32):14 229
35(32):23 295

36:7, 10 (33:9, 12) . . . 249
36(33):7 229
36:18-39:11 19
36:18-37:15 19
36:18-20 19-20
36:21-26 19-26

36:22 . . . . 110, 252

37:2 293
37:7-15 92
37:8 298
37:11 . . . 233-34, 246, 256
37:11a 92-93
37:17-18 312
37:18 259
37:29 229

38:3 224
38:7 219
38:16 . . . . 43, 256
38:18 293
38:24 289
38:25 234

39:4 224
39:10 307
39:19 256
39:30 . . . . 65, 235

40:1 . . . . 51, 289
40:5 288
40:17 255
40:18-26b 37
40:18-20 179-82
40:18 292
40:19, 23 37-38
40:19 256
40:20 277
40:22 252
40:26 . . . . 137, 291

41:1-4 124
41:2 281
41:2c 124
41:4 256
41:11 255
41:12 243
41:14-42:8 . . . . . . 49, 147
41:17-23 . . . 49, 125, 276
286
41:17-19a 49-50
41:17a 49-50
41:18 308
41:19a 302
41:19c 112. 273, 276
41:20-21 286
41:20b, 21c, 22a, 22b . . 125
126-27
41:20b 279

41:21 256
41:21a 266
41:22 223

42:1-8 . . . . 93, 225
42:1 292
42:1e 284
42:6 93-94
42:6a 246
42:8 240
42:8ab 124-25
42:9-14 . . . . . 142, 146-62
297-98
42:9-10 . . . . 73, 139
42:10ac 144
42:10b 138
42:11 . . . 107, 141-42, 229
42:11a . . 284, 295, 297-98
42:11cd 297
42:11c 231-32, 284
42:11f 281
42:12 . . . . . 21, 110, 252
42:14-16 225
42:14 223
42:15 147
42:16 196
42:21 197

43:9, 18 252
43:17 51
43:21 282

44:1 213
44:15 307-8
44:17, 20, 23 292
44:18, 20 255-56
44:19 243

45:17 259
45:18 308

46:1 . . . . 249, 292
46:7, 14 308
46:7 232
46:9 240
46:9c 259
46:10 266
46:11 90

47:3 250
47:4 223
47:7 . . . . 249, 307
47:12-22 89

47:19-20 260
47:19 . . . . 89-91, 259
47:19a 258
47:23 . . . . 213, 248

48:6 288
48:12 259
48:12-13 256
48:19 51

49:1 275-77
49:4 261
49:7 . . . . 51, 281
49:9 249

50:1 243
50:14 196
50:17 256
50:22 51
50:24 255
50:25-26 . . . . . 266, 312
50:25 249

51:2 . . . . . 232, 256, 307
51:9 228
51:13-22 207
51:16, 20, 26-27 292
51:18 253
51:20-21, 25 201
51:23 293
51:24 291
51:28 201